WELCOME TO TRANQUILITY

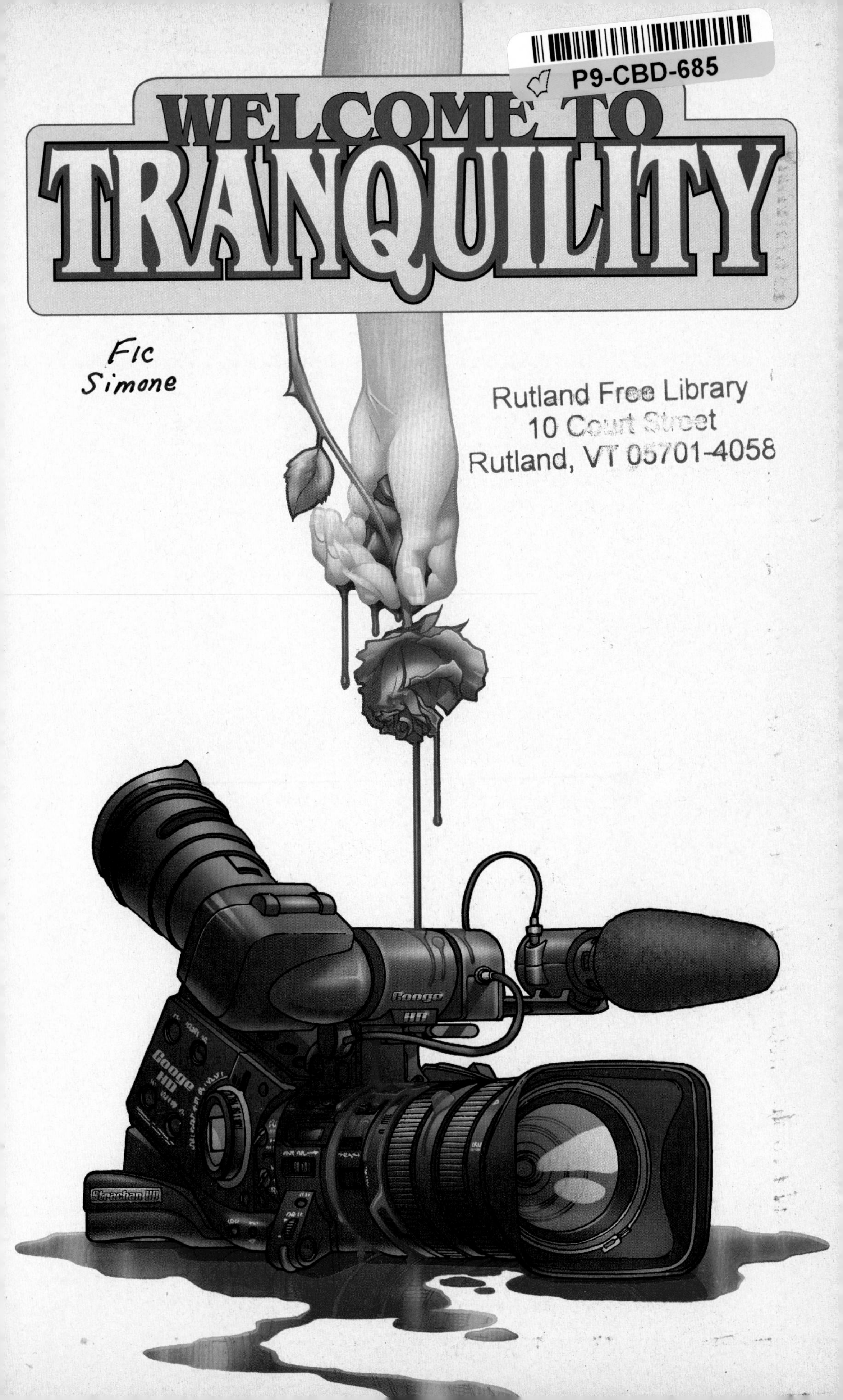
Googe
HD
Googe
HD
Strachan HD

Gail Simone: Writer
Neil Googe: Artist
Billy Dallas Patton: pencils #6 pp1-3, 19-21
Carrie Strachan: Colors
Travis Lanham: Letters

Collected Edition Cover and Original Series Covers by
Neil Googe and Carrie Strachan
Variant Cover #1 by J. Scott Campbell,
Avalon Studios and Studio F
Variant Cover #2 by Karl Kerschl
Variant Cover #3 by Dustin Nguyen
Variant Cover #4 by Gene Ha and Art Lyon
Character Designs by Neil Googe

WELCOME TO TRANQUILITY Book One, published by
WildStorm Productions. 888 Prospect St. #240, La Jolla,
CA 92037. Compilation and sketches copyright © 2008
WildStorm Productions, an imprint of DC Comics. All Rights
Reserved. WildStorm and logo, all characters, the distinctive
likenesses thereof and all related elements are trademarks of
DC Comics. Originally published in single magazine form as
Welcome to Tranquility #1-6 copyright © 2006, 2007 and
WorldStorm #1 © 2006. All Rights Reserved.

DC Comics, a Warner Bros. Entertainment Company. **WB**

ISBN: 978-1-4012-1516-3

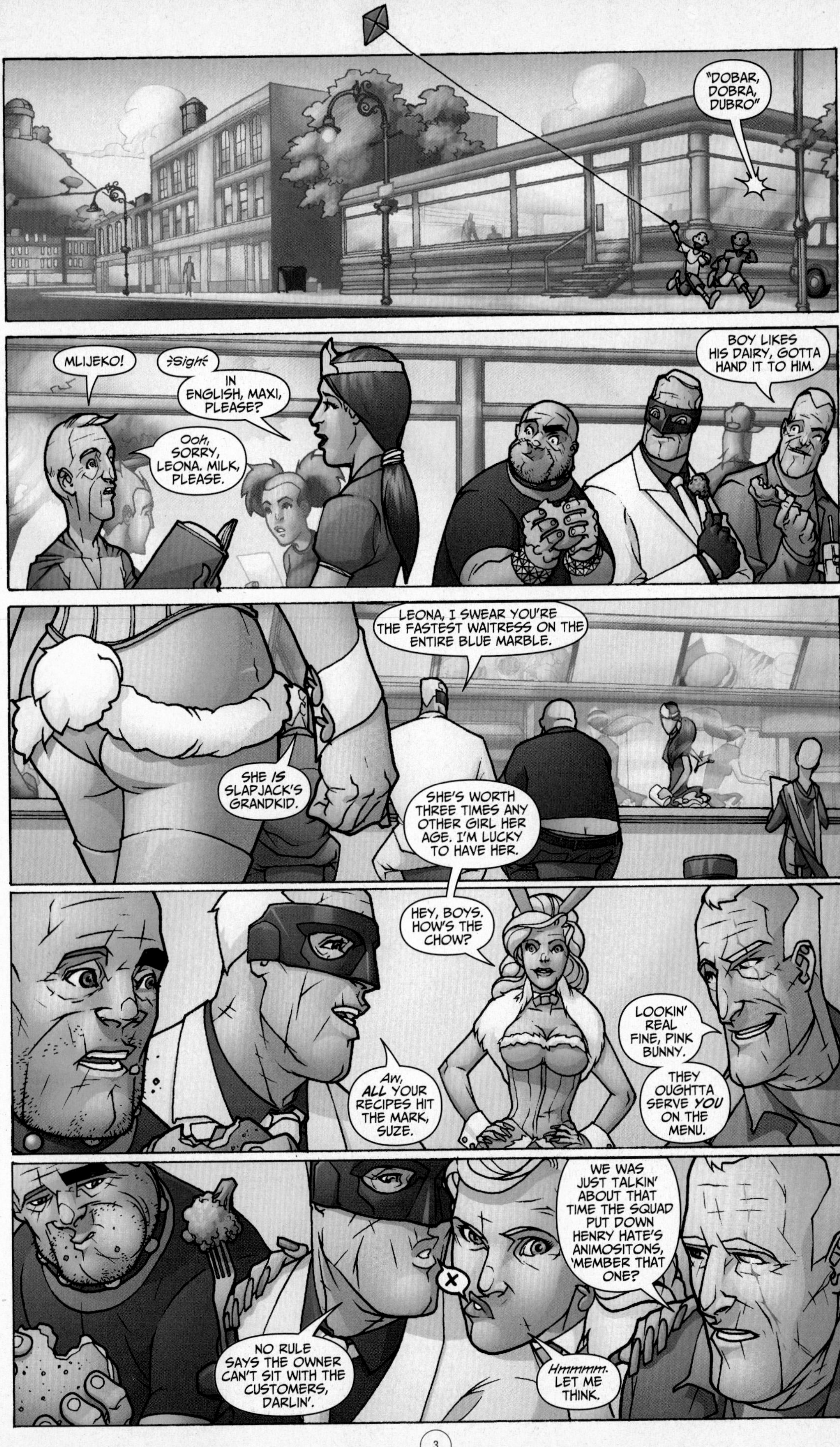

"DOBAR, DOBRA, DUBRO"
MLIJEKO!
Sigh
IN ENGLISH, MAXI, PLEASE?
Ooh, SORRY, LEONA. MILK, PLEASE.
BOY LIKES HIS DAIRY, GOTTA HAND IT TO HIM.
LEONA, I SWEAR YOU'RE THE FASTEST WAITRESS ON THE ENTIRE BLUE MARBLE.
SHE IS SLAPJACK'S GRANDKID.
SHE'S WORTH THREE TIMES ANY OTHER GIRL HER AGE. I'M LUCKY TO HAVE HER.
HEY, BOYS. HOW'S THE CHOW?
Aw, ALL YOUR RECIPES HIT THE MARK, SUZE.
LOOKIN' REAL FINE, PINK BUNNY.
THEY OUGHTTA SERVE YOU ON THE MENU.
WE WAS JUST TALKIN' ABOUT THAT TIME THE SQUAD PUT DOWN HENRY HATE'S ANIMOSITONS, 'MEMBER THAT ONE?
NO RULE SAYS THE OWNER CAN'T SIT WITH THE CUSTOMERS, DARLIN'.
Hmmmmm. LET ME THINK.

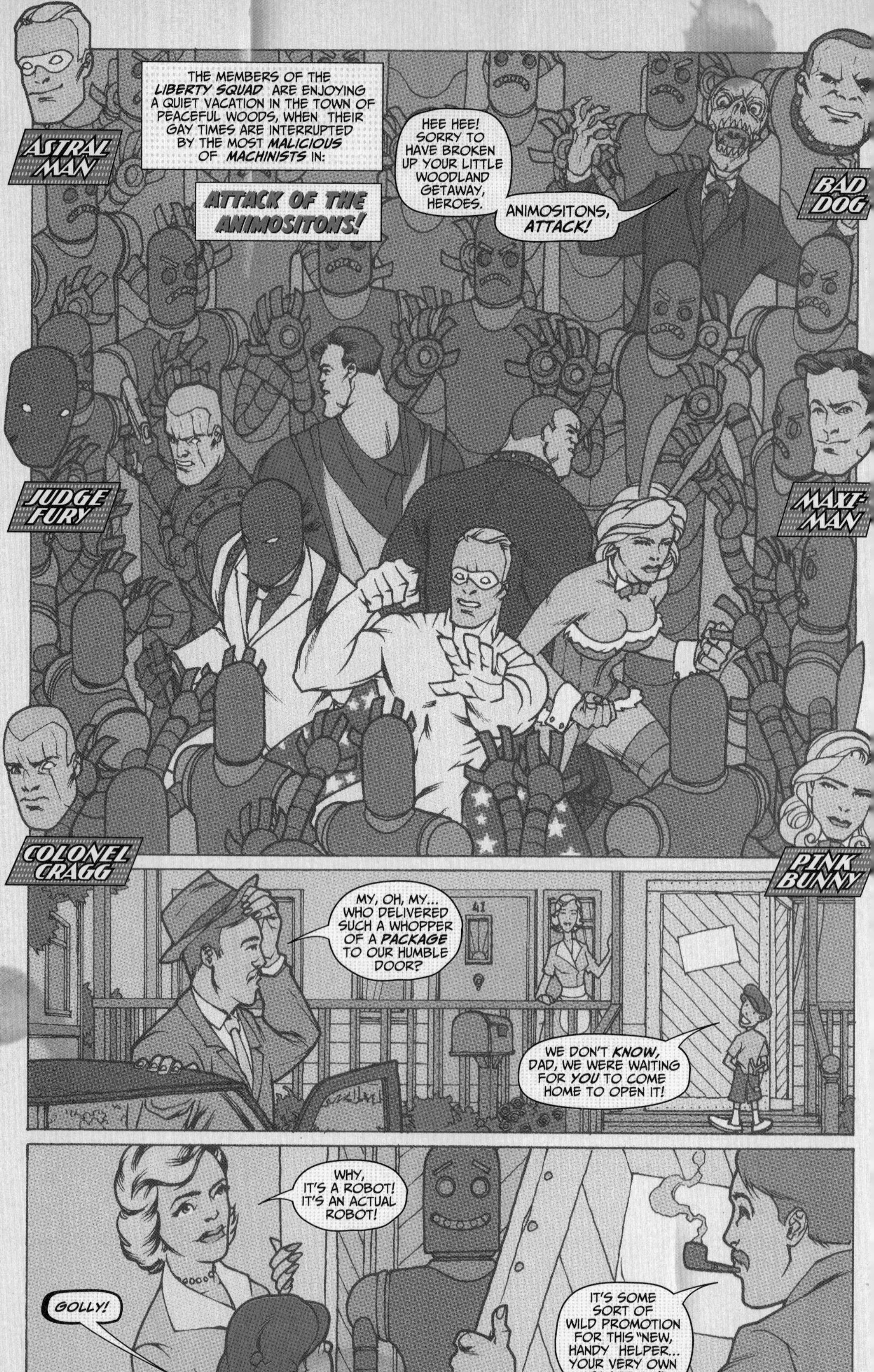

THE MEMBERS OF THE LIBERTY SQUAD ARE ENJOYING A QUIET VACATION IN THE TOWN OF PEACEFUL WOODS, WHEN THEIR GAY TIMES ARE INTERRUPTED BY THE MOST MALICIOUS OF MACHINISTS IN:
ATTACK OF THE ANIMOSITONS!
HEE HEE! SORRY TO HAVE BROKEN UP YOUR LITTLE WOODLAND GETAWAY, HEROES.
ANIMOSITONS, ATTACK!
ASTRAL MAN
BAD DOG
JUDGE FURY
MAXI-MAN
COLONEL CRAGG
PINK BUNNY
MY, OH, MY... WHO DELIVERED SUCH A WHOPPER OF A PACKAGE TO OUR HUMBLE DOOR?
41
WE DON'T KNOW, DAD, WE WERE WAITING FOR YOU TO COME HOME TO OPEN IT!
WHY, IT'S A ROBOT! IT'S AN ACTUAL ROBOT!
GOLLY!
IT'S SOME SORT OF WILD PROMOTION FOR THIS "NEW, HANDY HELPER... YOUR VERY OWN GLADBOT!"

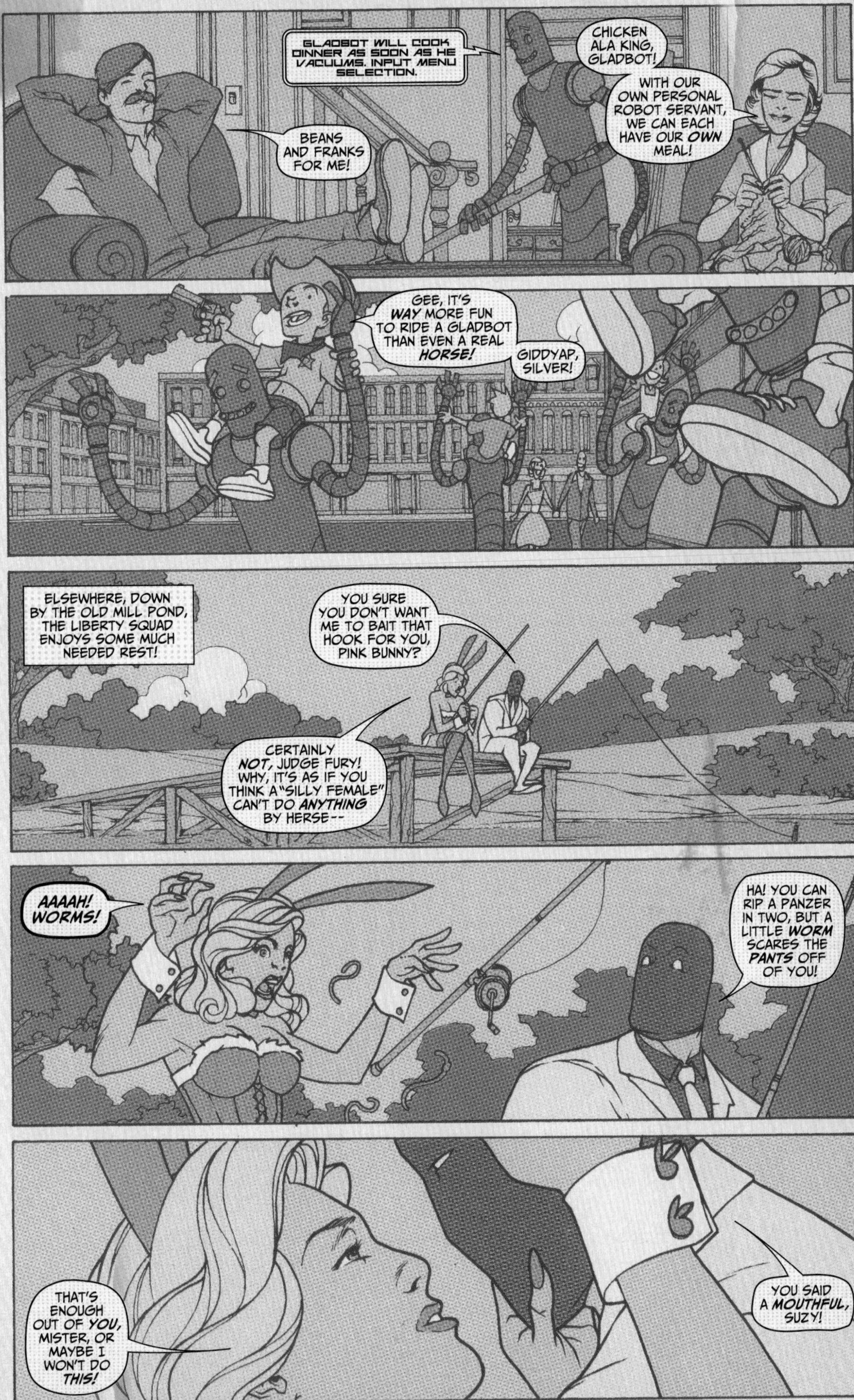
GLADBOT WILL COOK DINNER AS SOON AS HE VACUUMS. INPUT MENU SELECTION.
CHICKEN ALA KING, GLADBOT!
WITH OUR OWN PERSONAL ROBOT SERVANT, WE CAN EACH HAVE OUR OWN MEAL!
BEANS AND FRANKS FOR ME!
GEE, IT'S WAY MORE FUN TO RIDE A GLADBOT THAN EVEN A REAL HORSE!
GIDDYAP, SILVER!
ELSEWHERE, DOWN BY THE OLD MILL POND, THE LIBERTY SQUAD ENJOYS SOME MUCH NEEDED REST!
YOU SURE YOU DON'T WANT ME TO BAIT THAT HOOK FOR YOU, PINK BUNNY?
CERTAINLY NOT, JUDGE FURY! WHY, IT'S AS IF YOU THINK A "SILLY FEMALE" CAN'T DO ANYTHING BY HERSE--
AAAAH! WORMS!
HA! YOU CAN RIP A PANZER IN TWO, BUT A LITTLE WORM SCARES THE PANTS OFF OF YOU!
THAT'S ENOUGH OUT OF YOU, MISTER, OR MAYBE I WON'T DO THIS!
YOU SAID A MOUTHFUL, SUZY!

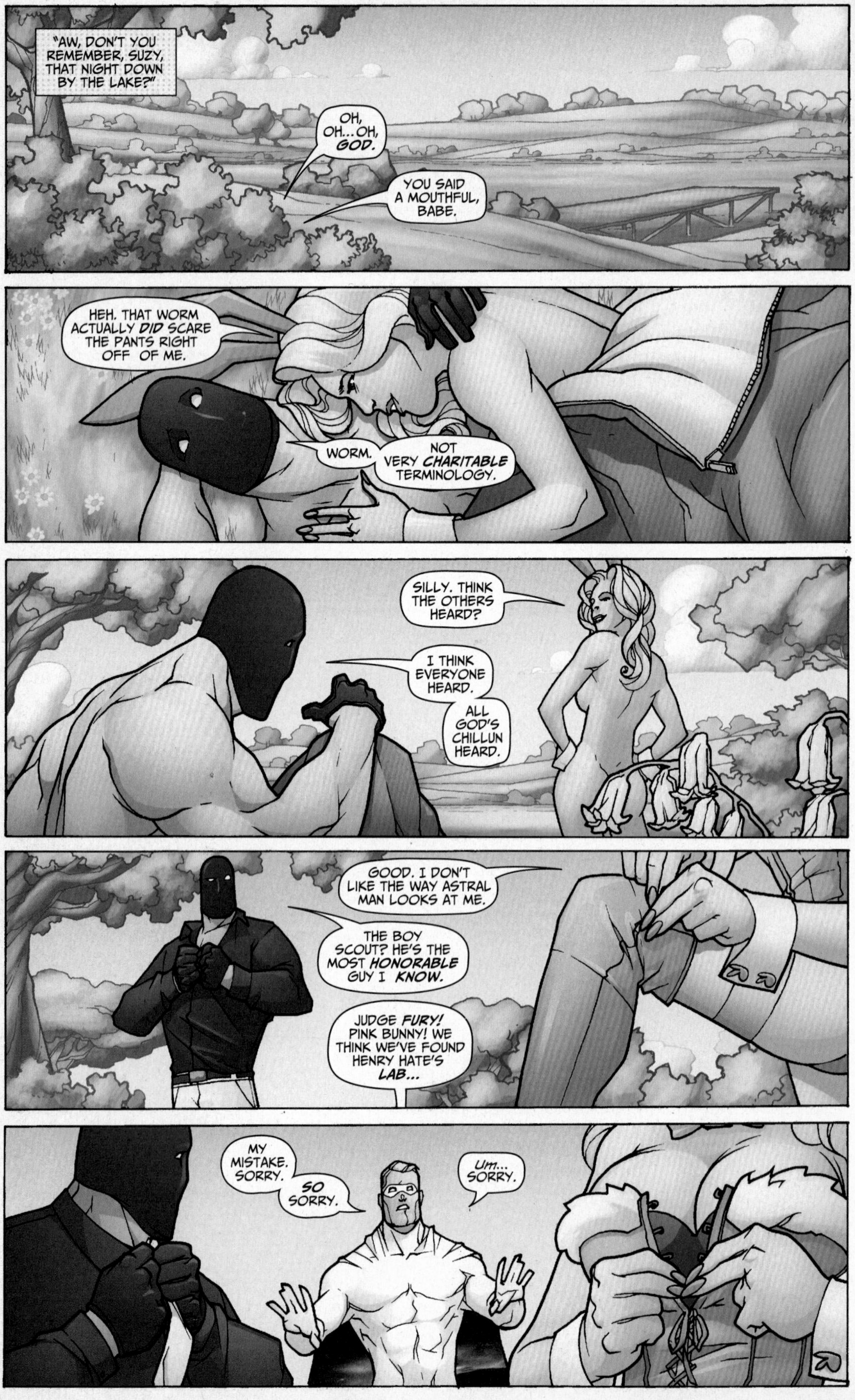
"AW, DON'T YOU REMEMBER, SUZY, THAT NIGHT DOWN BY THE LAKE?"
OH, OH...OH, GOD.
YOU SAID A MOUTHFUL, BABE.
HEH. THAT WORM ACTUALLY DID SCARE THE PANTS RIGHT OFF OF ME.
WORM.
NOT VERY CHARITABLE TERMINOLOGY.
SILLY. THINK THE OTHERS HEARD?
I THINK EVERYONE HEARD.
ALL GOD'S CHILLUN HEARD.
GOOD. I DON'T LIKE THE WAY ASTRAL MAN LOOKS AT ME.
THE BOY SCOUT? HE'S THE MOST HONORABLE GUY I KNOW.
JUDGE FURY! PINK BUNNY! WE THINK WE'VE FOUND HENRY HATE'S LAB...
MY MISTAKE. SORRY.
SO SORRY.
Um... SORRY.

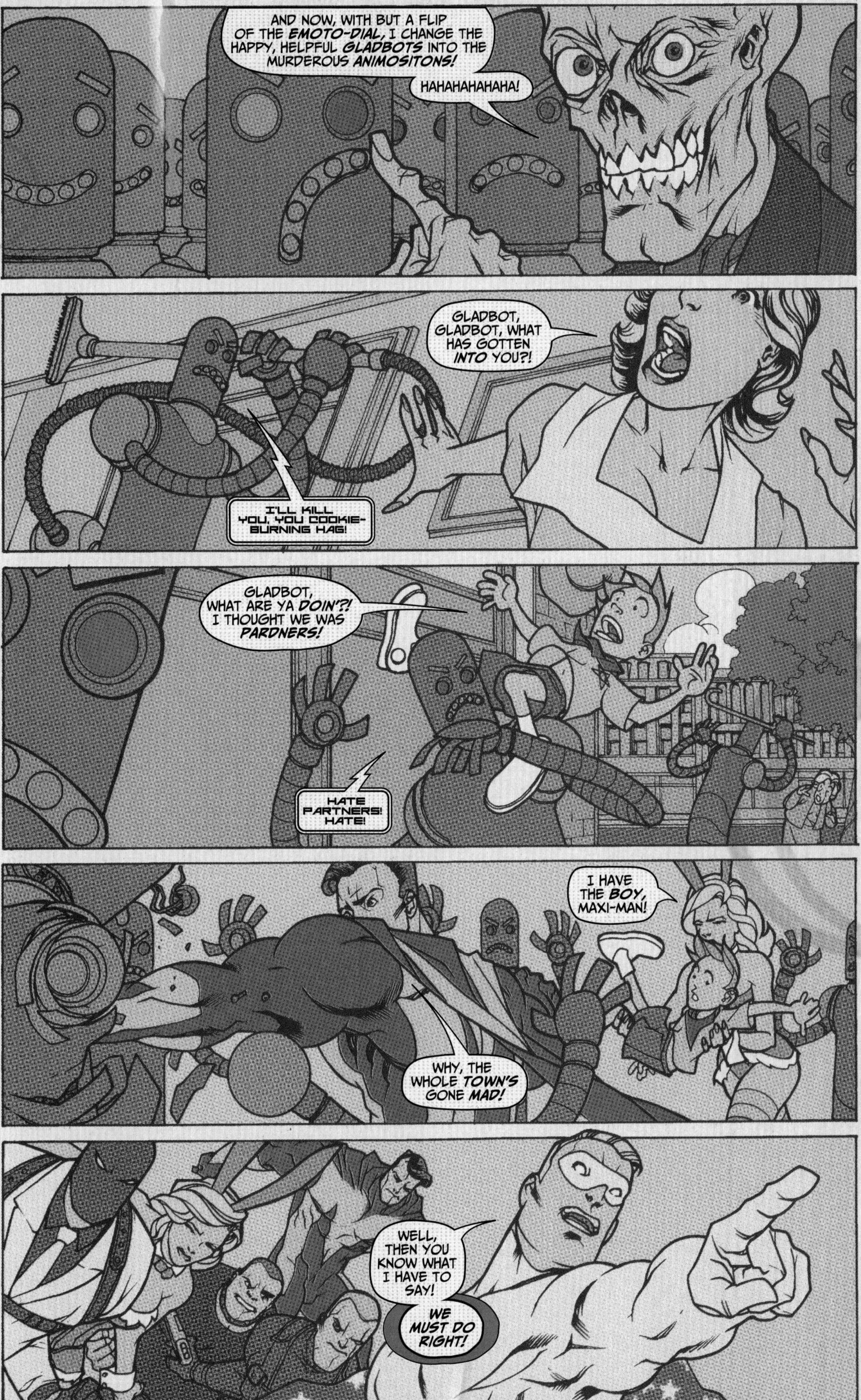
AND NOW, WITH BUT A FLIP OF THE EMOTO-DIAL, I CHANGE THE HAPPY, HELPFUL GLADBOTS INTO THE MURDEROUS ANIMOSITONS!
HAHAHAHAHAHA!
GLADBOT, GLADBOT, WHAT HAS GOTTEN INTO YOU?!
I'LL KILL YOU, YOU COOKIE-BURNING HAG!
GLADBOT, WHAT ARE YA DOIN'?! I THOUGHT WE WAS PARDNERS!
HATE PARTNERS! HATE!
I HAVE THE BOY, MAXI-MAN!
WHY, THE WHOLE TOWN'S GONE MAD!
WELL, THEN YOU KNOW WHAT I HAVE TO SAY!
WE MUST DO RIGHT!

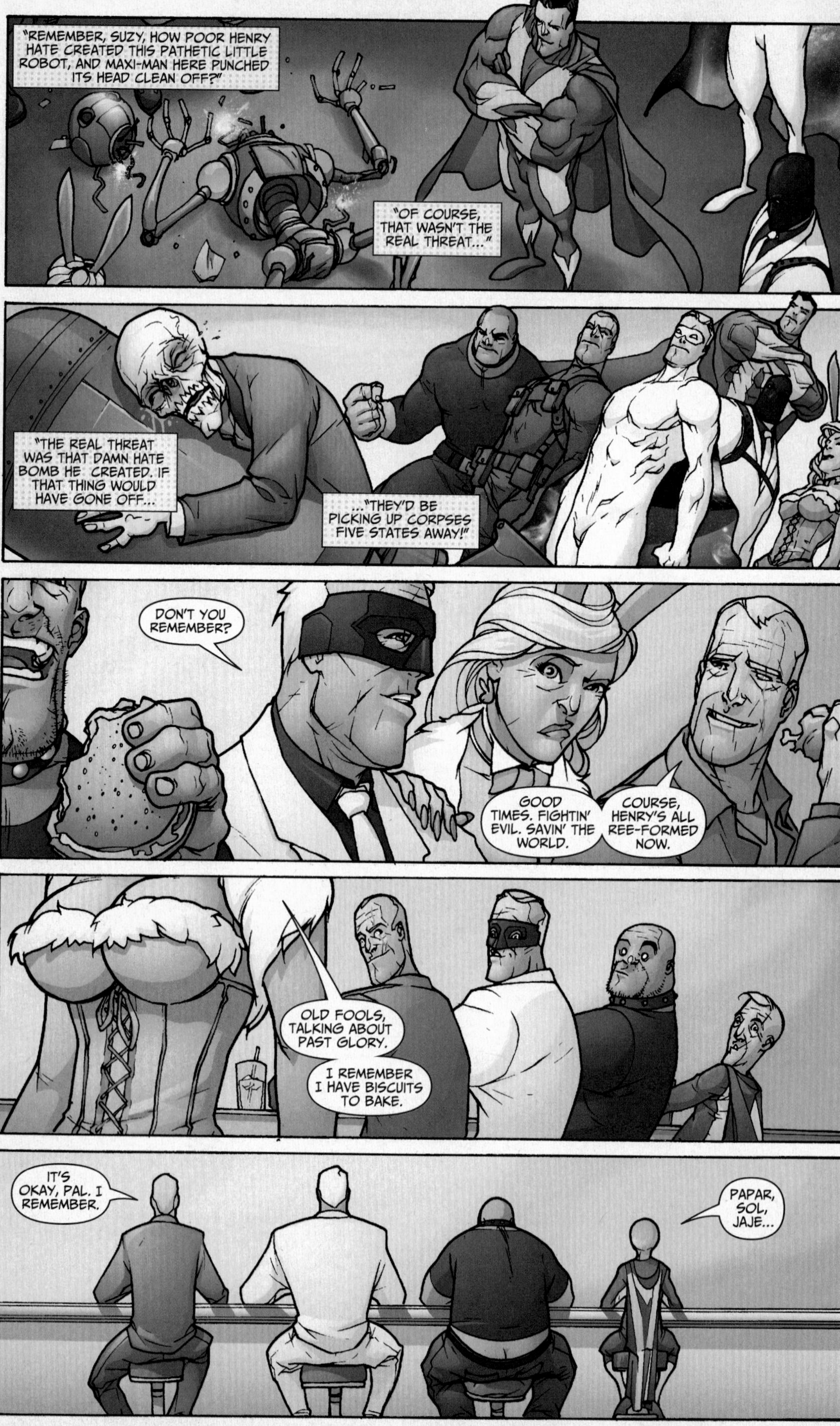
"REMEMBER, SUZY, HOW POOR HENRY HATE CREATED THIS PATHETIC LITTLE ROBOT, AND MAXI-MAN HERE PUNCHED ITS HEAD CLEAN OFF?"
"OF COURSE, THAT WASN'T THE REAL THREAT..."
"THE REAL THREAT WAS THAT DAMN HATE BOMB HE CREATED. IF THAT THING WOULD HAVE GONE OFF...
..."THEY'D BE PICKING UP CORPSES FIVE STATES AWAY!"
DON'T YOU REMEMBER?
GOOD TIMES. FIGHTIN' EVIL. SAVIN' THE WORLD.
COURSE, HENRY'S ALL REE-FORMED NOW.
OLD FOOLS, TALKING ABOUT PAST GLORY.
I REMEMBER I HAVE BISCUITS TO BAKE.
IT'S OKAY, PAL. I REMEMBER.
PAPAR, SOL, JAJE...

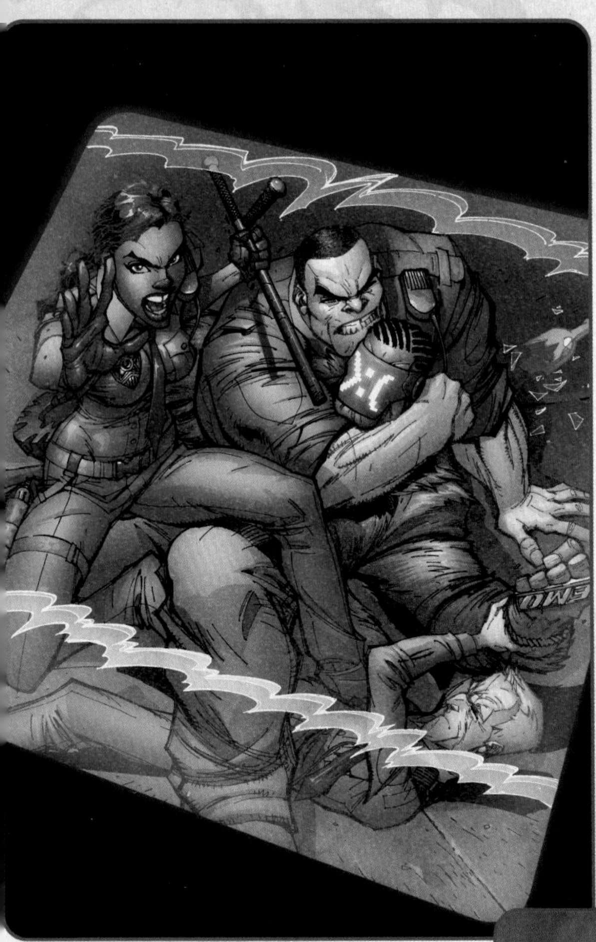

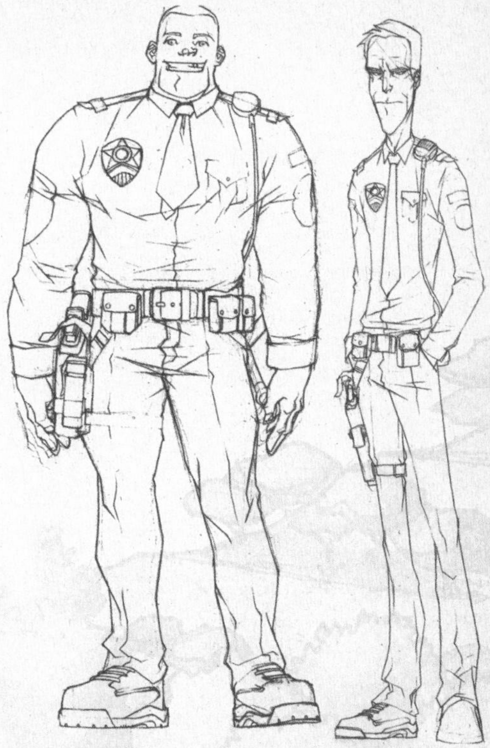

Variant Cover 1

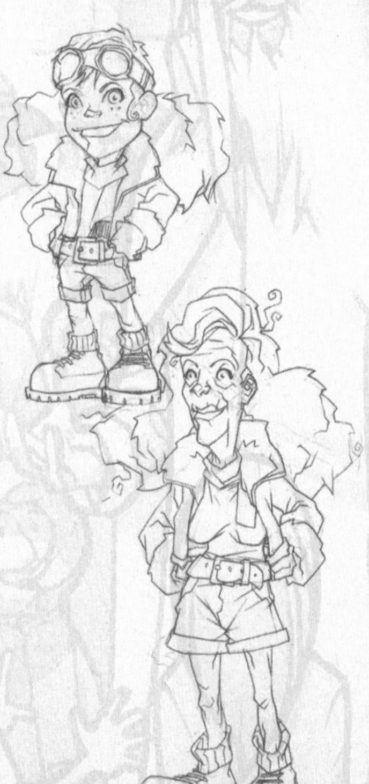

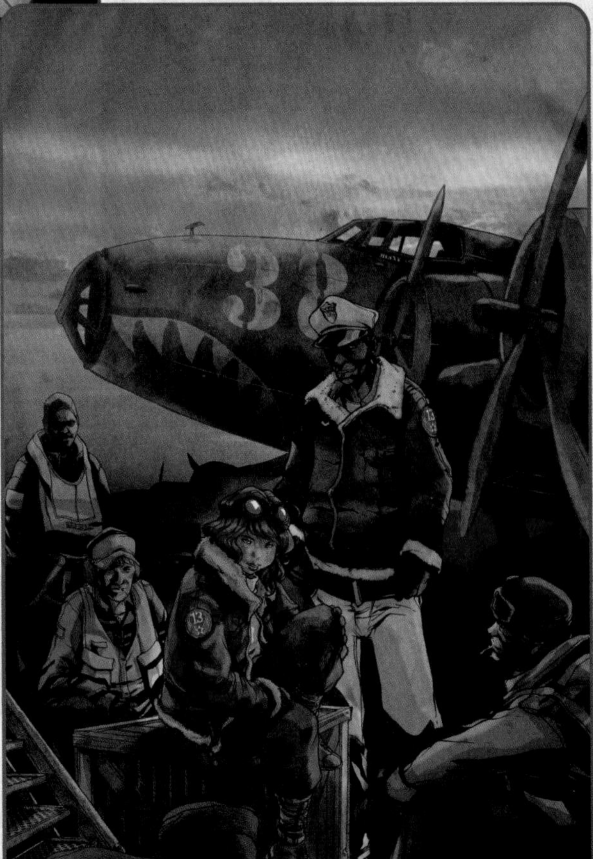
38

Variant Cover 2

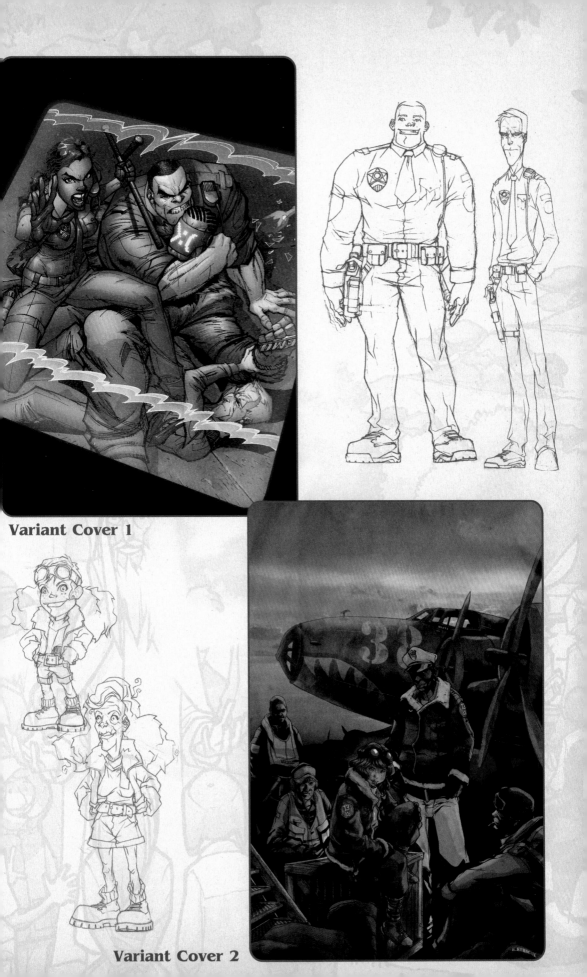

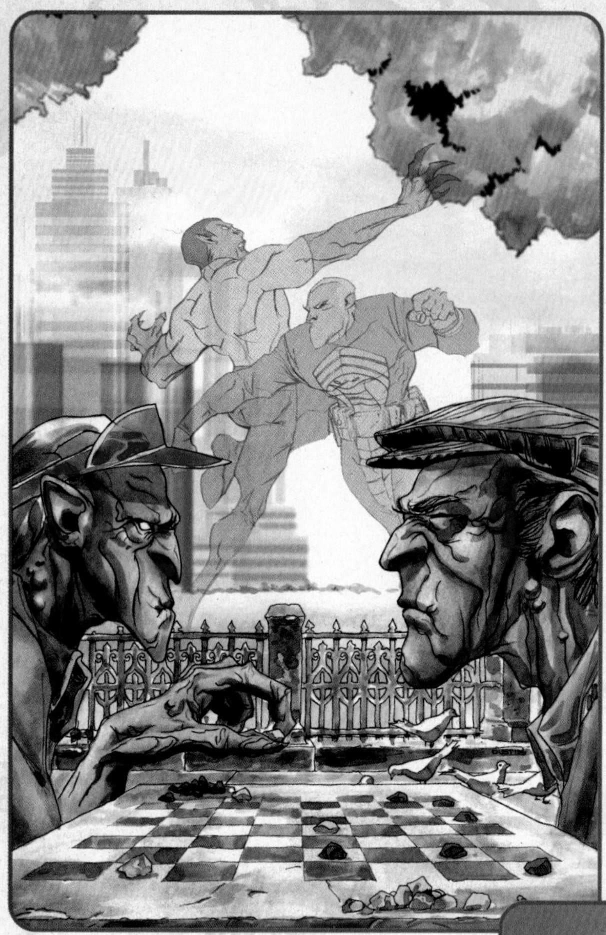

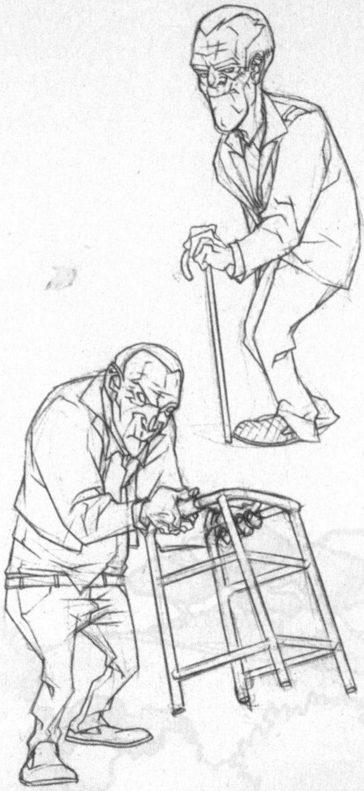

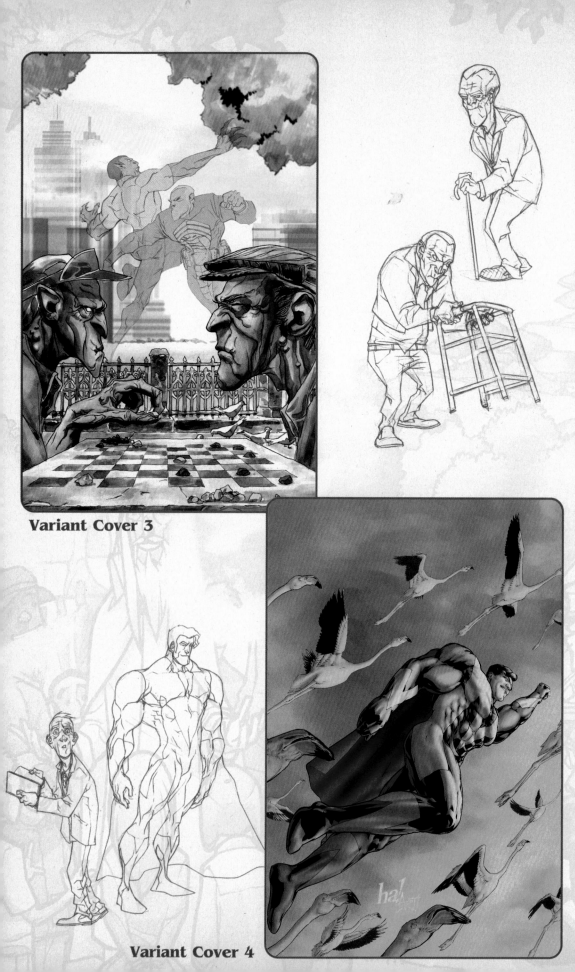

Variant Cover 3

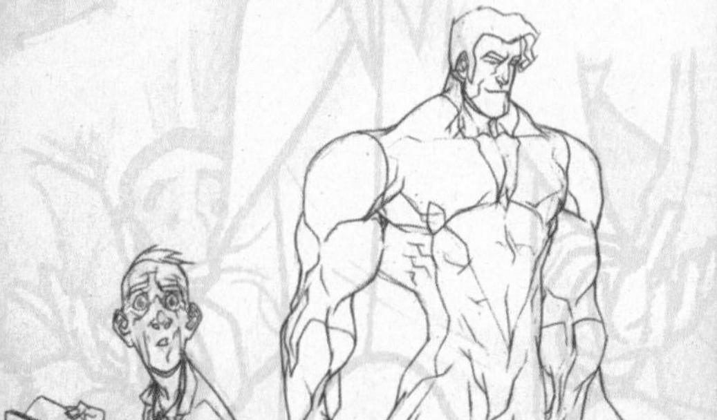

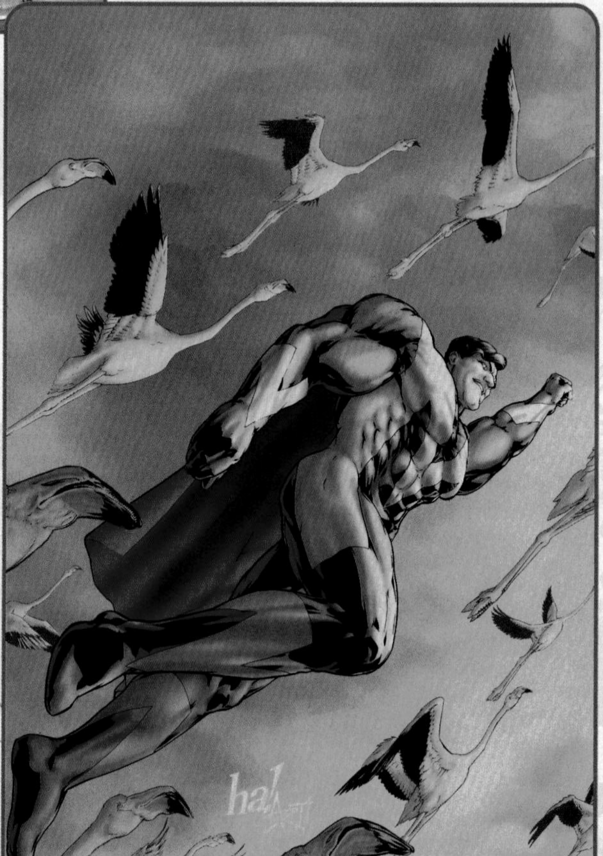

Variant Cover 4

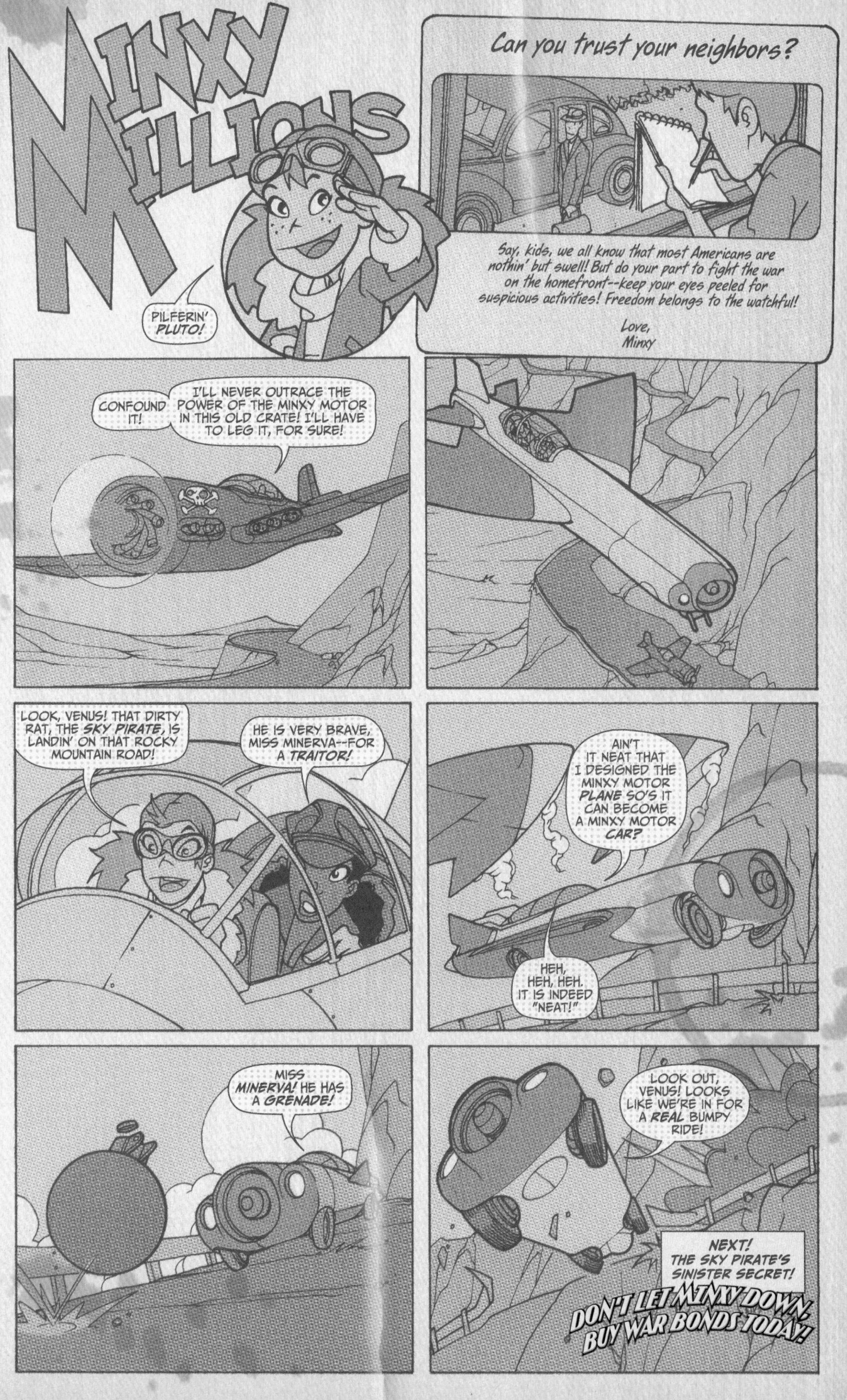
MINXY MILLIONS
Can you trust your neighbors?
Say, kids, we all know that most Americans are nothin' but swell! But do your part to fight the war on the homefront--keep your eyes peeled for suspicious activities! Freedom belongs to the watchful!
Love, Minxy
PILFERIN' PLUTO!
CONFOUND IT!
I'LL NEVER OUTRACE THE POWER OF THE MINXY MOTOR IN THIS OLD CRATE! I'LL HAVE TO LEG IT, FOR SURE!
LOOK, VENUS! THAT DIRTY RAT, THE SKY PIRATE, IS LANDIN' ON THAT ROCKY MOUNTAIN ROAD!
HE IS VERY BRAVE, MISS MINERVA--FOR A TRAITOR!
AIN'T IT NEAT THAT I DESIGNED THE MINXY MOTOR PLANE SO'S IT CAN BECOME A MINXY MOTOR CAR?
HEH, HEH, HEH. IT IS INDEED "NEAT!"
MISS MINERVA! HE HAS A GRENADE!
LOOK OUT, VENUS! LOOKS LIKE WE'RE IN FOR A REAL BUMPY RIDE!
NEXT! THE SKY PIRATE'S SINISTER SECRET!
DON'T LET MINXY DOWN, BUY WAR BONDS TODAY!

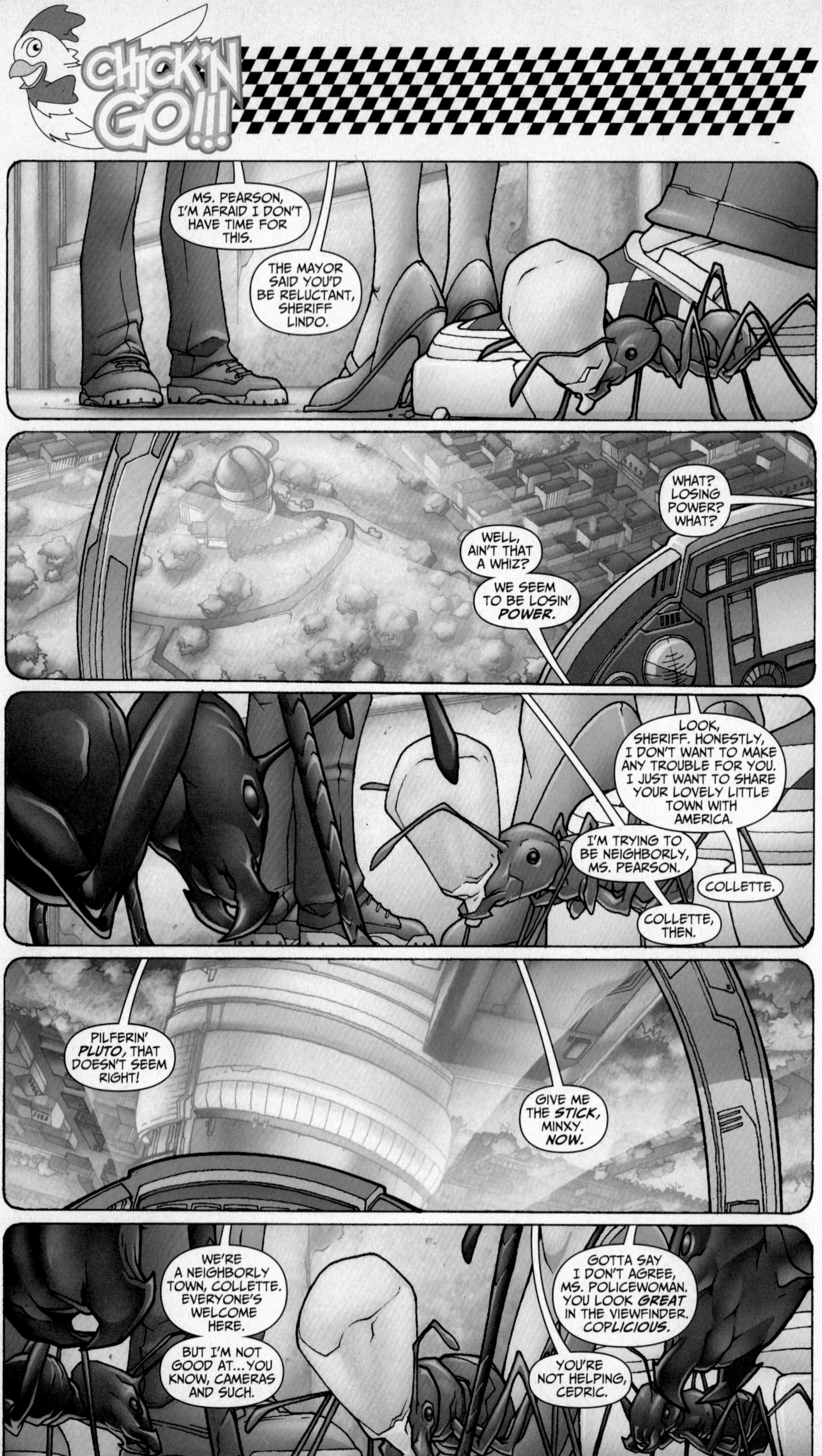
CHICK'N GO!!!
MS. PEARSON, I'M AFRAID I DON'T HAVE TIME FOR THIS.
THE MAYOR SAID YOU'D BE RELUCTANT, SHERIFF LINDO.
WHAT? LOSING POWER? WHAT?
WELL, AIN'T THAT A WHIZ?
WE SEEM TO BE LOSIN' POWER.
LOOK, SHERIFF. HONESTLY, I DON'T WANT TO MAKE ANY TROUBLE FOR YOU. I JUST WANT TO SHARE YOUR LOVELY LITTLE TOWN WITH AMERICA.
I'M TRYING TO BE NEIGHBORLY, MS. PEARSON.
COLLETTE.
COLLETTE, THEN.
PILFERIN' PLUTO, THAT DOESN'T SEEM RIGHT!
GIVE ME THE STICK, MINXY. NOW.
WE'RE A NEIGHBORLY TOWN, COLLETTE. EVERYONE'S WELCOME HERE.
BUT I'M NOT GOOD AT...YOU KNOW, CAMERAS AND SUCH.
GOTTA SAY I DON'T AGREE, MS. POLICEWOMAN. YOU LOOK GREAT IN THE VIEWFINDER. COPLICIOUS.
YOU'RE NOT HELPING, CEDRIC.

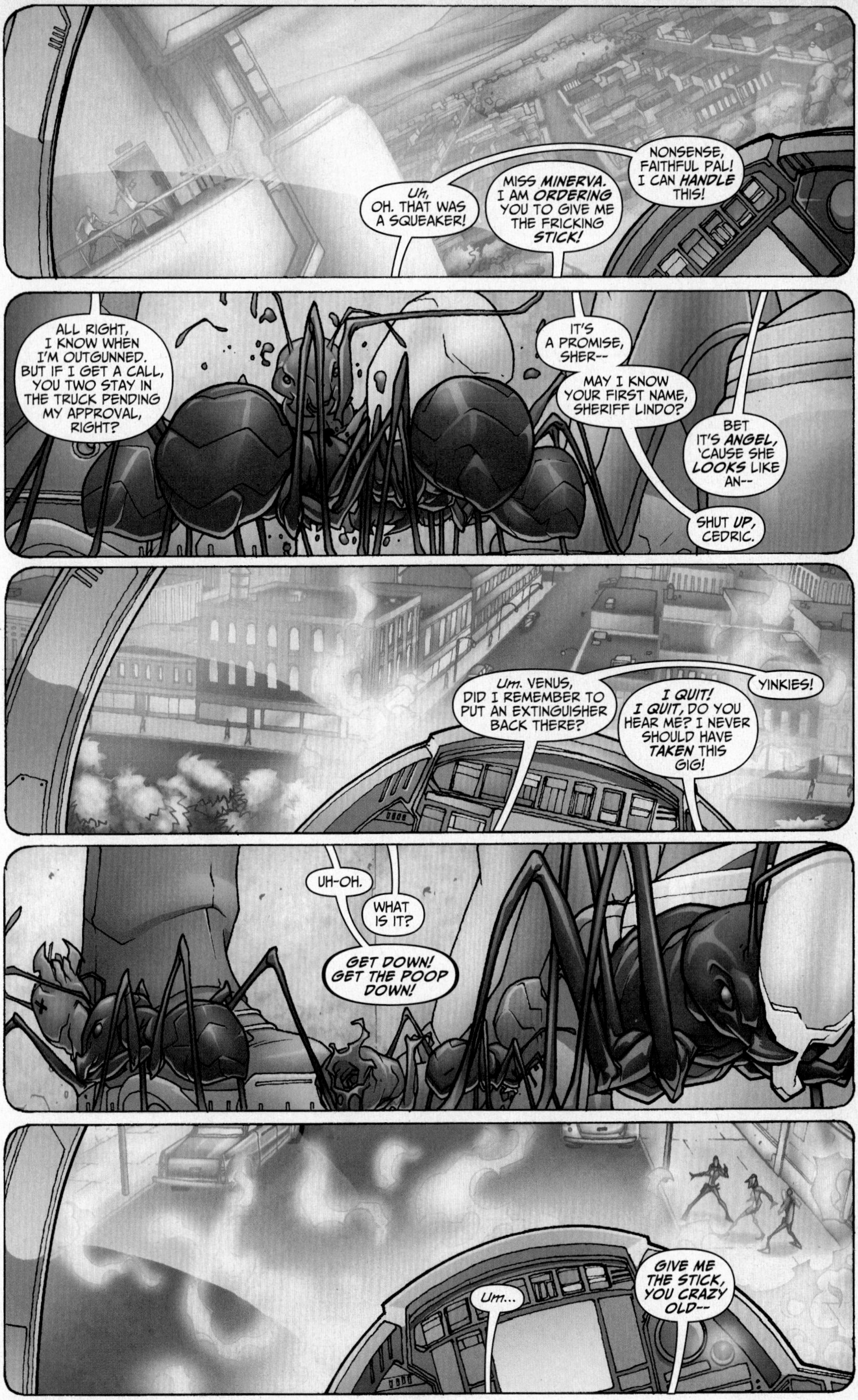
Uh, OH. THAT WAS A SQUEAKER!
MISS MINERVA. I AM ORDERING YOU TO GIVE ME THE FRICKING STICK!
NONSENSE, FAITHFUL PAL! I CAN HANDLE THIS!
ALL RIGHT, I KNOW WHEN I'M OUTGUNNED. BUT IF I GET A CALL, YOU TWO STAY IN THE TRUCK PENDING MY APPROVAL, RIGHT?
IT'S A PROMISE, SHER--
MAY I KNOW YOUR FIRST NAME, SHERIFF LINDO?
BET IT'S ANGEL, 'CAUSE SHE LOOKS LIKE AN--
SHUT UP, CEDRIC.
Um. VENUS, DID I REMEMBER TO PUT AN EXTINGUISHER BACK THERE?
YINKIES!
I QUIT! I QUIT, DO YOU HEAR ME? I NEVER SHOULD HAVE TAKEN THIS GIG!
UH-OH.
WHAT IS IT?
GET DOWN! GET THE POOP DOWN!
Um...
GIVE ME THE STICK, YOU CRAZY OLD--

CHICK'N GO!!!

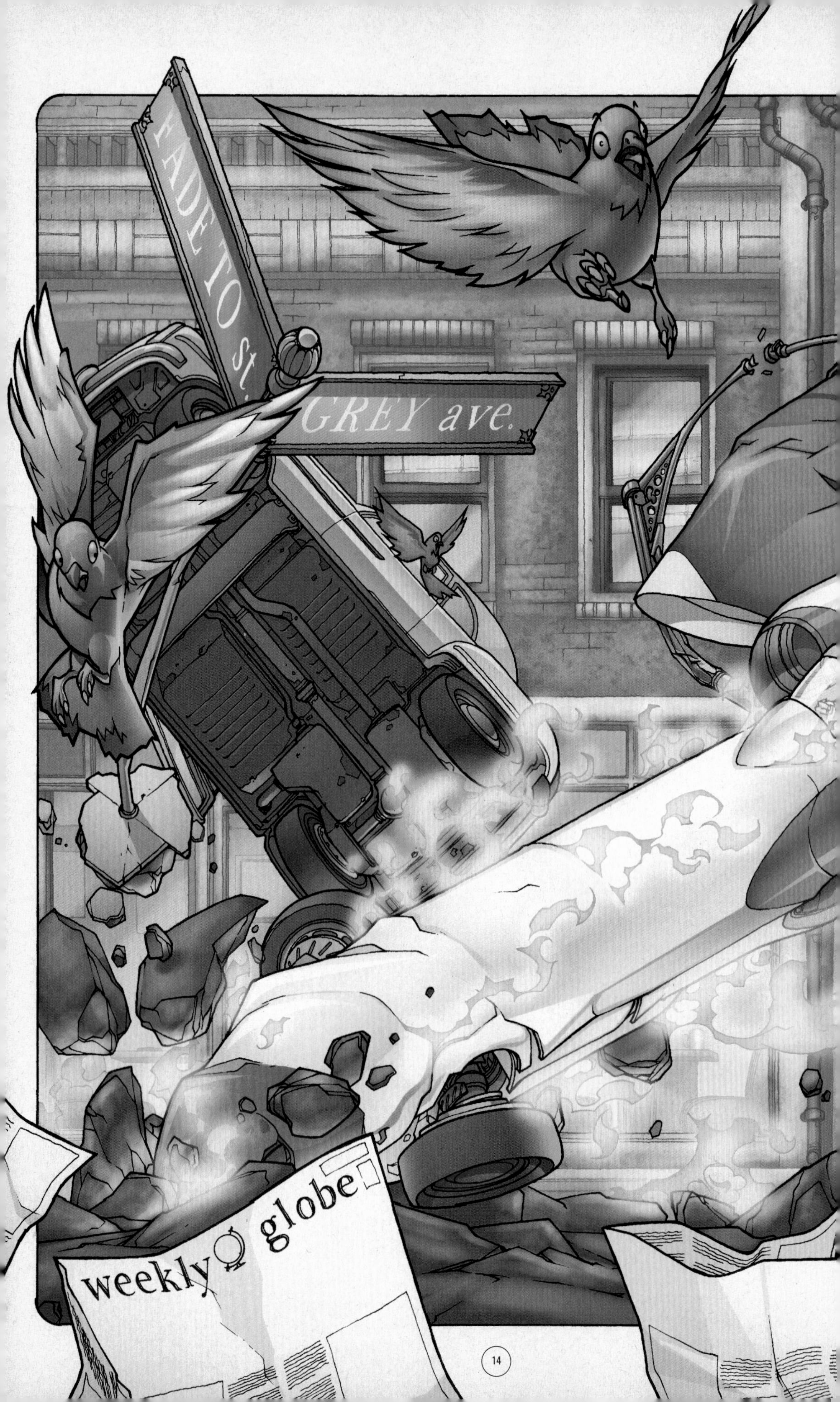
HADETO st.
GREY ave.
weekly globe

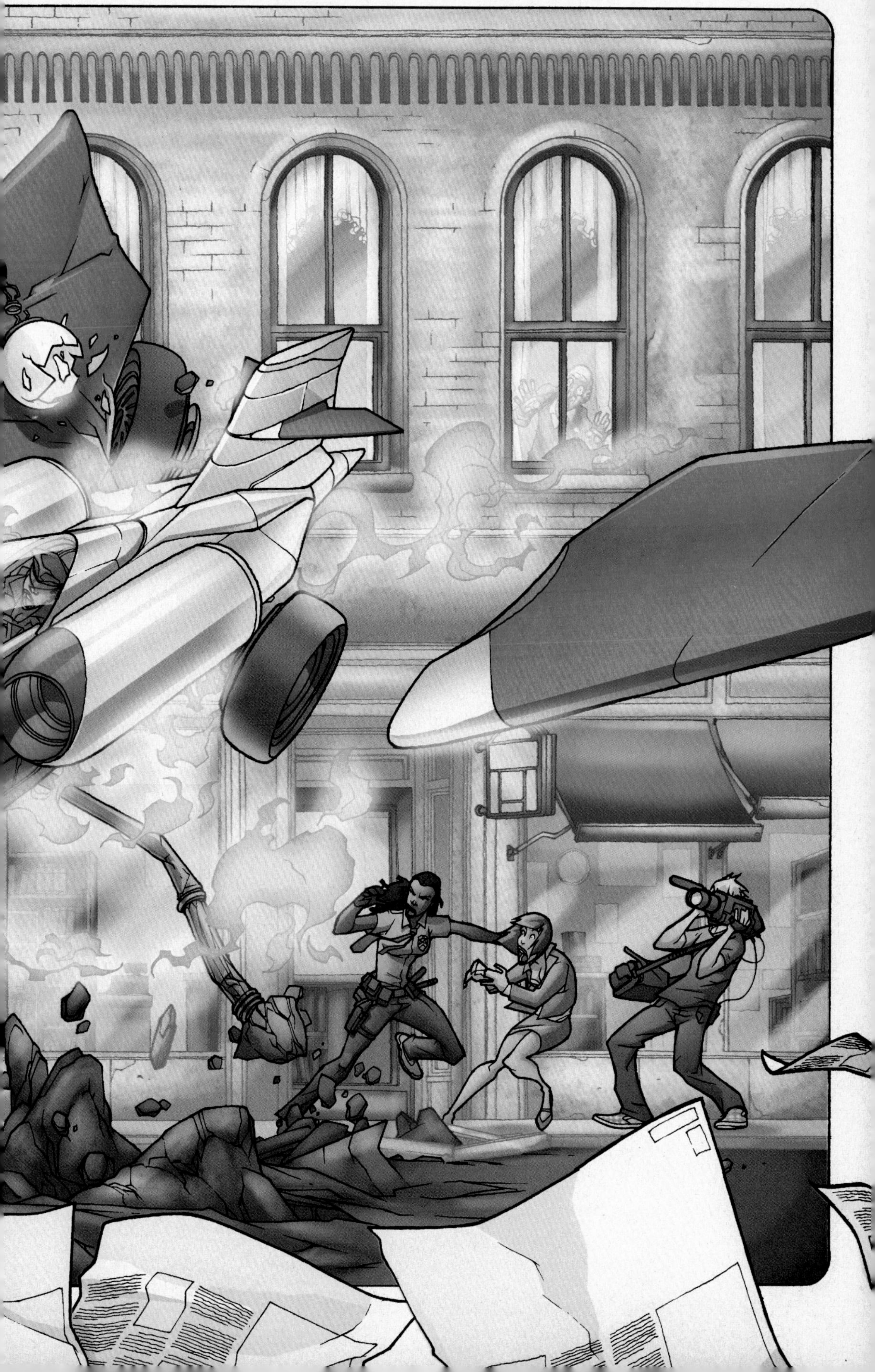

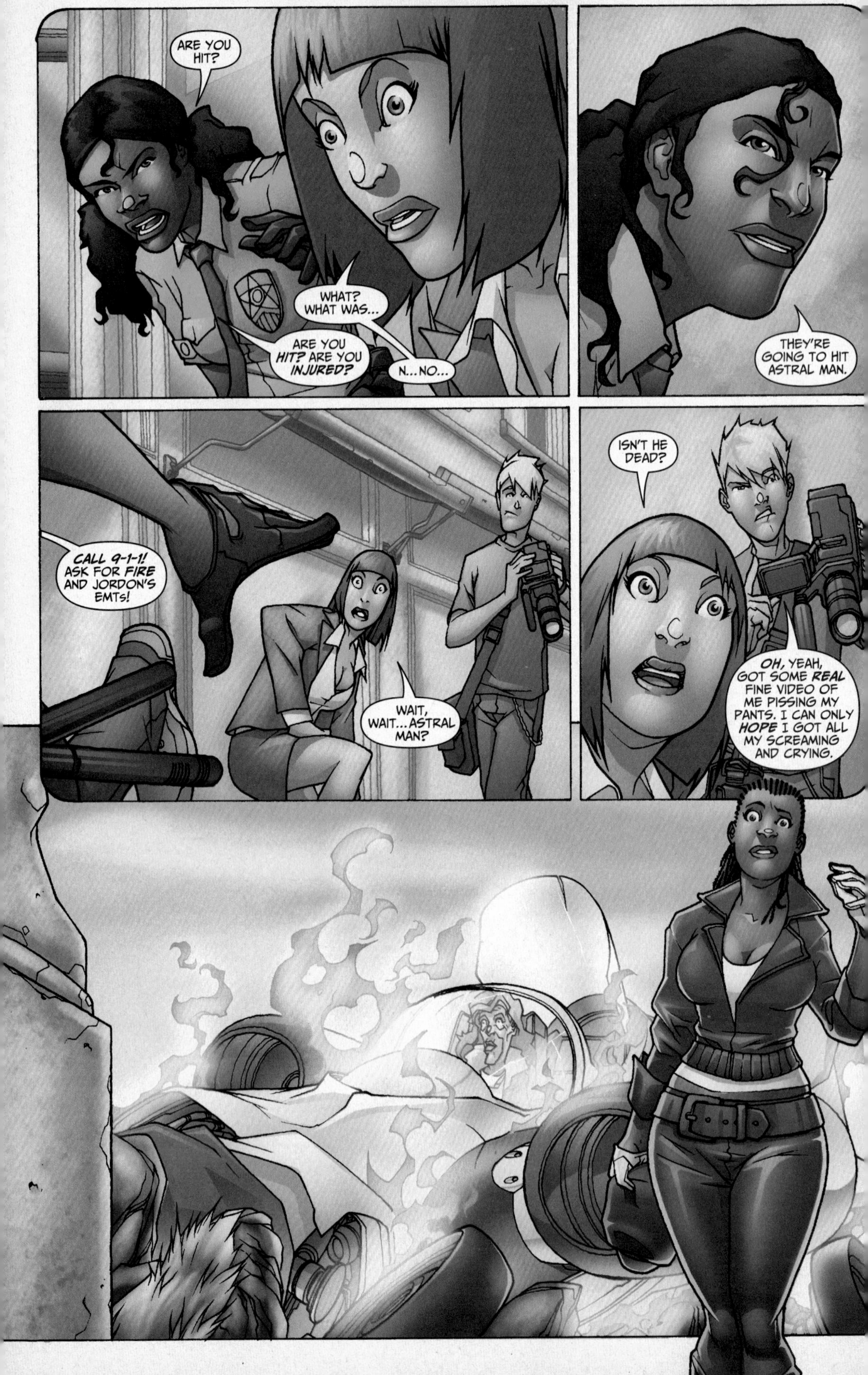

ARE YOU HIT?
WHAT? WHAT WAS...
ARE YOU *HIT?* ARE YOU *INJURED?*
N...NO...
THEY'RE GOING TO HIT ASTRAL MAN.
CALL 9-1-1! ASK FOR *FIRE* AND JORDON'S EMTs!
WAIT, WAIT...ASTRAL MAN?
ISN'T HE DEAD?
OH, YEAH, GOT SOME *REAL* FINE VIDEO OF ME PISSING MY PANTS. I CAN ONLY *HOPE* I GOT ALL MY SCREAMING AND CRYING.

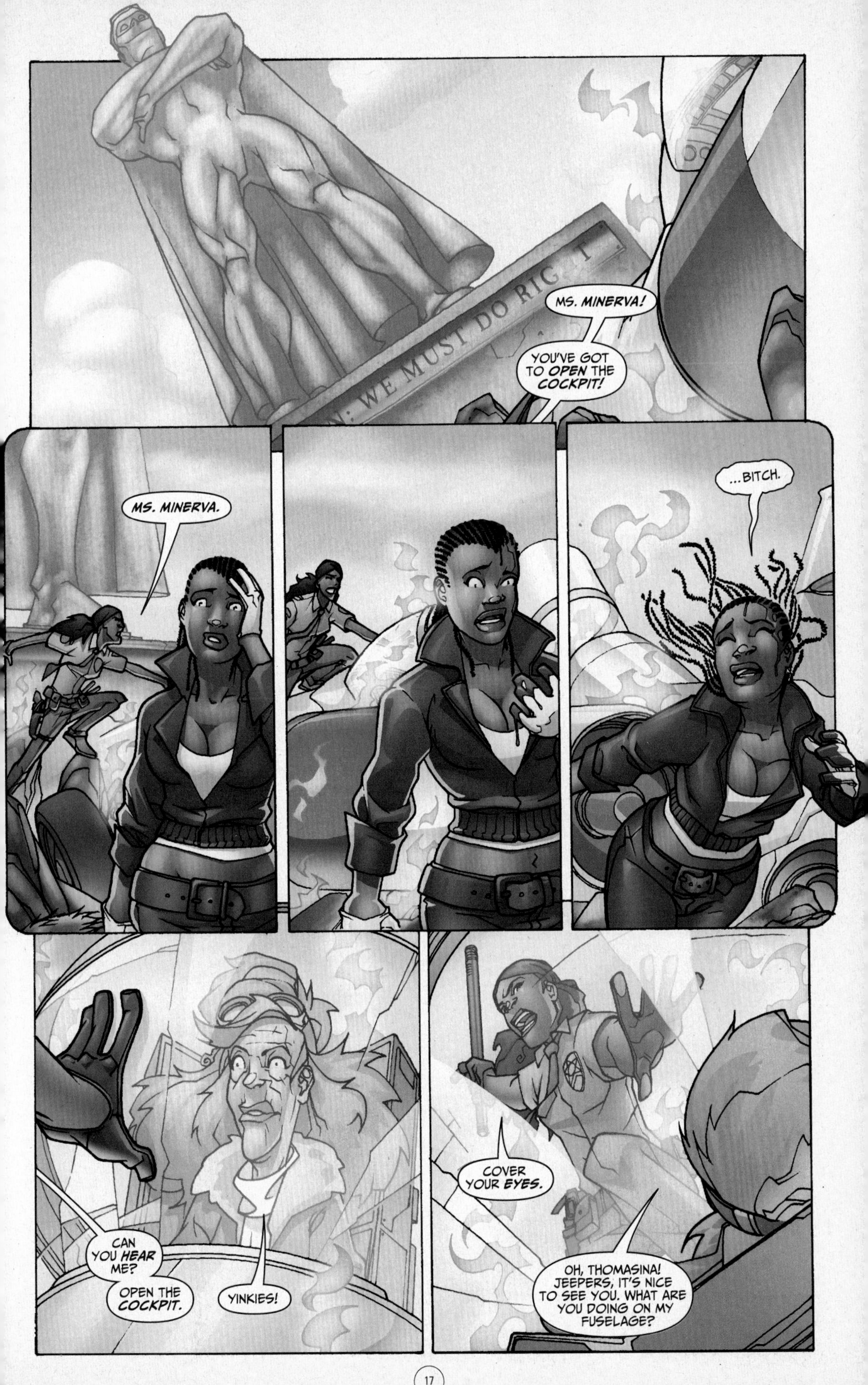
WE MUST DO RIG T
MS. MINERVA!
YOU'VE GOT TO OPEN THE COCKPIT!
MS. MINERVA.
...BITCH.
CAN YOU HEAR ME?
OPEN THE COCKPIT.
YINKIES!
COVER YOUR EYES.
OH, THOMASINA! JEEPERS, IT'S NICE TO SEE YOU. WHAT ARE YOU DOING ON MY FUSELAGE?

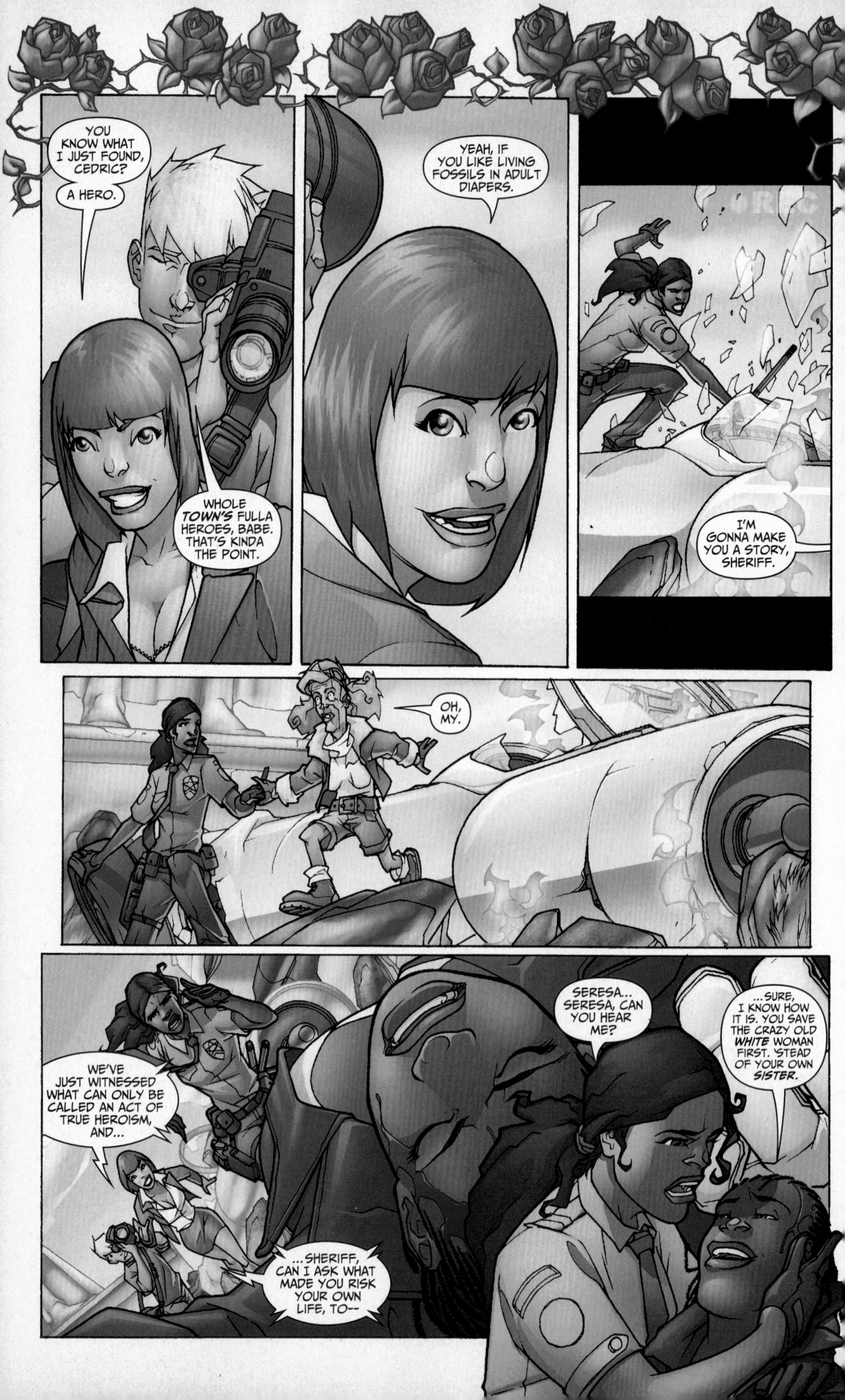
YOU KNOW WHAT I JUST FOUND, CEDRIC?
A HERO.
WHOLE *TOWN'S* FULLA HEROES, BABE. THAT'S KINDA THE POINT.
YEAH, IF YOU LIKE LIVING FOSSILS IN ADULT DIAPERS.
REC
I'M GONNA MAKE YOU A STORY, SHERIFF.
OH, MY.
WE'VE JUST WITNESSED WHAT CAN ONLY BE CALLED AN ACT OF TRUE HEROISM, AND...
...SHERIFF, CAN I ASK WHAT MADE YOU RISK YOUR OWN LIFE, TO--
SERESA... SERESA, CAN YOU HEAR ME?
...SURE, I KNOW HOW IT IS. YOU SAVE THE CRAZY OLD *WHITE* WOMAN FIRST. 'STEAD OF YOUR OWN *SISTER*.

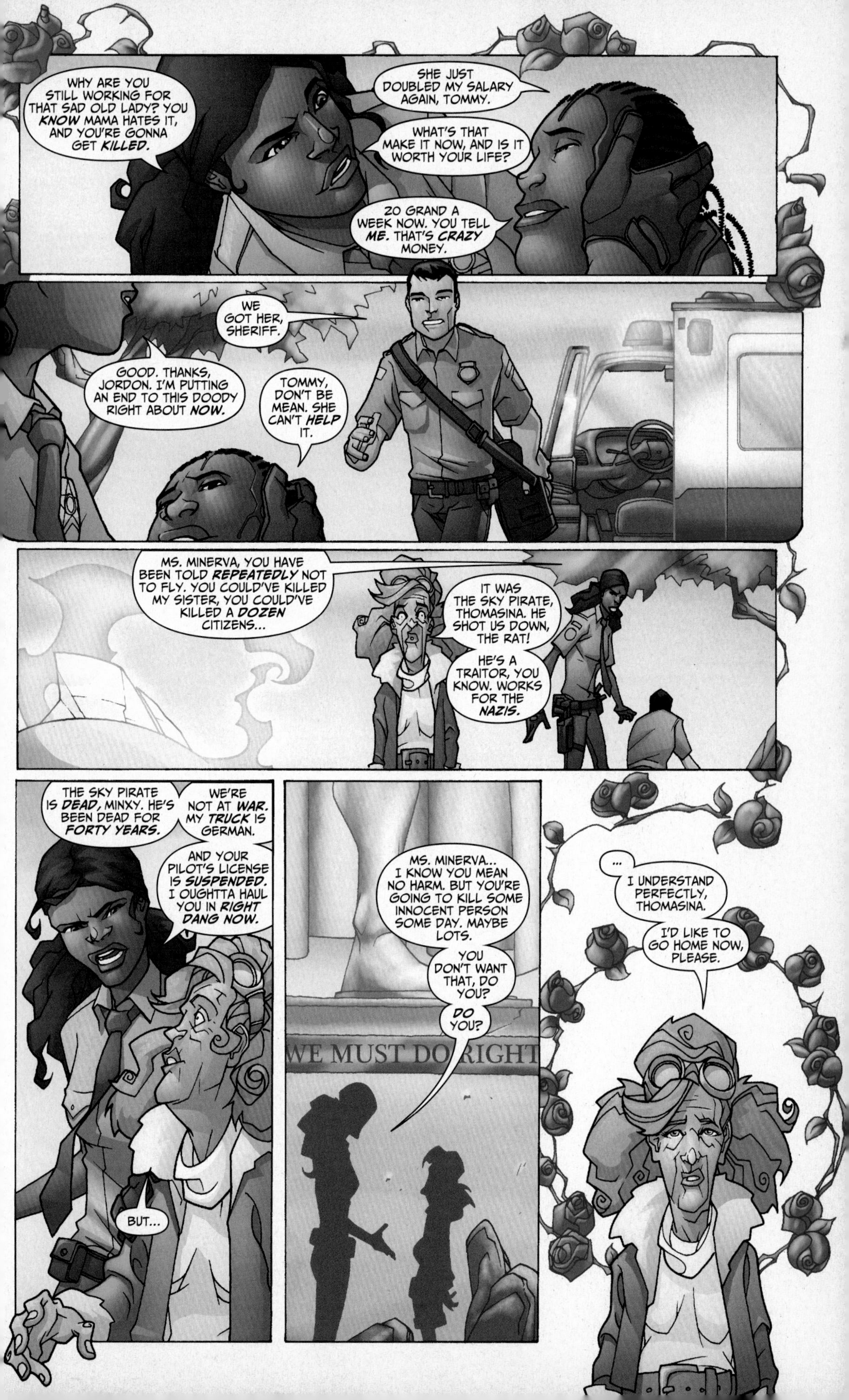
WHY ARE YOU STILL WORKING FOR THAT SAD OLD LADY? YOU KNOW MAMA HATES IT, AND YOU'RE GONNA GET KILLED.
SHE JUST DOUBLED MY SALARY AGAIN, TOMMY.
WHAT'S THAT MAKE IT NOW, AND IS IT WORTH YOUR LIFE?
20 GRAND A WEEK NOW. YOU TELL ME. THAT'S CRAZY MONEY.
WE GOT HER, SHERIFF.
GOOD. THANKS, JORDON. I'M PUTTING AN END TO THIS DOODY RIGHT ABOUT NOW.
TOMMY, DON'T BE MEAN. SHE CAN'T HELP IT.
MS. MINERVA, YOU HAVE BEEN TOLD REPEATEDLY NOT TO FLY. YOU COULD'VE KILLED MY SISTER, YOU COULD'VE KILLED A DOZEN CITIZENS...
IT WAS THE SKY PIRATE, THOMASINA. HE SHOT US DOWN, THE RAT!
HE'S A TRAITOR, YOU KNOW. WORKS FOR THE NAZIS.
THE SKY PIRATE IS DEAD, MINXY. HE'S BEEN DEAD FOR FORTY YEARS.
WE'RE NOT AT WAR. MY TRUCK IS GERMAN.
AND YOUR PILOT'S LICENSE IS SUSPENDED. I OUGHTTA HAUL YOU IN RIGHT DANG NOW.
BUT...
MS. MINERVA... I KNOW YOU MEAN NO HARM. BUT YOU'RE GOING TO KILL SOME INNOCENT PERSON SOME DAY. MAYBE LOTS.
YOU DON'T WANT THAT, DO YOU?
DO YOU?
WE MUST DO RIGHT
...
I UNDERSTAND PERFECTLY, THOMASINA.
I'D LIKE TO GO HOME NOW, PLEASE.

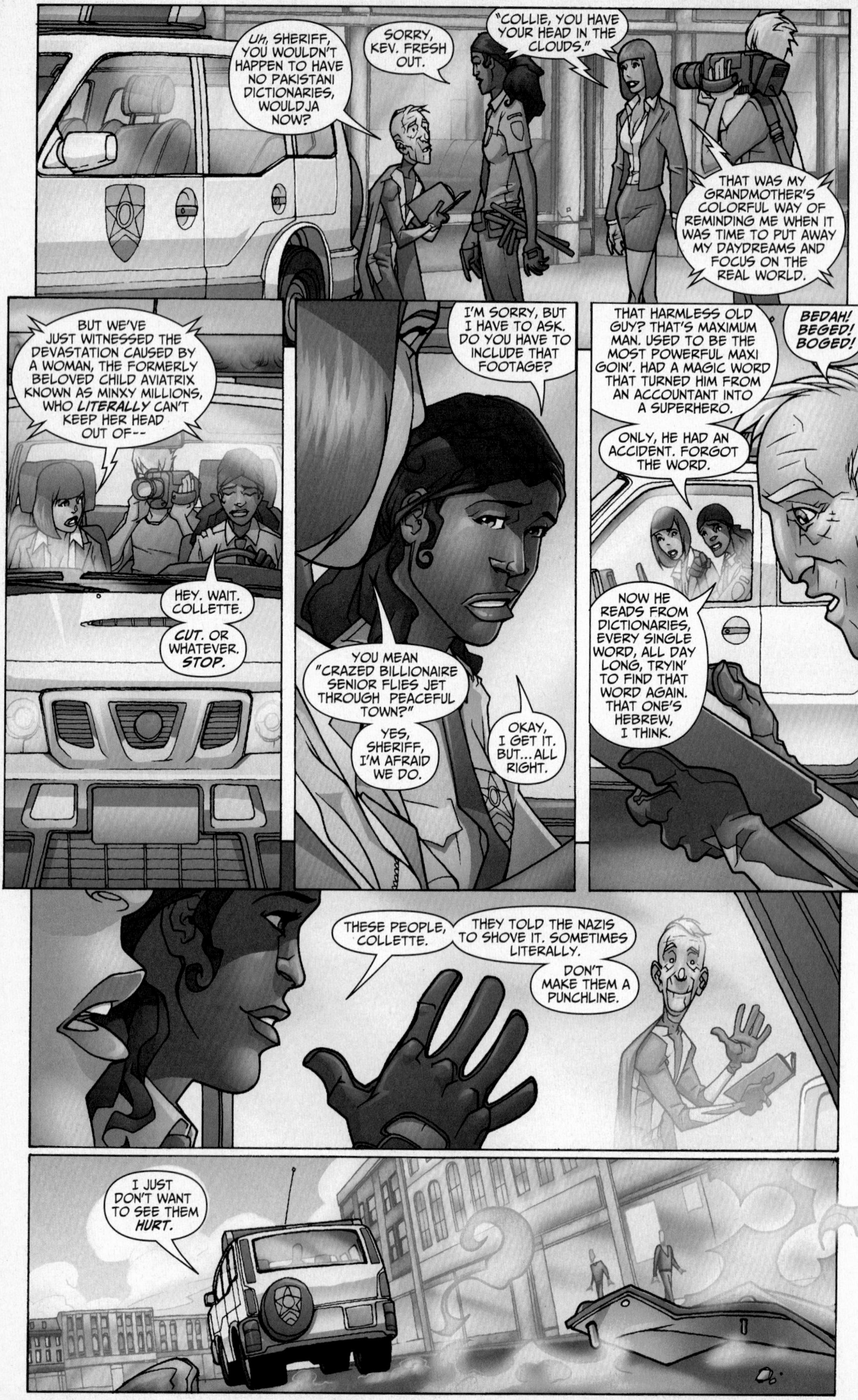
Uh, SHERIFF, YOU WOULDN'T HAPPEN TO HAVE NO PAKISTANI DICTIONARIES, WOULDJA NOW?
SORRY, KEV. FRESH OUT.
"COLLIE, YOU HAVE YOUR HEAD IN THE CLOUDS."
THAT WAS MY GRANDMOTHER'S COLORFUL WAY OF REMINDING ME WHEN IT WAS TIME TO PUT AWAY MY DAYDREAMS AND FOCUS ON THE REAL WORLD.
BUT WE'VE JUST WITNESSED THE DEVASTATION CAUSED BY A WOMAN, THE FORMERLY BELOVED CHILD AVIATRIX KNOWN AS MINXY MILLIONS, WHO LITERALLY CAN'T KEEP HER HEAD OUT OF--
HEY. WAIT. COLLETTE.
CUT. OR WHATEVER. STOP.
I'M SORRY, BUT I HAVE TO ASK. DO YOU HAVE TO INCLUDE THAT FOOTAGE?
YOU MEAN "CRAZED BILLIONAIRE SENIOR FLIES JET THROUGH PEACEFUL TOWN?"
YES, SHERIFF, I'M AFRAID WE DO.
OKAY, I GET IT. BUT... ALL RIGHT.
THAT HARMLESS OLD GUY? THAT'S MAXIMUM MAN. USED TO BE THE MOST POWERFUL MAXI GOIN'. HAD A MAGIC WORD THAT TURNED HIM FROM AN ACCOUNTANT INTO A SUPERHERO.
BEDAH! BEGED! BOGED!
ONLY, HE HAD AN ACCIDENT. FORGOT THE WORD.
NOW HE READS FROM DICTIONARIES, EVERY SINGLE WORD, ALL DAY LONG, TRYIN' TO FIND THAT WORD AGAIN. THAT ONE'S HEBREW, I THINK.
THESE PEOPLE, COLLETTE.
THEY TOLD THE NAZIS TO SHOVE IT. SOMETIMES LITERALLY.
DON'T MAKE THEM A PUNCHLINE.
I JUST DON'T WANT TO SEE THEM HURT.

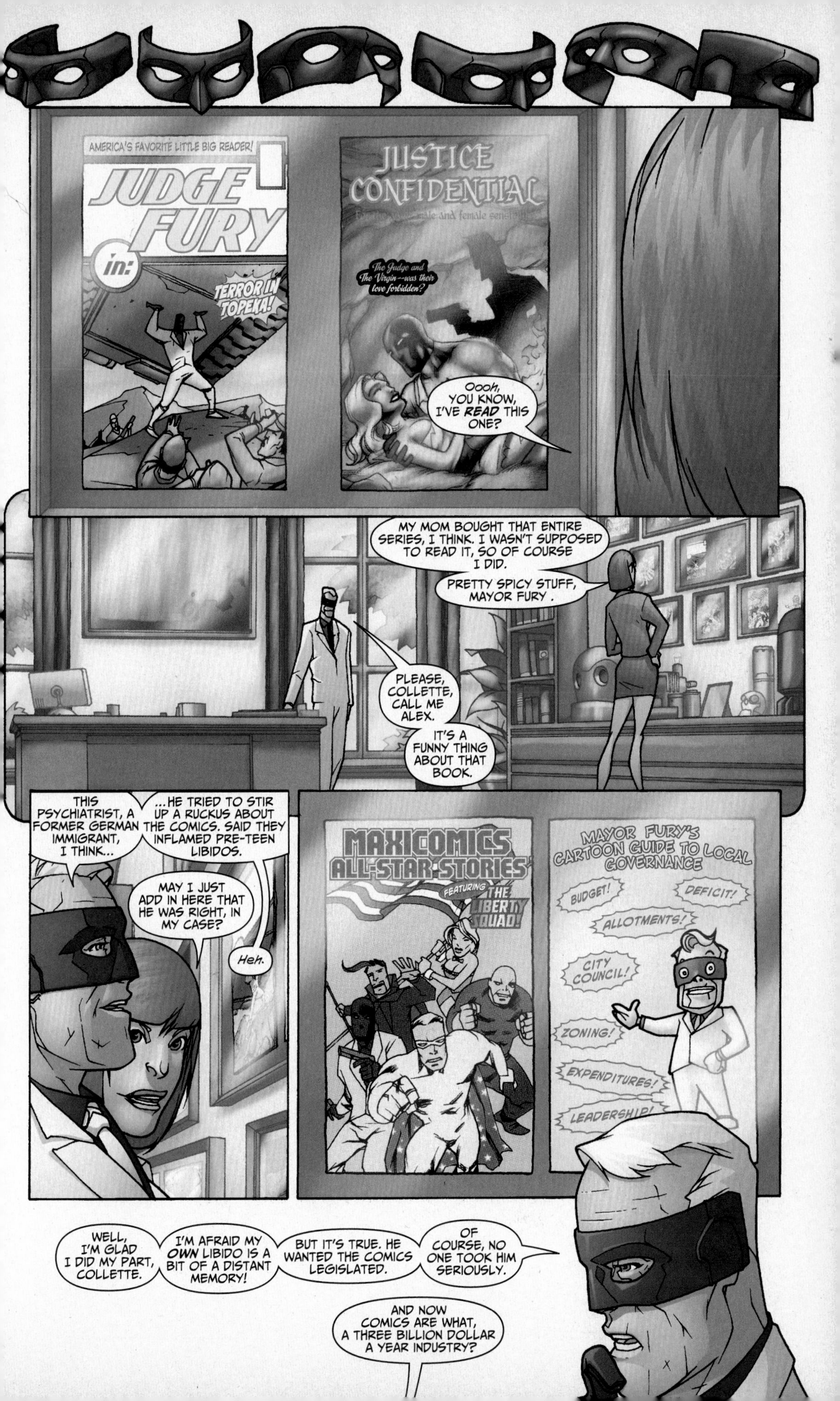
AMERICA'S FAVORITE LITTLE BIG READER!
JUDGE FURY in:
TERROR IN TOPEKA!
JUSTICE CONFIDENTIAL
The Judge and The Virgin--was their love forbidden?
Oooh, YOU KNOW, I'VE READ THIS ONE?
MY MOM BOUGHT THAT ENTIRE SERIES, I THINK. I WASN'T SUPPOSED TO READ IT, SO OF COURSE I DID.
PRETTY SPICY STUFF, MAYOR FURY .
PLEASE, COLLETTE, CALL ME ALEX.
IT'S A FUNNY THING ABOUT THAT BOOK.
THIS PSYCHIATRIST, A FORMER GERMAN IMMIGRANT, I THINK...
...HE TRIED TO STIR UP A RUCKUS ABOUT THE COMICS. SAID THEY INFLAMED PRE-TEEN LIBIDOS.
MAY I JUST ADD IN HERE THAT HE WAS RIGHT, IN MY CASE?
Heh.
MAXICOMICS ALL-STAR STORIES
FEATURING THE LIBERTY SQUAD!
MAYOR FURY'S CARTOON GUIDE TO LOCAL GOVERNANCE
BUDGET!
DEFICIT!
ALLOTMENTS!
CITY COUNCIL!
ZONING!
EXPENDITURES!
LEADERSHIP!
WELL, I'M GLAD I DID MY PART, COLLETTE.
I'M AFRAID MY OWN LIBIDO IS A BIT OF A DISTANT MEMORY!
BUT IT'S TRUE. HE WANTED THE COMICS LEGISLATED.
OF COURSE, NO ONE TOOK HIM SERIOUSLY.
AND NOW COMICS ARE WHAT, A THREE BILLION DOLLAR A YEAR INDUSTRY?

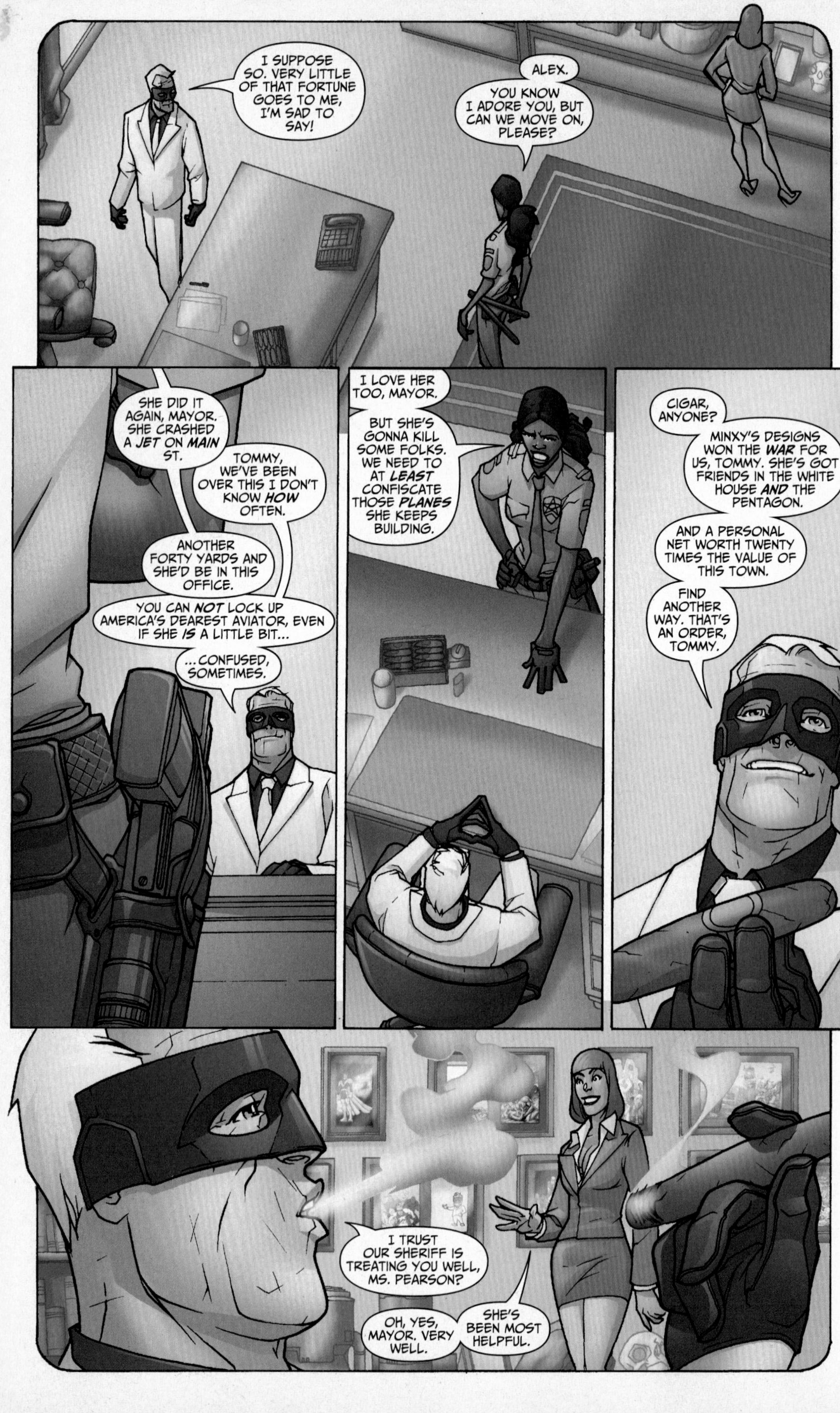

I SUPPOSE SO. VERY LITTLE OF THAT FORTUNE GOES TO ME, I'M SAD TO SAY!
ALEX.
YOU KNOW I ADORE YOU, BUT CAN WE MOVE ON, PLEASE?
SHE DID IT AGAIN, MAYOR. SHE CRASHED A JET ON MAIN ST.
TOMMY, WE'VE BEEN OVER THIS I DON'T KNOW HOW OFTEN.
ANOTHER FORTY YARDS AND SHE'D BE IN THIS OFFICE.
YOU CAN NOT LOCK UP AMERICA'S DEAREST AVIATOR, EVEN IF SHE IS A LITTLE BIT...
...CONFUSED, SOMETIMES.
I LOVE HER TOO, MAYOR.
BUT SHE'S GONNA KILL SOME FOLKS. WE NEED TO AT LEAST CONFISCATE THOSE PLANES SHE KEEPS BUILDING.
CIGAR, ANYONE?
MINXY'S DESIGNS WON THE WAR FOR US, TOMMY. SHE'S GOT FRIENDS IN THE WHITE HOUSE AND THE PENTAGON.
AND A PERSONAL NET WORTH TWENTY TIMES THE VALUE OF THIS TOWN.
FIND ANOTHER WAY. THAT'S AN ORDER, TOMMY.
I TRUST OUR SHERIFF IS TREATING YOU WELL, MS. PEARSON?
OH, YES, MAYOR. VERY WELL.
SHE'S BEEN MOST HELPFUL.

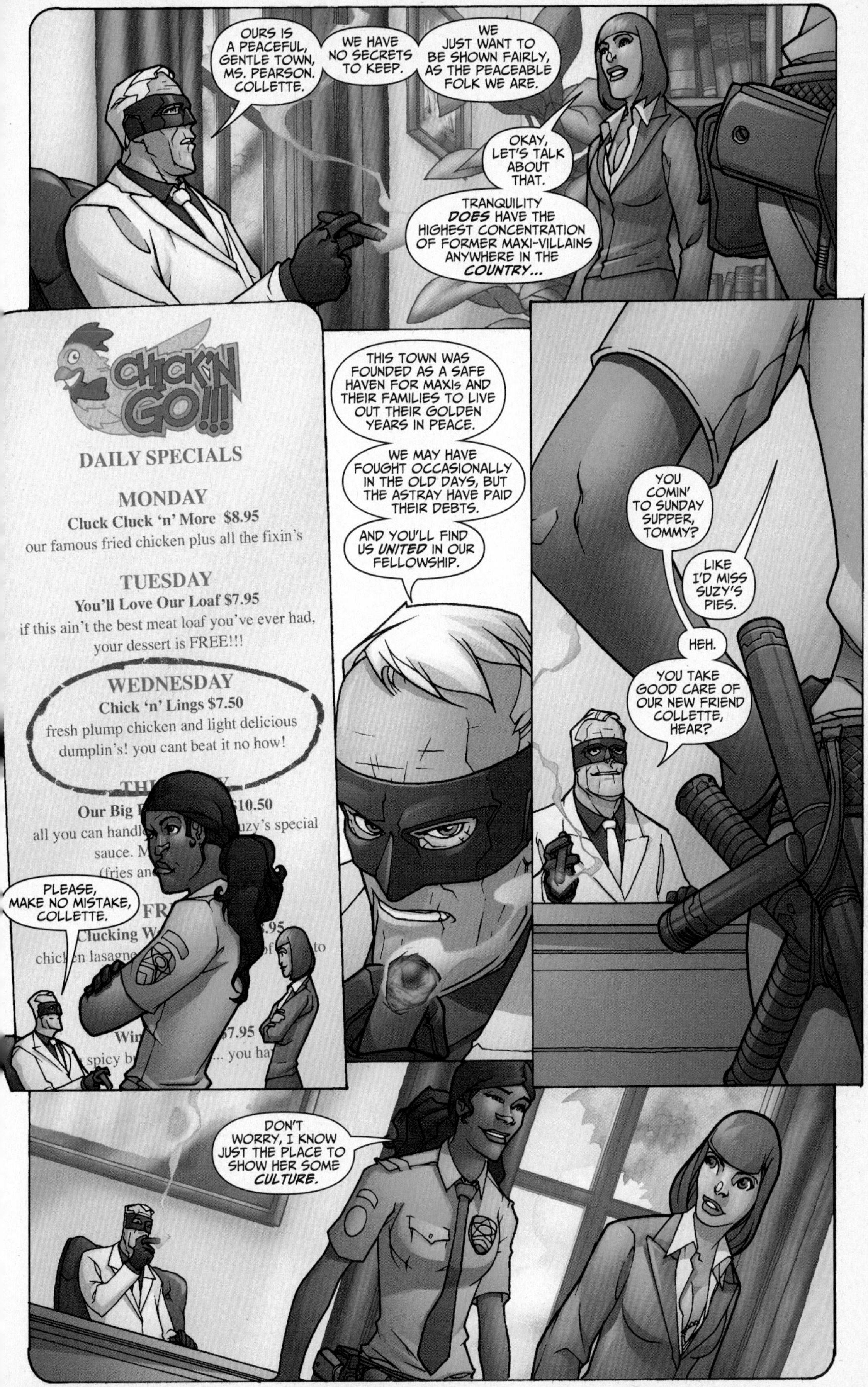

OURS IS A PEACEFUL, GENTLE TOWN, MS. PEARSON. COLLETTE.
WE HAVE NO SECRETS TO KEEP.
WE JUST WANT TO BE SHOWN FAIRLY, AS THE PEACEABLE FOLK WE ARE.
OKAY, LET'S TALK ABOUT THAT.
TRANQUILITY DOES HAVE THE HIGHEST CONCENTRATION OF FORMER MAXI-VILLAINS ANYWHERE IN THE COUNTRY...
CHICK'N GO!!!
DAILY SPECIALS
MONDAY
Cluck Cluck 'n' More $8.95
our famous fried chicken plus all the fixin's
TUESDAY
You'll Love Our Loaf $7.95
if this ain't the best meat loaf you've ever had, your dessert is FREE!!!
WEDNESDAY
Chick 'n' Lings $7.50
fresh plump chicken and light delicious dumplin's! you cant beat it no how!
PLEASE, MAKE NO MISTAKE, COLLETTE.
THIS TOWN WAS FOUNDED AS A SAFE HAVEN FOR MAXIS AND THEIR FAMILIES TO LIVE OUT THEIR GOLDEN YEARS IN PEACE.
WE MAY HAVE FOUGHT OCCASIONALLY IN THE OLD DAYS, BUT THE ASTRAY HAVE PAID THEIR DEBTS.
AND YOU'LL FIND US UNITED IN OUR FELLOWSHIP.
YOU COMIN' TO SUNDAY SUPPER, TOMMY?
LIKE I'D MISS SUZY'S PIES.
HEH.
YOU TAKE GOOD CARE OF OUR NEW FRIEND COLLETTE, HEAR?
DON'T WORRY, I KNOW JUST THE PLACE TO SHOW HER SOME CULTURE.

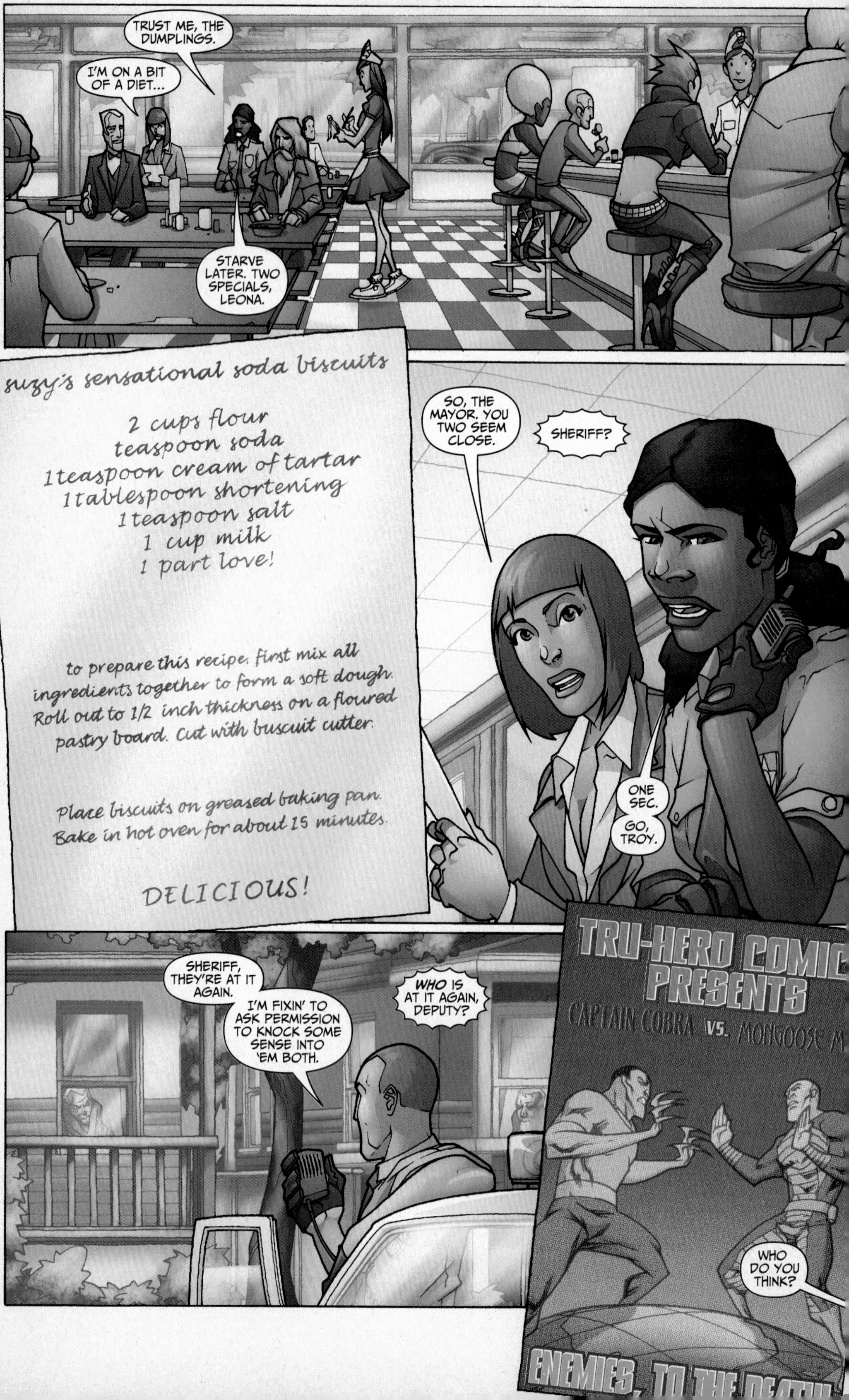

TRUST ME, THE DUMPLINGS.
I'M ON A BIT OF A DIET...
STARVE LATER. TWO SPECIALS, LEONA.
suzy's sensational soda biscuits
2 cups flour
teaspoon soda
1teaspoon cream of tartar
1tablespoon shortening
1teaspoon salt
1 cup milk
1 part love!
to prepare this recipe, first mix all ingredients together to form a soft dough. Roll out to 1/2 inch thickness on a floured pastry board. Cut with buscuit cutter.
Place biscuits on greased baking pan. Bake in hot oven for about 15 minutes.
DELICIOUS!
SO, THE MAYOR. YOU TWO SEEM CLOSE.
SHERIFF?
ONE SEC.
GO, TROY.
SHERIFF, THEY'RE AT IT AGAIN.
I'M FIXIN' TO ASK PERMISSION TO KNOCK SOME SENSE INTO 'EM BOTH.
WHO IS AT IT AGAIN, DEPUTY?
TRU-HERO COMIC PRESENTS
CAPTAIN COBRA VS. MONGOOSE M
WHO DO YOU THINK?
ENEMIES, TO THE DEATH

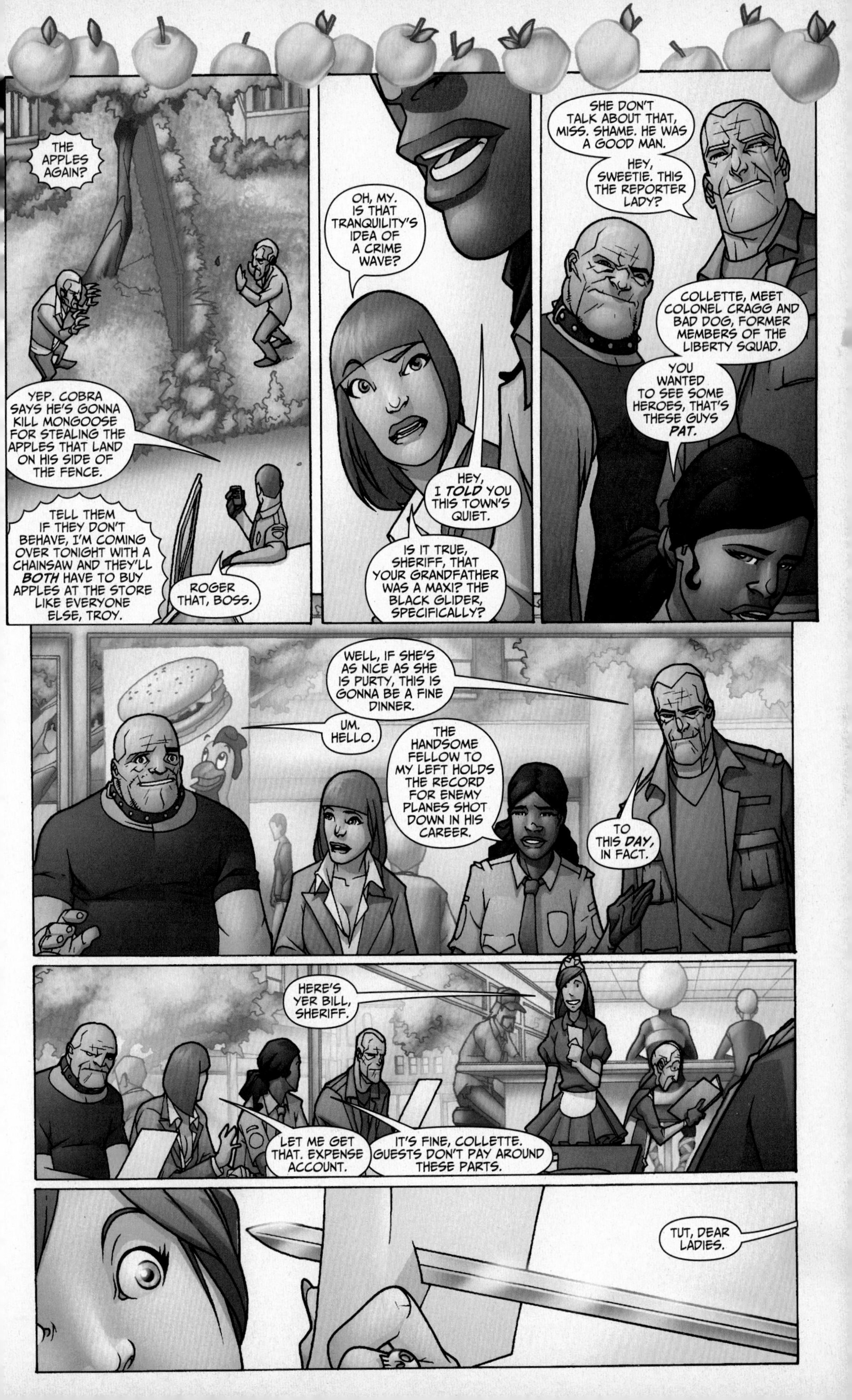
THE APPLES AGAIN?
YEP. COBRA SAYS HE'S GONNA KILL MONGOOSE FOR STEALING THE APPLES THAT LAND ON HIS SIDE OF THE FENCE.
TELL THEM IF THEY DON'T BEHAVE, I'M COMING OVER TONIGHT WITH A CHAINSAW AND THEY'LL BOTH HAVE TO BUY APPLES AT THE STORE LIKE EVERYONE ELSE, TROY.
ROGER THAT, BOSS.
OH, MY. IS THAT TRANQUILITY'S IDEA OF A CRIME WAVE?
HEY, I TOLD YOU THIS TOWN'S QUIET.
IS IT TRUE, SHERIFF, THAT YOUR GRANDFATHER WAS A MAXI? THE BLACK GLIDER, SPECIFICALLY?
SHE DON'T TALK ABOUT THAT, MISS. SHAME. HE WAS A GOOD MAN.
HEY, SWEETIE. THIS THE REPORTER LADY?
COLLETTE, MEET COLONEL CRAGG AND BAD DOG, FORMER MEMBERS OF THE LIBERTY SQUAD.
YOU WANTED TO SEE SOME HEROES, THAT'S THESE GUYS PAT.
WELL, IF SHE'S AS NICE AS SHE IS PURTY, THIS IS GONNA BE A FINE DINNER.
UM. HELLO.
THE HANDSOME FELLOW TO MY LEFT HOLDS THE RECORD FOR ENEMY PLANES SHOT DOWN IN HIS CAREER.
TO THIS DAY, IN FACT.
HERE'S YER BILL, SHERIFF.
LET ME GET THAT. EXPENSE ACCOUNT.
IT'S FINE, COLLETTE. GUESTS DON'T PAY AROUND THESE PARTS.
TUT, DEAR LADIES.

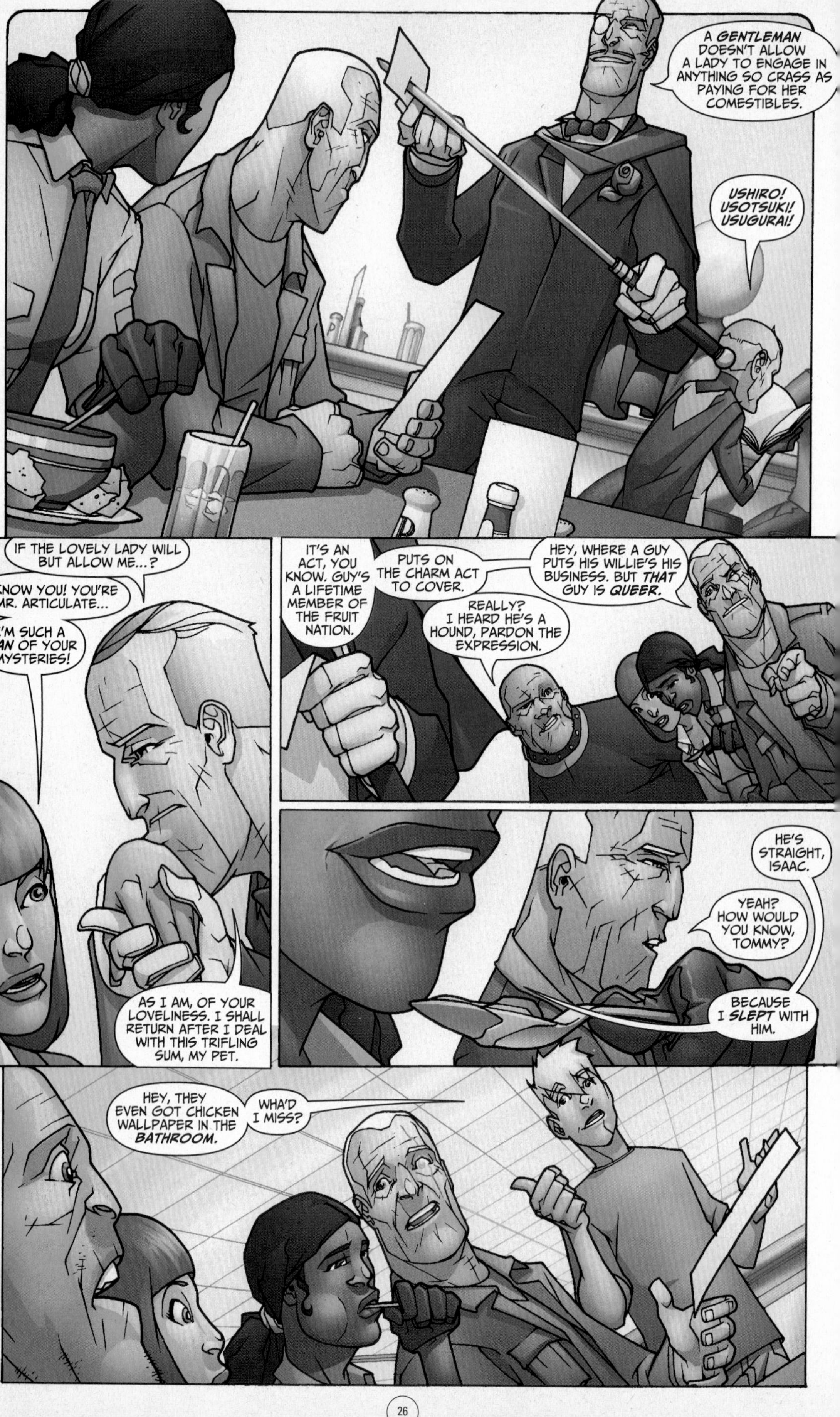
A GENTLEMAN DOESN'T ALLOW A LADY TO ENGAGE IN ANYTHING SO CRASS AS PAYING FOR HER COMESTIBLES.
USHIRO! USOTSUKI! USUGURAI!
IF THE LOVELY LADY WILL BUT ALLOW ME...?
I KNOW YOU! YOU'RE MR. ARTICULATE...
I'M SUCH A FAN OF YOUR MYSTERIES!
AS I AM, OF YOUR LOVELINESS. I SHALL RETURN AFTER I DEAL WITH THIS TRIFLING SUM, MY PET.
IT'S AN ACT, YOU KNOW. GUY'S A LIFETIME MEMBER OF THE FRUIT NATION.
PUTS ON THE CHARM ACT TO COVER.
HEY, WHERE A GUY PUTS HIS WILLIE'S HIS BUSINESS. BUT THAT GUY IS QUEER.
REALLY? I HEARD HE'S A HOUND, PARDON THE EXPRESSION.
HE'S STRAIGHT, ISAAC.
YEAH? HOW WOULD YOU KNOW, TOMMY?
BECAUSE I SLEPT WITH HIM.
HEY, THEY EVEN GOT CHICKEN WALLPAPER IN THE BATHROOM.
WHA'D I MISS?

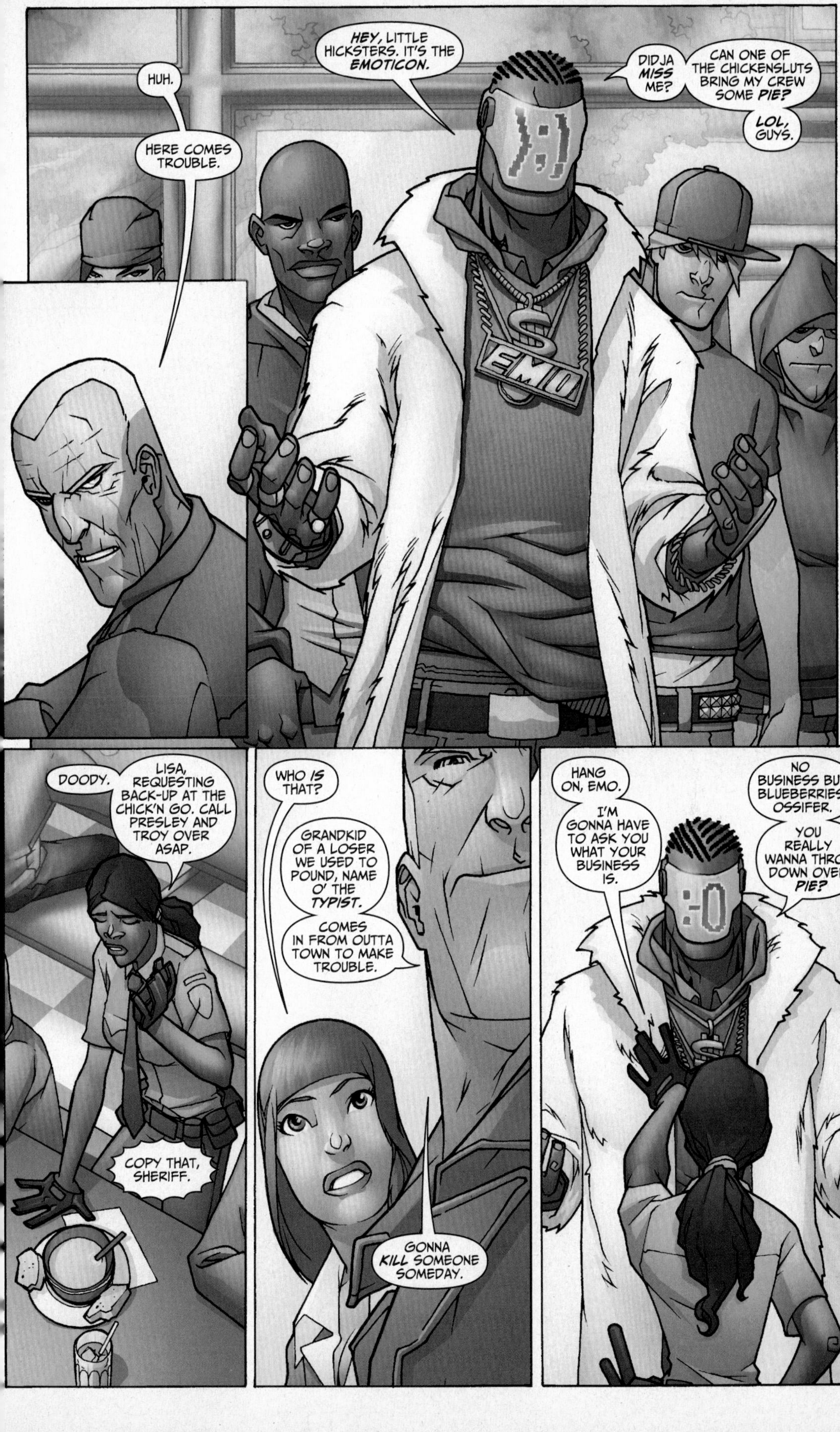
HUH.
HERE COMES TROUBLE.
HEY, LITTLE HICKSTERS. IT'S THE EMOTICON.
DIDJA MISS ME?
CAN ONE OF THE CHICKENSLUTS BRING MY CREW SOME PIE?
LOL, GUYS.
EMO
DOODY.
LISA, REQUESTING BACK-UP AT THE CHICK'N GO. CALL PRESLEY AND TROY OVER ASAP.
COPY THAT, SHERIFF.
WHO IS THAT?
GRANDKID OF A LOSER WE USED TO POUND, NAME O' THE TYPIST.
COMES IN FROM OUTTA TOWN TO MAKE TROUBLE.
GONNA KILL SOMEONE SOMEDAY.
HANG ON, EMO.
I'M GONNA HAVE TO ASK YOU WHAT YOUR BUSINESS IS.
NO BUSINESS BUT BLUEBERRIES, OSSIFER.
YOU REALLY WANNA THROW DOWN OVER PIE?

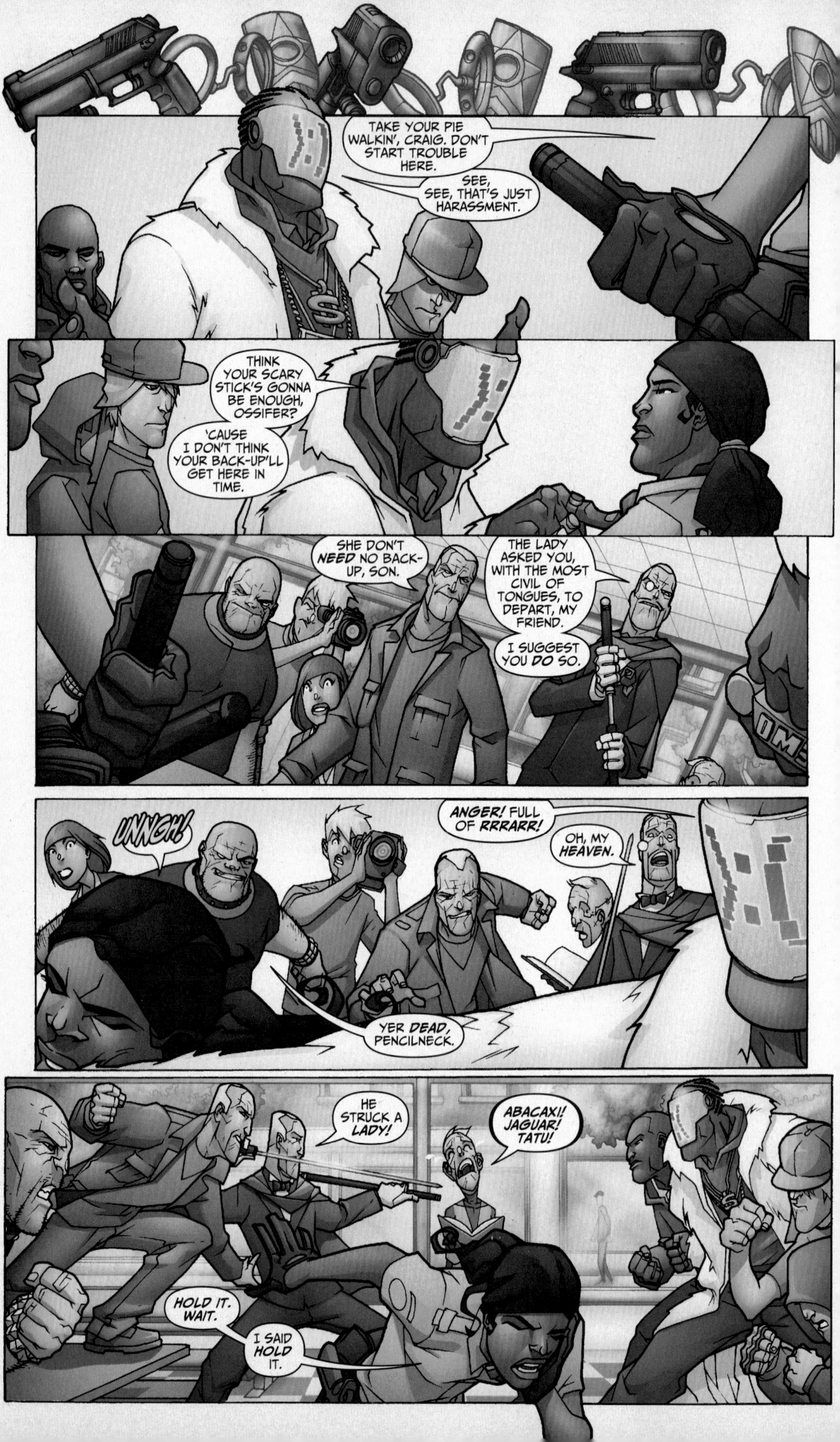

TAKE YOUR PIE WALKIN', CRAIG. DON'T START TROUBLE HERE.
SEE, SEE, THAT'S JUST HARASSMENT.
THINK YOUR SCARY STICK'S GONNA BE ENOUGH, OSSIFER?
'CAUSE I DON'T THINK YOUR BACK-UP'LL GET HERE IN TIME.
SHE DON'T NEED NO BACK-UP, SON.
THE LADY ASKED YOU, WITH THE MOST CIVIL OF TONGUES, TO DEPART, MY FRIEND.
I SUGGEST YOU DO SO.
UNNGH!
ANGER! FULL OF RRRARR!
OH, MY HEAVEN.
YER DEAD, PENCILNECK.
HE STRUCK A LADY!
ABACAXI! JAGUAR! TATU!
HOLD IT. WAIT.
I SAID HOLD IT.

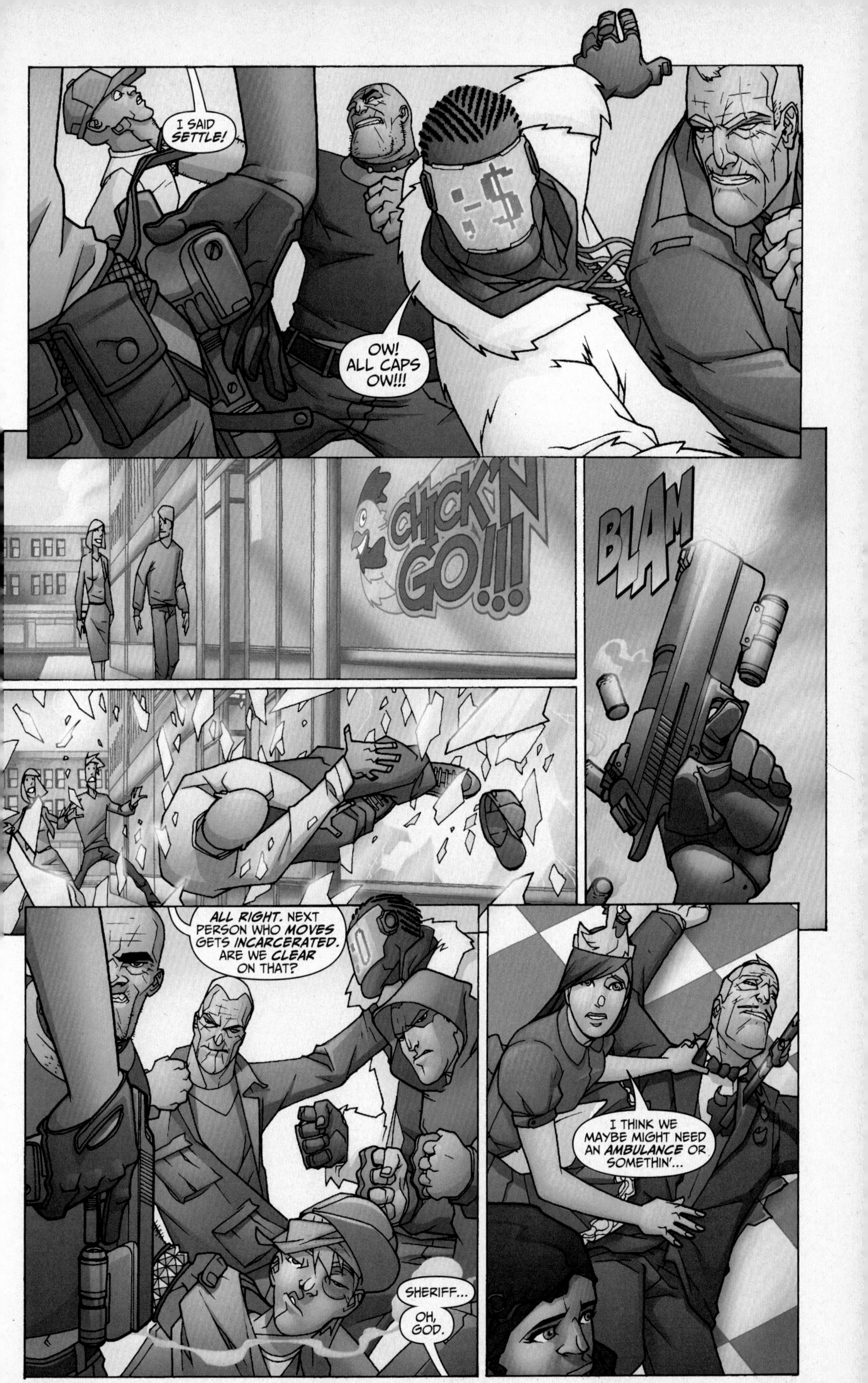
I SAID SETTLE!
OW! ALL CAPS OW!!!
CHICK'N GO!!!
BLAM
ALL RIGHT. NEXT PERSON WHO MOVES GETS INCARCERATED. ARE WE CLEAR ON THAT?
SHERIFF...
OH, GOD.
I THINK WE MAYBE MIGHT NEED AN AMBULANCE OR SOMETHIN'...

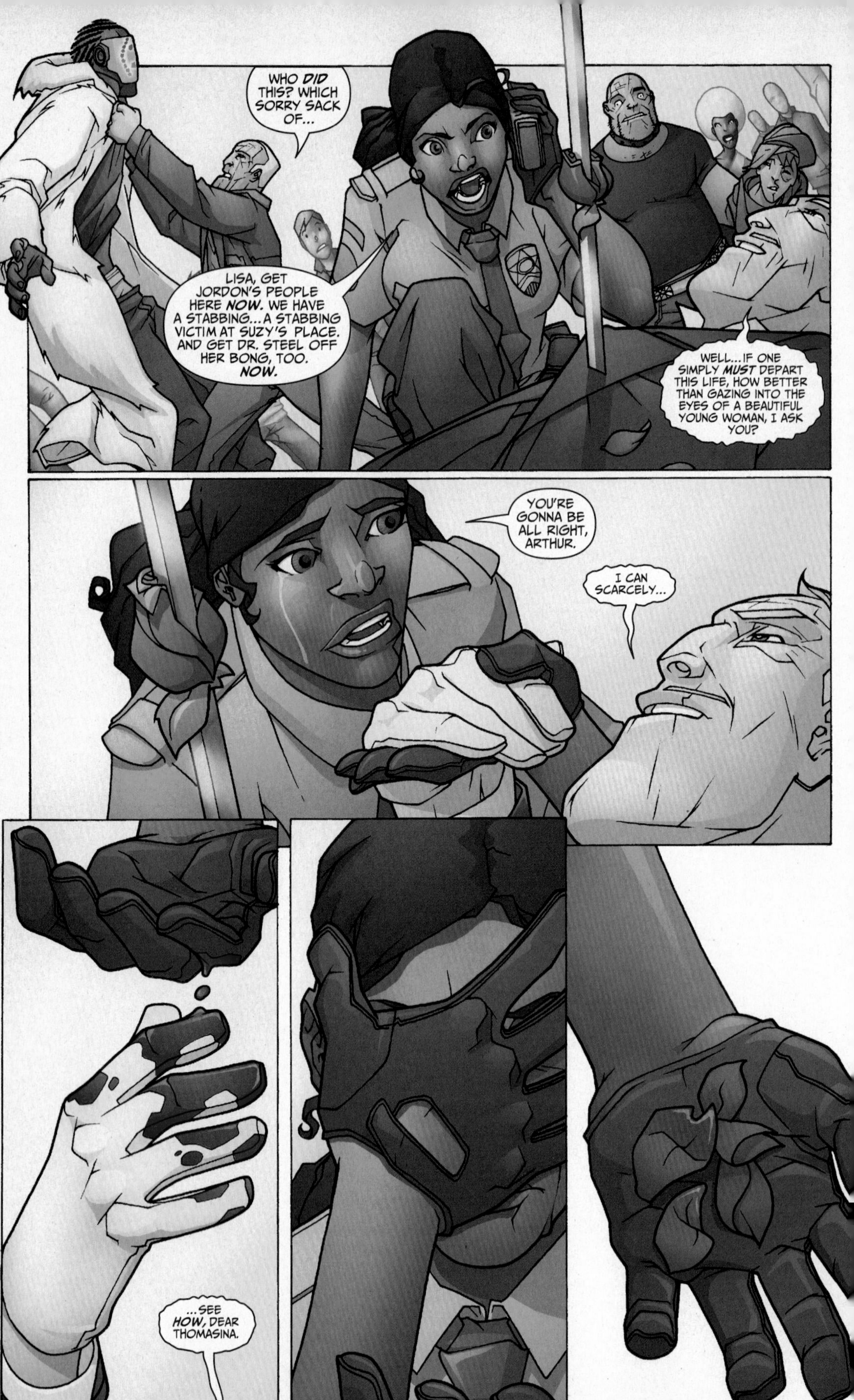
WHO DID THIS? WHICH SORRY SACK OF...
LISA, GET JORDON'S PEOPLE HERE NOW. WE HAVE A STABBING...A STABBING VICTIM AT SUZY'S PLACE. AND GET DR. STEEL OFF HER BONG, TOO. NOW.
WELL...IF ONE SIMPLY MUST DEPART THIS LIFE, HOW BETTER THAN GAZING INTO THE EYES OF A BEAUTIFUL YOUNG WOMAN, I ASK YOU?
YOU'RE GONNA BE ALL RIGHT, ARTHUR.
I CAN SCARCELY...
...SEE HOW, DEAR THOMASINA.

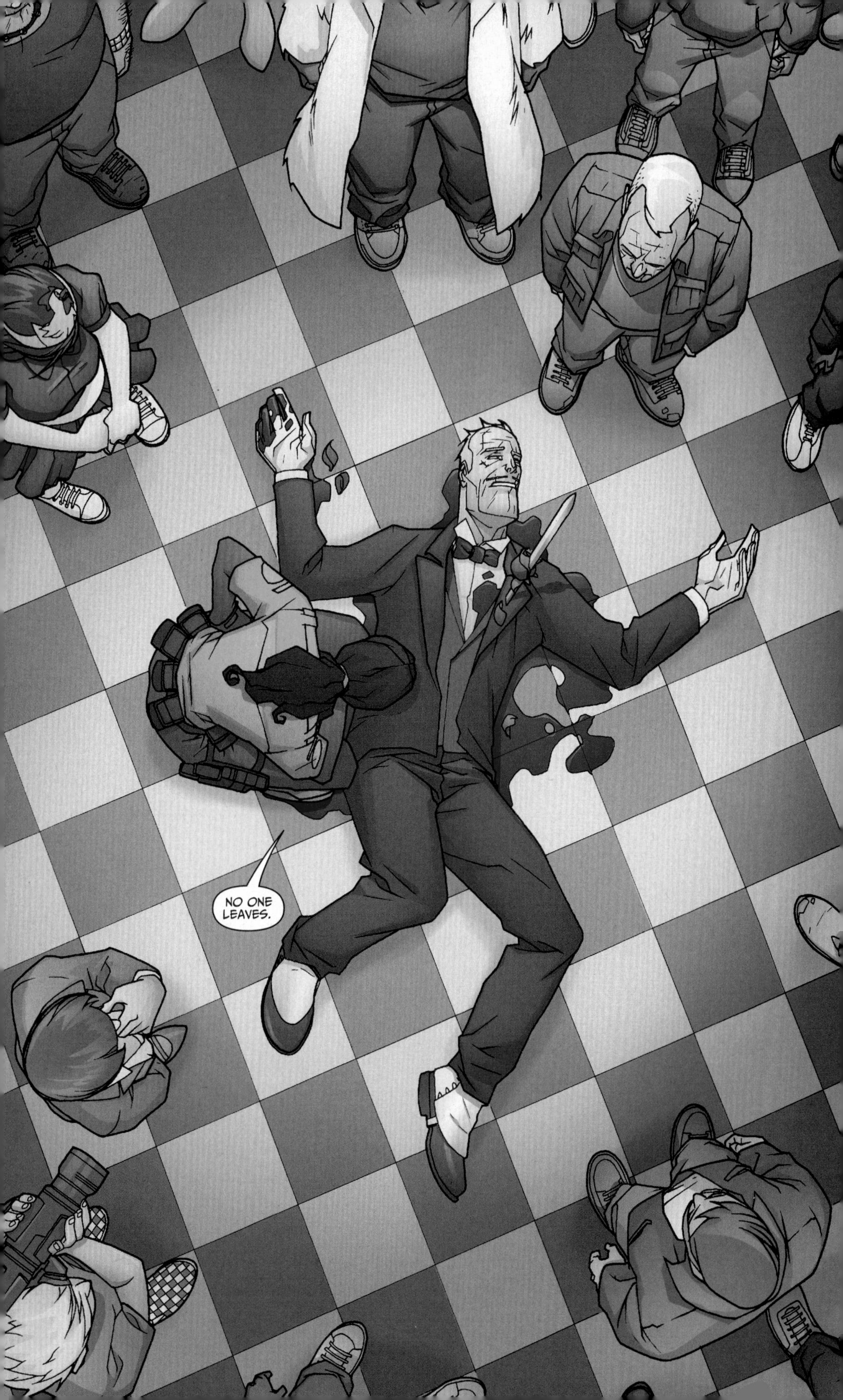
NO ONE LEAVES.

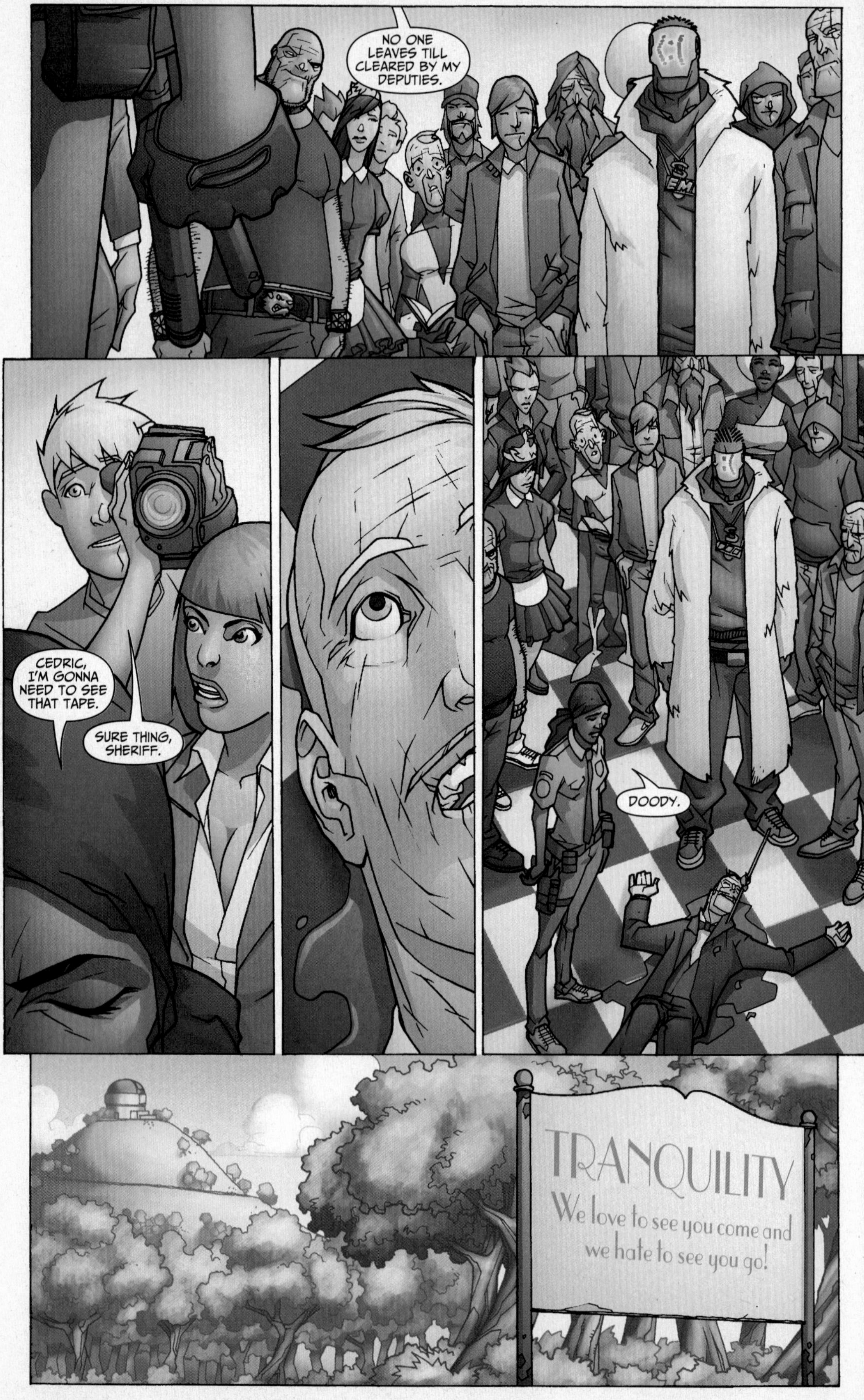
NO ONE LEAVES TILL CLEARED BY MY DEPUTIES.
CEDRIC, I'M GONNA NEED TO SEE THAT TAPE.
SURE THING, SHERIFF.
DOODY.
TRANQUILITY
We love to see you come and we hate to see you go!

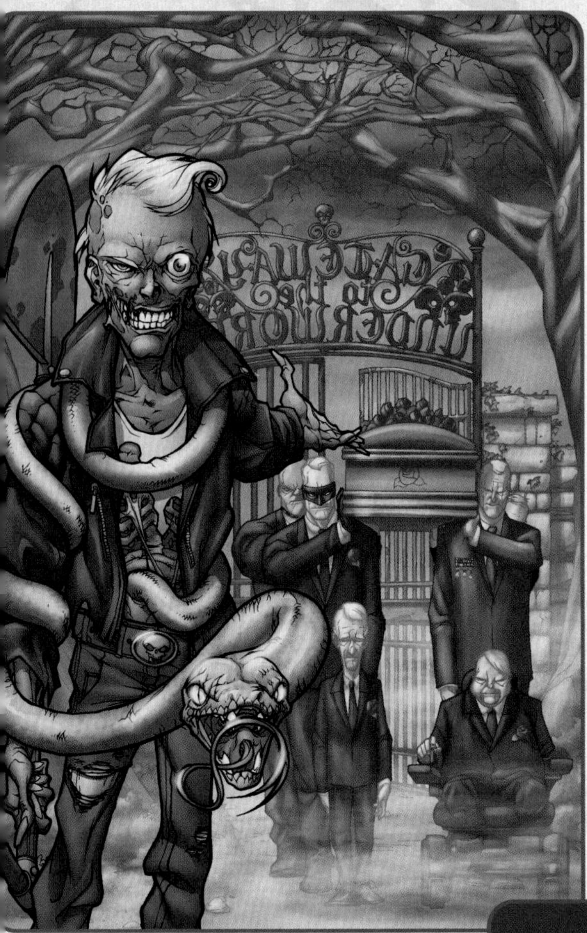

Cover 2

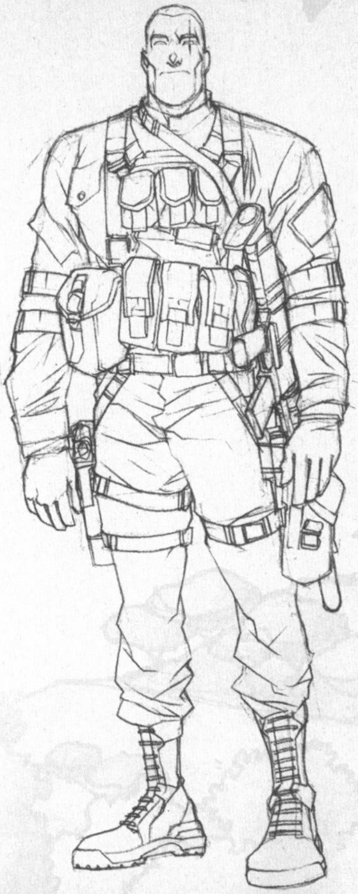

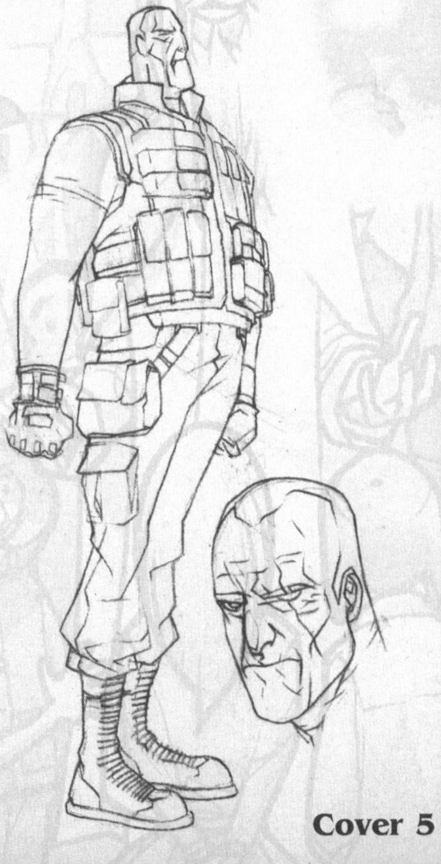

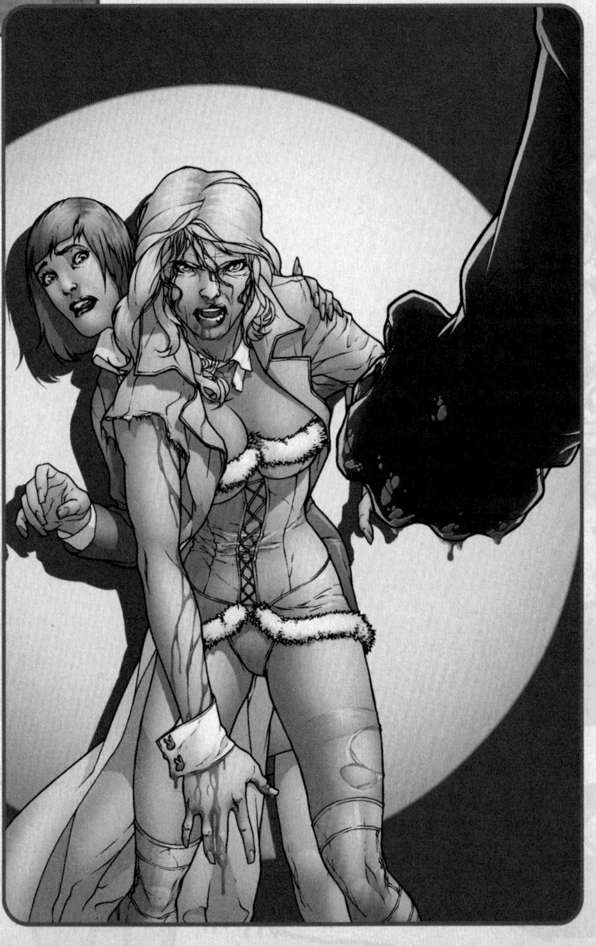

Cover 5

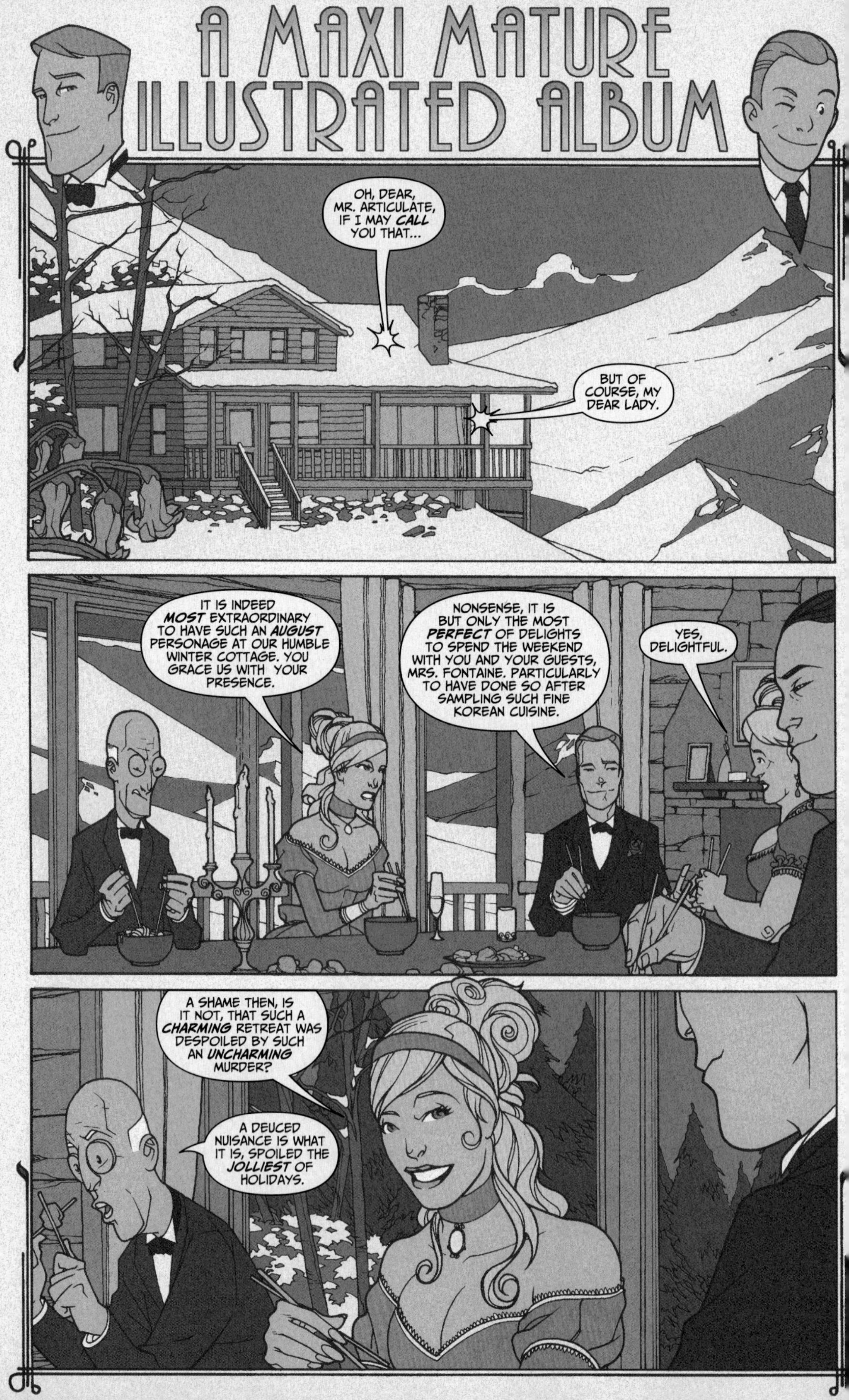
A MAXI MATURE ILLUSTRATED ALBUM
OH, DEAR, MR. ARTICULATE, IF I MAY CALL YOU THAT...
BUT OF COURSE, MY DEAR LADY.
IT IS INDEED MOST EXTRAORDINARY TO HAVE SUCH AN AUGUST PERSONAGE AT OUR HUMBLE WINTER COTTAGE. YOU GRACE US WITH YOUR PRESENCE.
NONSENSE, IT IS BUT ONLY THE MOST PERFECT OF DELIGHTS TO SPEND THE WEEKEND WITH YOU AND YOUR GUESTS, MRS. FONTAINE. PARTICULARLY TO HAVE DONE SO AFTER SAMPLING SUCH FINE KOREAN CUISINE.
YES, DELIGHTFUL.
A SHAME THEN, IS IT NOT, THAT SUCH A CHARMING RETREAT WAS DESPOILED BY SUCH AN UNCHARMING MURDER?
A DEUCED NUISANCE IS WHAT IT IS, SPOILED THE JOLLIEST OF HOLIDAYS.

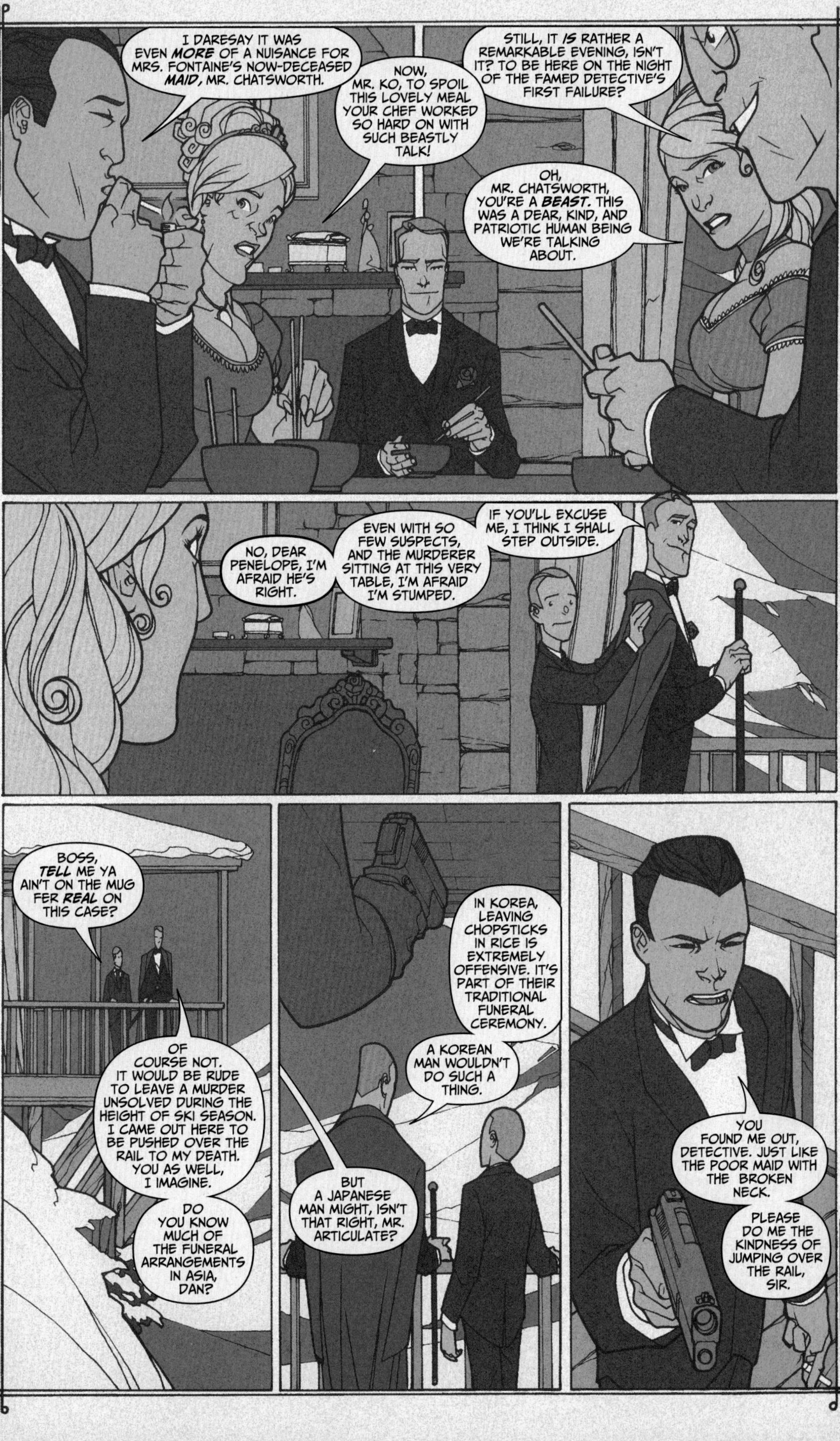
I DARESAY IT WAS EVEN MORE OF A NUISANCE FOR MRS. FONTAINE'S NOW-DECEASED MAID, MR. CHATSWORTH.
NOW, MR. KO, TO SPOIL THIS LOVELY MEAL YOUR CHEF WORKED SO HARD ON WITH SUCH BEASTLY TALK!
STILL, IT IS RATHER A REMARKABLE EVENING, ISN'T IT? TO BE HERE ON THE NIGHT OF THE FAMED DETECTIVE'S FIRST FAILURE?
OH, MR. CHATSWORTH, YOU'RE A BEAST. THIS WAS A DEAR, KIND, AND PATRIOTIC HUMAN BEING WE'RE TALKING ABOUT.
NO, DEAR PENELOPE, I'M AFRAID HE'S RIGHT.
EVEN WITH SO FEW SUSPECTS, AND THE MURDERER SITTING AT THIS VERY TABLE, I'M AFRAID I'M STUMPED.
IF YOU'LL EXCUSE ME, I THINK I SHALL STEP OUTSIDE.
BOSS, TELL ME YA AIN'T ON THE MUG FER REAL ON THIS CASE?
OF COURSE NOT. IT WOULD BE RUDE TO LEAVE A MURDER UNSOLVED DURING THE HEIGHT OF SKI SEASON. I CAME OUT HERE TO BE PUSHED OVER THE RAIL TO MY DEATH. YOU AS WELL, I IMAGINE.
DO YOU KNOW MUCH OF THE FUNERAL ARRANGEMENTS IN ASIA, DAN?
IN KOREA, LEAVING CHOPSTICKS IN RICE IS EXTREMELY OFFENSIVE. IT'S PART OF THEIR TRADITIONAL FUNERAL CEREMONY.
A KOREAN MAN WOULDN'T DO SUCH A THING.
BUT A JAPANESE MAN MIGHT, ISN'T THAT RIGHT, MR. ARTICULATE?
YOU FOUND ME OUT, DETECTIVE. JUST LIKE THE POOR MAID WITH THE BROKEN NECK.
PLEASE DO ME THE KINDNESS OF JUMPING OVER THE RAIL, SIR.

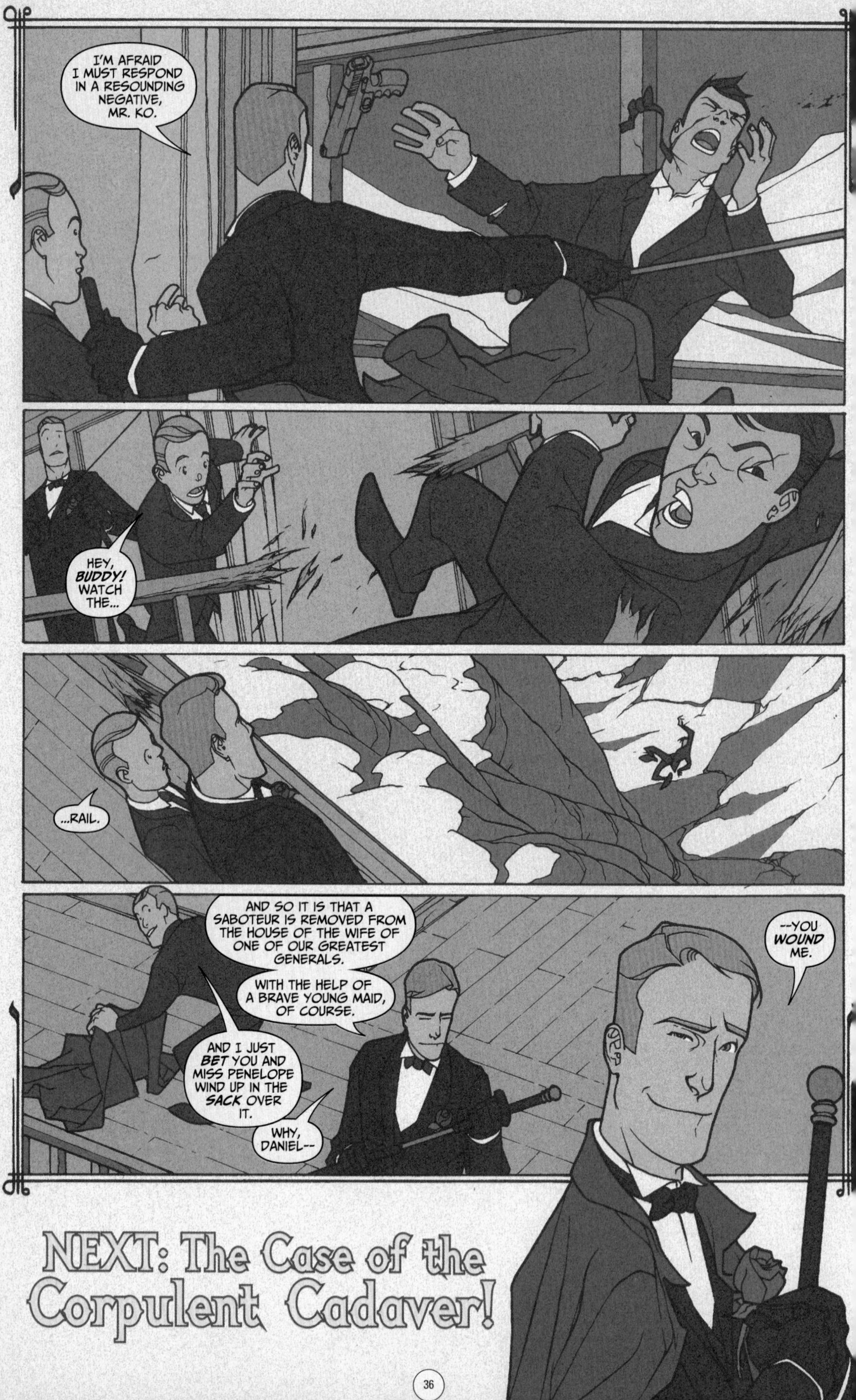
I'M AFRAID I MUST RESPOND IN A RESOUNDING NEGATIVE, MR. KO.
HEY, BUDDY! WATCH THE...
...RAIL.
AND SO IT IS THAT A SABOTEUR IS REMOVED FROM THE HOUSE OF THE WIFE OF ONE OF OUR GREATEST GENERALS.
WITH THE HELP OF A BRAVE YOUNG MAID, OF COURSE.
AND I JUST BET YOU AND MISS PENELOPE WIND UP IN THE SACK OVER IT.
WHY, DANIEL--
--YOU WOUND ME.
NEXT: The Case of the Corpulent Cadaver!

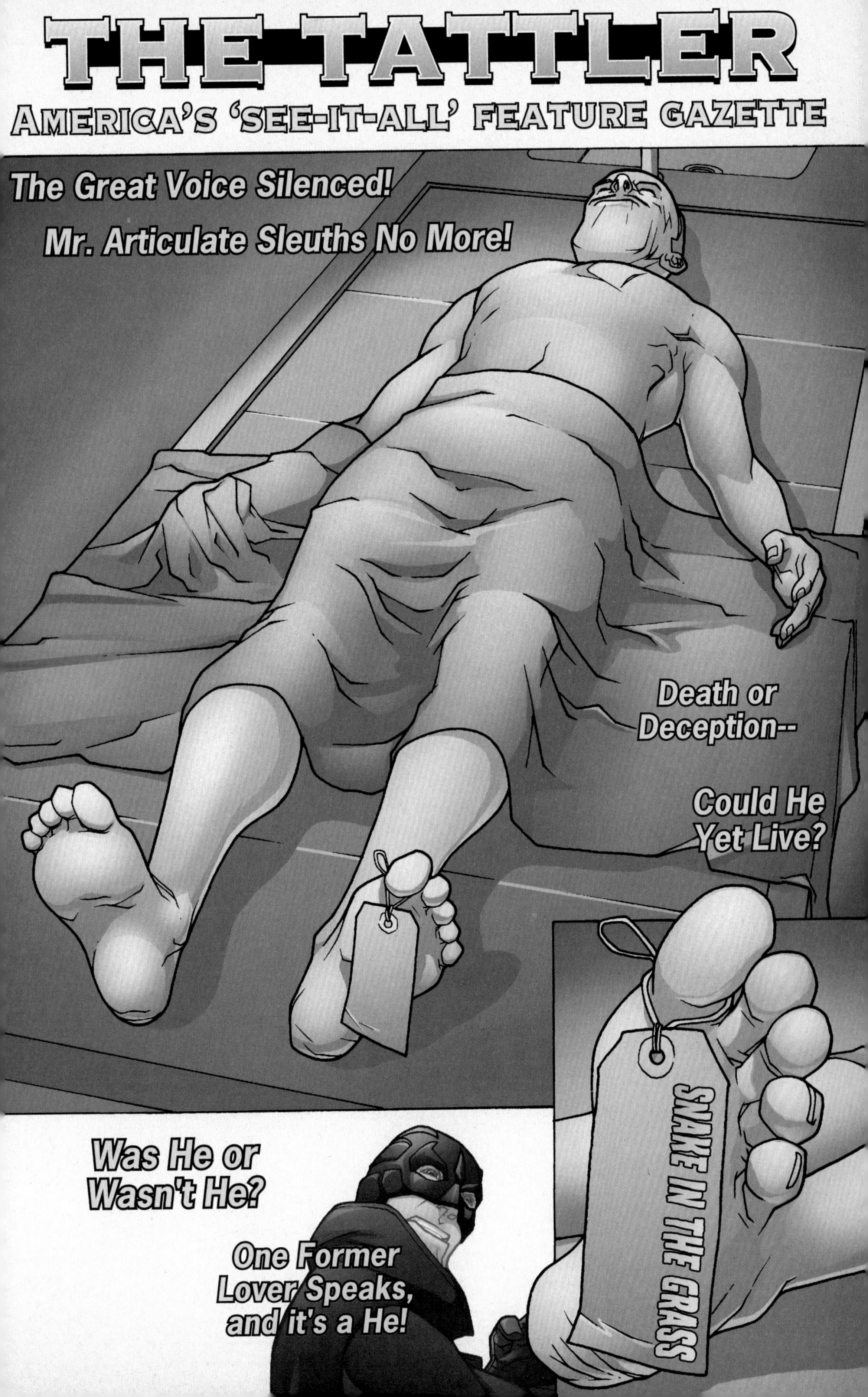
THE TATTLER
AMERICA'S 'SEE-IT-ALL' FEATURE GAZETTE
The Great Voice Silenced!
Mr. Articulate Sleuths No More!
Death or Deception--
Could He Yet Live?
Was He or Wasn't He?
One Former Lover Speaks, and it's a He!
SNAKE IN THE GRASS

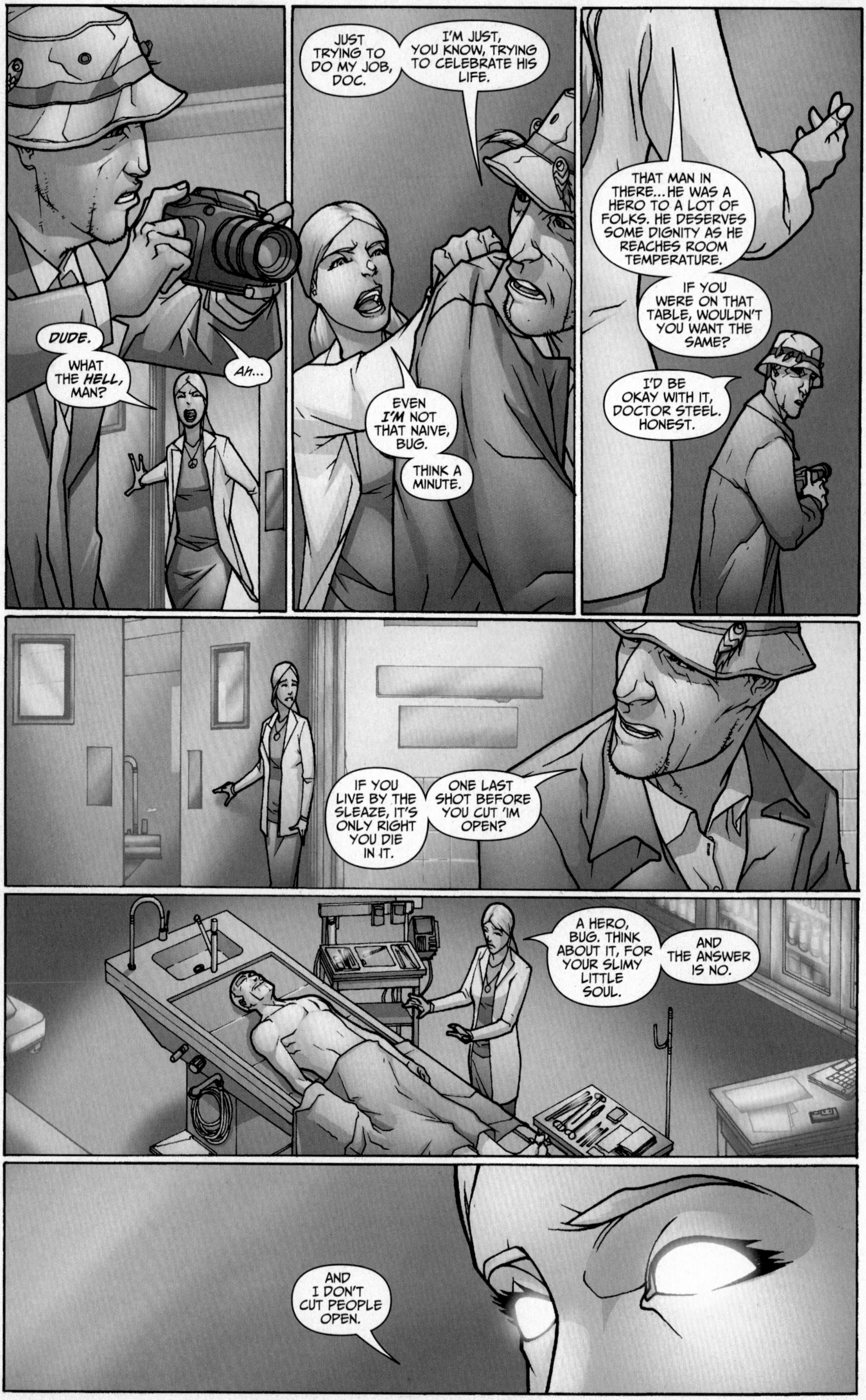

DUDE.
WHAT THE HELL, MAN?
Ah...
JUST TRYING TO DO MY JOB, DOC.
I'M JUST, YOU KNOW, TRYING TO CELEBRATE HIS LIFE.
EVEN I'M NOT THAT NAIVE, BUG.
THINK A MINUTE.
THAT MAN IN THERE... HE WAS A HERO TO A LOT OF FOLKS. HE DESERVES SOME DIGNITY AS HE REACHES ROOM TEMPERATURE.
IF YOU WERE ON THAT TABLE, WOULDN'T YOU WANT THE SAME?
I'D BE OKAY WITH IT, DOCTOR STEEL. HONEST.
IF YOU LIVE BY THE SLEAZE, IT'S ONLY RIGHT YOU DIE IN IT.
ONE LAST SHOT BEFORE YOU CUT 'IM OPEN?
A HERO, BUG. THINK ABOUT IT, FOR YOUR SLIMY LITTLE SOUL.
AND THE ANSWER IS NO.
AND I DON'T CUT PEOPLE OPEN.

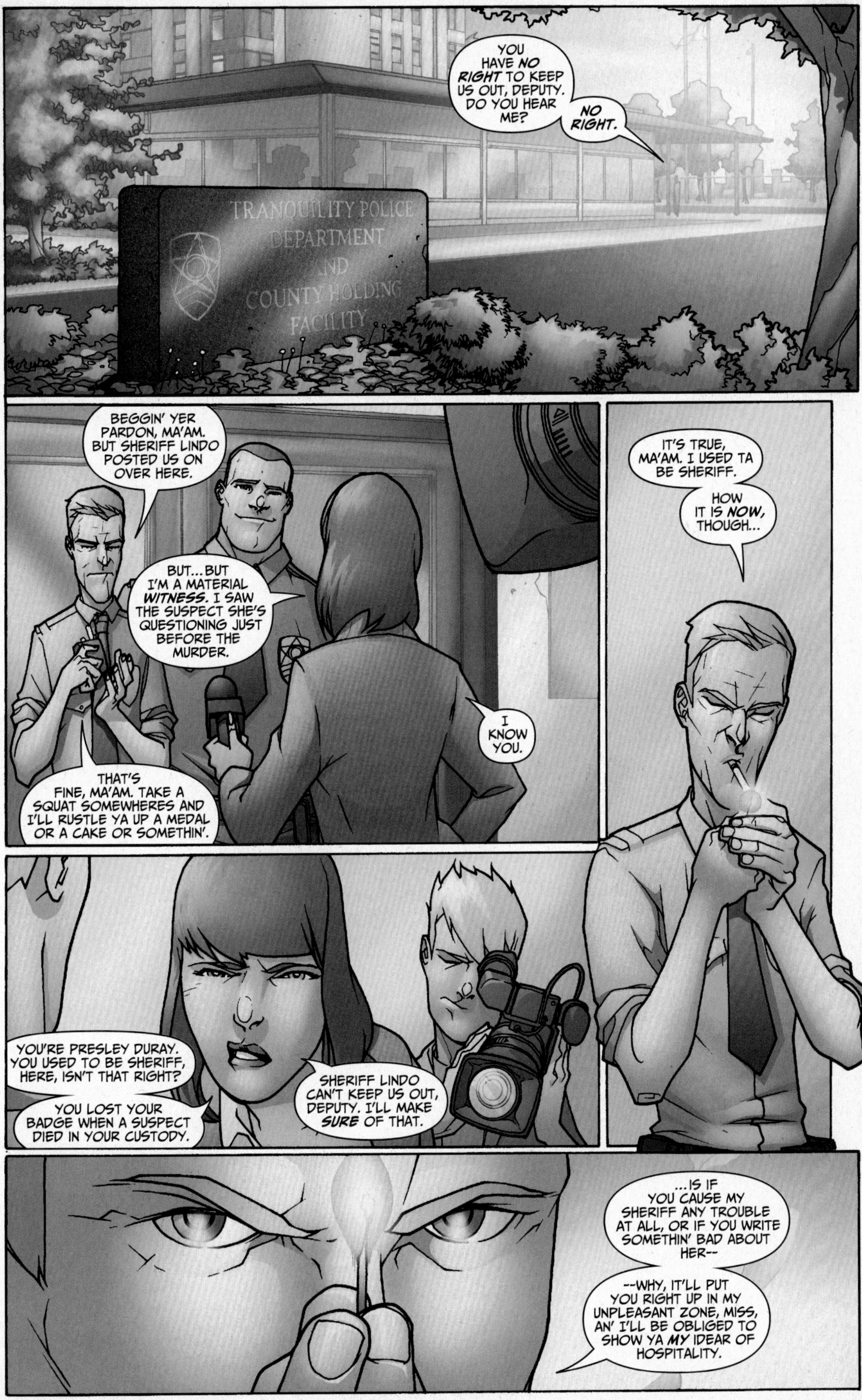
TRANQUILITY POLICE DEPARTMENT AND COUNTY HOLDING FACILITY
YOU HAVE NO RIGHT TO KEEP US OUT, DEPUTY. DO YOU HEAR ME?
NO RIGHT.
BEGGIN' YER PARDON, MA'AM. BUT SHERIFF LINDO POSTED US ON OVER HERE.
BUT... BUT I'M A MATERIAL WITNESS. I SAW THE SUSPECT SHE'S QUESTIONING JUST BEFORE THE MURDER.
THAT'S FINE, MA'AM. TAKE A SQUAT SOMEWHERES AND I'LL RUSTLE YA UP A MEDAL OR A CAKE OR SOMETHIN'.
I KNOW YOU.
YOU'RE PRESLEY DURAY. YOU USED TO BE SHERIFF, HERE, ISN'T THAT RIGHT?
YOU LOST YOUR BADGE WHEN A SUSPECT DIED IN YOUR CUSTODY.
SHERIFF LINDO CAN'T KEEP US OUT, DEPUTY. I'LL MAKE SURE OF THAT.
IT'S TRUE, MA'AM. I USED TA BE SHERIFF.
HOW IT IS NOW, THOUGH...
...IS IF YOU CAUSE MY SHERIFF ANY TROUBLE AT ALL, OR IF YOU WRITE SOMETHIN' BAD ABOUT HER--
--WHY, IT'LL PUT YOU RIGHT UP IN MY UNPLEASANT ZONE, MISS, AN' I'LL BE OBLIGED TO SHOW YA MY IDEAR OF HOSPITALITY.

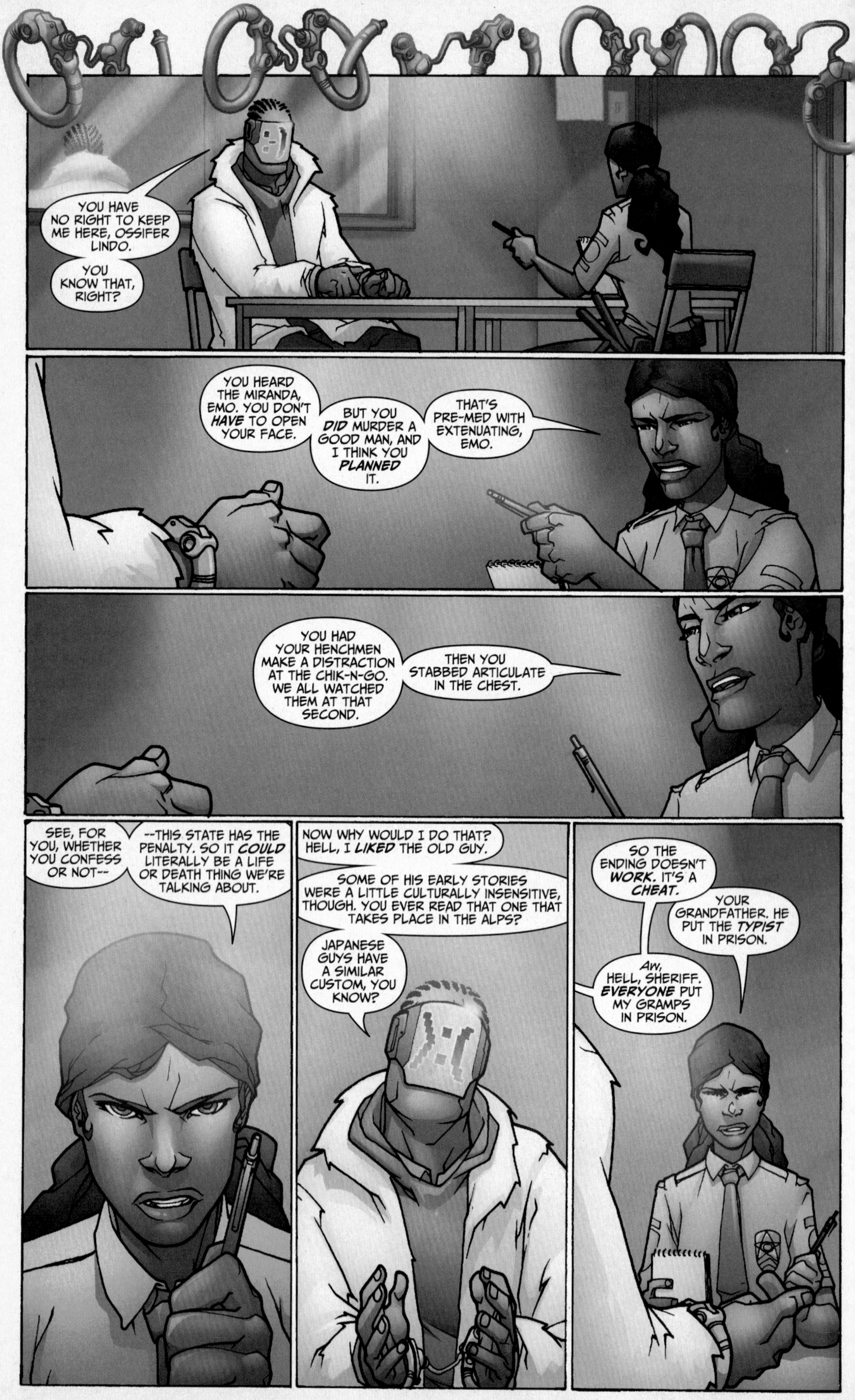
YOU HAVE NO RIGHT TO KEEP ME HERE, OSSIFER LINDO.
YOU KNOW THAT, RIGHT?
YOU HEARD THE MIRANDA, EMO. YOU DON'T *HAVE* TO OPEN YOUR FACE.
BUT YOU *DID* MURDER A GOOD MAN, AND I THINK YOU *PLANNED* IT.
THAT'S PRE-MED WITH EXTENUATING, EMO.
YOU HAD YOUR HENCHMEN MAKE A DISTRACTION AT THE CHIK-N-GO. WE ALL WATCHED THEM AT THAT SECOND.
THEN YOU STABBED ARTICULATE IN THE CHEST.
SEE, FOR YOU, WHETHER YOU CONFESS OR NOT--
--THIS STATE HAS THE PENALTY. SO IT *COULD* LITERALLY BE A LIFE OR DEATH THING WE'RE TALKING ABOUT.
NOW WHY WOULD I DO THAT? HELL, I *LIKED* THE OLD GUY.
SOME OF HIS EARLY STORIES WERE A LITTLE CULTURALLY INSENSITIVE, THOUGH. YOU EVER READ THAT ONE THAT TAKES PLACE IN THE ALPS?
JAPANESE GUYS HAVE A SIMILAR CUSTOM, YOU KNOW?
SO THE ENDING DOESN'T *WORK*. IT'S A *CHEAT.*
YOUR GRANDFATHER. HE PUT THE *TYPIST* IN PRISON.
AW, HELL, SHERIFF. *EVERYONE* PUT MY GRAMPS IN PRISON.

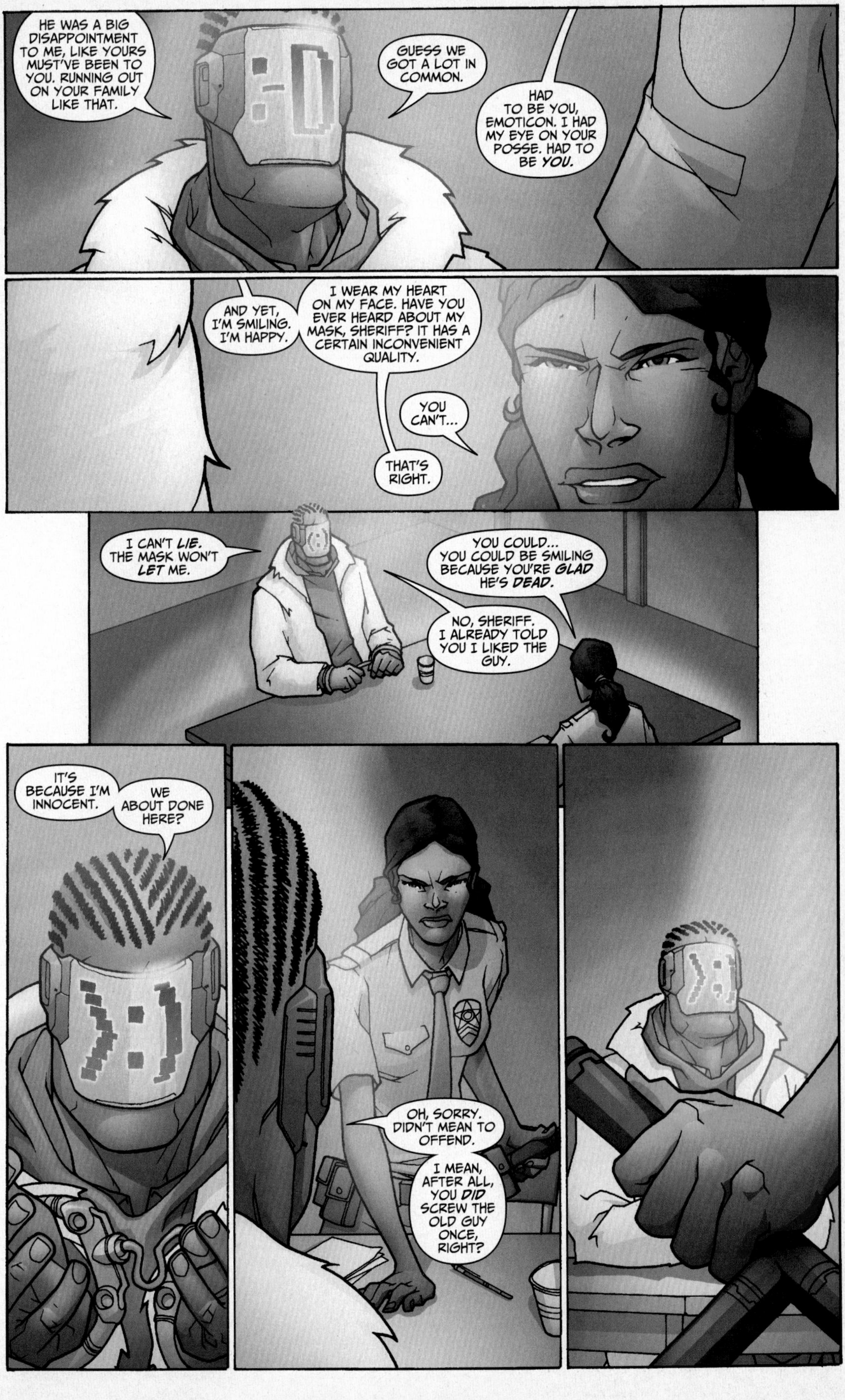

HE WAS A BIG DISAPPOINTMENT TO ME, LIKE YOURS MUST'VE BEEN TO YOU. RUNNING OUT ON YOUR FAMILY LIKE THAT.
GUESS WE GOT A LOT IN COMMON.
HAD TO BE YOU, EMOTICON. I HAD MY EYE ON YOUR POSSE. HAD TO BE *YOU.*
AND YET, I'M SMILING. I'M HAPPY.
I WEAR MY HEART ON MY FACE. HAVE YOU EVER HEARD ABOUT MY MASK, SHERIFF? IT HAS A CERTAIN INCONVENIENT QUALITY.
YOU CAN'T...
THAT'S RIGHT.
I CAN'T *LIE.* THE MASK WON'T *LET* ME.
YOU COULD... YOU COULD BE SMILING BECAUSE YOU'RE *GLAD* HE'S *DEAD.*
NO, SHERIFF. I ALREADY TOLD YOU I LIKED THE GUY.
IT'S BECAUSE I'M INNOCENT.
WE ABOUT DONE HERE?
OH, SORRY. DIDN'T MEAN TO OFFEND.
I MEAN, AFTER ALL, YOU *DID* SCREW THE OLD GUY ONCE, RIGHT?

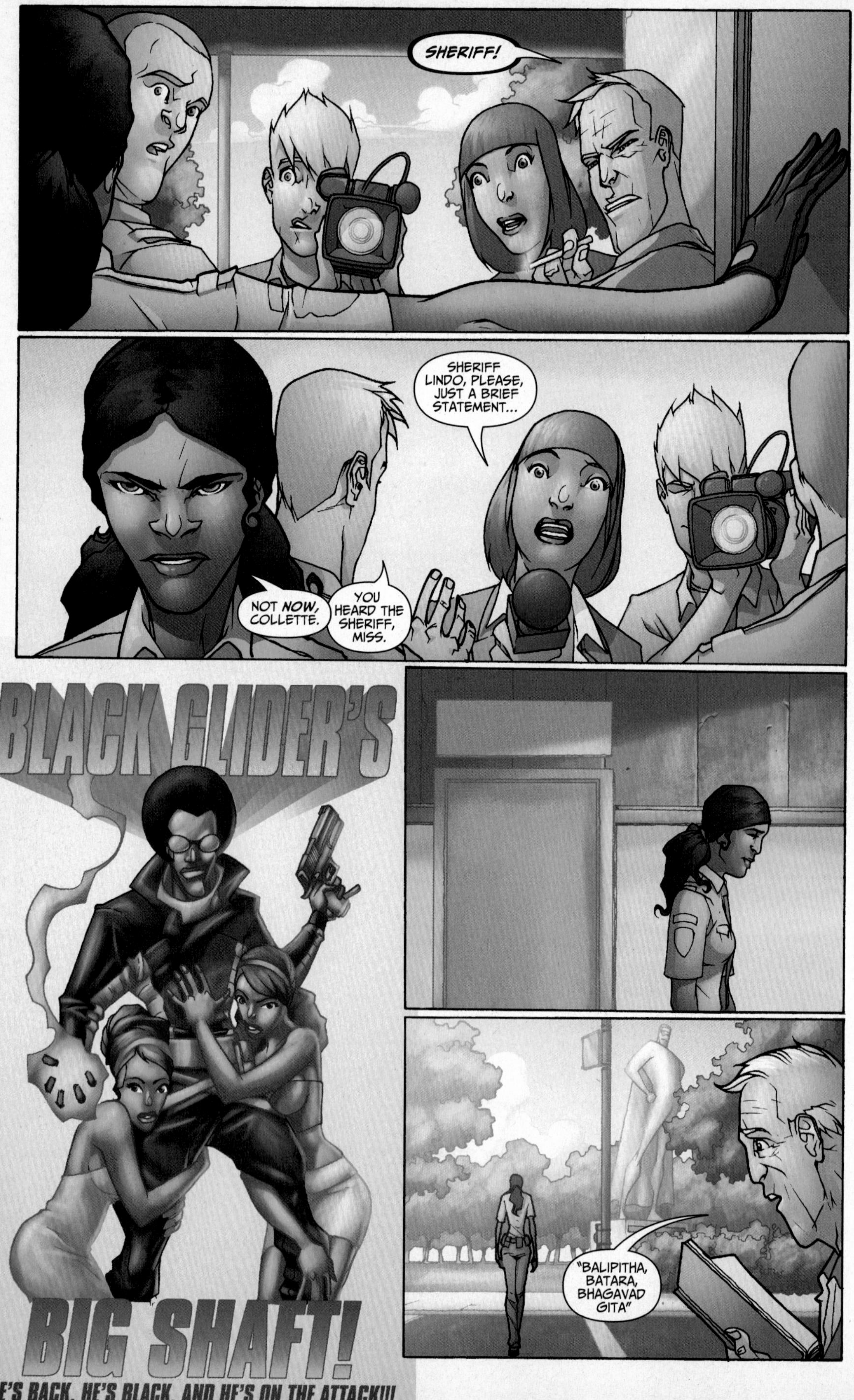
SHERIFF!
SHERIFF LINDO, PLEASE, JUST A BRIEF STATEMENT...
NOT NOW, COLLETTE.
YOU HEARD THE SHERIFF, MISS.
BLACK GLIDER'S
BIG SHAFT!
HE'S BACK, HE'S BLACK, AND HE'S ON THE ATTACK!!!
"BALIPITHA, BATARA, BHAGAVAD GITA"

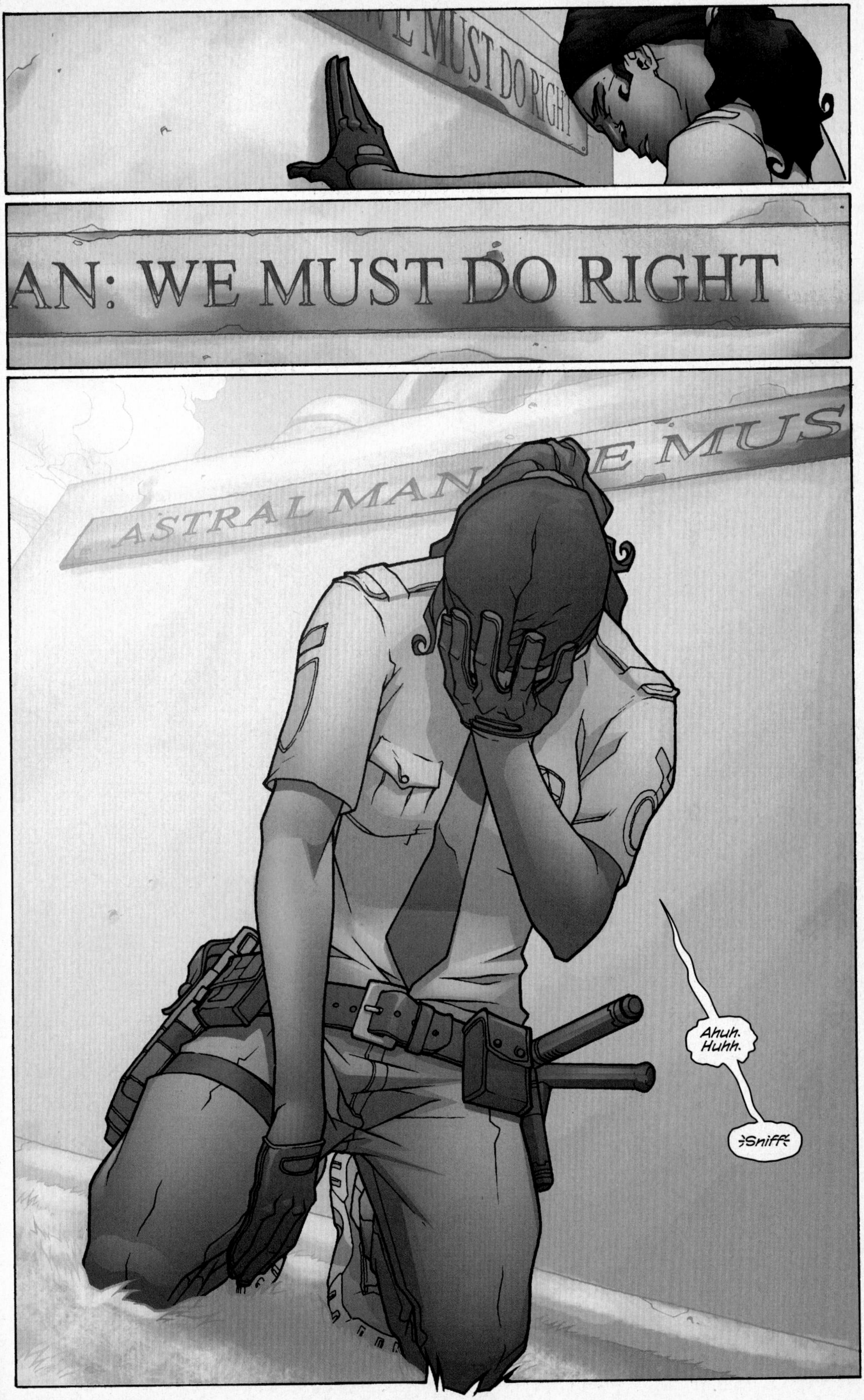
WE MUST DO RIGHT
AN: WE MUST DO RIGHT
ASTRAL MAN
E MUS
Ahuh. Huhh.
Sniff

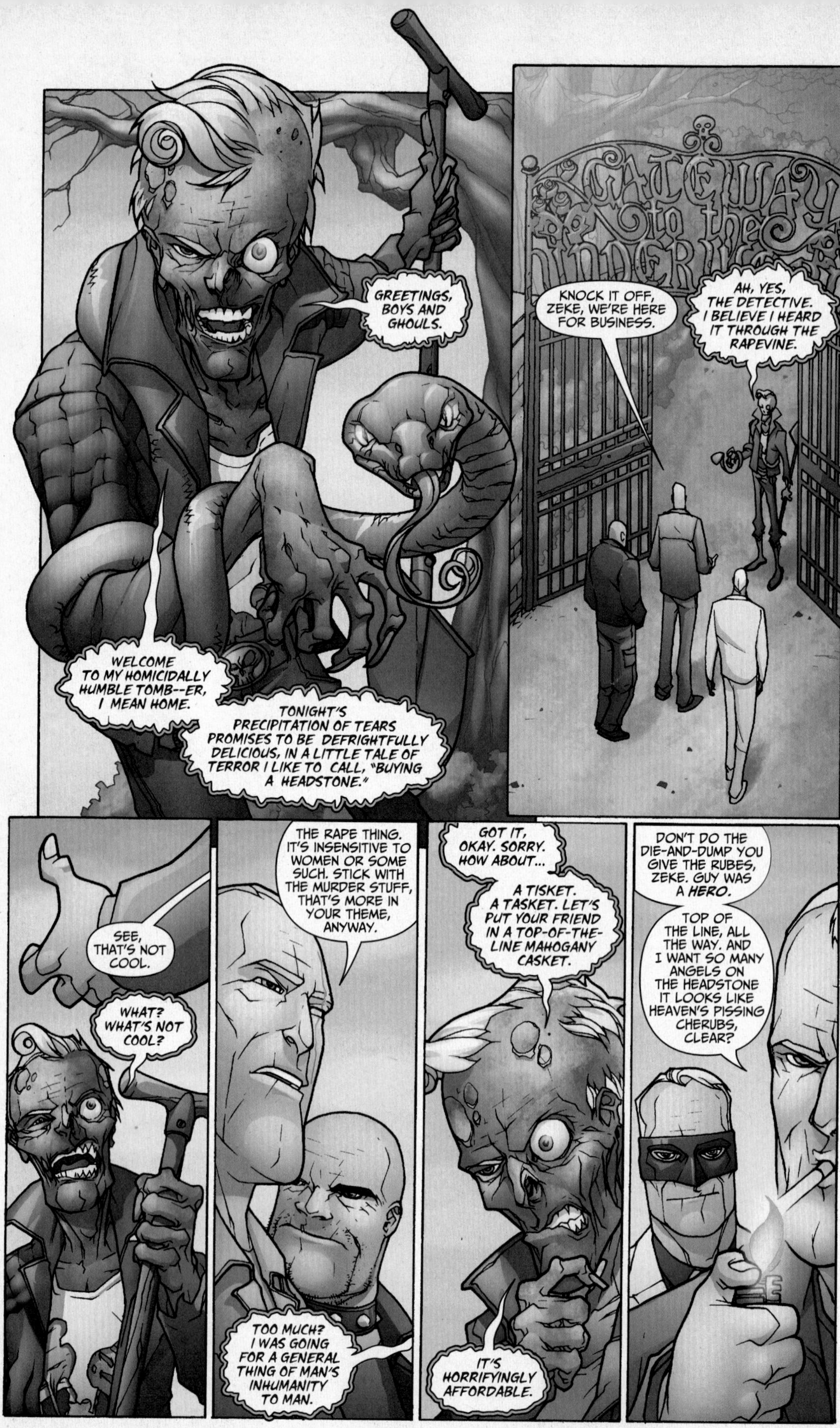
GREETINGS, BOYS AND GHOULS.
WELCOME TO MY HOMICIDALLY HUMBLE TOMB--ER, I MEAN HOME.
TONIGHT'S PRECIPITATION OF TEARS PROMISES TO BE DEFRIGHTFULLY DELICIOUS, IN A LITTLE TALE OF TERROR I LIKE TO CALL, "BUYING A HEADSTONE."
KNOCK IT OFF, ZEKE, WE'RE HERE FOR BUSINESS.
AH, YES, THE DETECTIVE. I BELIEVE I HEARD IT THROUGH THE RAPEVINE.
SEE, THAT'S NOT COOL.
WHAT? WHAT'S NOT COOL?
THE RAPE THING. IT'S INSENSITIVE TO WOMEN OR SOME SUCH. STICK WITH THE MURDER STUFF, THAT'S MORE IN YOUR THEME, ANYWAY.
TOO MUCH? I WAS GOING FOR A GENERAL THING OF MAN'S INHUMANITY TO MAN.
GOT IT, OKAY. SORRY. HOW ABOUT...
A TISKET. A TASKET. LET'S PUT YOUR FRIEND IN A TOP-OF-THE-LINE MAHOGANY CASKET.
IT'S HORRIFYINGLY AFFORDABLE.
DON'T DO THE DIE-AND-DUMP YOU GIVE THE RUBES, ZEKE. GUY WAS A HERO.
TOP OF THE LINE, ALL THE WAY. AND I WANT SO MANY ANGELS ON THE HEADSTONE IT LOOKS LIKE HEAVEN'S PISSING CHERUBS, CLEAR?

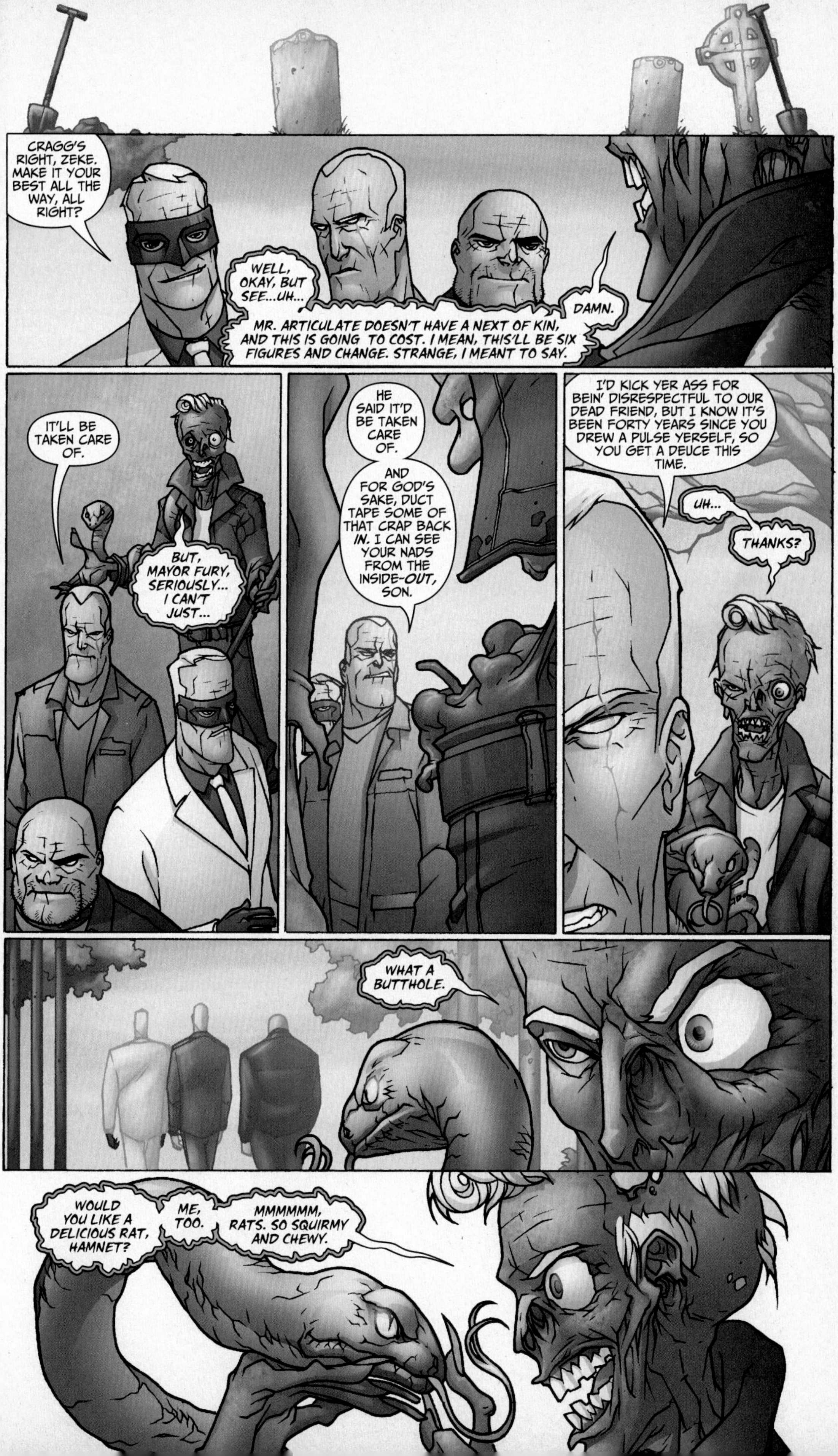

CRAGG'S RIGHT, ZEKE. MAKE IT YOUR BEST ALL THE WAY, ALL RIGHT?
WELL, OKAY, BUT SEE...UH...
MR. ARTICULATE DOESN'T HAVE A NEXT OF KIN, AND THIS IS GOING TO COST. I MEAN, THIS'LL BE SIX FIGURES AND CHANGE. STRANGE, I MEANT TO SAY.
DAMN.
IT'LL BE TAKEN CARE OF.
BUT, MAYOR FURY, SERIOUSLY... I CAN'T JUST...
HE SAID IT'D BE TAKEN CARE OF.
AND FOR GOD'S SAKE, DUCT TAPE SOME OF THAT CRAP BACK IN. I CAN SEE YOUR NADS FROM THE INSIDE-OUT, SON.
I'D KICK YER ASS FOR BEIN' DISRESPECTFUL TO OUR DEAD FRIEND, BUT I KNOW IT'S BEEN FORTY YEARS SINCE YOU DREW A PULSE YERSELF, SO YOU GET A DEUCE THIS TIME.
UH...
THANKS?
WHAT A BUTTHOLE.
WOULD YOU LIKE A DELICIOUS RAT, HAMNET?
ME, TOO.
MMMMMM, RATS. SO SQUIRMY AND CHEWY.

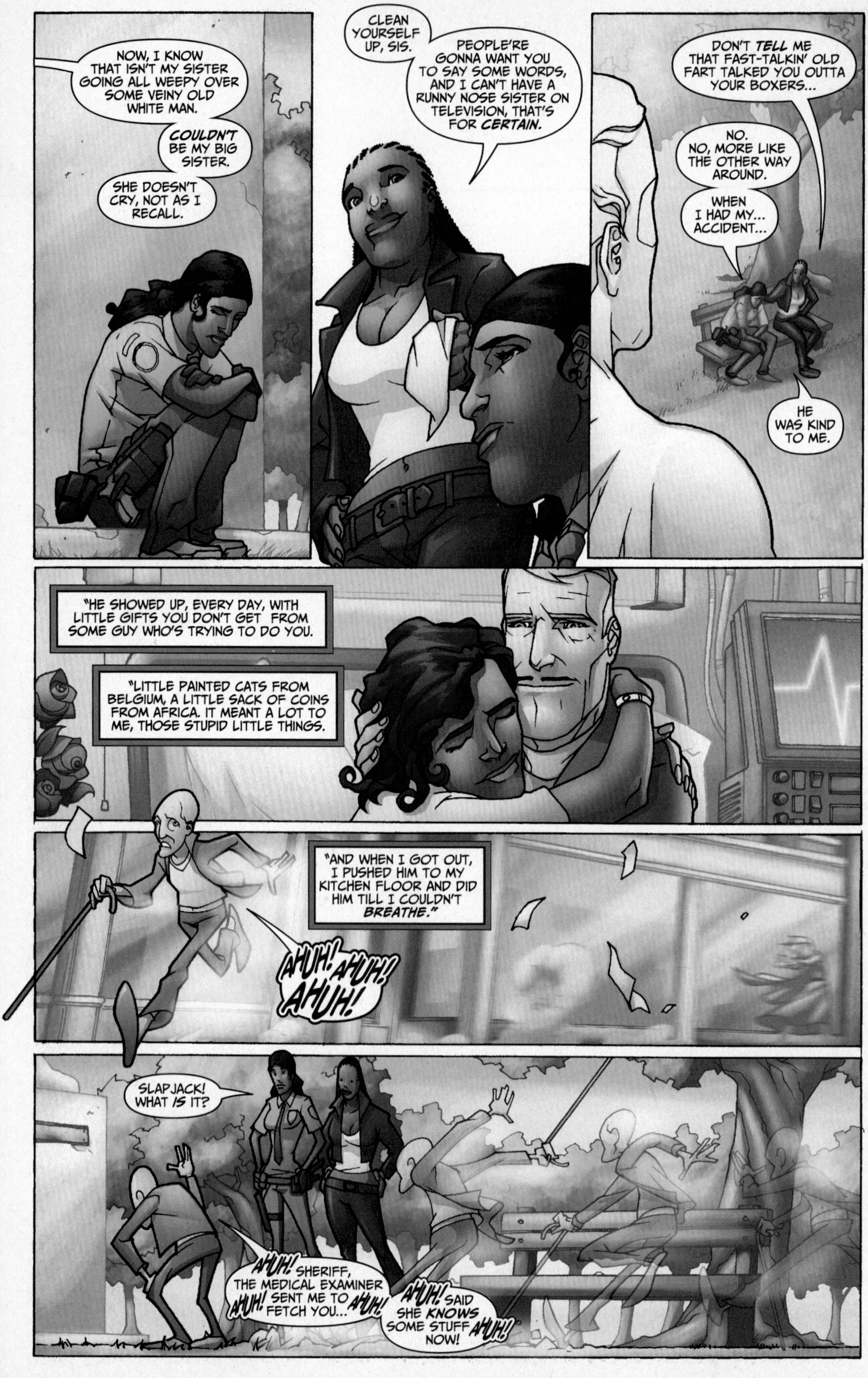

NOW, I KNOW THAT ISN'T MY SISTER GOING ALL WEEPY OVER SOME VEINY OLD WHITE MAN.
COULDN'T BE MY BIG SISTER.
SHE DOESN'T CRY, NOT AS I RECALL.
CLEAN YOURSELF UP, SIS.
PEOPLE'RE GONNA WANT YOU TO SAY SOME WORDS, AND I CAN'T HAVE A RUNNY NOSE SISTER ON TELEVISION, THAT'S FOR CERTAIN.
DON'T TELL ME THAT FAST-TALKIN' OLD FART TALKED YOU OUTTA YOUR BOXERS...
NO. NO, MORE LIKE THE OTHER WAY AROUND.
WHEN I HAD MY... ACCIDENT...
HE WAS KIND TO ME.
"HE SHOWED UP, EVERY DAY, WITH LITTLE GIFTS YOU DON'T GET FROM SOME GUY WHO'S TRYING TO DO YOU.
"LITTLE PAINTED CATS FROM BELGIUM, A LITTLE SACK OF COINS FROM AFRICA. IT MEANT A LOT TO ME, THOSE STUPID LITTLE THINGS.
"AND WHEN I GOT OUT, I PUSHED HIM TO MY KITCHEN FLOOR AND DID HIM TILL I COULDN'T BREATHE."
AHUH! AHUH! AHUH!
SLAPJACK! WHAT IS IT?
AHUH! SHERIFF, THE MEDICAL EXAMINER AHUH! SENT ME TO AHUH! FETCH YOU...
AHUH! SAID SHE KNOWS SOME STUFF AHUH! NOW!

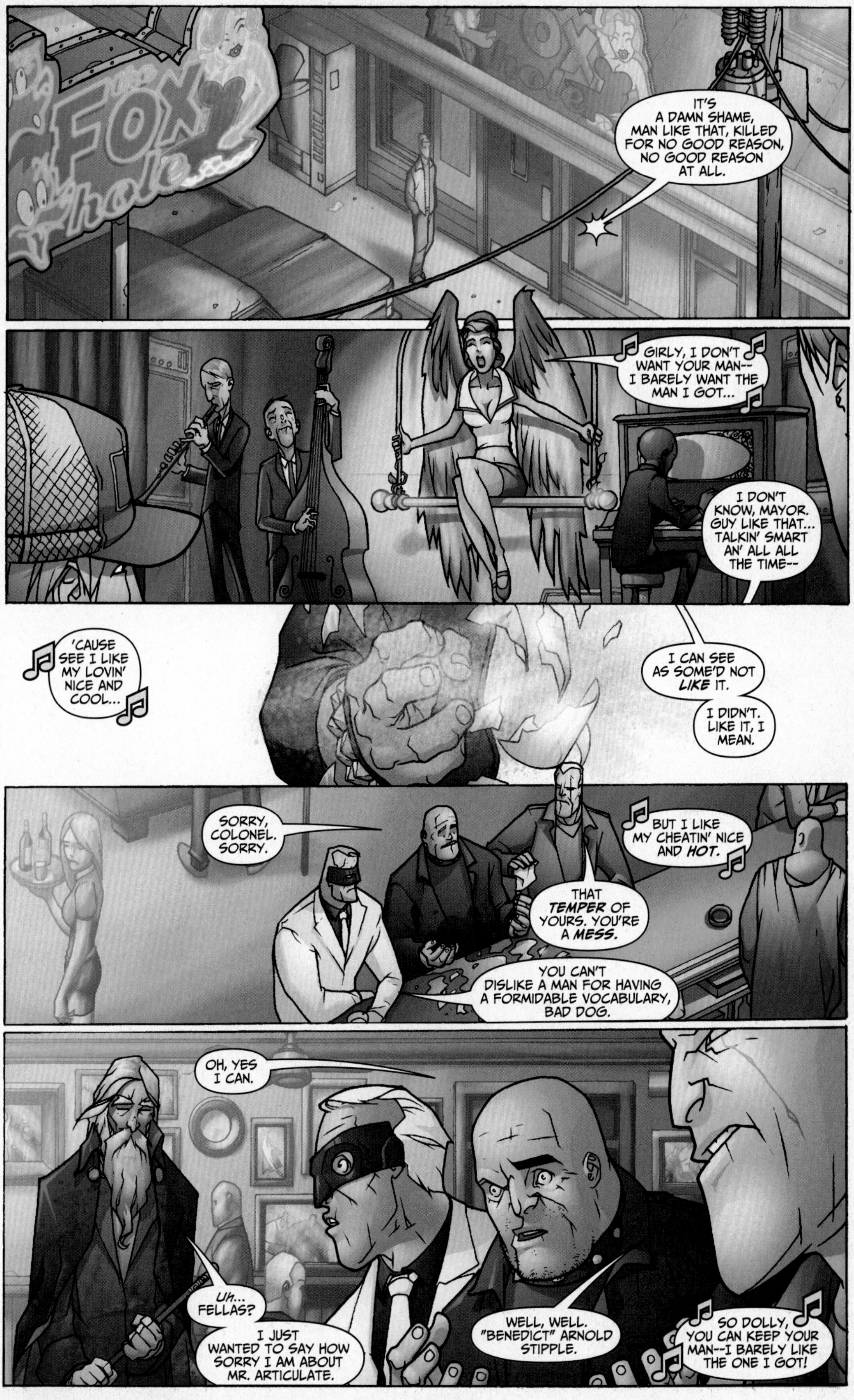

IT'S A DAMN SHAME, MAN LIKE THAT, KILLED FOR NO GOOD REASON, NO GOOD REASON AT ALL.
GIRLY, I DON'T WANT YOUR MAN-- I BARELY WANT THE MAN I GOT...
I DON'T KNOW, MAYOR. GUY LIKE THAT... TALKIN' SMART AN' ALL ALL THE TIME--
'CAUSE SEE I LIKE MY LOVIN' NICE AND COOL...
I CAN SEE AS SOME'D NOT LIKE IT.
I DIDN'T. LIKE IT, I MEAN.
SORRY, COLONEL. SORRY.
BUT I LIKE MY CHEATIN' NICE AND HOT.
THAT TEMPER OF YOURS. YOU'RE A MESS.
YOU CAN'T DISLIKE A MAN FOR HAVING A FORMIDABLE VOCABULARY, BAD DOG.
OH, YES I CAN.
UH... FELLAS?
I JUST WANTED TO SAY HOW SORRY I AM ABOUT MR. ARTICULATE.
WELL, WELL. "BENEDICT" ARNOLD STIPPLE.
SO DOLLY, YOU CAN KEEP YOUR MAN--I BARELY LIKE THE ONE I GOT!

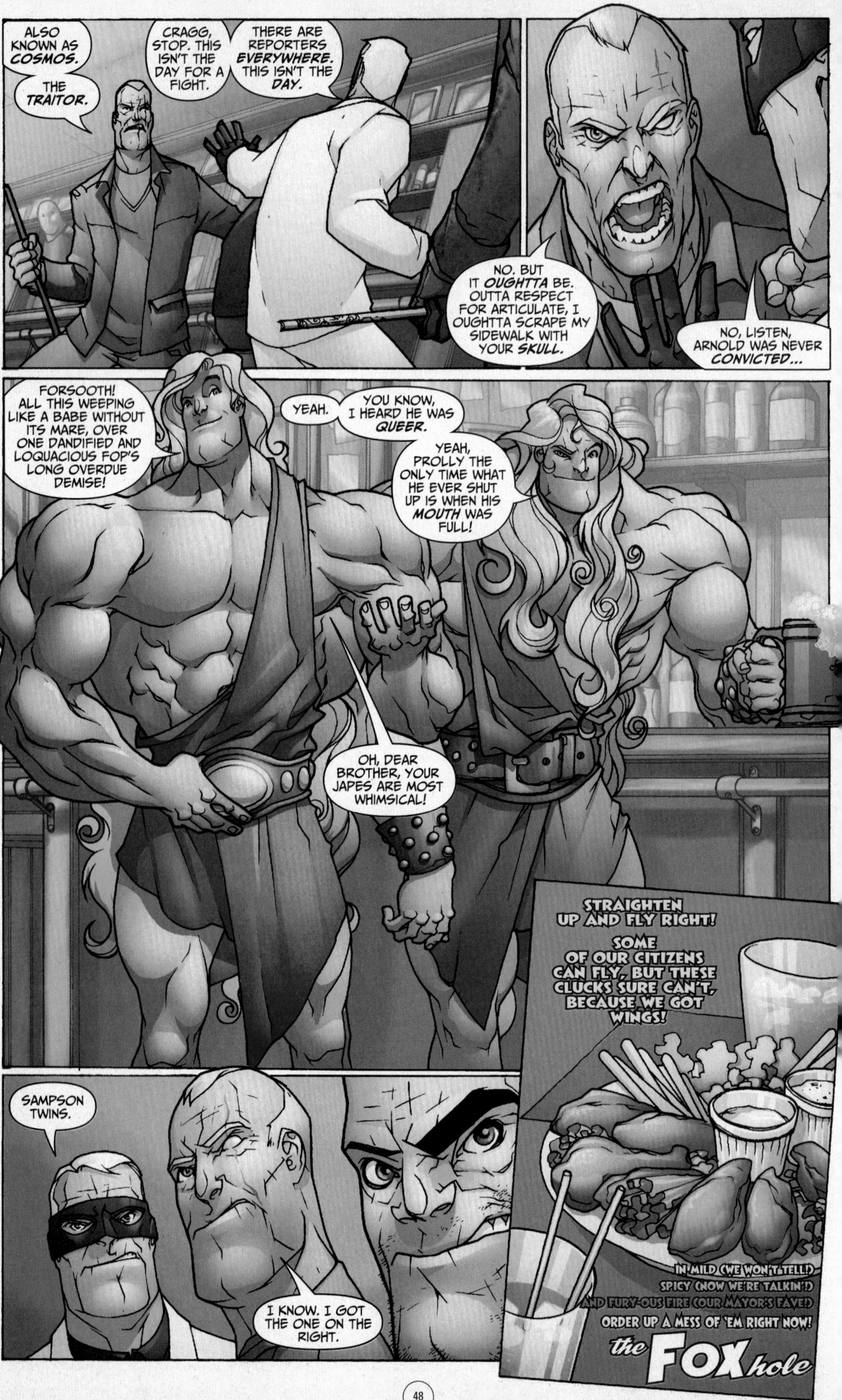
ALSO KNOWN AS *COSMOS.*
THE *TRAITOR.*
CRAGG, STOP. THIS ISN'T THE DAY FOR A FIGHT.
THERE ARE REPORTERS *EVERYWHERE.* THIS ISN'T THE *DAY.*
NO. BUT IT *OUGHTTA* BE. OUTTA RESPECT FOR ARTICULATE, I OUGHTTA SCRAPE MY SIDEWALK WITH YOUR *SKULL.*
NO, LISTEN, ARNOLD WAS NEVER *CONVICTED...*
FORSOOTH! ALL THIS WEEPING LIKE A BABE WITHOUT ITS MARE, OVER ONE DANDIFIED AND LOQUACIOUS FOP'S LONG OVERDUE DEMISE!
YEAH.
YOU KNOW, I HEARD HE WAS *QUEER.*
YEAH, PROLLY THE ONLY TIME WHAT HE EVER SHUT UP IS WHEN HIS *MOUTH* WAS FULL!
OH, DEAR BROTHER, YOUR JAPES ARE MOST WHIMSICAL!
STRAIGHTEN UP AND FLY RIGHT!
SOME OF OUR CITIZENS CAN FLY, BUT THESE CLUCKS SURE CAN'T, BECAUSE WE GOT WINGS!
IN MILD (WE WON'T TELL!)
SPICY (NOW WE'RE TALKIN'!)
AND FURY-OUS FIRE (OUR MAYOR'S FAVE!)
ORDER UP A MESS OF 'EM RIGHT NOW!
the FOX hole
SAMPSON TWINS.
I KNOW. I GOT THE ONE ON THE RIGHT.

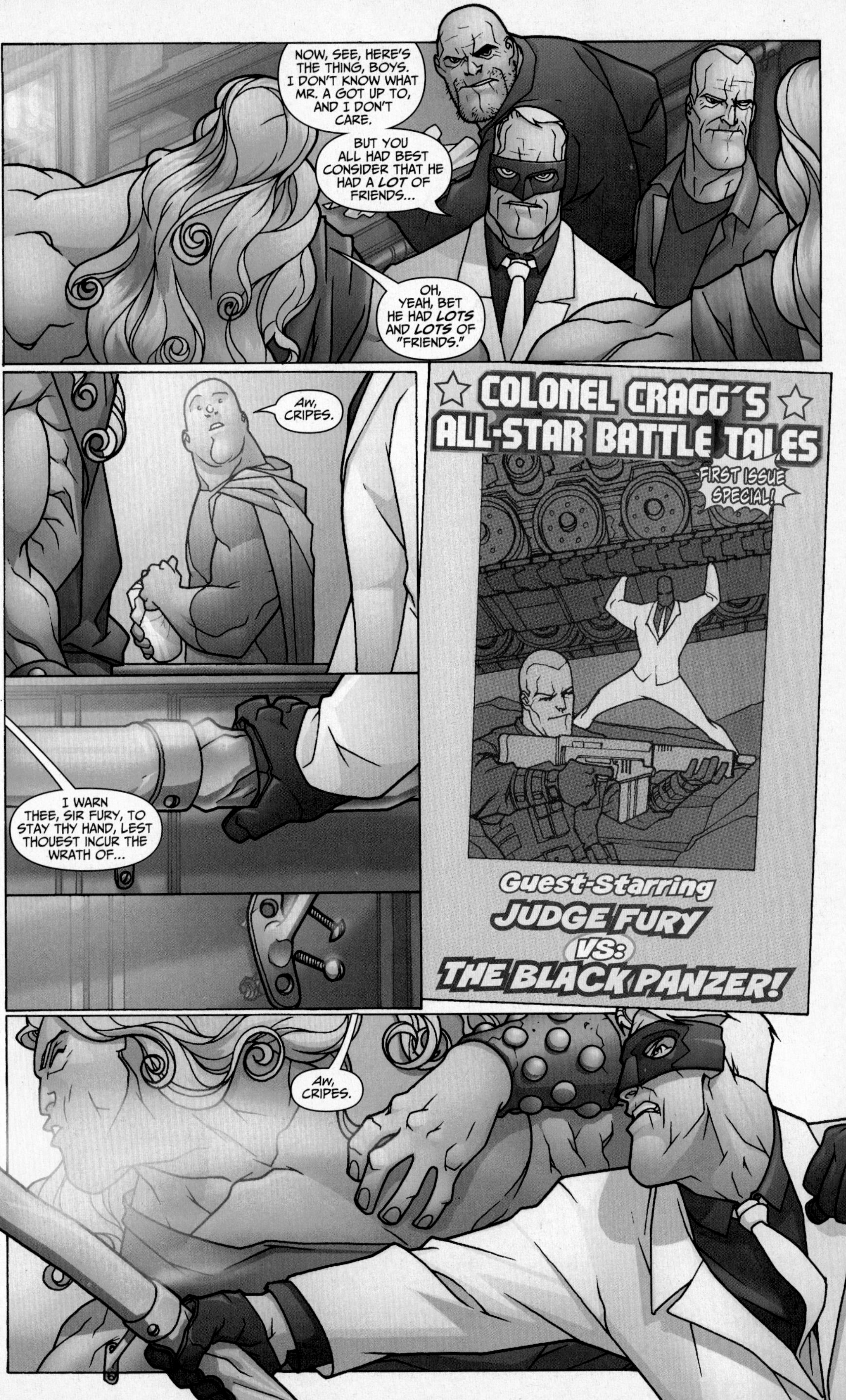

NOW, SEE, HERE'S THE THING, BOYS. I DON'T KNOW WHAT MR. A GOT UP TO, AND I DON'T CARE.
BUT YOU ALL HAD BEST CONSIDER THAT HE HAD A LOT OF FRIENDS...
OH, YEAH, BET HE HAD LOTS AND LOTS OF "FRIENDS."
AW, CRIPES.
COLONEL CRAGG'S ALL-STAR BATTLE TALES
FIRST ISSUE SPECIAL!
Guest-Starring
JUDGE FURY
VS:
THE BLACK PANZER!
I WARN THEE, SIR FURY, TO STAY THY HAND, LEST THOUEST INCUR THE WRATH OF...
AW, CRIPES.

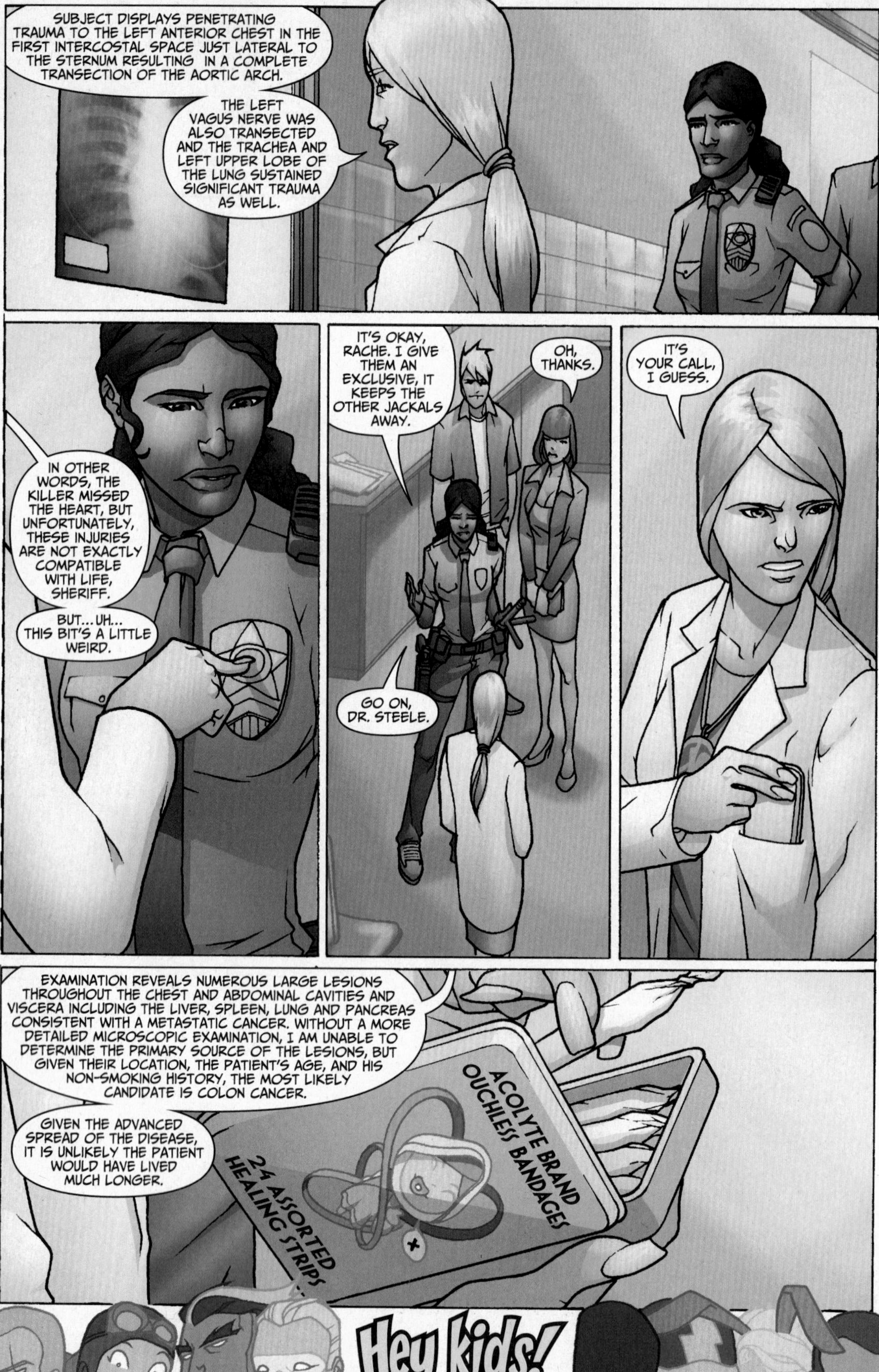
SUBJECT DISPLAYS PENETRATING TRAUMA TO THE LEFT ANTERIOR CHEST IN THE FIRST INTERCOSTAL SPACE JUST LATERAL TO THE STERNUM RESULTING IN A COMPLETE TRANSECTION OF THE AORTIC ARCH.
THE LEFT VAGUS NERVE WAS ALSO TRANSECTED AND THE TRACHEA AND LEFT UPPER LOBE OF THE LUNG SUSTAINED SIGNIFICANT TRAUMA AS WELL.
IN OTHER WORDS, THE KILLER MISSED THE HEART, BUT UNFORTUNATELY, THESE INJURIES ARE NOT EXACTLY COMPATIBLE WITH LIFE, SHERIFF.
BUT... UH... THIS BIT'S A LITTLE WEIRD.
IT'S OKAY, RACHE. I GIVE THEM AN EXCLUSIVE, IT KEEPS THE OTHER JACKALS AWAY.
OH, THANKS.
GO ON, DR. STEELE.
IT'S YOUR CALL, I GUESS.
EXAMINATION REVEALS NUMEROUS LARGE LESIONS THROUGHOUT THE CHEST AND ABDOMINAL CAVITIES AND VISCERA INCLUDING THE LIVER, SPLEEN, LUNG AND PANCREAS CONSISTENT WITH A METASTATIC CANCER. WITHOUT A MORE DETAILED MICROSCOPIC EXAMINATION, I AM UNABLE TO DETERMINE THE PRIMARY SOURCE OF THE LESIONS, BUT GIVEN THEIR LOCATION, THE PATIENT'S AGE, AND HIS NON-SMOKING HISTORY, THE MOST LIKELY CANDIDATE IS COLON CANCER.
GIVEN THE ADVANCED SPREAD OF THE DISEASE, IT IS UNLIKELY THE PATIENT WOULD HAVE LIVED MUCH LONGER.
ACOLYTE BRAND OUCHLESS BANDAGES
24 ASSORTED HEALING STRIPS
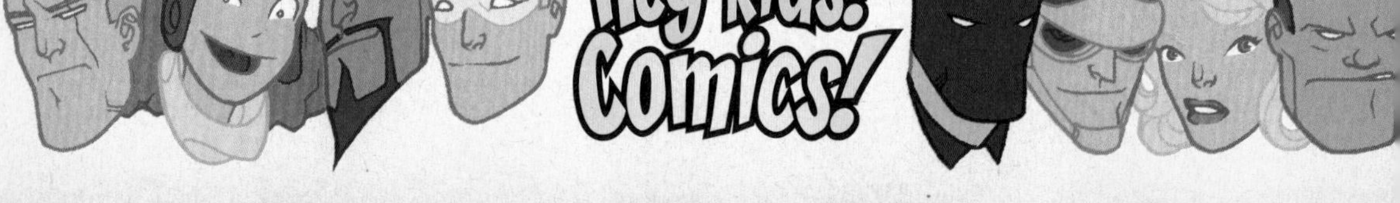
Hey kids! Comics!

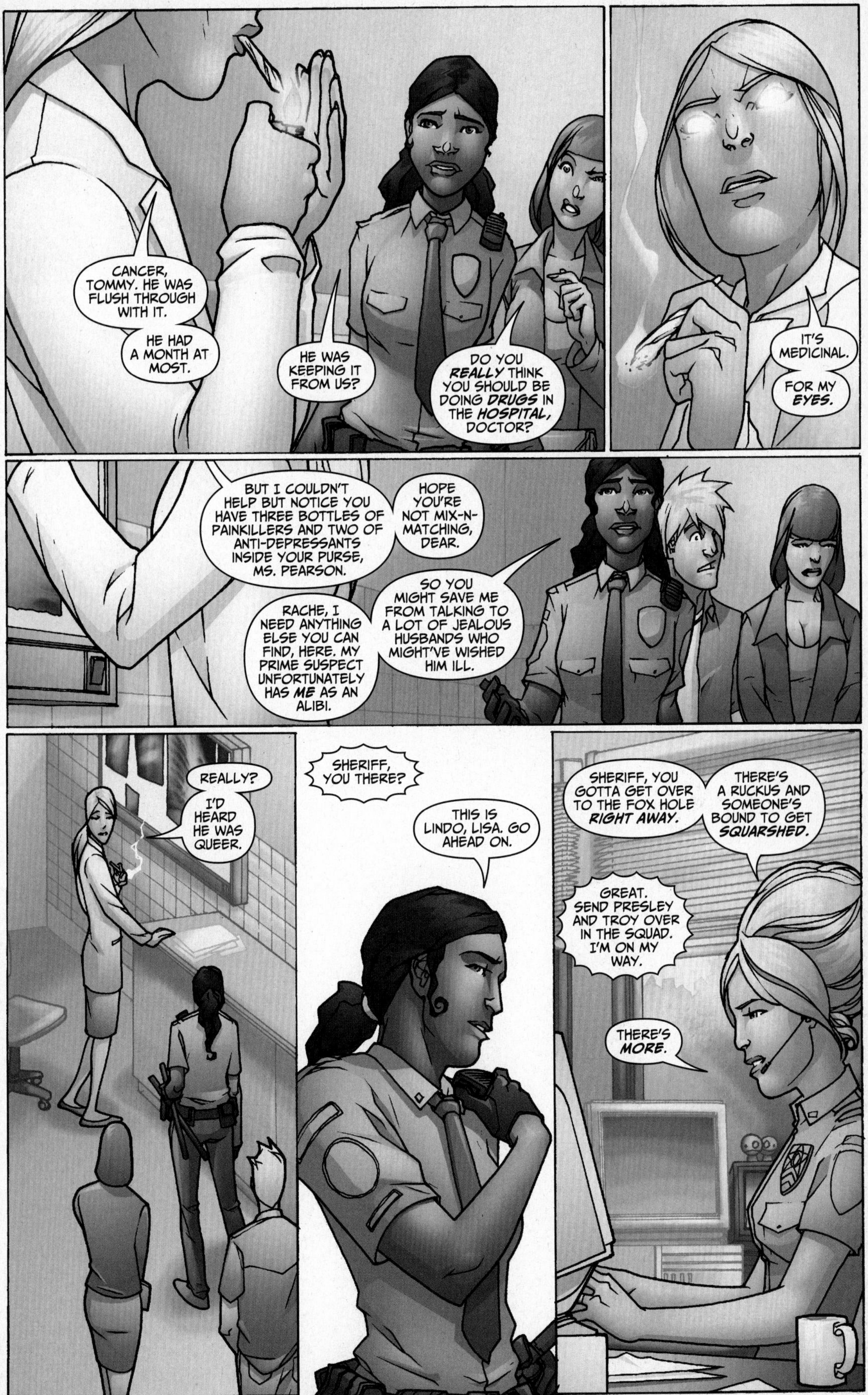
CANCER, TOMMY. HE WAS FLUSH THROUGH WITH IT.
HE HAD A MONTH AT MOST.
HE WAS KEEPING IT FROM US?
DO YOU *REALLY* THINK YOU SHOULD BE DOING *DRUGS* IN THE *HOSPITAL,* DOCTOR?
IT'S MEDICINAL.
FOR MY *EYES.*
BUT I COULDN'T HELP BUT NOTICE YOU HAVE THREE BOTTLES OF PAINKILLERS AND TWO OF ANTI-DEPRESSANTS INSIDE YOUR PURSE, MS. PEARSON.
HOPE YOU'RE NOT MIX-N-MATCHING, DEAR.
RACHE, I NEED ANYTHING ELSE YOU CAN FIND, HERE. MY PRIME SUSPECT UNFORTUNATELY HAS *ME* AS AN ALIBI.
SO YOU MIGHT SAVE ME FROM TALKING TO A LOT OF JEALOUS HUSBANDS WHO MIGHT'VE WISHED HIM ILL.
REALLY?
I'D HEARD HE WAS QUEER.
SHERIFF, YOU THERE?
THIS IS LINDO, LISA. GO AHEAD ON.
SHERIFF, YOU GOTTA GET OVER TO THE FOX HOLE *RIGHT AWAY.*
THERE'S A RUCKUS AND SOMEONE'S BOUND TO GET *SQUARSHED.*
GREAT. SEND PRESLEY AND TROY OVER IN THE SQUAD. I'M ON MY WAY.
THERE'S *MORE.*

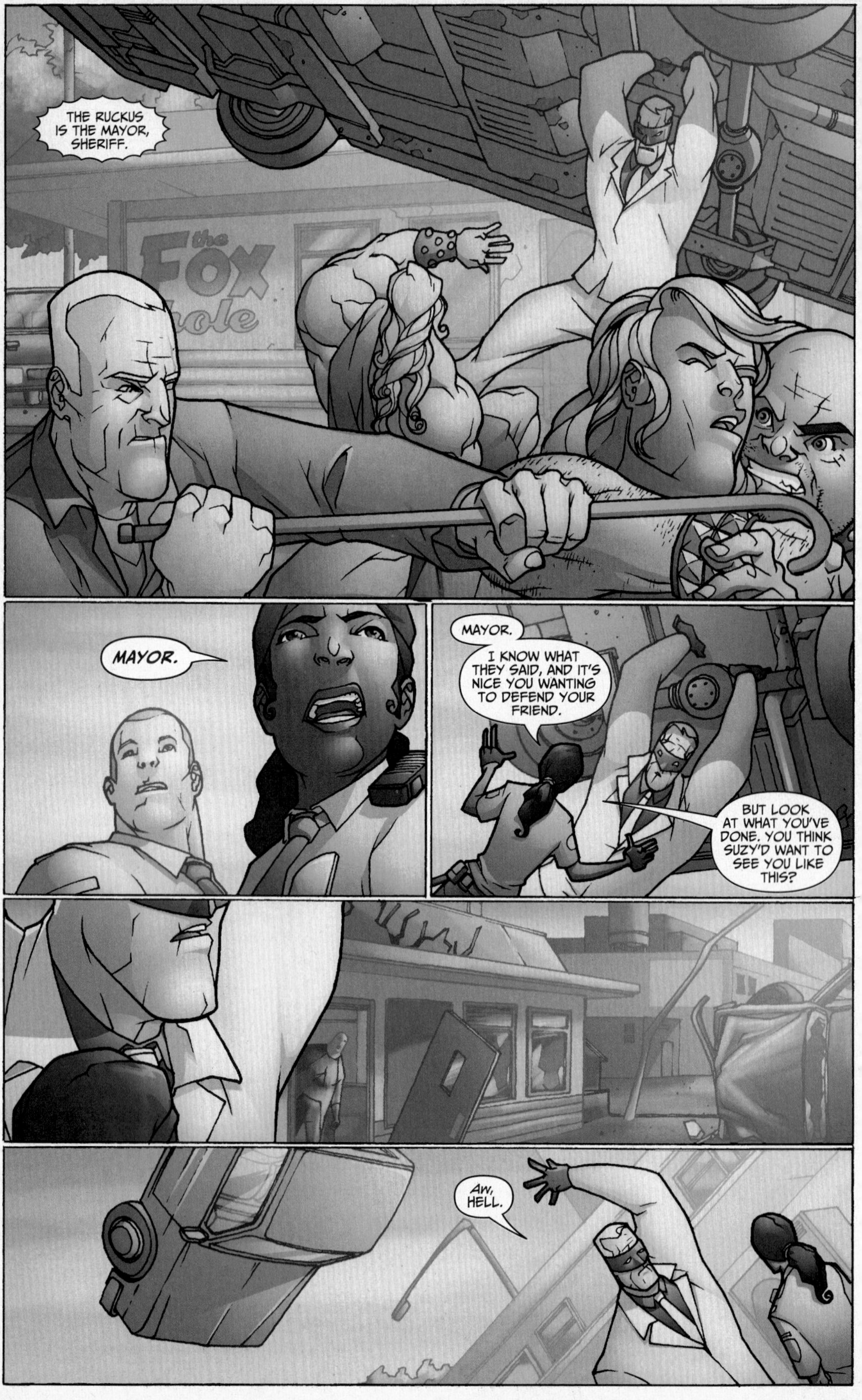
THE RUCKUS IS THE MAYOR, SHERIFF.
the FOX hole
MAYOR.
MAYOR.
I KNOW WHAT THEY SAID, AND IT'S NICE YOU WANTING TO DEFEND YOUR FRIEND.
BUT LOOK AT WHAT YOU'VE DONE. YOU THINK SUZY'D WANT TO SEE YOU LIKE THIS?
AW, HELL.

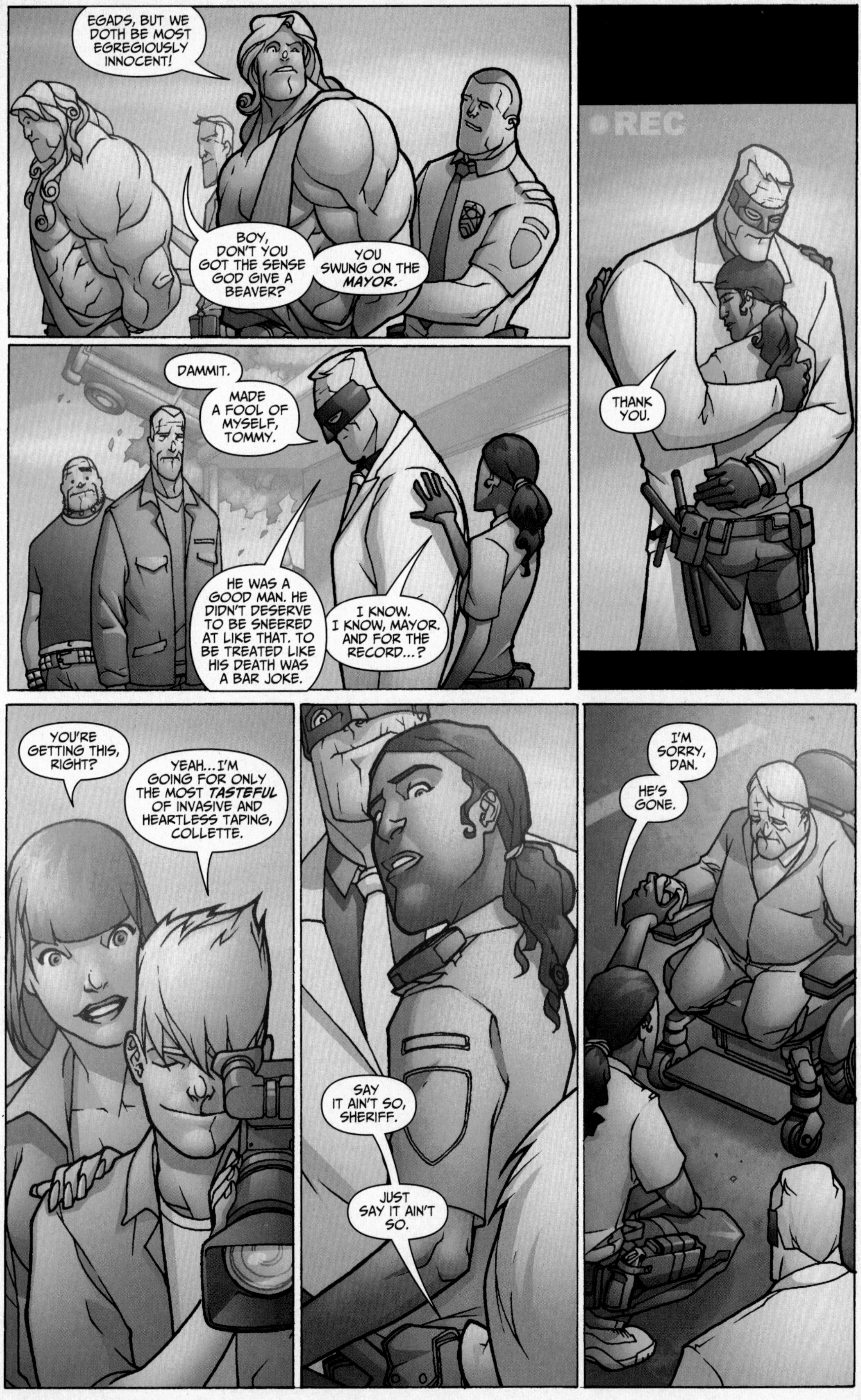
EGADS, BUT WE DOTH BE MOST EGREGIOUSLY INNOCENT!
BOY, DON'T YOU GOT THE SENSE GOD GIVE A BEAVER?
YOU SWUNG ON THE *MAYOR.*
DAMMIT.
MADE A FOOL OF MYSELF, TOMMY.
HE WAS A GOOD MAN. HE DIDN'T DESERVE TO BE SNEERED AT LIKE THAT. TO BE TREATED LIKE HIS DEATH WAS A BAR JOKE.
I KNOW. I KNOW, MAYOR. AND FOR THE RECORD...?
REC
THANK YOU.
YOU'RE GETTING THIS, RIGHT?
YEAH...I'M GOING FOR ONLY THE MOST *TASTEFUL* OF INVASIVE AND HEARTLESS TAPING, COLLETTE.
SAY IT AIN'T SO, SHERIFF.
JUST SAY IT AIN'T SO.
I'M SORRY, DAN.
HE'S GONE.

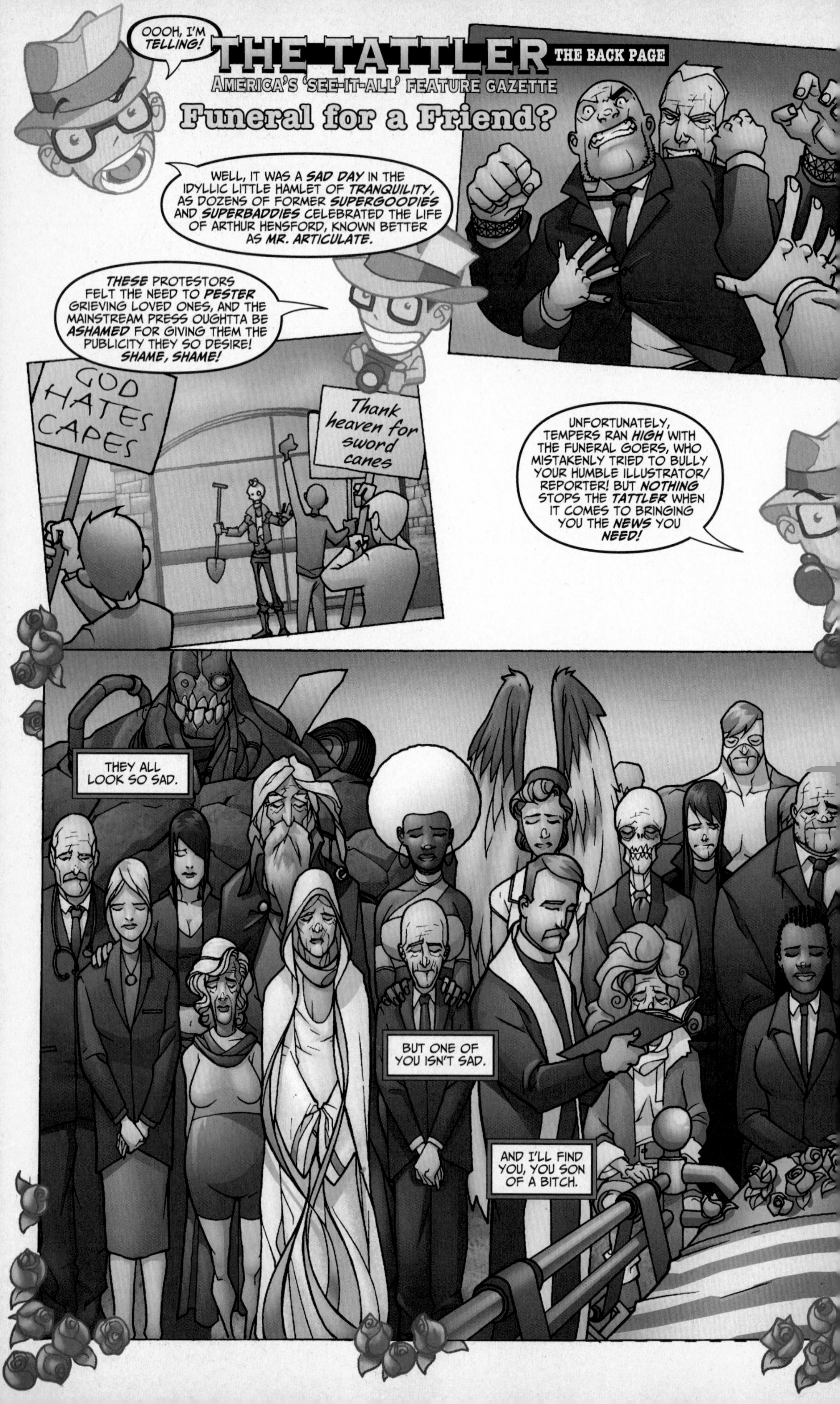
OOOH, I'M TELLING!
THE TATTLER
THE BACK PAGE
AMERICA'S 'SEE-IT-ALL' FEATURE GAZETTE
Funeral for a Friend?
WELL, IT WAS A SAD DAY IN THE IDYLLIC LITTLE HAMLET OF TRANQUILITY, AS DOZENS OF FORMER SUPERGOODIES AND SUPERBADDIES CELEBRATED THE LIFE OF ARTHUR HENSFORD, KNOWN BETTER AS MR. ARTICULATE.
THESE PROTESTORS FELT THE NEED TO PESTER GRIEVING LOVED ONES, AND THE MAINSTREAM PRESS OUGHTTA BE ASHAMED FOR GIVING THEM THE PUBLICITY THEY SO DESIRE! SHAME, SHAME!
GOD HATES CAPES
Thank heaven for sword canes
UNFORTUNATELY, TEMPERS RAN HIGH WITH THE FUNERAL GOERS, WHO MISTAKENLY TRIED TO BULLY YOUR HUMBLE ILLUSTRATOR/ REPORTER! BUT NOTHING STOPS THE TATTLER WHEN IT COMES TO BRINGING YOU THE NEWS YOU NEED!
THEY ALL LOOK SO SAD.
BUT ONE OF YOU ISN'T SAD.
AND I'LL FIND YOU, YOU SON OF A BITCH.

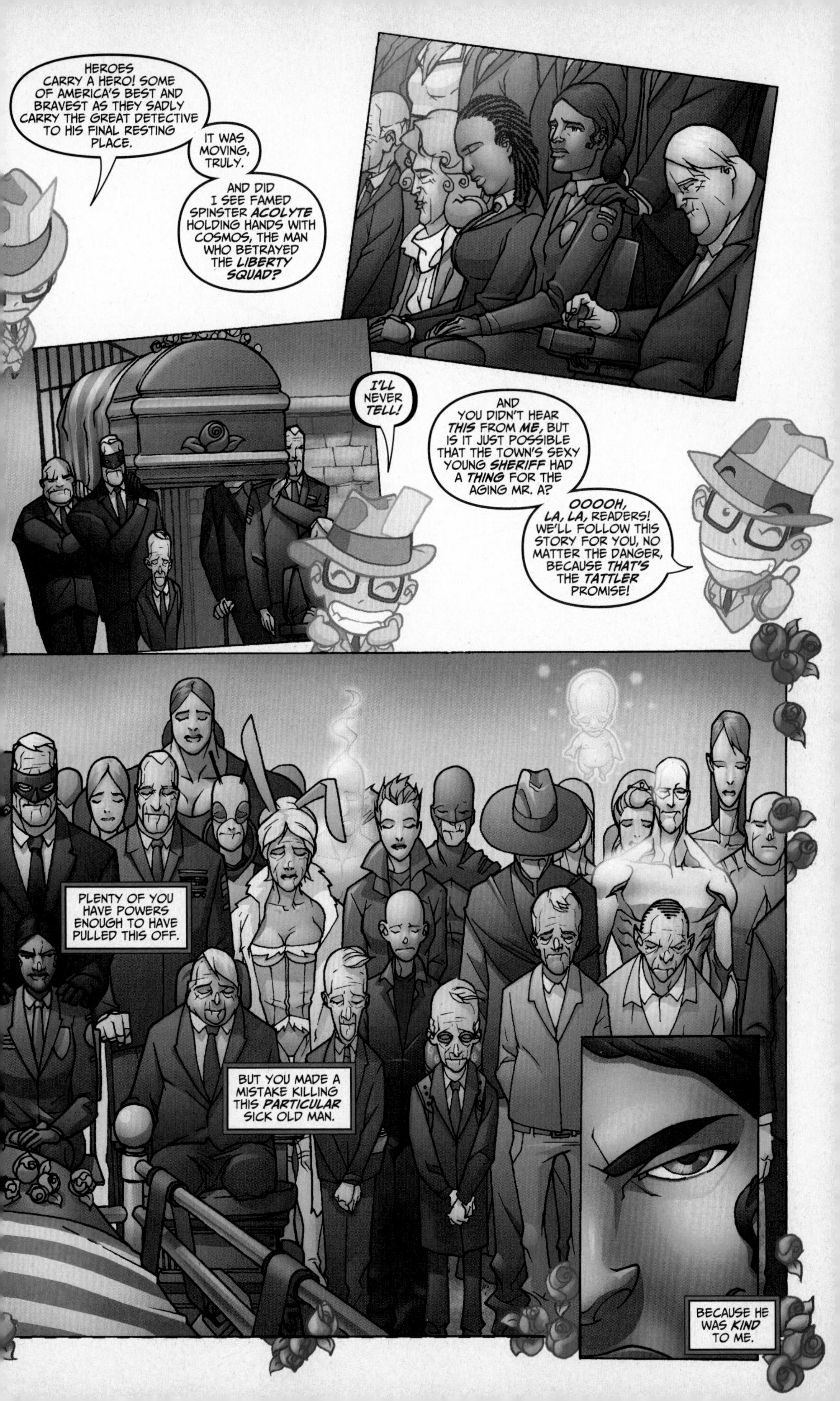

HEROES CARRY A HERO! SOME OF AMERICA'S BEST AND BRAVEST AS THEY SADLY CARRY THE GREAT DETECTIVE TO HIS FINAL RESTING PLACE.
IT WAS MOVING, TRULY.
AND DID I SEE FAMED SPINSTER ACOLYTE HOLDING HANDS WITH COSMOS, THE MAN WHO BETRAYED THE LIBERTY SQUAD?
I'LL NEVER TELL!
AND YOU DIDN'T HEAR THIS FROM ME, BUT IS IT JUST POSSIBLE THAT THE TOWN'S SEXY YOUNG SHERIFF HAD A THING FOR THE AGING MR. A?
OOOOH, LA, LA, READERS! WE'LL FOLLOW THIS STORY FOR YOU, NO MATTER THE DANGER, BECAUSE THAT'S THE TATTLER PROMISE!
PLENTY OF YOU HAVE POWERS ENOUGH TO HAVE PULLED THIS OFF.
BUT YOU MADE A MISTAKE KILLING THIS PARTICULAR SICK OLD MAN.
BECAUSE HE WAS KIND TO ME.

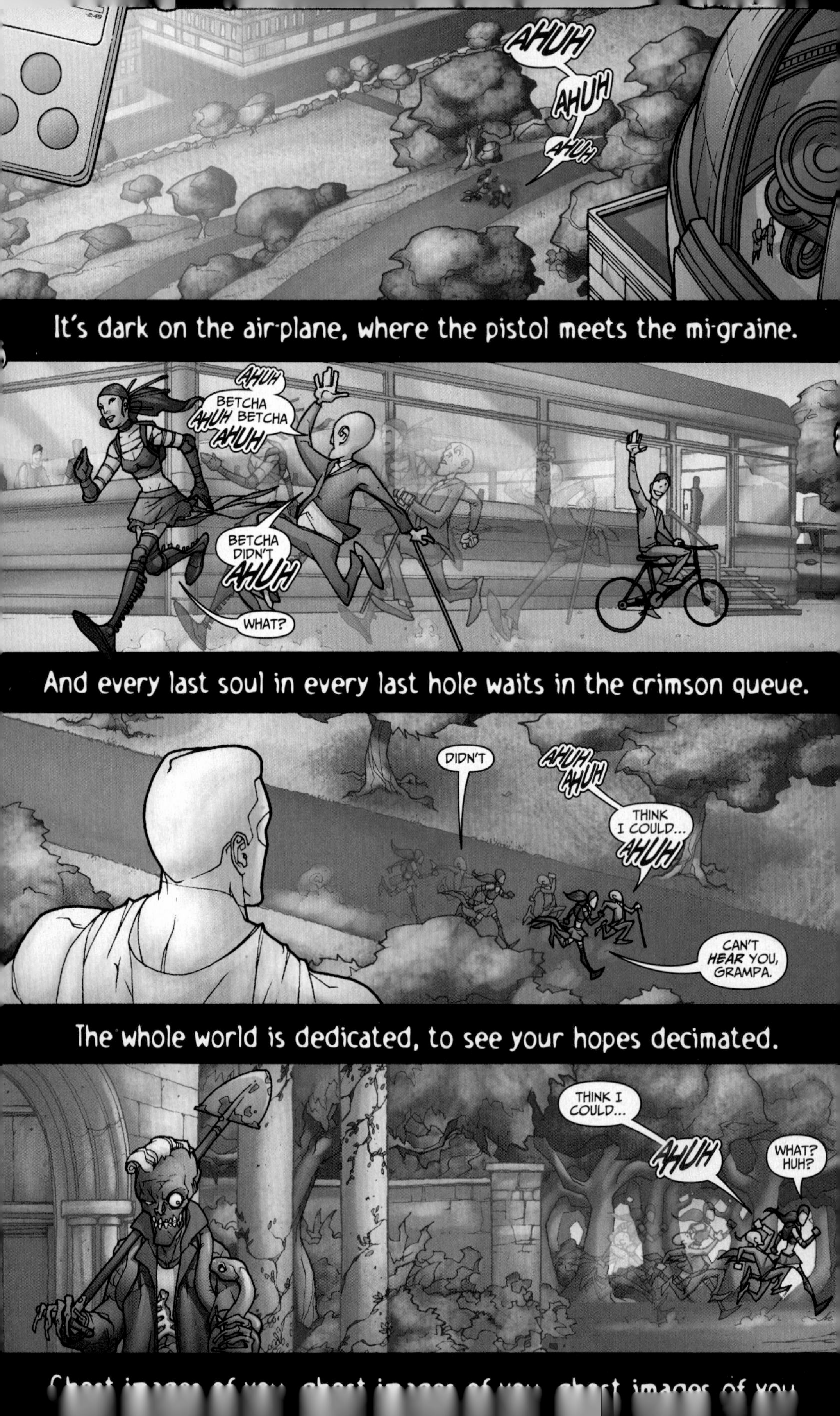
AHUH
AHUH
AHUH
It's dark on the air-plane, where the pistol meets the mi-graine.
AHUH
BETCHA AHUH BETCHA AHUH
BETCHA DIDN'T AHUH
WHAT?
And every last soul in every last hole waits in the crimson queue.
DIDN'T
AHUH AHUH
THINK I COULD... AHUH
CAN'T HEAR YOU, GRAMPA.
The whole world is dedicated, to see your hopes decimated.
THINK I COULD...
AHUH
WHAT? HUH?

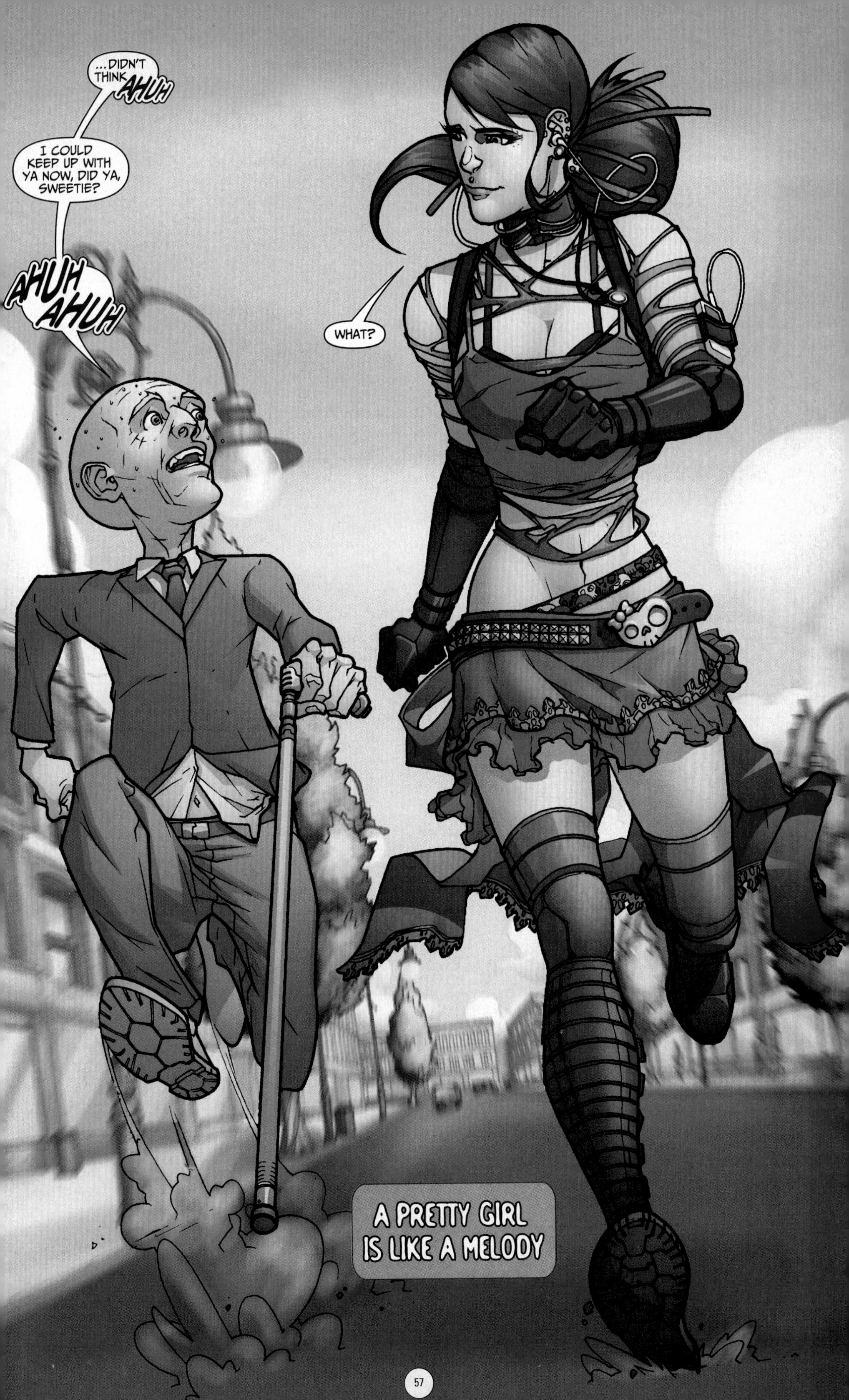

...DIDN'T THINK AHUH
I COULD KEEP UP WITH YA NOW, DID YA, SWEETIE?
AHUH AHUH
WHAT?
A PRETTY GIRL IS LIKE A MELODY

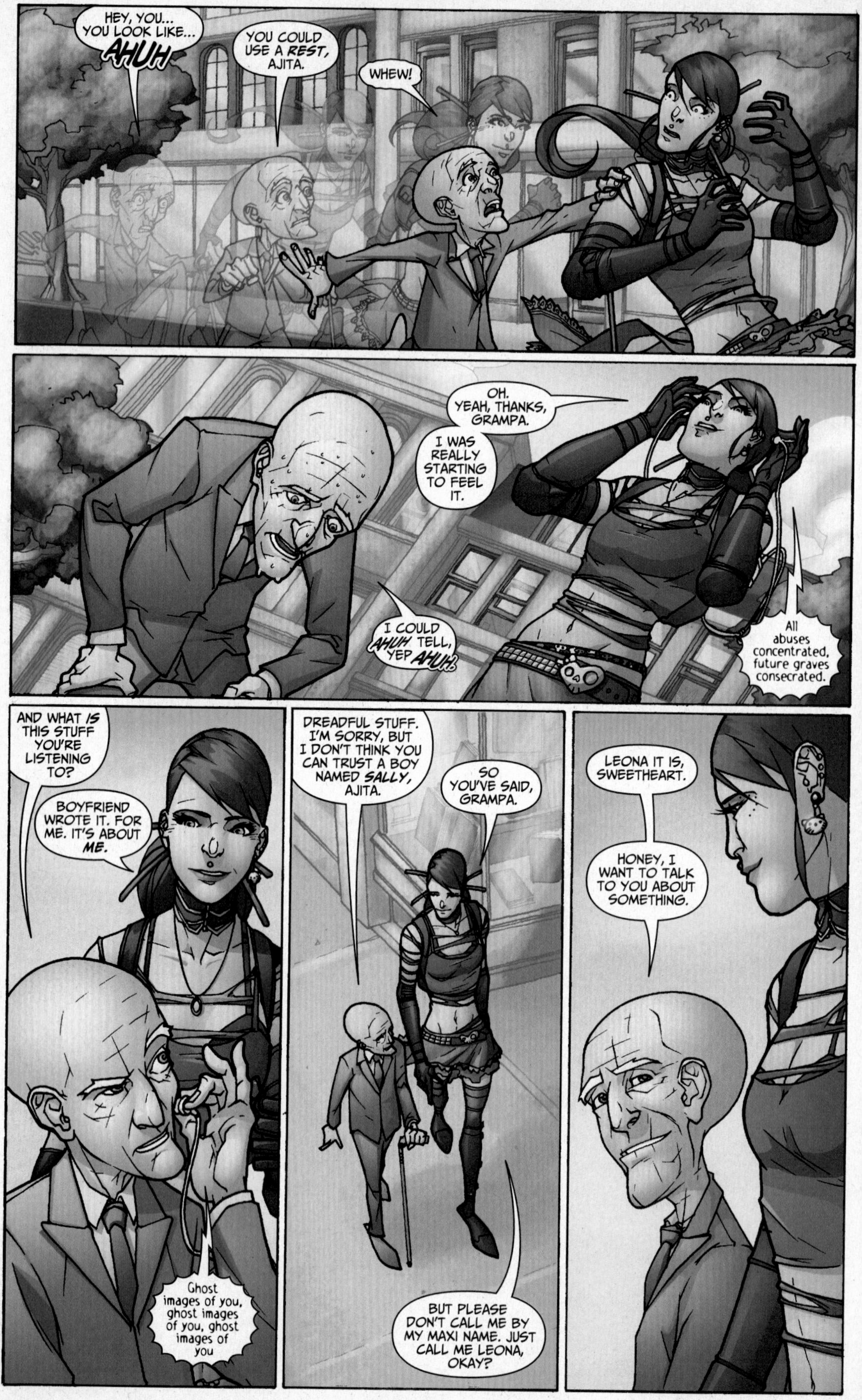
HEY, YOU... YOU LOOK LIKE... AHUH
YOU COULD USE A REST, AJITA.
WHEW!
OH. YEAH, THANKS, GRAMPA.
I WAS REALLY STARTING TO FEEL IT.
I COULD AHUH TELL, YEP AHUH.
All abuses concentrated, future graves consecrated.
AND WHAT IS THIS STUFF YOU'RE LISTENING TO?
BOYFRIEND WROTE IT. FOR ME. IT'S ABOUT ME.
Ghost images of you, ghost images of you, ghost images of you
DREADFUL STUFF. I'M SORRY, BUT I DON'T THINK YOU CAN TRUST A BOY NAMED SALLY, AJITA.
SO YOU'VE SAID, GRAMPA.
BUT PLEASE DON'T CALL ME BY MY MAXI NAME. JUST CALL ME LEONA, OKAY?
LEONA IT IS, SWEETHEART.
HONEY, I WANT TO TALK TO YOU ABOUT SOMETHING.

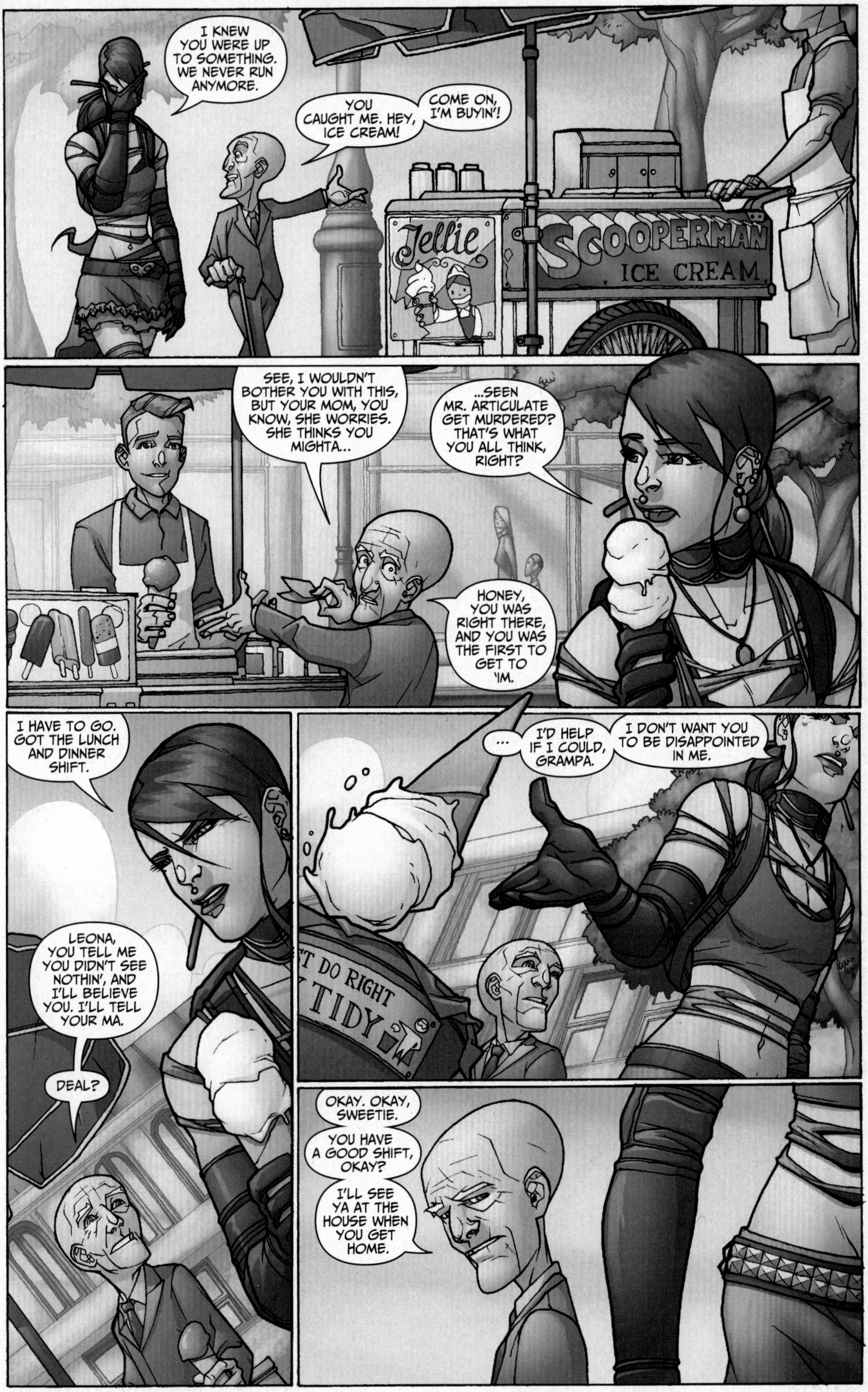
I KNEW YOU WERE UP TO SOMETHING. WE NEVER RUN ANYMORE.
YOU CAUGHT ME. HEY, ICE CREAM!
COME ON, I'M BUYIN'!
Jellie
SCOOPERMAN ICE CREAM
SEE, I WOULDN'T BOTHER YOU WITH THIS, BUT YOUR MOM, YOU KNOW, SHE WORRIES. SHE THINKS YOU MIGHTA...
...SEEN MR. ARTICULATE GET MURDERED? THAT'S WHAT YOU ALL THINK, RIGHT?
HONEY, YOU WAS RIGHT THERE, AND YOU WAS THE FIRST TO GET TO 'IM.
I HAVE TO GO. GOT THE LUNCH AND DINNER SHIFT.
LEONA, YOU TELL ME YOU DIDN'T SEE NOTHIN', AND I'LL BELIEVE YOU. I'LL TELL YOUR MA.
DEAL?
...
I'D HELP IF I COULD, GRAMPA.
I DON'T WANT YOU TO BE DISAPPOINTED IN ME.
T DO RIGHT
TIDY
OKAY. OKAY, SWEETIE.
YOU HAVE A GOOD SHIFT, OKAY?
I'LL SEE YA AT THE HOUSE WHEN YOU GET HOME.

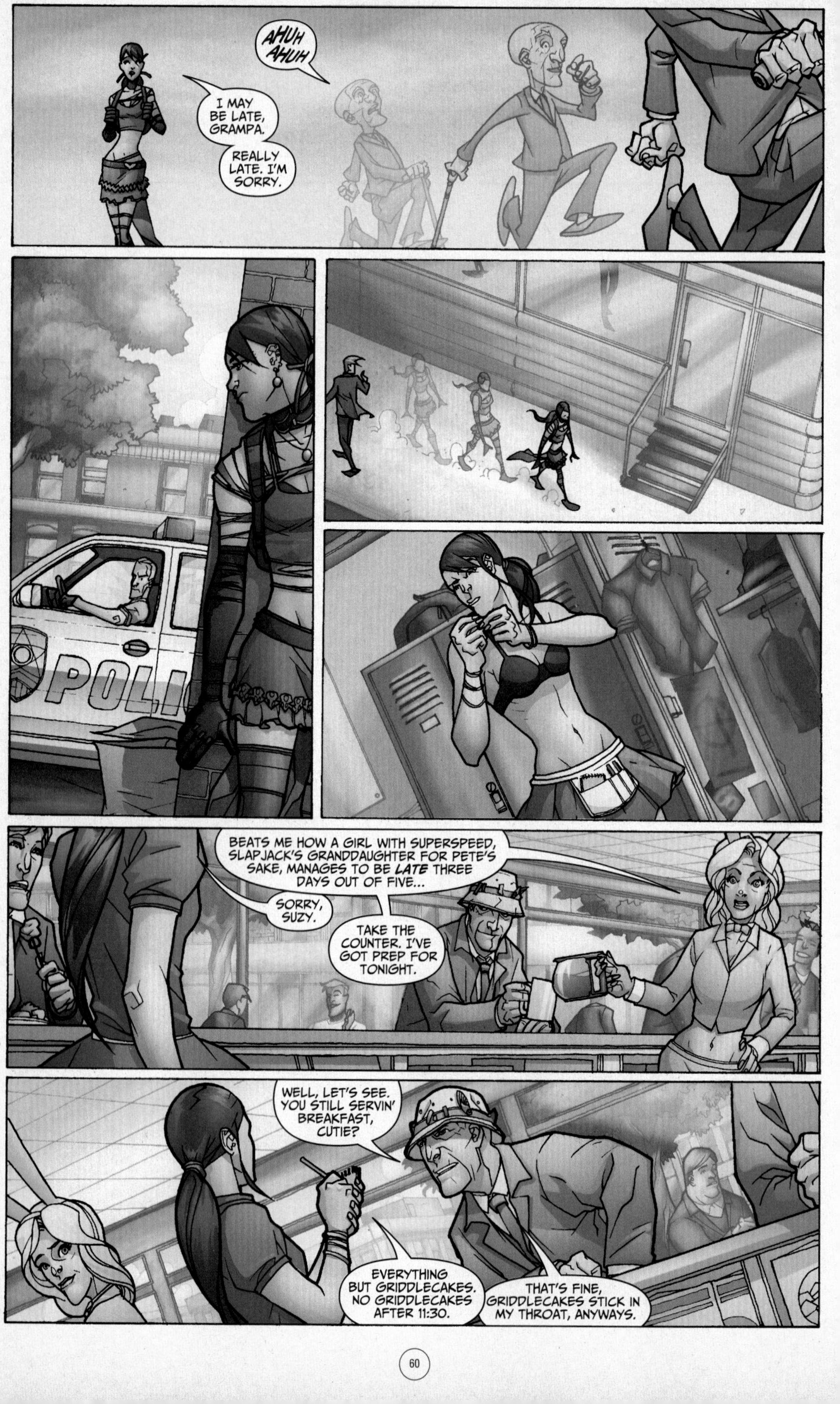
AHUH AHUH
I MAY BE LATE, GRAMPA.
REALLY LATE. I'M SORRY.
POLI
BEATS ME HOW A GIRL WITH SUPERSPEED, SLAPJACK'S GRANDDAUGHTER FOR PETE'S SAKE, MANAGES TO BE LATE THREE DAYS OUT OF FIVE...
SORRY, SUZY.
TAKE THE COUNTER. I'VE GOT PREP FOR TONIGHT.
WELL, LET'S SEE. YOU STILL SERVIN' BREAKFAST, CUTIE?
EVERYTHING BUT GRIDDLECAKES. NO GRIDDLECAKES AFTER 11:30.
THAT'S FINE, GRIDDLECAKES STICK IN MY THROAT, ANYWAYS.

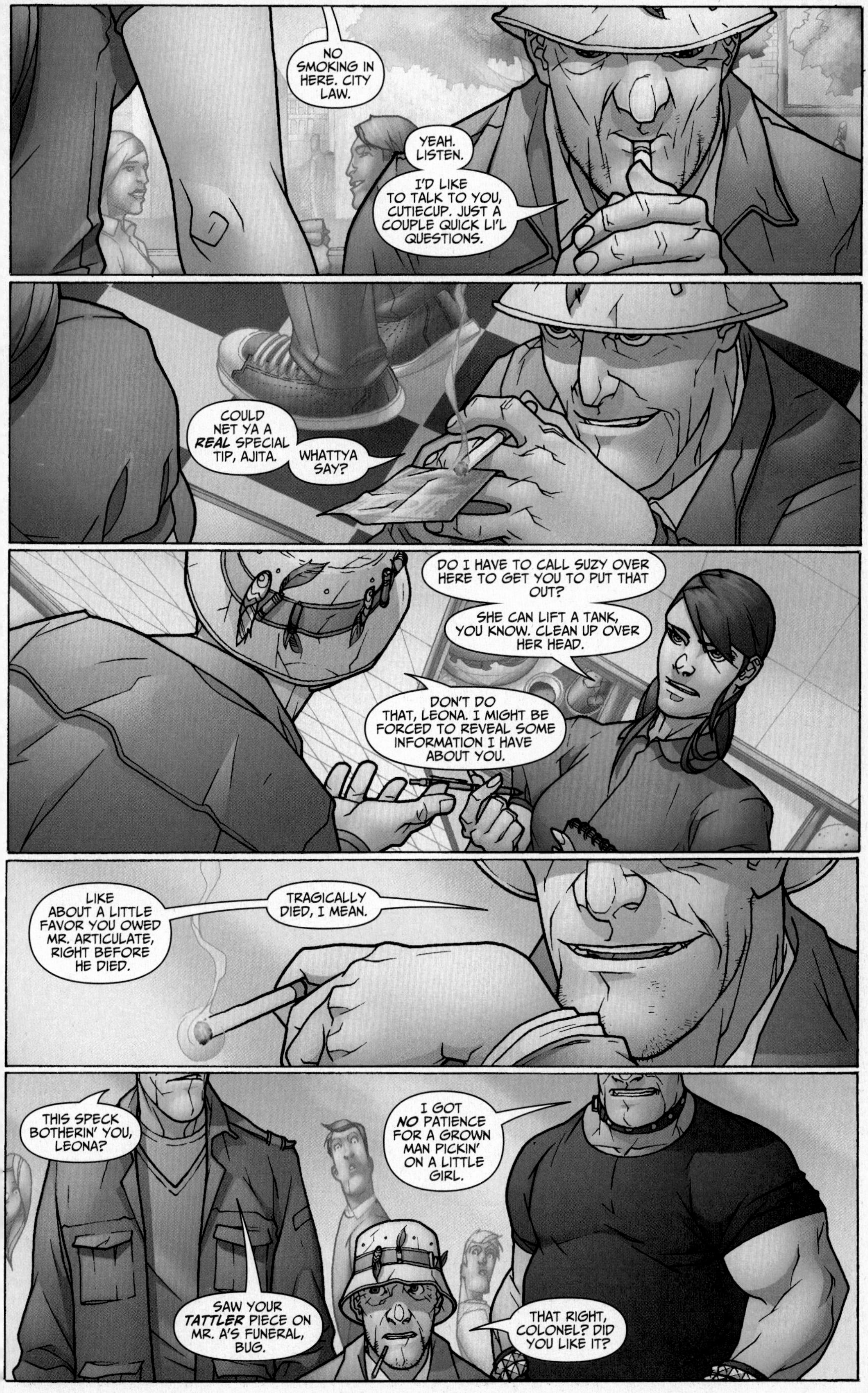
NO SMOKING IN HERE. CITY LAW.
YEAH. LISTEN.
I'D LIKE TO TALK TO YOU, CUTIECUP. JUST A COUPLE QUICK LI'L QUESTIONS.
COULD NET YA A *REAL* SPECIAL TIP, AJITA.
WHATTYA SAY?
DO I HAVE TO CALL SUZY OVER HERE TO GET YOU TO PUT THAT OUT?
SHE CAN LIFT A TANK, YOU KNOW. CLEAN UP OVER HER HEAD.
DON'T DO THAT, LEONA. I MIGHT BE FORCED TO REVEAL SOME INFORMATION I HAVE ABOUT YOU.
LIKE ABOUT A LITTLE FAVOR YOU OWED MR. ARTICULATE, RIGHT BEFORE HE DIED.
TRAGICALLY DIED, I MEAN.
THIS SPECK BOTHERIN' YOU, LEONA?
I GOT *NO* PATIENCE FOR A GROWN MAN PICKIN' ON A LITTLE GIRL.
SAW YOUR *TATTLER* PIECE ON MR. A'S FUNERAL, BUG.
THAT RIGHT, COLONEL? DID YOU LIKE IT?

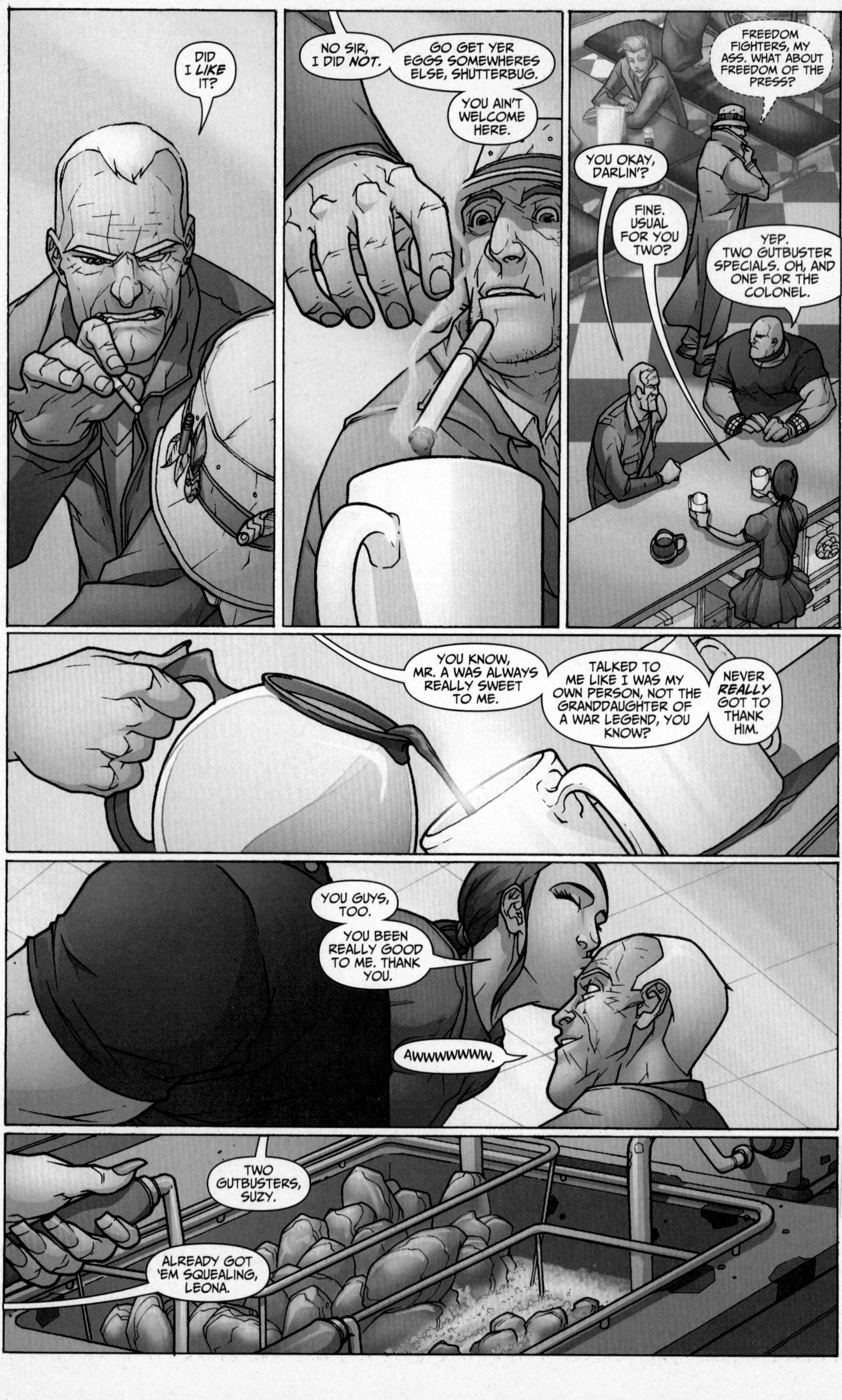

DID I LIKE IT?
NO SIR, I DID NOT.
GO GET YER EGGS SOMEWHERES ELSE, SHUTTERBUG.
YOU AIN'T WELCOME HERE.
FREEDOM FIGHTERS, MY ASS. WHAT ABOUT FREEDOM OF THE PRESS?
YOU OKAY, DARLIN'?
FINE. USUAL FOR YOU TWO?
YEP. TWO GUTBUSTER SPECIALS. OH, AND ONE FOR THE COLONEL.
YOU KNOW, MR. A WAS ALWAYS REALLY SWEET TO ME.
TALKED TO ME LIKE I WAS MY OWN PERSON, NOT THE GRANDDAUGHTER OF A WAR LEGEND, YOU KNOW?
NEVER REALLY GOT TO THANK HIM.
YOU GUYS, TOO.
YOU BEEN REALLY GOOD TO ME. THANK YOU.
AWWWWWWW.
TWO GUTBUSTERS, SUZY.
ALREADY GOT 'EM SQUEALING, LEONA.

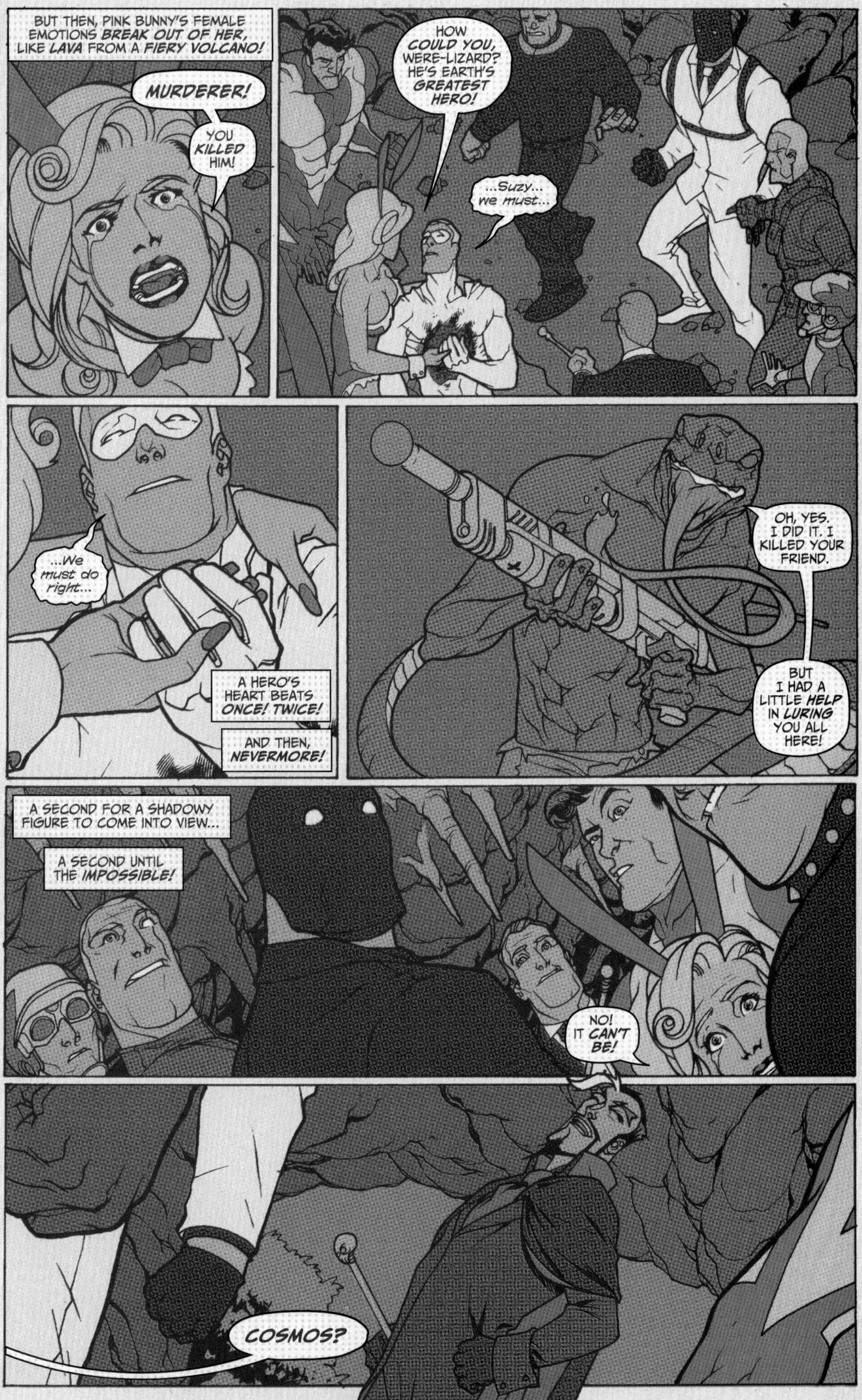
BUT THEN, PINK BUNNY'S FEMALE EMOTIONS BREAK OUT OF HER, LIKE LAVA FROM A FIERY VOLCANO!
MURDERER!
YOU KILLED HIM!
HOW COULD YOU, WERE-LIZARD? HE'S EARTH'S GREATEST HERO!
...Suzy... we must...
...We must do right...
A HERO'S HEART BEATS ONCE! TWICE!
AND THEN, NEVERMORE!
OH, YES. I DID IT. I KILLED YOUR FRIEND.
BUT I HAD A LITTLE HELP IN LURING YOU ALL HERE!
A SECOND FOR A SHADOWY FIGURE TO COME INTO VIEW...
A SECOND UNTIL THE IMPOSSIBLE!
NO! IT CAN'T BE!
COSMOS?

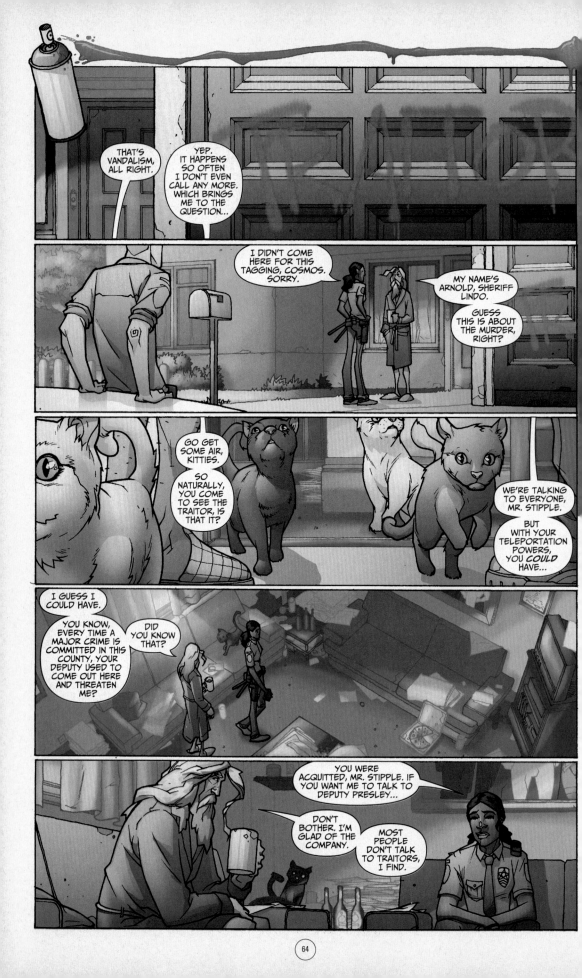

THAT'S VANDALISM, ALL RIGHT.

YEP. IT HAPPENS SO OFTEN I DON'T EVEN CALL ANY MORE. WHICH BRINGS ME TO THE QUESTION...

I DIDN'T COME HERE FOR THIS TAGGING, COSMOS. SORRY.

MY NAME'S ARNOLD, SHERIFF LINDO.

GUESS THIS IS ABOUT THE MURDER, RIGHT?

GO GET SOME AIR, KITTIES.

SO NATURALLY, YOU COME TO SEE THE TRAITOR, IS THAT IT?

WE'RE TALKING TO EVERYONE, MR. STIPPLE.

BUT WITH YOUR TELEPORTATION POWERS, YOU COULD HAVE...

I GUESS I COULD HAVE.

YOU KNOW, EVERY TIME A MAJOR CRIME IS COMMITTED IN THIS COUNTY, YOUR DEPUTY USED TO COME OUT HERE AND THREATEN ME?

DID YOU KNOW THAT?

YOU WERE ACQUITTED, MR. STIPPLE. IF YOU WANT ME TO TALK TO DEPUTY PRESLEY...

DON'T BOTHER. I'M GLAD OF THE COMPANY.

MOST PEOPLE DON'T TALK TO TRAITORS, I FIND.

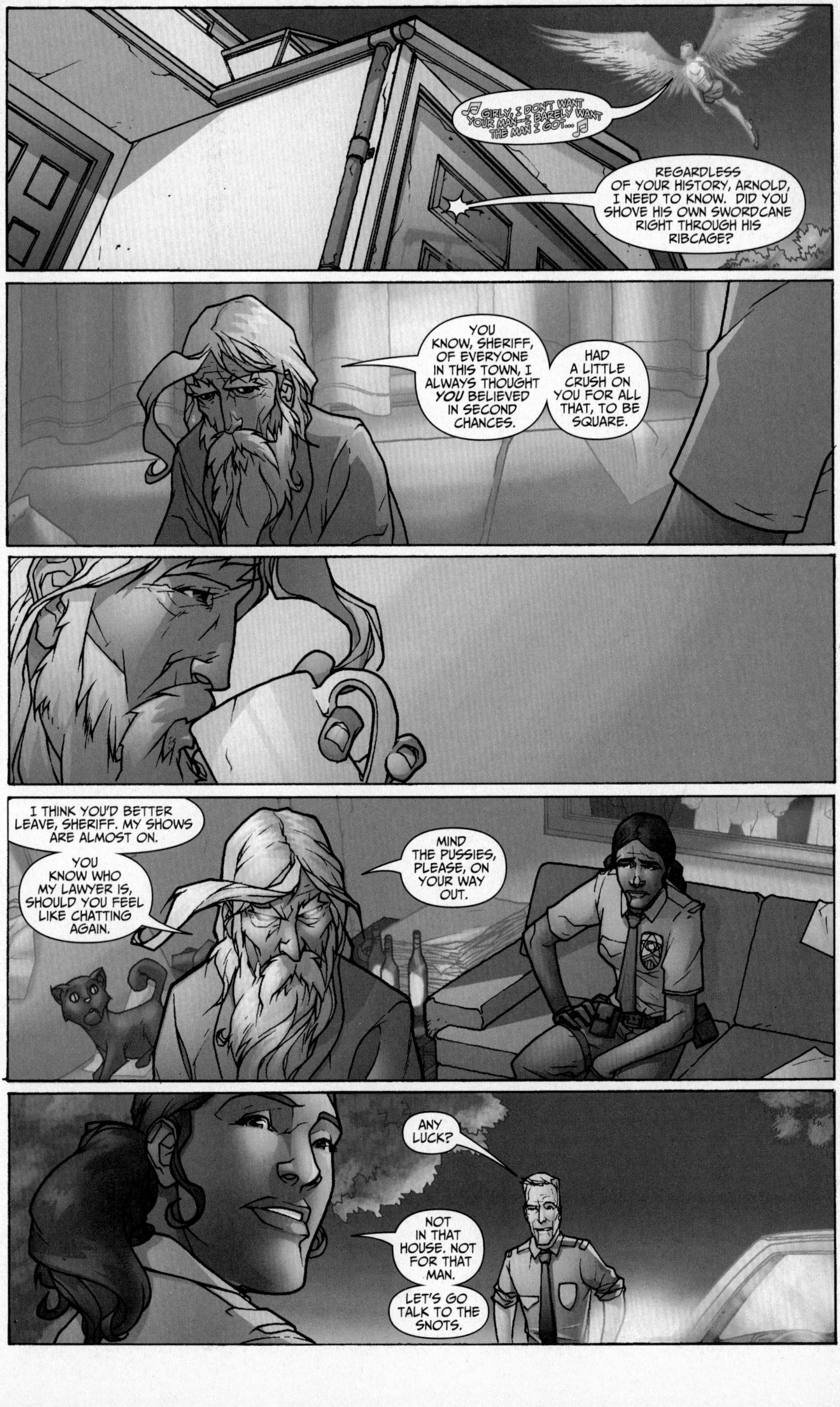
♫ GIRLY, I DON'T WANT YOUR MAN--I BARELY WANT THE MAN I GOT... ♫
REGARDLESS OF YOUR HISTORY, ARNOLD, I NEED TO KNOW. DID YOU SHOVE HIS OWN SWORDCANE RIGHT THROUGH HIS RIBCAGE?
YOU KNOW, SHERIFF, OF EVERYONE IN THIS TOWN, I ALWAYS THOUGHT *YOU* BELIEVED IN SECOND CHANCES.
HAD A LITTLE CRUSH ON YOU FOR ALL THAT, TO BE SQUARE.
I THINK YOU'D BETTER LEAVE, SHERIFF. MY SHOWS ARE ALMOST ON.
YOU KNOW WHO MY LAWYER IS, SHOULD YOU FEEL LIKE CHATTING AGAIN.
MIND THE PUSSIES, PLEASE, ON YOUR WAY OUT.
ANY LUCK?
NOT IN THAT HOUSE. NOT FOR THAT MAN.
LET'S GO TALK TO THE SNOTS.

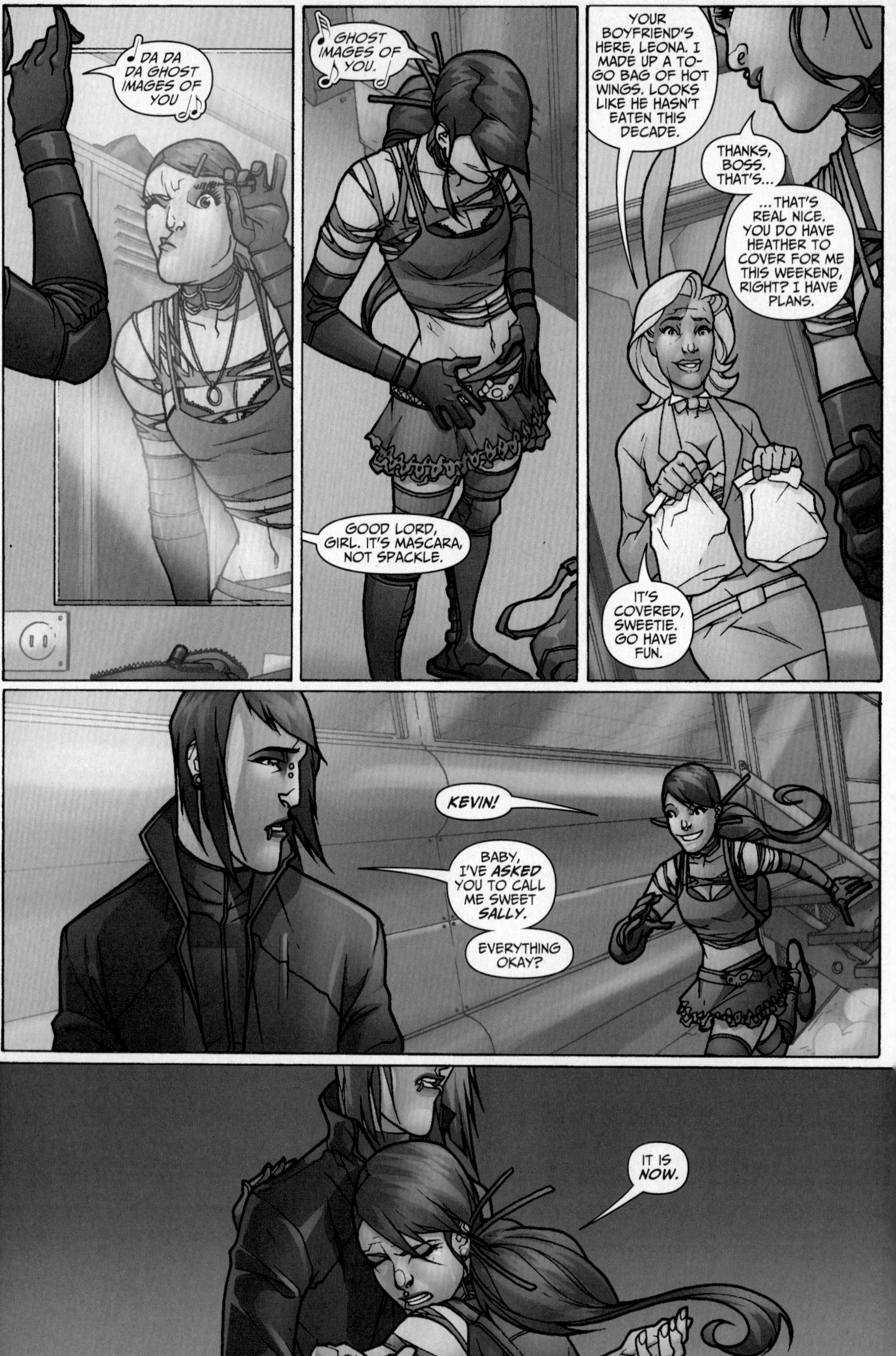
DA DA DA GHOST IMAGES OF YOU
GHOST IMAGES OF YOU.
GOOD LORD, GIRL. IT'S MASCARA, NOT SPACKLE.
YOUR BOYFRIEND'S HERE, LEONA. I MADE UP A TO-GO BAG OF HOT WINGS. LOOKS LIKE HE HASN'T EATEN THIS DECADE.
THANKS, BOSS. THAT'S...
...THAT'S REAL NICE. YOU DO HAVE HEATHER TO COVER FOR ME THIS WEEKEND, RIGHT? I HAVE PLANS.
IT'S COVERED, SWEETIE. GO HAVE FUN.
KEVIN!
BABY, I'VE ASKED YOU TO CALL ME SWEET SALLY.
EVERYTHING OKAY?
IT IS NOW.

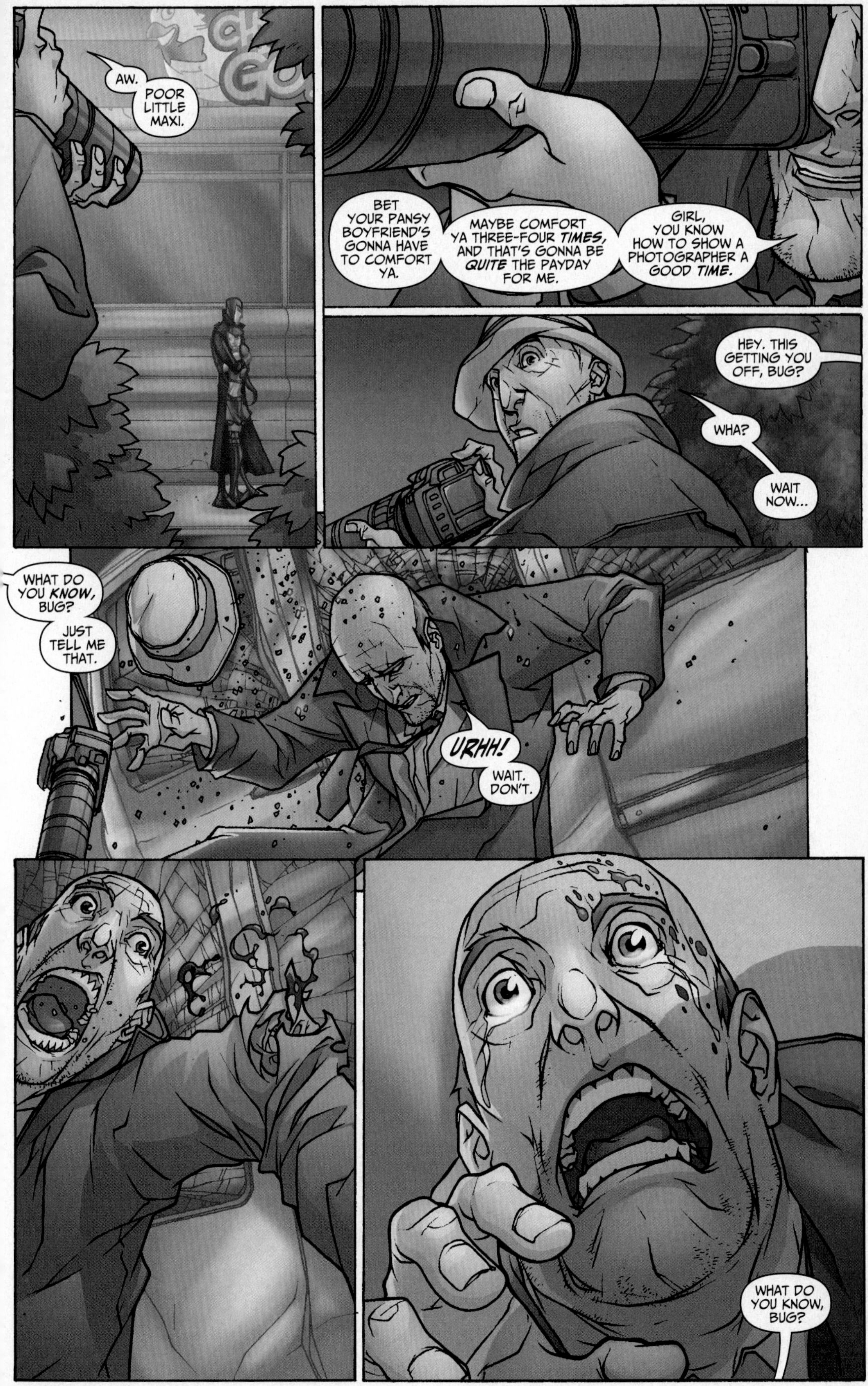

AW. POOR LITTLE MAXI.
GIRL, YOU KNOW HOW TO SHOW A PHOTOGRAPHER A GOOD *TIME.*
MAYBE COMFORT YA THREE-FOUR *TIMES,* AND THAT'S GONNA BE *QUITE* THE PAYDAY FOR ME.
BET YOUR PANSY BOYFRIEND'S GONNA HAVE TO COMFORT YA.
HEY. THIS GETTING YOU OFF, BUG?
WHA?
WAIT NOW...
WHAT DO YOU *KNOW,* BUG?
JUST TELL ME THAT.
URHH!
WAIT. DON'T.
WHAT DO YOU KNOW, BUG?

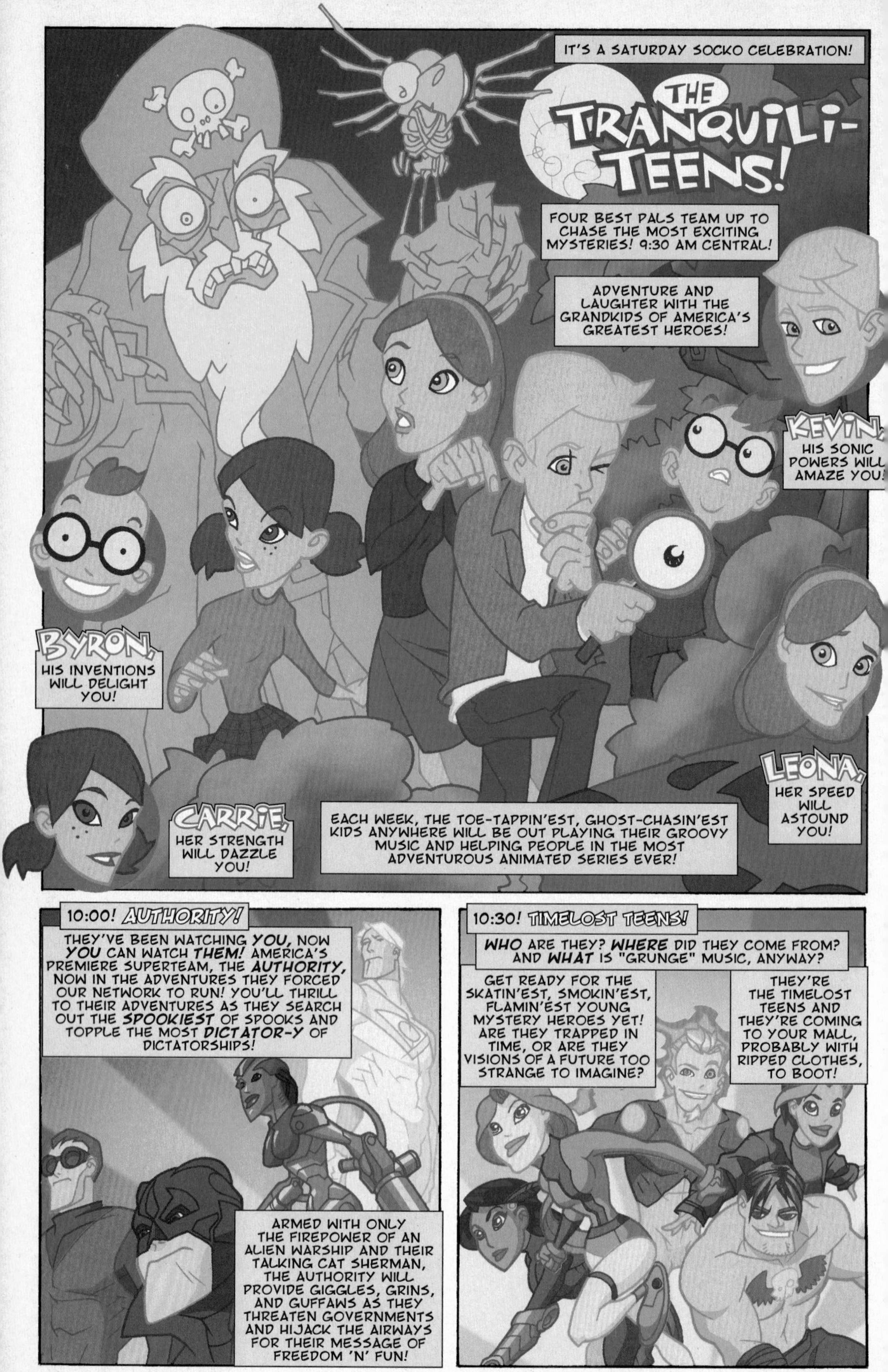
IT'S A SATURDAY SOCKO CELEBRATION!
THE TRANQUILI-TEENS!
FOUR BEST PALS TEAM UP TO CHASE THE MOST EXCITING MYSTERIES! 9:30 AM CENTRAL!
ADVENTURE AND LAUGHTER WITH THE GRANDKIDS OF AMERICA'S GREATEST HEROES!
KEVIN, HIS SONIC POWERS WILL AMAZE YOU!
BYRON, HIS INVENTIONS WILL DELIGHT YOU!
LEONA, HER SPEED WILL ASTOUND YOU!
CARRIE, HER STRENGTH WILL DAZZLE YOU!
EACH WEEK, THE TOE-TAPPIN'EST, GHOST-CHASIN'EST KIDS ANYWHERE WILL BE OUT PLAYING THEIR GROOVY MUSIC AND HELPING PEOPLE IN THE MOST ADVENTUROUS ANIMATED SERIES EVER!
10:00! AUTHORITY!
THEY'VE BEEN WATCHING YOU, NOW YOU CAN WATCH THEM! AMERICA'S PREMIERE SUPERTEAM, THE AUTHORITY, NOW IN THE ADVENTURES THEY FORCED OUR NETWORK TO RUN! YOU'LL THRILL TO THEIR ADVENTURES AS THEY SEARCH OUT THE SPOOKIEST OF SPOOKS AND TOPPLE THE MOST DICTATOR-Y OF DICTATORSHIPS!
ARMED WITH ONLY THE FIREPOWER OF AN ALIEN WARSHIP AND THEIR TALKING CAT SHERMAN, THE AUTHORITY WILL PROVIDE GIGGLES, GRINS, AND GUFFAWS AS THEY THREATEN GOVERNMENTS AND HIJACK THE AIRWAYS FOR THEIR MESSAGE OF FREEDOM 'N' FUN!
10:30! TIMELOST TEENS!
WHO ARE THEY? WHERE DID THEY COME FROM? AND WHAT IS "GRUNGE" MUSIC, ANYWAY?
GET READY FOR THE SKATIN'EST, SMOKIN'EST, FLAMIN'EST YOUNG MYSTERY HEROES YET! ARE THEY TRAPPED IN TIME, OR ARE THEY VISIONS OF A FUTURE TOO STRANGE TO IMAGINE?
THEY'RE THE TIMELOST TEENS AND THEY'RE COMING TO YOUR MALL, PROBABLY WITH RIPPED CLOTHES, TO BOOT!

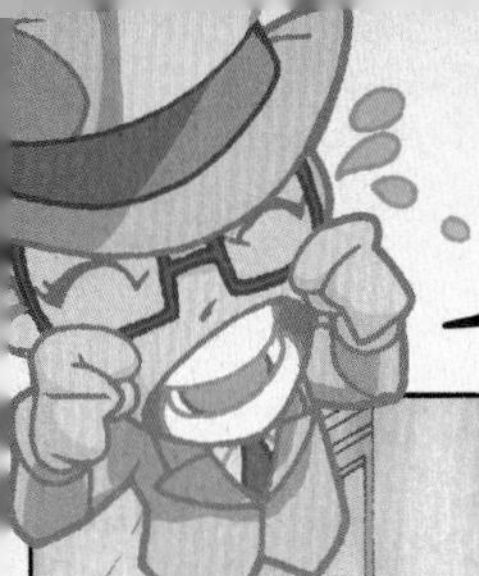

What The Heck Happened?

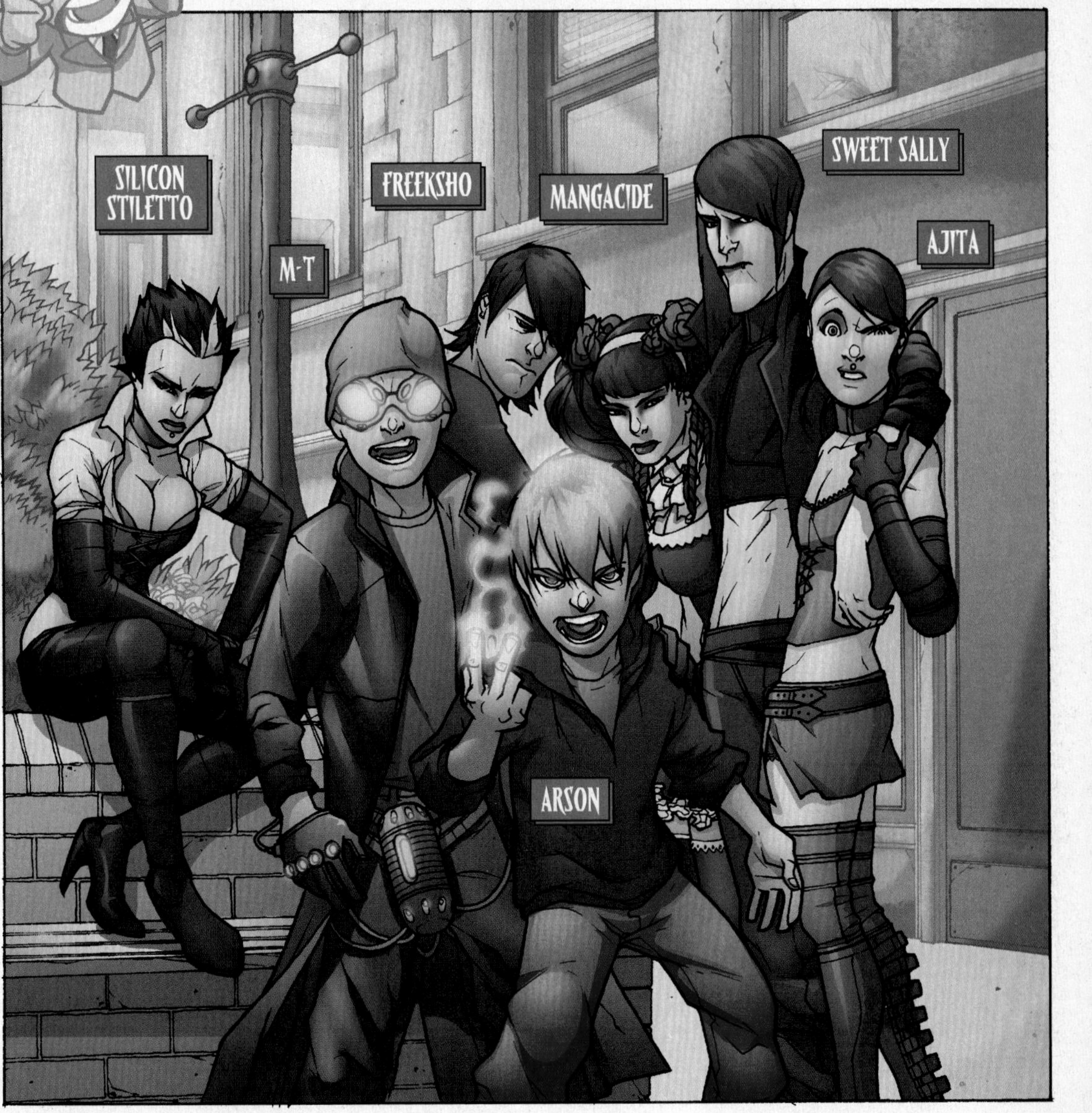

SILICON STILETTO
M-T
FREEKSHO
MANGACIDE
SWEET SALLY
AJITA
ARSON

I DON'T KNOW, GANG. YOU TELL ***ME.***

DO ***THESE*** LOOK LIKE THE HAPPY, HEALTHY, TUNEFUL KIDS THAT USED TO HAVE ONE OF THE MOST POPULAR CARTOONS ON ***KIDS' TELEVISION*** ONLY A FEW YEARS AGO?

YOUR EYES DON'T DECEIVE YOU, THESE ARE THE ***SAME*** KIDS, WITH SOME NEW ADDITIONS THAT SEEM EVERY BIT AS NUTS!

IT SEEMS BEING BELOVED BY AMERICA WAS NOT ***ENOUGH*** FOR THESE SPOILED SPARROWS...NOW THEY (EVEN THE ***BOYS!***) WEAR ENOUGH MAKE-UP TO MAKE PINK BUNNY LOOK AMISH! THEY DRESS IN BLACK, AND GET THIS...THEY STILL PLAY "MUSIC," IF YOU CAN CALL IT THAT! WITH THEIR MOST RECENT SONG BEING CALLED ***"I EAT SOULS,"*** I DON'T THINK YOU'RE GOING TO BE SEEING ***THESE*** BRATS ON ANY SCHOOL LUNCHBOXES AGAIN ANY TIME SOON!

AND YOU MIGHT WELL ASK HOW CAN THE GRANDKIDS OF GREAT AMERICAN ICONS LIKE PINK BUNNY, SLAPJACK, AND DR. TOMORROW HAVE BECOME, AS THEY CALL THEMSELVES NOW (I APOLOGIZE FOR EVEN HAVING TO ***SAY*** IT!), "THE ***LIBERTY SNOTS?"***

WELL, ***THIS*** REPORTER HAS A SECRET HE KNOWS ABOUT ONE OF THEIR ***ROTTENEST*** MEMBERS, LEONA, AKA ***AJITA!*** AND BECAUSE WE'RE ***SO*** DISAPPOINTED IN HER BEHAVIOR, WE'LL BE ***REVEALING*** THAT SECRET IN NEXT WEEK'S ***TATTLER!***

AND ***SHE*** USED TO BE THE ***INNOCENT ONE!***

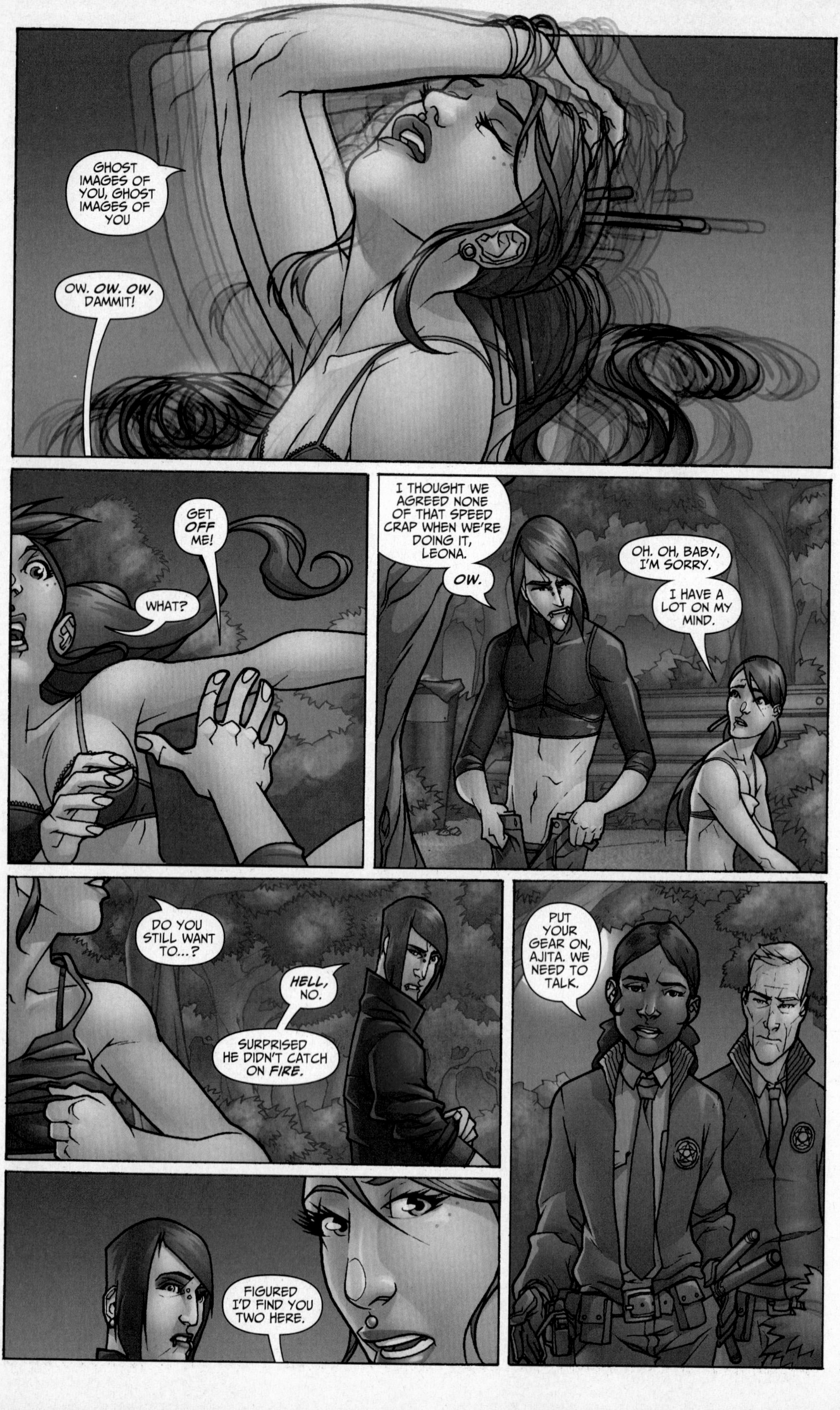
GHOST IMAGES OF YOU, GHOST IMAGES OF YOU
OW. OW. OW, DAMMIT!
GET OFF ME!
WHAT?
I THOUGHT WE AGREED NONE OF THAT SPEED CRAP WHEN WE'RE DOING IT, LEONA.
OW.
OH. OH, BABY, I'M SORRY.
I HAVE A LOT ON MY MIND.
DO YOU STILL WANT TO...?
HELL, NO.
SURPRISED HE DIDN'T CATCH ON FIRE.
FIGURED I'D FIND YOU TWO HERE.
PUT YOUR GEAR ON, AJITA. WE NEED TO TALK.

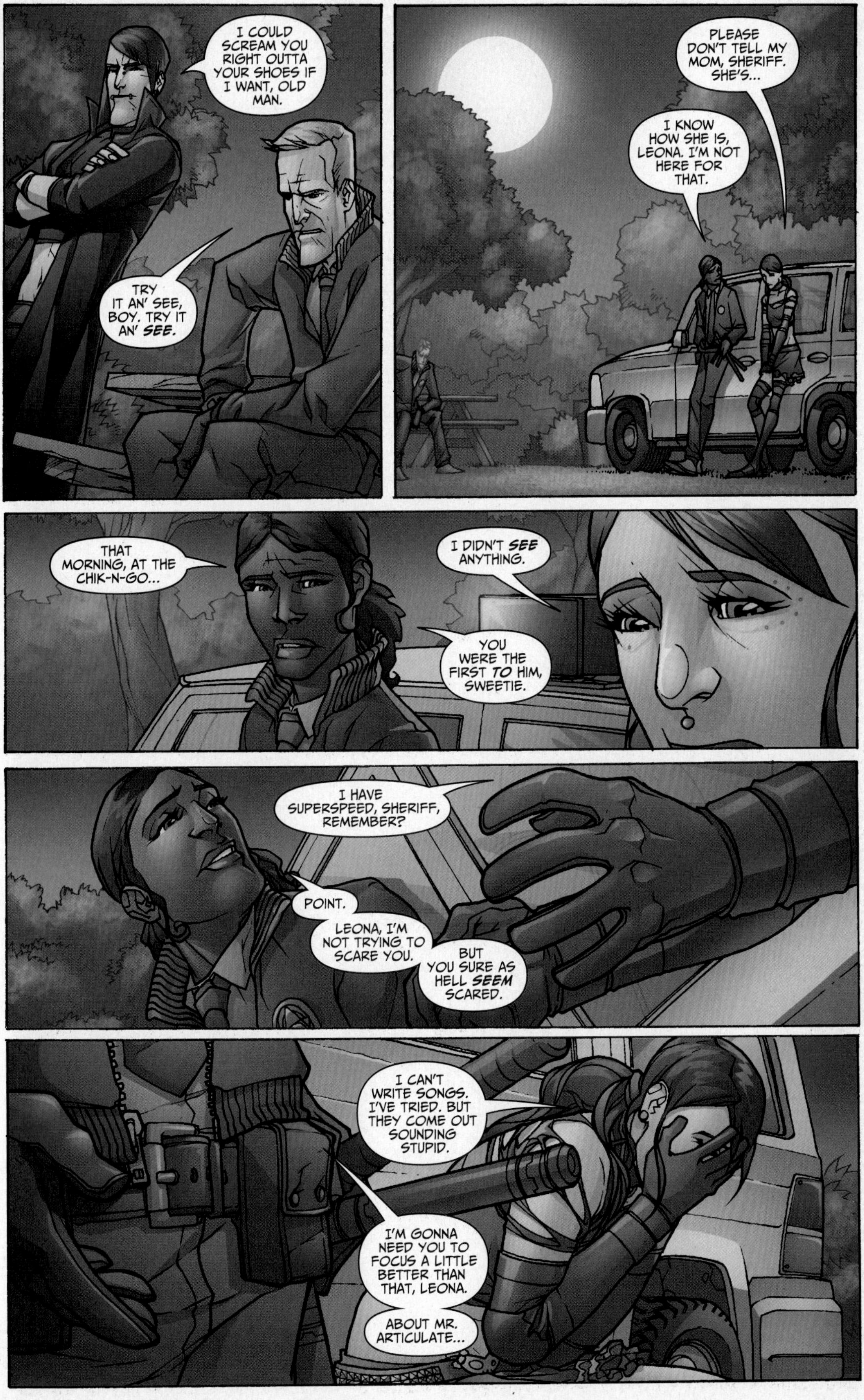
I COULD SCREAM YOU RIGHT OUTTA YOUR SHOES IF I WANT, OLD MAN.
TRY IT AN' SEE, BOY. TRY IT AN' SEE.
PLEASE DON'T TELL MY MOM, SHERIFF. SHE'S...
I KNOW HOW SHE IS, LEONA. I'M NOT HERE FOR THAT.
THAT MORNING, AT THE CHIK-N-GO...
I DIDN'T SEE ANYTHING.
YOU WERE THE FIRST TO HIM, SWEETIE.
I HAVE SUPERSPEED, SHERIFF, REMEMBER?
POINT.
LEONA, I'M NOT TRYING TO SCARE YOU.
BUT YOU SURE AS HELL SEEM SCARED.
I CAN'T WRITE SONGS. I'VE TRIED. BUT THEY COME OUT SOUNDING STUPID.
I'M GONNA NEED YOU TO FOCUS A LITTLE BETTER THAN THAT, LEONA.
ABOUT MR. ARTICULATE...

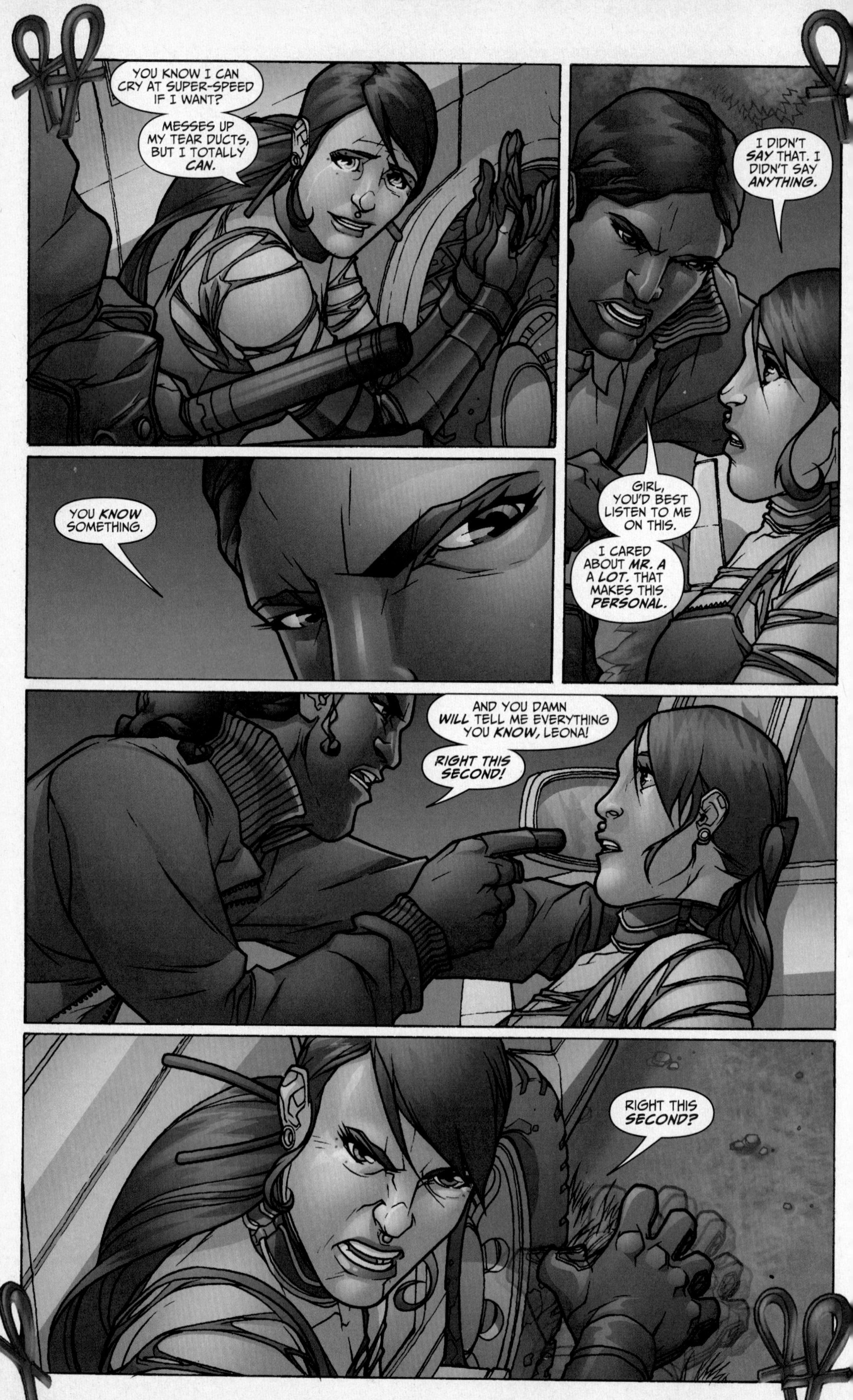
YOU KNOW I CAN CRY AT SUPER-SPEED IF I WANT?
MESSES UP MY TEAR DUCTS, BUT I TOTALLY CAN.
I DIDN'T SAY THAT. I DIDN'T SAY ANYTHING.
YOU KNOW SOMETHING.
GIRL, YOU'D BEST LISTEN TO ME ON THIS.
I CARED ABOUT MR. A A LOT. THAT MAKES THIS PERSONAL.
AND YOU DAMN WILL TELL ME EVERYTHING YOU KNOW, LEONA!
RIGHT THIS SECOND!
RIGHT THIS SECOND?

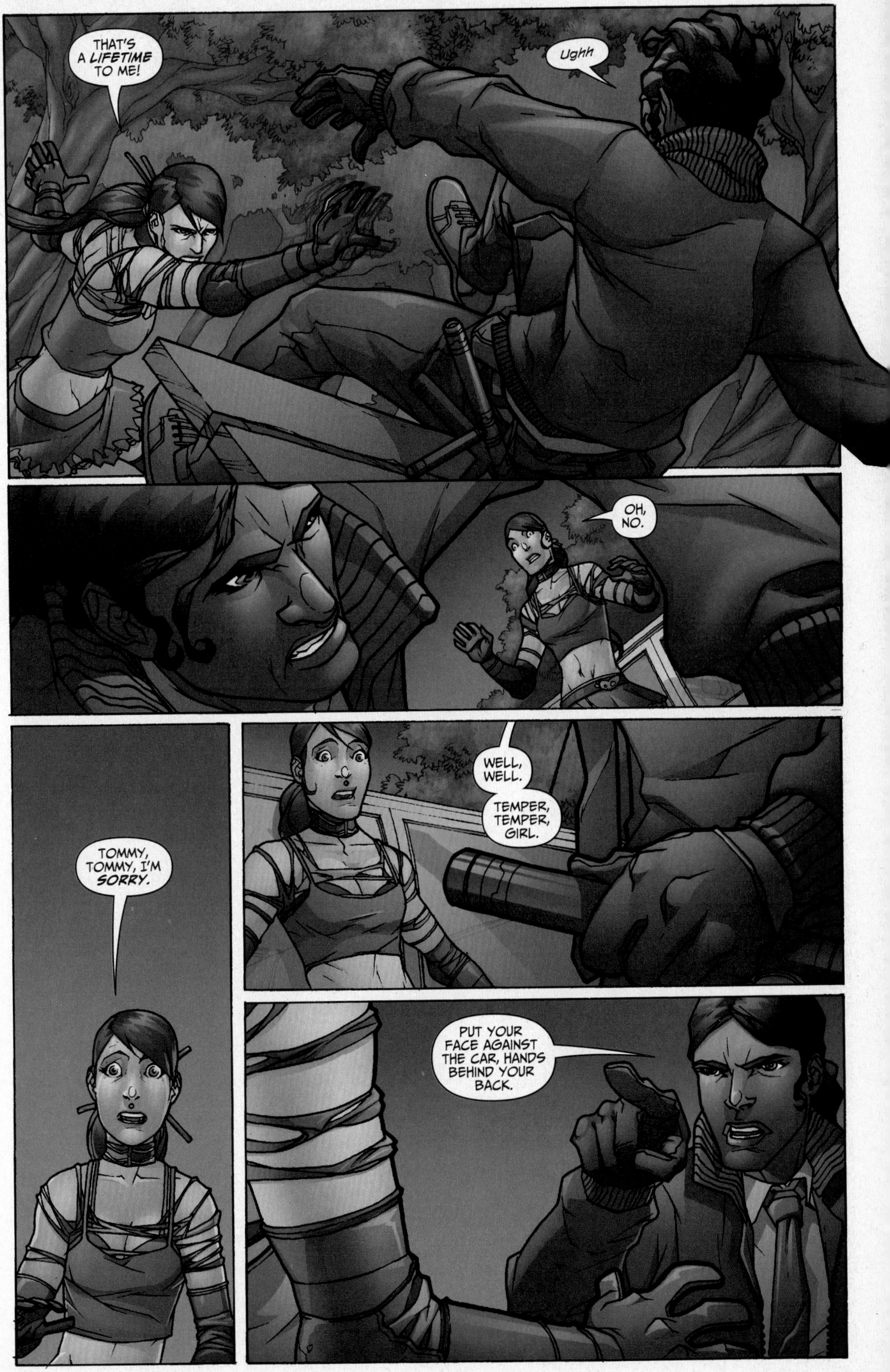

THAT'S A LIFETIME TO ME!
Ughh
OH, NO.
TOMMY, TOMMY, I'M SORRY.
WELL, WELL.
TEMPER, TEMPER, GIRL.
PUT YOUR FACE AGAINST THE CAR, HANDS BEHIND YOUR BACK.

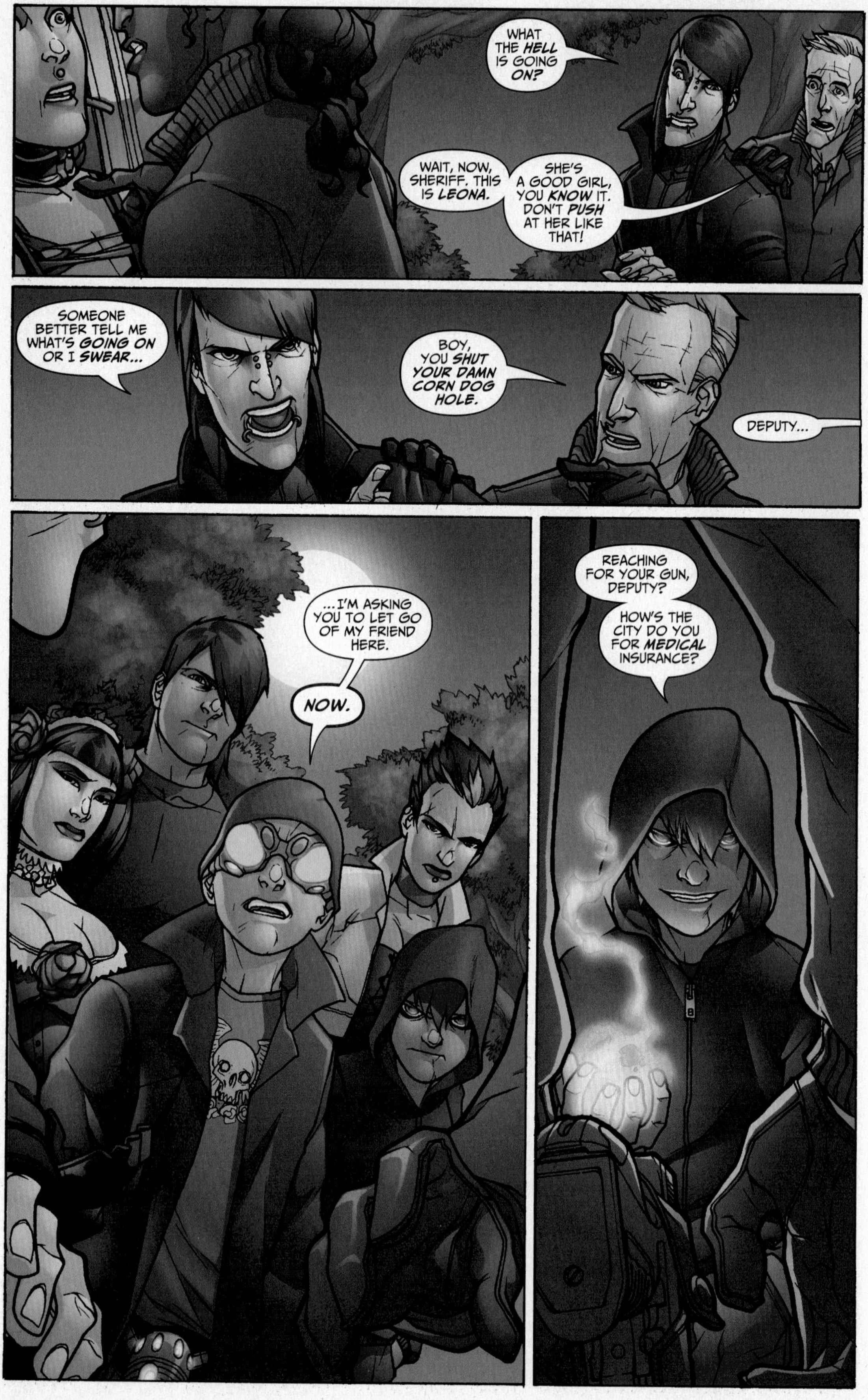
WHAT THE HELL IS GOING ON?
WAIT, NOW, SHERIFF. THIS IS LEONA.
SHE'S A GOOD GIRL, YOU KNOW IT. DON'T PUSH AT HER LIKE THAT!
SOMEONE BETTER TELL ME WHAT'S GOING ON OR I SWEAR...
BOY, YOU SHUT YOUR DAMN CORN DOG HOLE.
DEPUTY...
...I'M ASKING YOU TO LET GO OF MY FRIEND HERE.
NOW.
REACHING FOR YOUR GUN, DEPUTY?
HOW'S THE CITY DO YOU FOR MEDICAL INSURANCE?

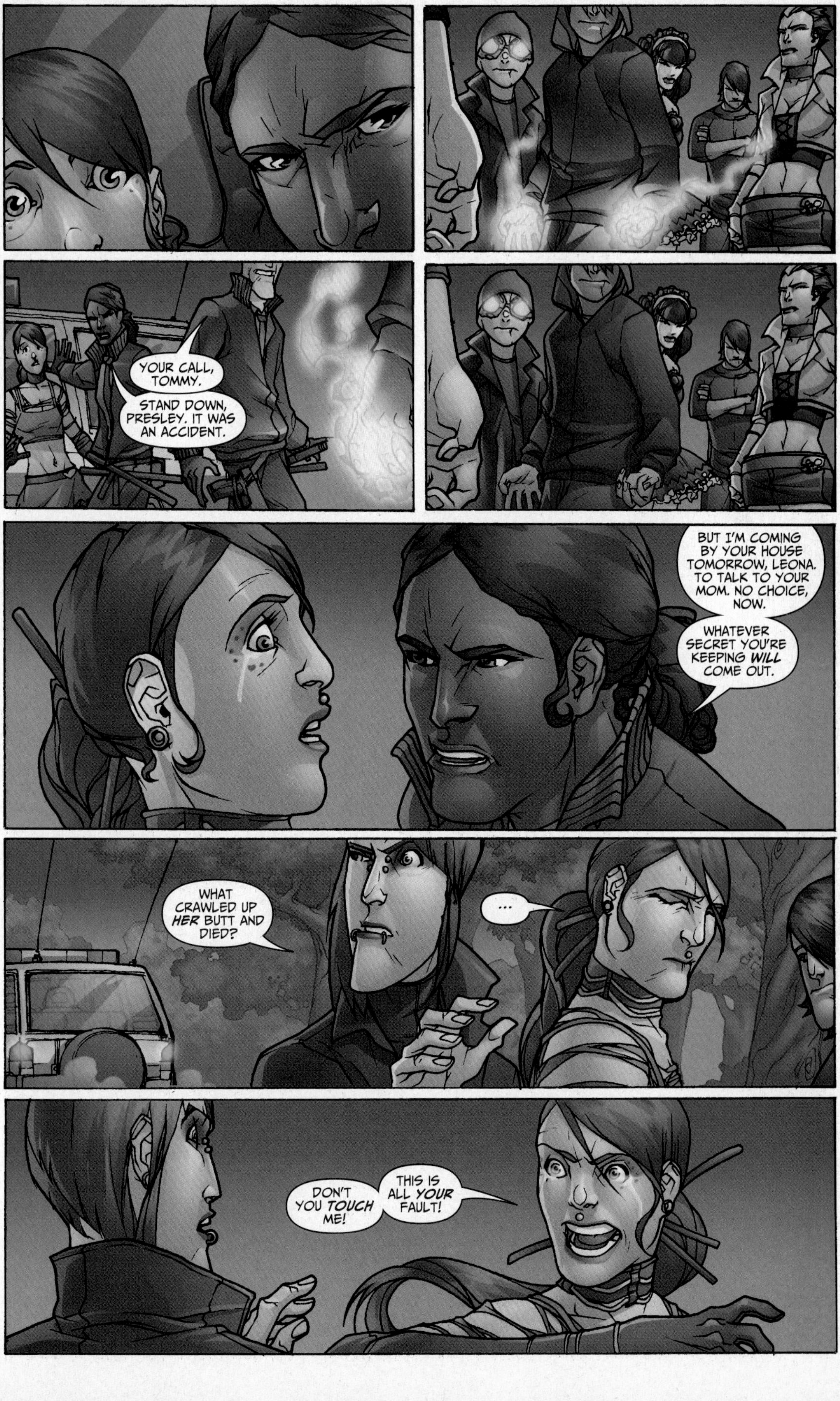
YOUR CALL, TOMMY.
STAND DOWN, PRESLEY. IT WAS AN ACCIDENT.
BUT I'M COMING BY YOUR HOUSE TOMORROW, LEONA. TO TALK TO YOUR MOM. NO CHOICE, NOW.
WHATEVER SECRET YOU'RE KEEPING WILL COME OUT.
WHAT CRAWLED UP HER BUTT AND DIED?
...
THIS IS ALL YOUR FAULT!
DON'T YOU TOUCH ME!

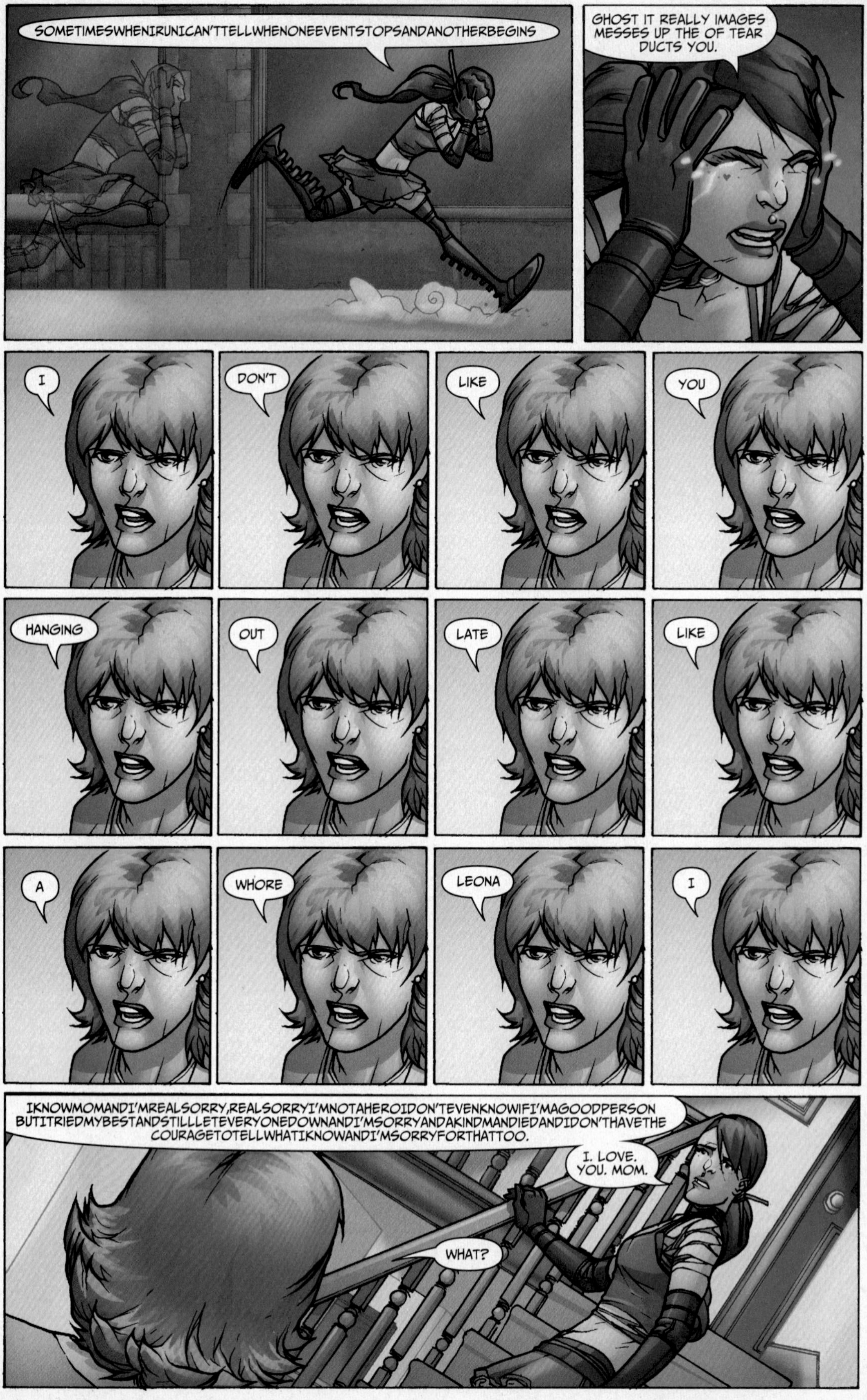
SOMETIMESWHENIRUNICAN'TTELLWHENONEEVENTSTOPSANDANOTHERBEGINS
GHOST IT REALLY IMAGES MESSES UP THE OF TEAR DUCTS YOU.
I
DON'T
LIKE
YOU
HANGING
OUT
LATE
LIKE
A
WHORE
LEONA
I
IKNOWMOMANDI'MREALSORRY,REALSORRYI'MNOTAHEROIDON'TEVENKNOWIFI'MAGOODPERSON BUTITRIEDMYBESTANDSTILLLETEVERYONEDOWNANDI'MSORRYANDAKINDMANDIEDANDIDON'THAVETHE COURAGETOTELLWHATIKNOWANDI'MSORRYFORTHATTOO.
I. LOVE. YOU. MOM.
WHAT?

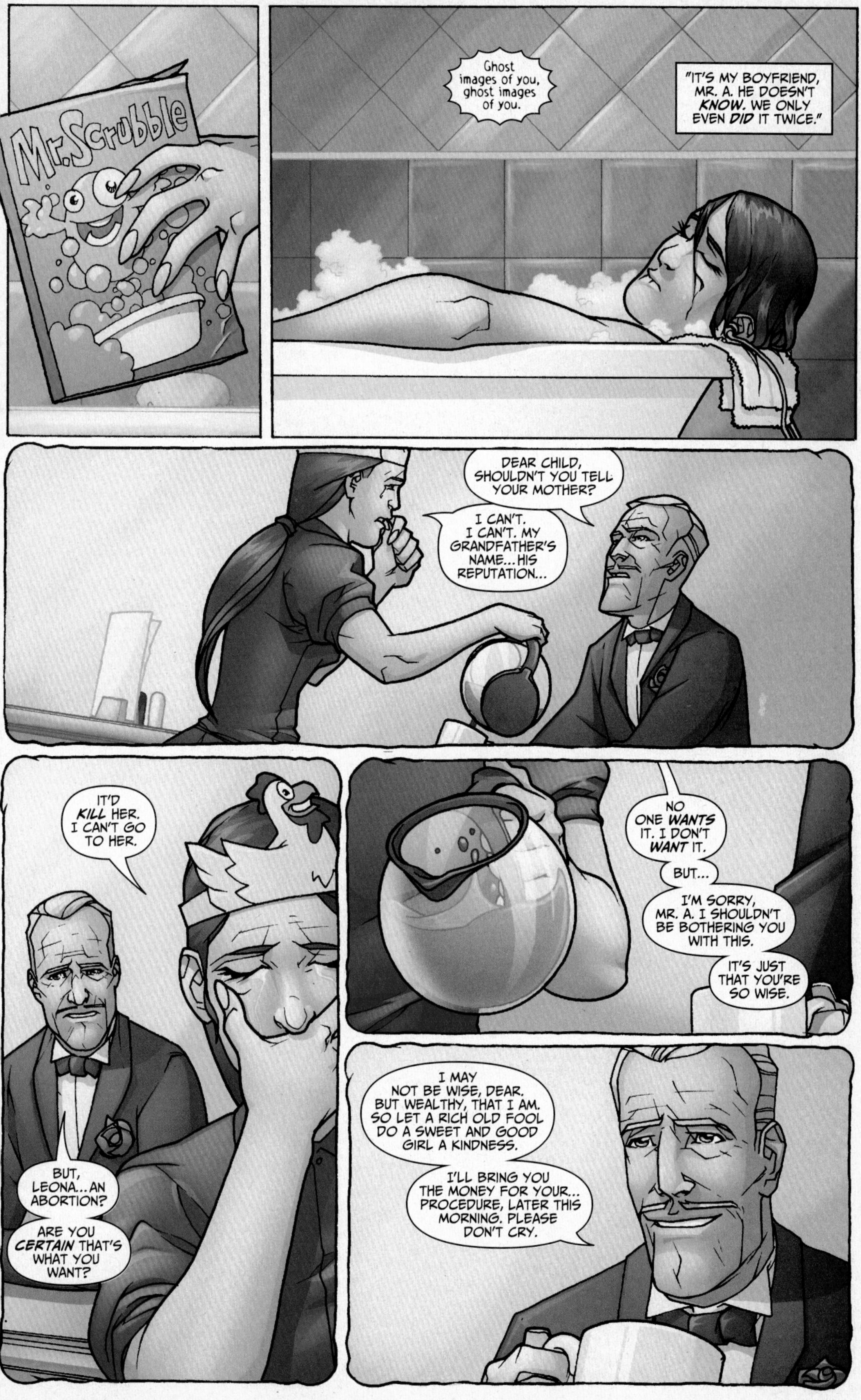

Mr.Scrubble
Ghost images of you, ghost images of you.
"IT'S MY BOYFRIEND, MR. A. HE DOESN'T *KNOW*. WE ONLY EVEN *DID* IT TWICE."
DEAR CHILD, SHOULDN'T YOU TELL YOUR MOTHER?
I CAN'T. I CAN'T. MY GRANDFATHER'S NAME...HIS REPUTATION...
IT'D *KILL* HER. I CAN'T GO TO HER.
BUT, LEONA...AN ABORTION?
ARE YOU *CERTAIN* THAT'S WHAT YOU WANT?
NO ONE *WANTS* IT. I DON'T *WANT* IT.
BUT...
I'M SORRY, MR. A. I SHOULDN'T BE BOTHERING YOU WITH THIS.
IT'S JUST THAT YOU'RE SO WISE.
I MAY NOT BE WISE, DEAR. BUT WEALTHY, THAT I AM. SO LET A RICH OLD FOOL DO A SWEET AND GOOD GIRL A KINDNESS.
I'LL BRING YOU THE MONEY FOR YOUR... PROCEDURE, LATER THIS MORNING. PLEASE DON'T CRY.

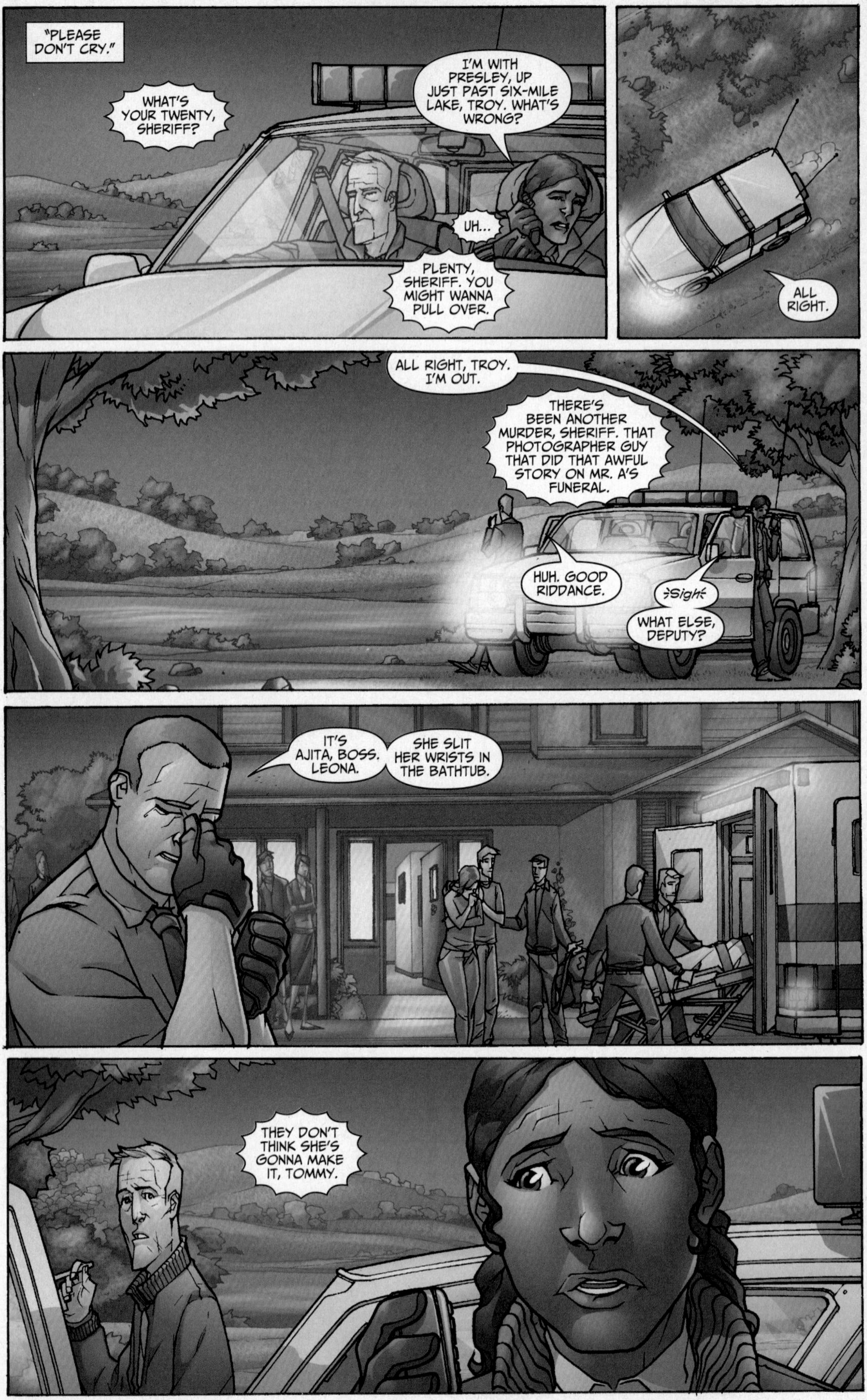
"PLEASE DON'T CRY."
WHAT'S YOUR TWENTY, SHERIFF?
I'M WITH PRESLEY, UP JUST PAST SIX-MILE LAKE, TROY. WHAT'S WRONG?
UH...
PLENTY, SHERIFF. YOU MIGHT WANNA PULL OVER.
ALL RIGHT.
ALL RIGHT, TROY. I'M OUT.
THERE'S BEEN ANOTHER MURDER, SHERIFF. THAT PHOTOGRAPHER GUY THAT DID THAT AWFUL STORY ON MR. A'S FUNERAL.
HUH. GOOD RIDDANCE.
Sigh
WHAT ELSE, DEPUTY?
IT'S AJITA, BOSS. LEONA.
SHE SLIT HER WRISTS IN THE BATHTUB.
THEY DON'T THINK SHE'S GONNA MAKE IT, TOMMY.

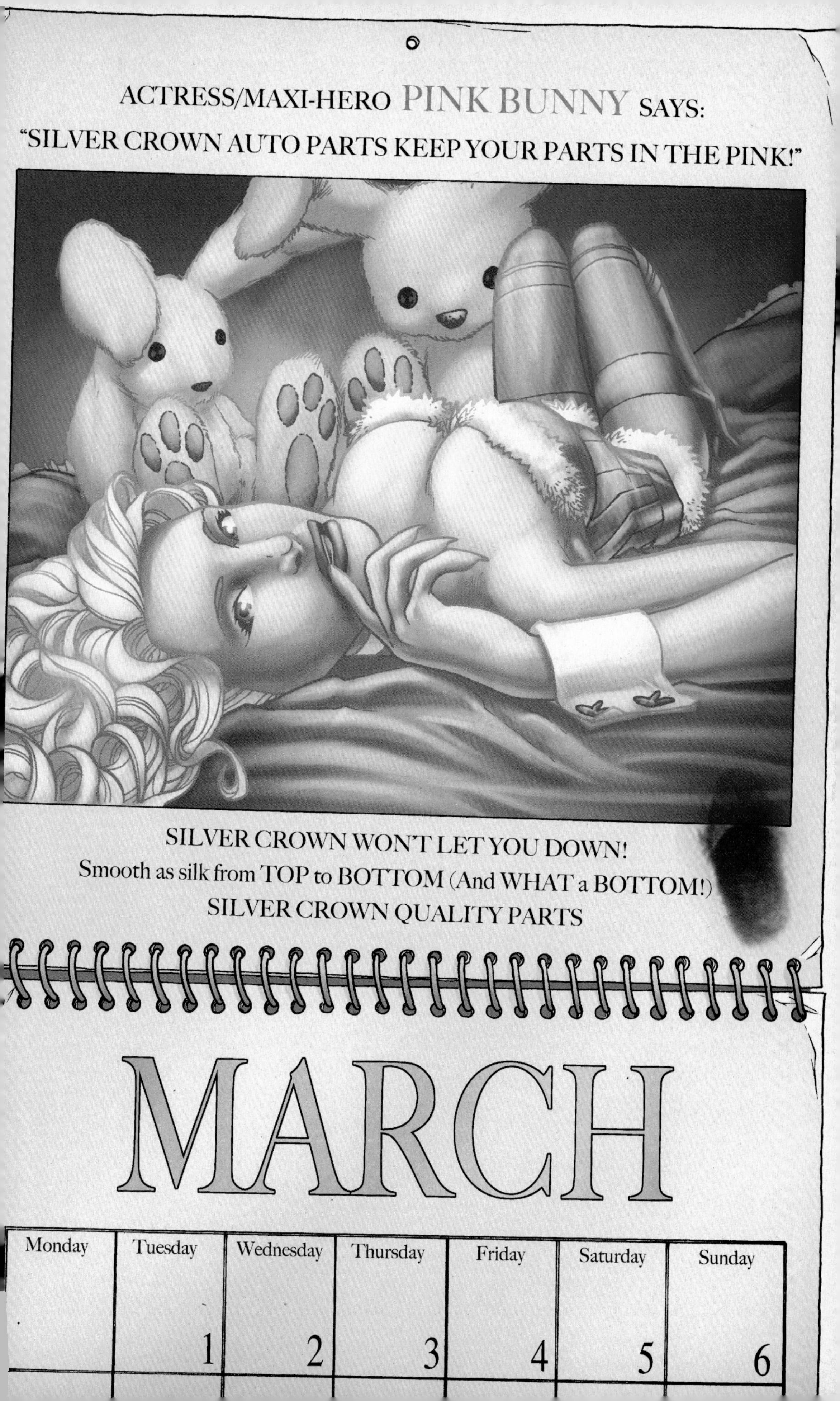

ACTRESS/MAXI-HERO PINK BUNNY SAYS:
"SILVER CROWN AUTO PARTS KEEP YOUR PARTS IN THE PINK!"
SILVER CROWN WON'T LET YOU DOWN!
Smooth as silk from TOP to BOTTOM (And WHAT a BOTTOM!)
SILVER CROWN QUALITY PARTS
MARCH
Monday
Tuesday
Wednesday
Thursday
Friday
Saturday
Sunday
1
2
3
4
5
6

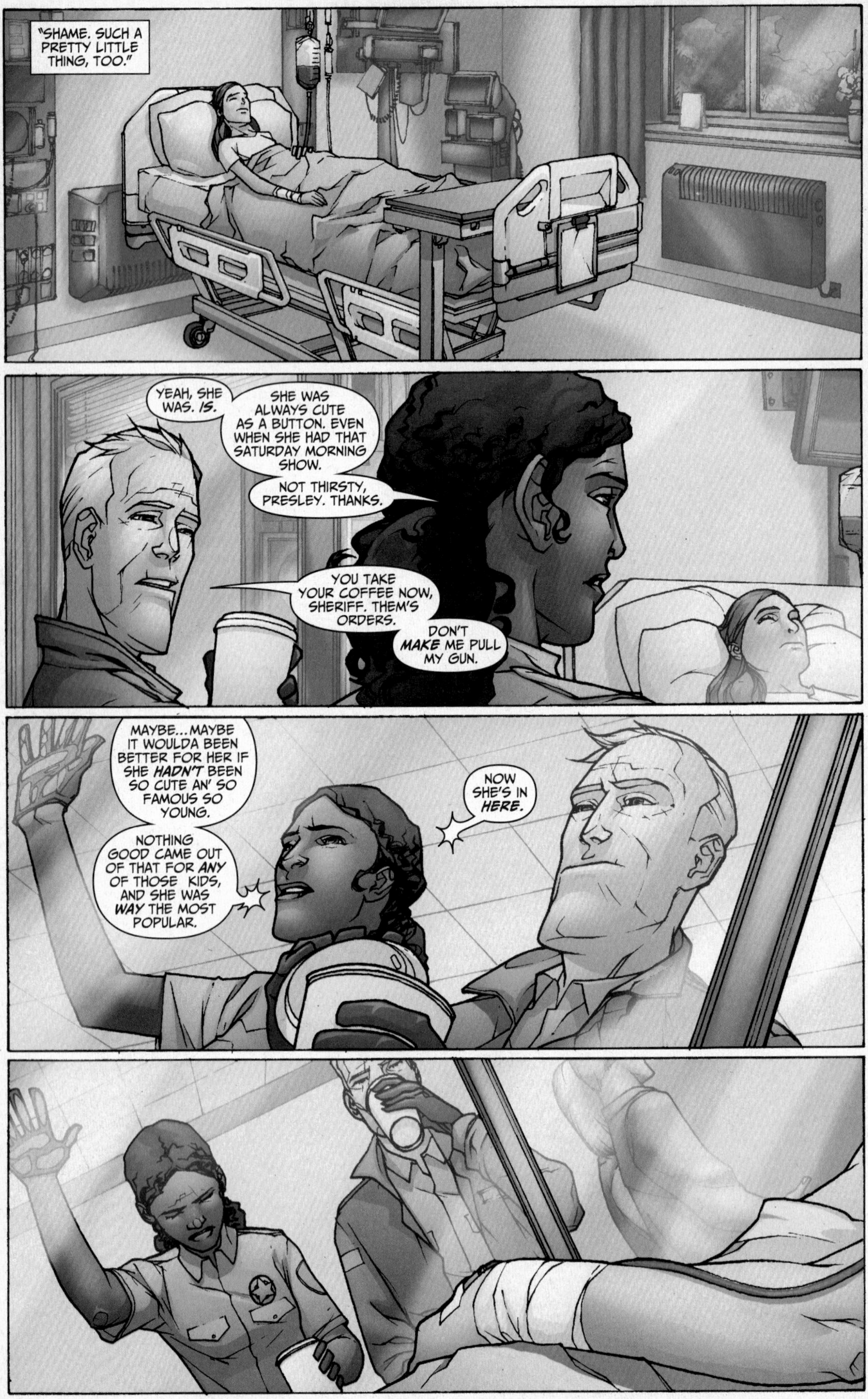
"SHAME. SUCH A PRETTY LITTLE THING, TOO."
YEAH, SHE WAS. *IS.*
SHE WAS ALWAYS CUTE AS A BUTTON. EVEN WHEN SHE HAD THAT SATURDAY MORNING SHOW.
NOT THIRSTY, PRESLEY. THANKS.
YOU TAKE YOUR COFFEE NOW, SHERIFF. THEM'S ORDERS.
DON'T *MAKE* ME PULL MY GUN.
MAYBE...MAYBE IT WOULDA BEEN BETTER FOR HER IF SHE *HADN'T* BEEN SO CUTE AN' SO FAMOUS SO YOUNG.
NOTHING GOOD CAME OUT OF THAT FOR *ANY* OF THOSE KIDS, AND SHE WAS *WAY* THE MOST POPULAR.
NOW SHE'S IN *HERE.*

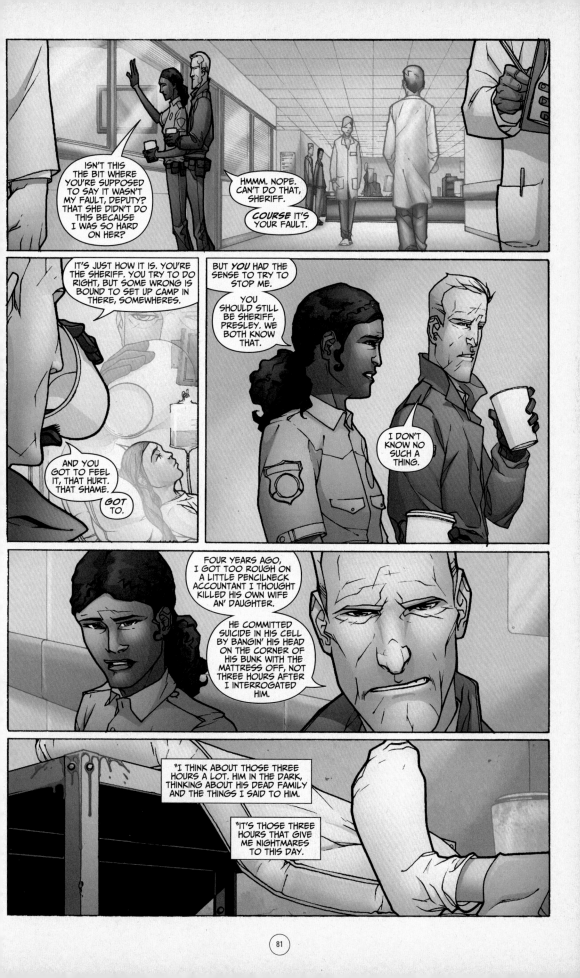

ISN'T THIS THE BIT WHERE YOU'RE SUPPOSED TO SAY IT WASN'T MY FAULT, DEPUTY? THAT SHE DIDN'T DO THIS BECAUSE I WAS SO HARD ON HER?

HMMM. NOPE. CAN'T DO THAT, SHERIFF.

COURSE IT'S YOUR FAULT.

IT'S JUST HOW IT IS. YOU'RE THE SHERIFF. YOU TRY TO DO RIGHT, BUT SOME WRONG IS BOUND TO SET UP CAMP IN THERE, SOMEWHERES.

BUT *YOU* HAD THE SENSE TO TRY TO STOP ME.

YOU SHOULD STILL BE SHERIFF, PRESLEY. WE BOTH KNOW THAT.

I DON'T KNOW NO SUCH A THING.

AND YOU GOT TO FEEL IT, THAT HURT. THAT SHAME.

GOT TO.

FOUR YEARS AGO, I GOT TOO ROUGH ON A LITTLE PENCILNECK ACCOUNTANT I THOUGHT KILLED HIS OWN WIFE AN' DAUGHTER.

HE COMMITTED SUICIDE IN HIS CELL BY BANGIN' HIS HEAD ON THE CORNER OF HIS BUNK WITH THE MATTRESS OFF, NOT THREE HOURS AFTER I INTERROGATED HIM.

"I THINK ABOUT THOSE THREE HOURS A LOT. HIM IN THE DARK, THINKING ABOUT HIS DEAD FAMILY AND THE THINGS I SAID TO HIM.

"IT'S THOSE THREE HOURS THAT GIVE ME NIGHTMARES TO THIS DAY.

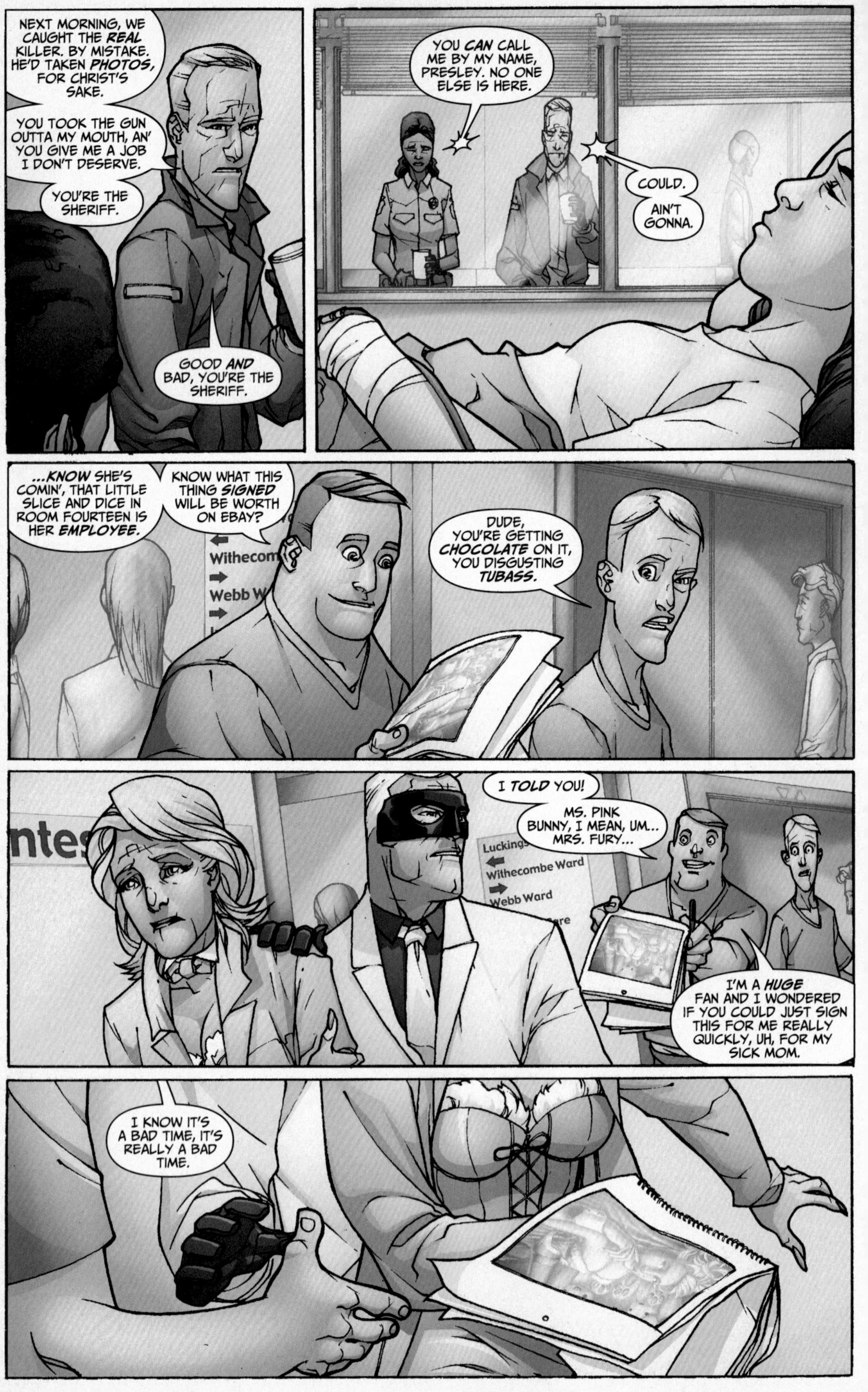
NEXT MORNING, WE CAUGHT THE REAL KILLER. BY MISTAKE. HE'D TAKEN PHOTOS, FOR CHRIST'S SAKE.
YOU TOOK THE GUN OUTTA MY MOUTH, AN' YOU GIVE ME A JOB I DON'T DESERVE.
YOU'RE THE SHERIFF.
GOOD AND BAD, YOU'RE THE SHERIFF.
YOU CAN CALL ME BY MY NAME, PRESLEY. NO ONE ELSE IS HERE.
COULD.
AIN'T GONNA.
...KNOW SHE'S COMIN', THAT LITTLE SLICE AND DICE IN ROOM FOURTEEN IS HER EMPLOYEE.
KNOW WHAT THIS THING SIGNED WILL BE WORTH ON EBAY?
Withecom
Webb W
DUDE, YOU'RE GETTING CHOCOLATE ON IT, YOU DISGUSTING TUBASS.
I TOLD YOU!
MS. PINK BUNNY, I MEAN, UM... MRS. FURY...
Withecombe Ward
Webb Ward
I'M A HUGE FAN AND I WONDERED IF YOU COULD JUST SIGN THIS FOR ME REALLY QUICKLY, UH, FOR MY SICK MOM.
I KNOW IT'S A BAD TIME, IT'S REALLY A BAD TIME.

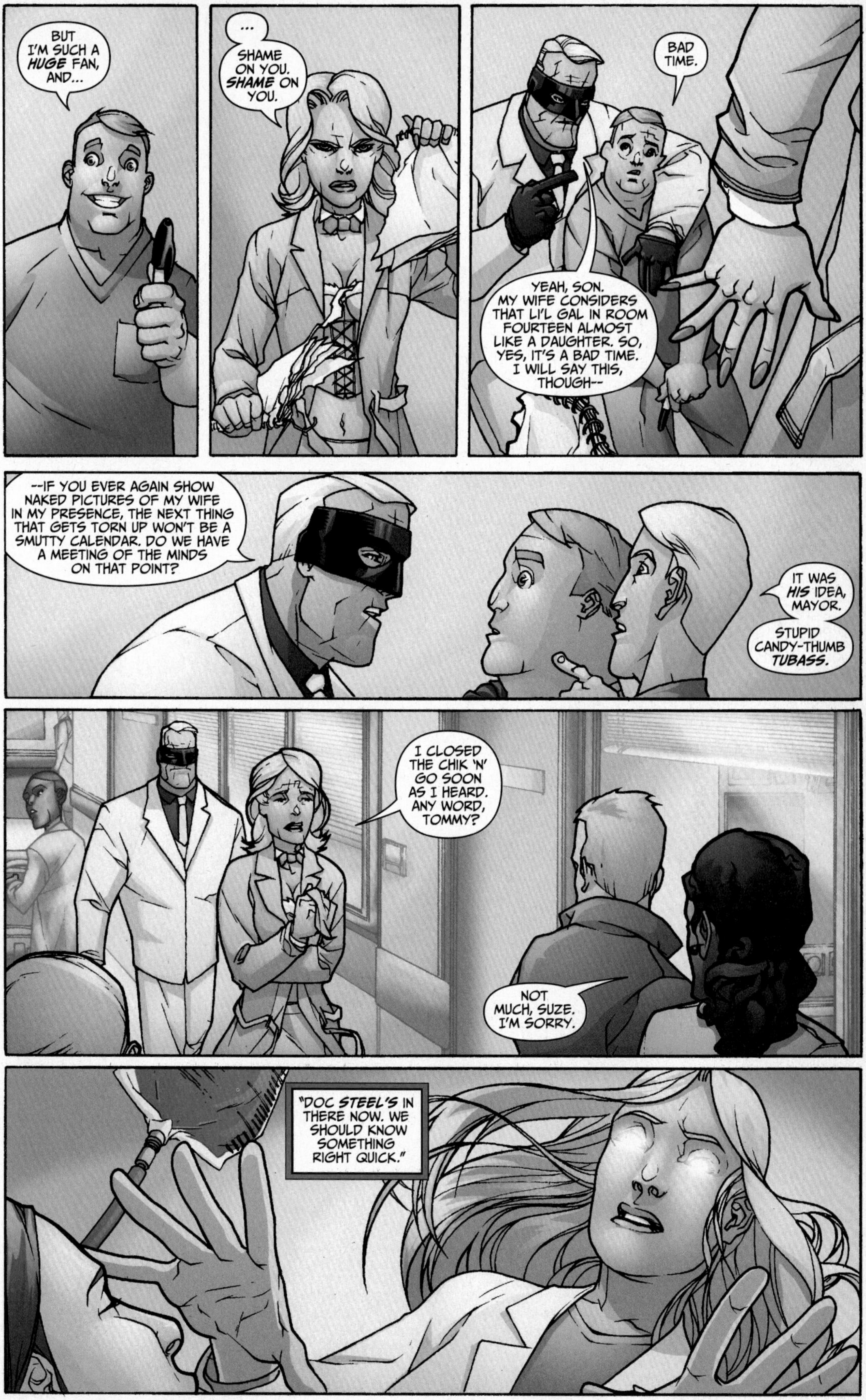
BUT I'M SUCH A *HUGE* FAN, AND...
...
SHAME ON YOU. *SHAME* ON YOU.
BAD TIME.
YEAH, SON. MY WIFE CONSIDERS THAT LI'L GAL IN ROOM FOURTEEN ALMOST LIKE A DAUGHTER. SO, YES, IT'S A BAD TIME. I WILL SAY THIS, THOUGH--
--IF YOU EVER AGAIN SHOW NAKED PICTURES OF MY WIFE IN MY PRESENCE, THE NEXT THING THAT GETS TORN UP WON'T BE A SMUTTY CALENDAR. DO WE HAVE A MEETING OF THE MINDS ON THAT POINT?
IT WAS *HIS* IDEA, MAYOR.
STUPID CANDY-THUMB *TUBASS.*
I CLOSED THE CHIK 'N' GO SOON AS I HEARD. ANY WORD, TOMMY?
NOT MUCH, SUZE. I'M SORRY.
"DOC *STEEL'S* IN THERE NOW. WE SHOULD KNOW SOMETHING RIGHT QUICK."

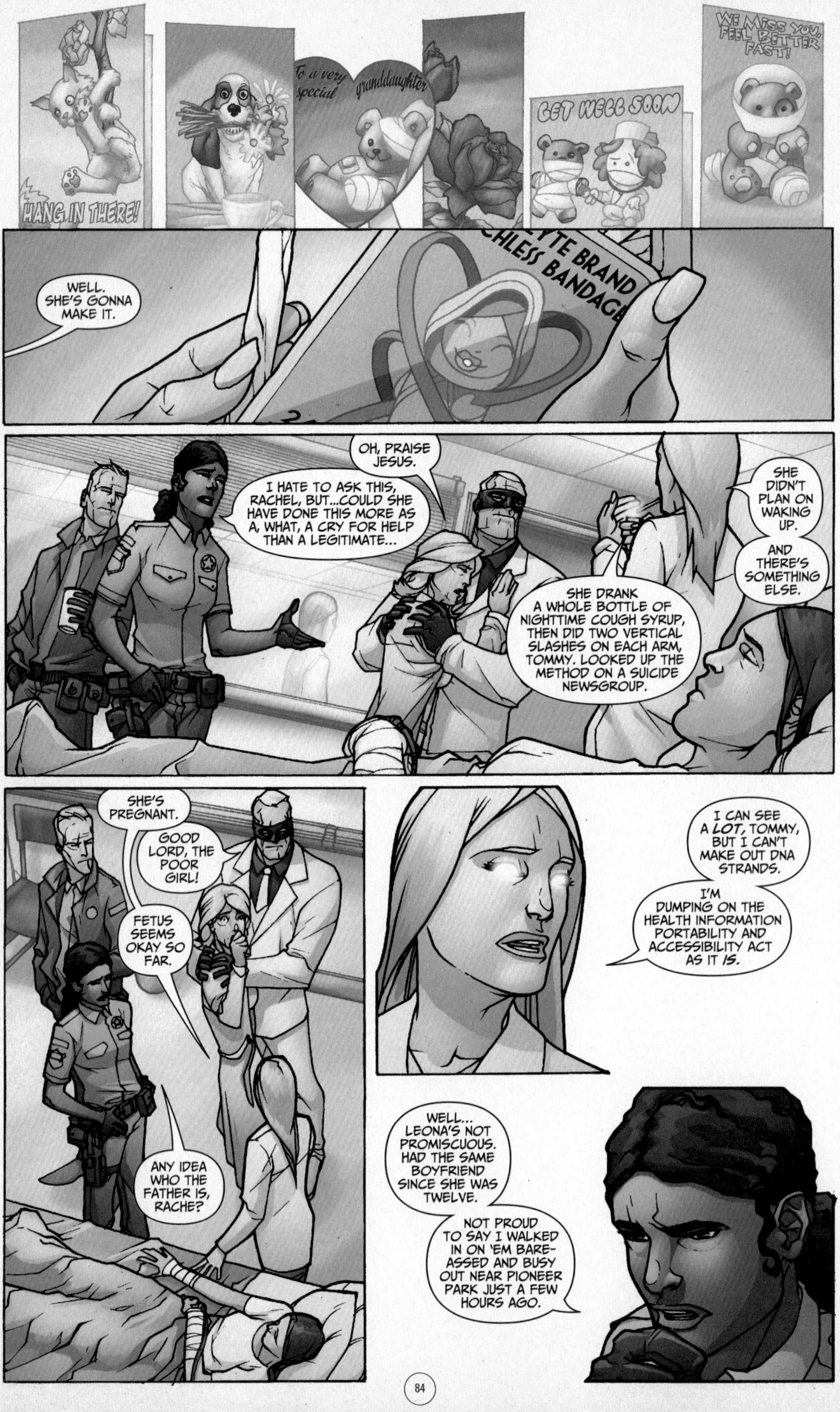

HANG IN THERE!
To a very special granddaughter
GET WELL SOON
WE MISS YOU, FEEL BETTER FAST!
WELL. SHE'S GONNA MAKE IT.
OH, PRAISE JESUS.
I HATE TO ASK THIS, RACHEL, BUT...COULD SHE HAVE DONE THIS MORE AS A, WHAT, A CRY FOR HELP THAN A LEGITIMATE...
SHE DRANK A WHOLE BOTTLE OF NIGHTTIME COUGH SYRUP, THEN DID TWO VERTICAL SLASHES ON EACH ARM, TOMMY. LOOKED UP THE METHOD ON A SUICIDE NEWSGROUP.
SHE DIDN'T PLAN ON WAKING UP.
AND THERE'S SOMETHING ELSE.
SHE'S PREGNANT.
GOOD LORD, THE POOR GIRL!
FETUS SEEMS OKAY SO FAR.
ANY IDEA WHO THE FATHER IS, RACHE?
I CAN SEE A *LOT*, TOMMY, BUT I CAN'T MAKE OUT DNA STRANDS.
I'M DUMPING ON THE HEALTH INFORMATION PORTABILITY AND ACCESSIBILITY ACT AS IT *IS*.
WELL... LEONA'S NOT PROMISCUOUS. HAD THE SAME BOYFRIEND SINCE SHE WAS TWELVE.
NOT PROUD TO SAY I WALKED IN ON 'EM BARE-ASSED AND BUSY OUT NEAR PIONEER PARK JUST A FEW HOURS AGO.

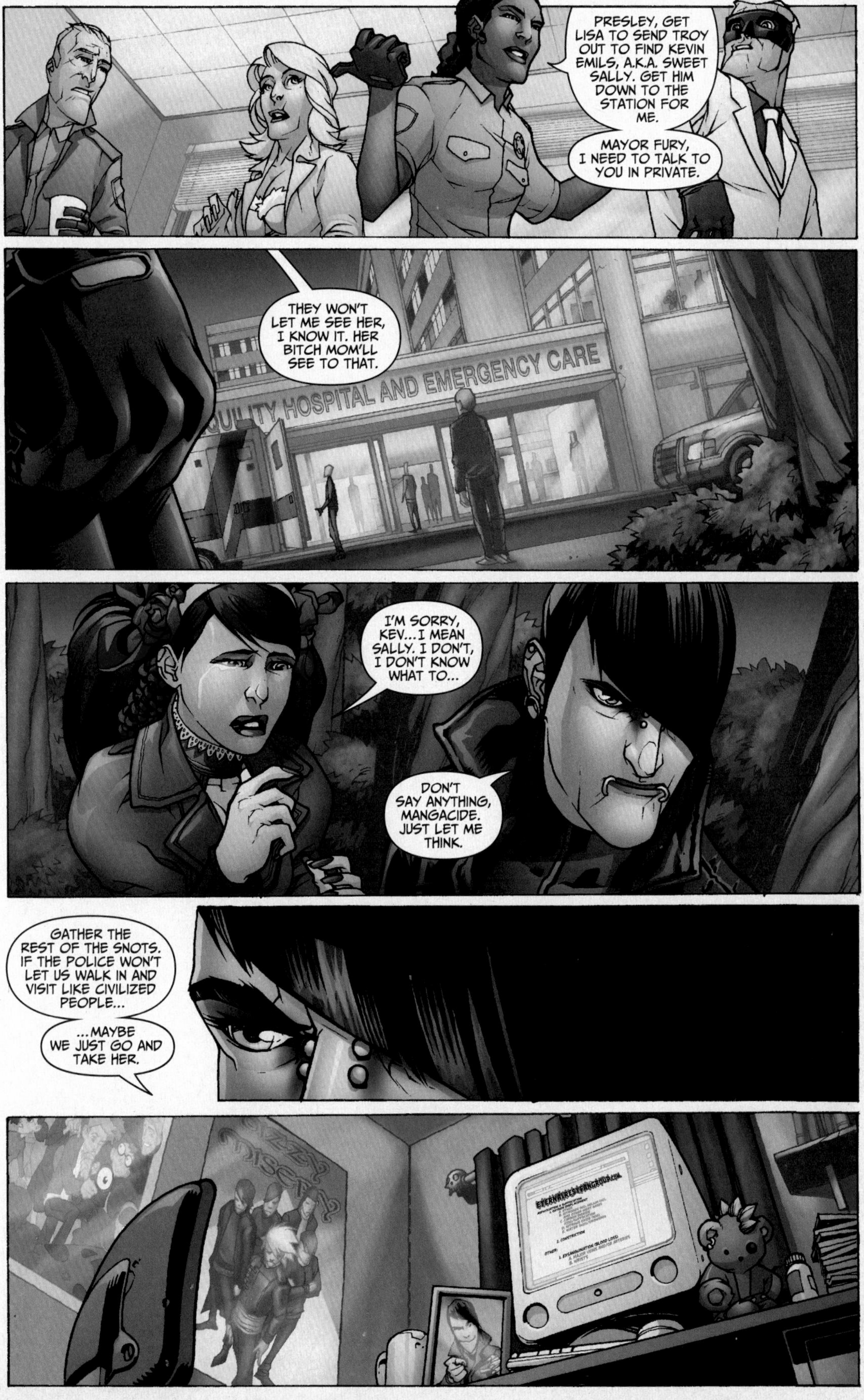
PRESLEY, GET LISA TO SEND TROY OUT TO FIND KEVIN EMILS, A.K.A. SWEET SALLY. GET HIM DOWN TO THE STATION FOR ME.
MAYOR FURY, I NEED TO TALK TO YOU IN PRIVATE.
THEY WON'T LET ME SEE HER, I KNOW IT. HER BITCH MOM'LL SEE TO THAT.
HOSPITAL AND EMERGENCY CARE
I'M SORRY, KEV...I MEAN SALLY. I DON'T, I DON'T KNOW WHAT TO...
DON'T SAY ANYTHING, MANGACIDE. JUST LET ME THINK.
GATHER THE REST OF THE SNOTS. IF THE POLICE WON'T LET US WALK IN AND VISIT LIKE CIVILIZED PEOPLE...
...MAYBE WE JUST GO AND TAKE HER.

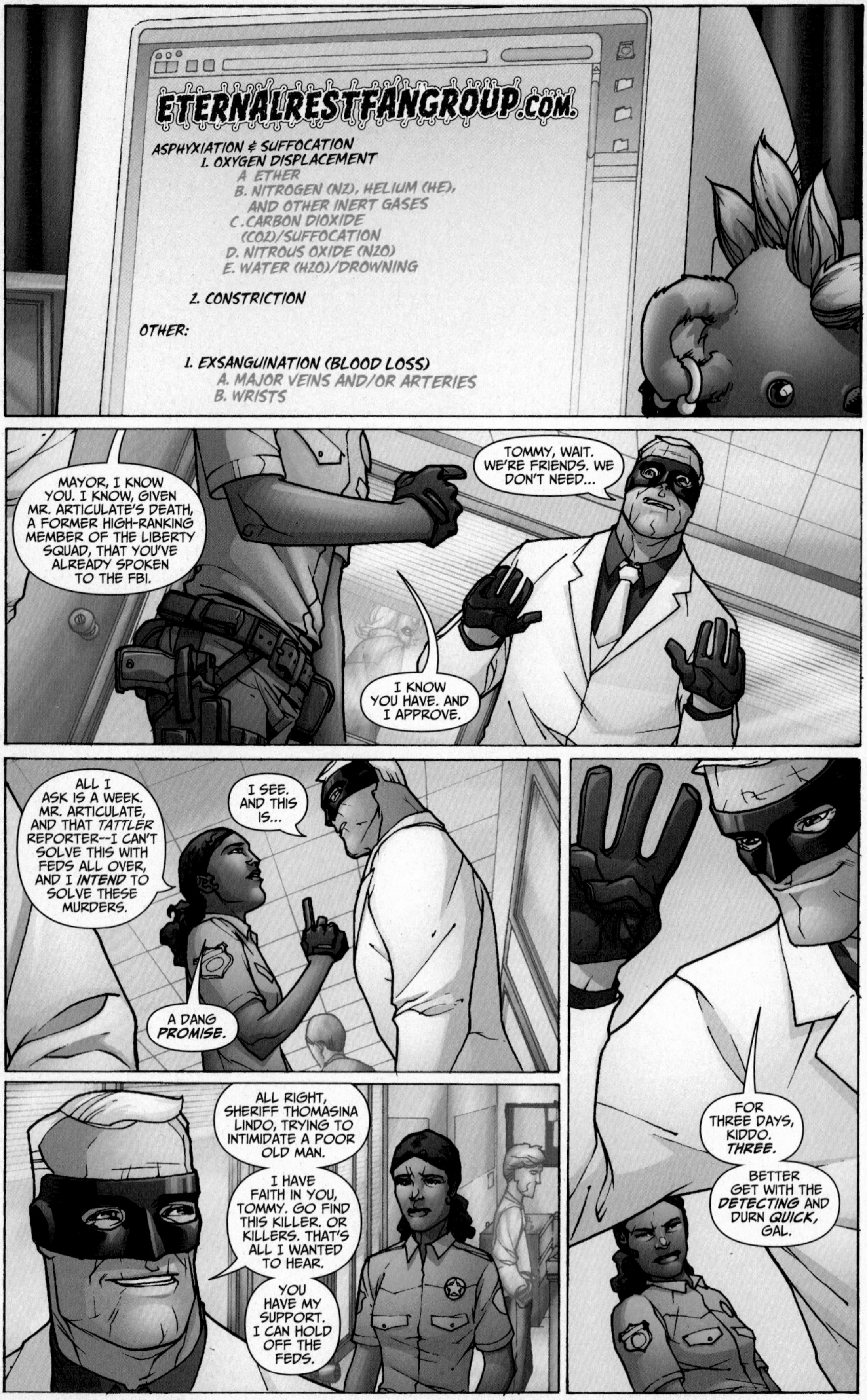
ETERNALRESTFANGROUP.com.
ASPHYXIATION & SUFFOCATION
1. OXYGEN DISPLACEMENT
A. ETHER
B. NITROGEN (N2), HELIUM (HE), AND OTHER INERT GASES
C. CARBON DIOXIDE (CO2)/SUFFOCATION
D. NITROUS OXIDE (N2O)
E. WATER (H2O)/DROWNING
2. CONSTRICTION
OTHER:
1. EXSANGUINATION (BLOOD LOSS)
A. MAJOR VEINS AND/OR ARTERIES
B. WRISTS
MAYOR, I KNOW YOU. I KNOW, GIVEN MR. ARTICULATE'S DEATH, A FORMER HIGH-RANKING MEMBER OF THE LIBERTY SQUAD, THAT YOU'VE ALREADY SPOKEN TO THE FBI.
TOMMY, WAIT. WE'RE FRIENDS. WE DON'T NEED...
I KNOW YOU HAVE. AND I APPROVE.
ALL I ASK IS A WEEK. MR. ARTICULATE, AND THAT TATTLER REPORTER--I CAN'T SOLVE THIS WITH FEDS ALL OVER, AND I INTEND TO SOLVE THESE MURDERS.
I SEE. AND THIS IS...
A DANG PROMISE.
FOR THREE DAYS, KIDDO. THREE.
BETTER GET WITH THE DETECTING AND DURN QUICK, GAL.
ALL RIGHT, SHERIFF THOMASINA LINDO, TRYING TO INTIMIDATE A POOR OLD MAN.
I HAVE FAITH IN YOU, TOMMY. GO FIND THIS KILLER. OR KILLERS. THAT'S ALL I WANTED TO HEAR.
YOU HAVE MY SUPPORT. I CAN HOLD OFF THE FEDS.

OFFICIAL MAXI-COMICS TRADING STAMP CLUB BOOK!

MAXIMUM MAN

Channeling the mighty forces of the Indian Fakirs, MAXIMUM MAN is the most powerful maxi hero alive! As Kevin Trueblood, he is an unassuming and timid mailman, but when he says his secret word, LOOK OUT EVIL!

POWERS: Flight, super strength, invulnerability!

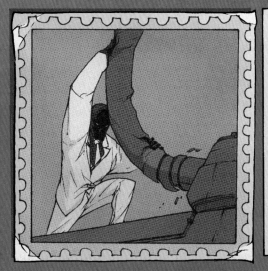

JUDGE FURY

BOOM bangs the gavel of justice when ALEX FURY, strongman crusader, appears on the scene! Leader of the LIBERTY SQUAD (stamp 49, collectors!), he makes evildoers say HELL HATH NO FURY like FURY!

POWERS: Super combat skills and strength, and near-invulnerability

HENRY HATE

Born the bad half of a set of twins, Henry Hate (real name, Henry HYDE) murdered his brother while still an infant! A master inventor, Henry claims to be working on a bomb which DESTROYS humans while PRESERVING material goods! Maximum Man's DEADLIEST FOE!

POWERS: Super criminal genius

PINK BUNNY

One look at her and the crooks happily go to jail. Wouldn't you? Actress, dancer, and Liberty Squad secretary, this gal's got her hands full, and brother, she's quite a handful herself!

POWERS: Beauty, super strength, poise

COLONEL CRAGG

America's supreme soldier! The only man in history to be enlisted in three branches of the military at the same time! An ace pilot, unstoppable foot soldier, an unequaled sailor, Colonel Cragg is the enemy's nightmare!

POWERS: Sharpshooting, aerial dogfighting, unarmed combat

BAD DOG

Colonel Cragg's fiercely loyal second-in-command, Bad Dog might not be the smartest soldier, but he's one of the toughest! It's said that once he clamps his jaws on his prey, he never lets go!

POWERS: Toughness, unarmed combat

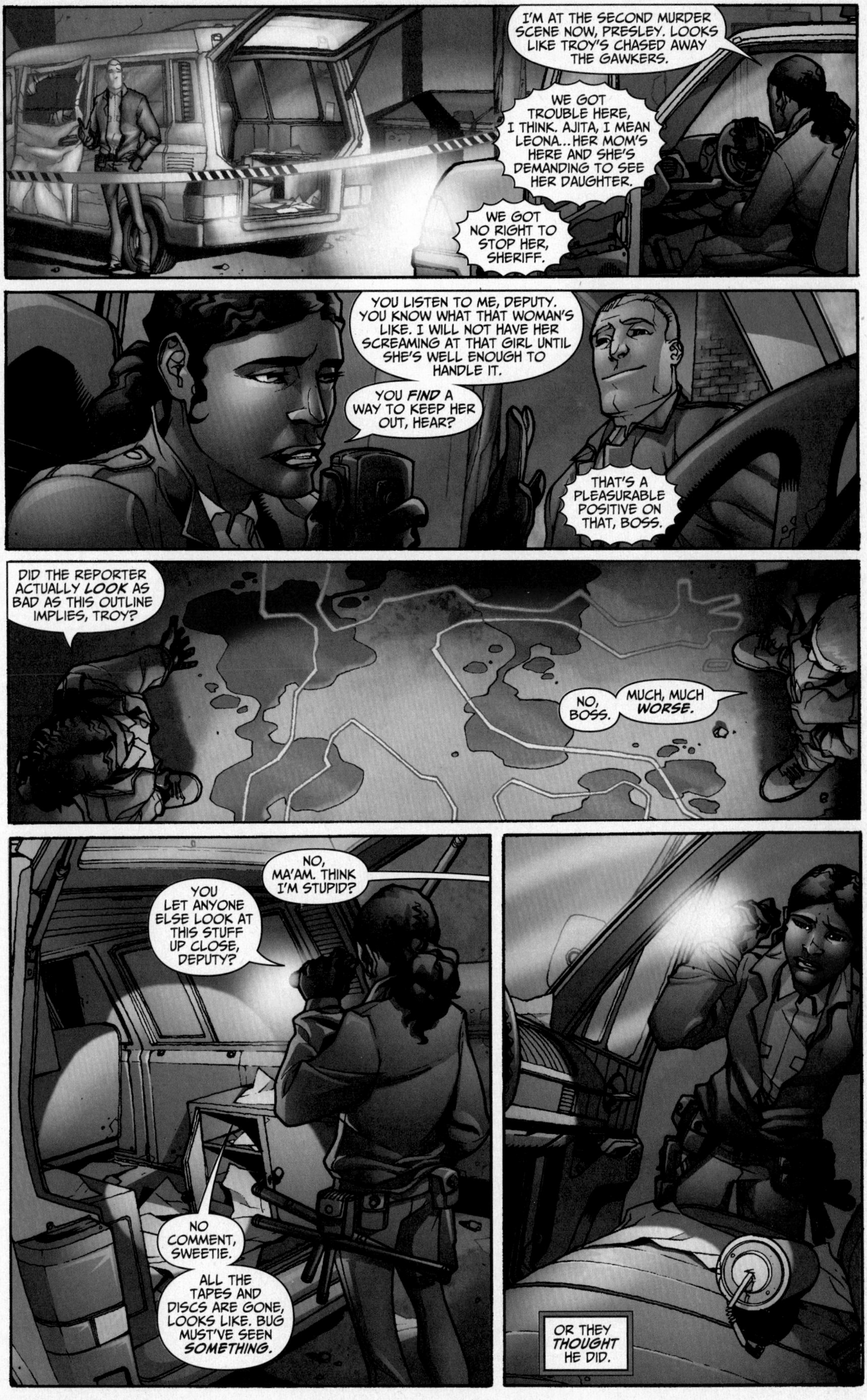
I'M AT THE SECOND MURDER SCENE NOW, PRESLEY. LOOKS LIKE TROY'S CHASED AWAY THE GAWKERS.
WE GOT TROUBLE HERE, I THINK. AJITA, I MEAN LEONA...HER MOM'S HERE AND SHE'S DEMANDING TO SEE HER DAUGHTER.
WE GOT NO RIGHT TO STOP HER, SHERIFF.
YOU LISTEN TO ME, DEPUTY. YOU KNOW WHAT THAT WOMAN'S LIKE. I WILL NOT HAVE HER SCREAMING AT THAT GIRL UNTIL SHE'S WELL ENOUGH TO HANDLE IT.
YOU *FIND* A WAY TO KEEP HER OUT, HEAR?
THAT'S A PLEASURABLE POSITIVE ON THAT, BOSS.
DID THE REPORTER ACTUALLY *LOOK* AS BAD AS THIS OUTLINE IMPLIES, TROY?
NO, BOSS.
MUCH, MUCH *WORSE.*
YOU LET ANYONE ELSE LOOK AT THIS STUFF UP CLOSE, DEPUTY?
NO, MA'AM. THINK I'M STUPID?
NO COMMENT, SWEETIE.
ALL THE TAPES AND DISCS ARE GONE, LOOKS LIKE. BUG MUST'VE SEEN *SOMETHING.*
OR THEY *THOUGHT* HE DID.

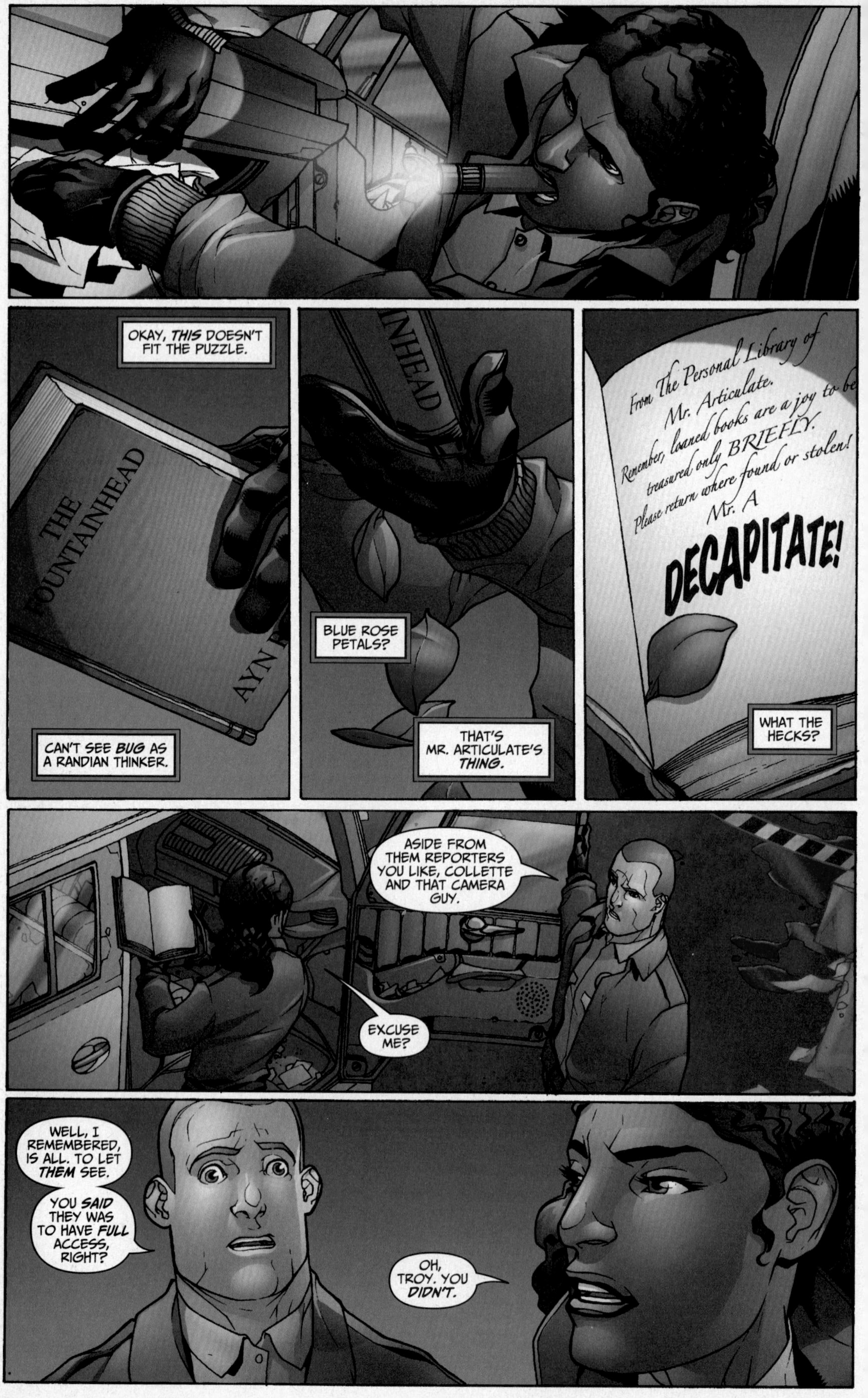
OKAY, THIS DOESN'T FIT THE PUZZLE.
THE FOUNTAINHEAD
AYN
CAN'T SEE BUG AS A RANDIAN THINKER.
INHEAD
BLUE ROSE PETALS?
THAT'S MR. ARTICULATE'S THING.
From The Personal Library of Mr. Articulate. Remember, loaned books are a joy to be treasured only BRIEFLY. Please return where found or stolen! Mr. A
DECAPITATE!
WHAT THE HECKS?
ASIDE FROM THEM REPORTERS YOU LIKE, COLLETTE AND THAT CAMERA GUY.
EXCUSE ME?
WELL, I REMEMBERED, IS ALL. TO LET THEM SEE.
YOU SAID THEY WAS TO HAVE FULL ACCESS, RIGHT?
OH, TROY. YOU DIDN'T.

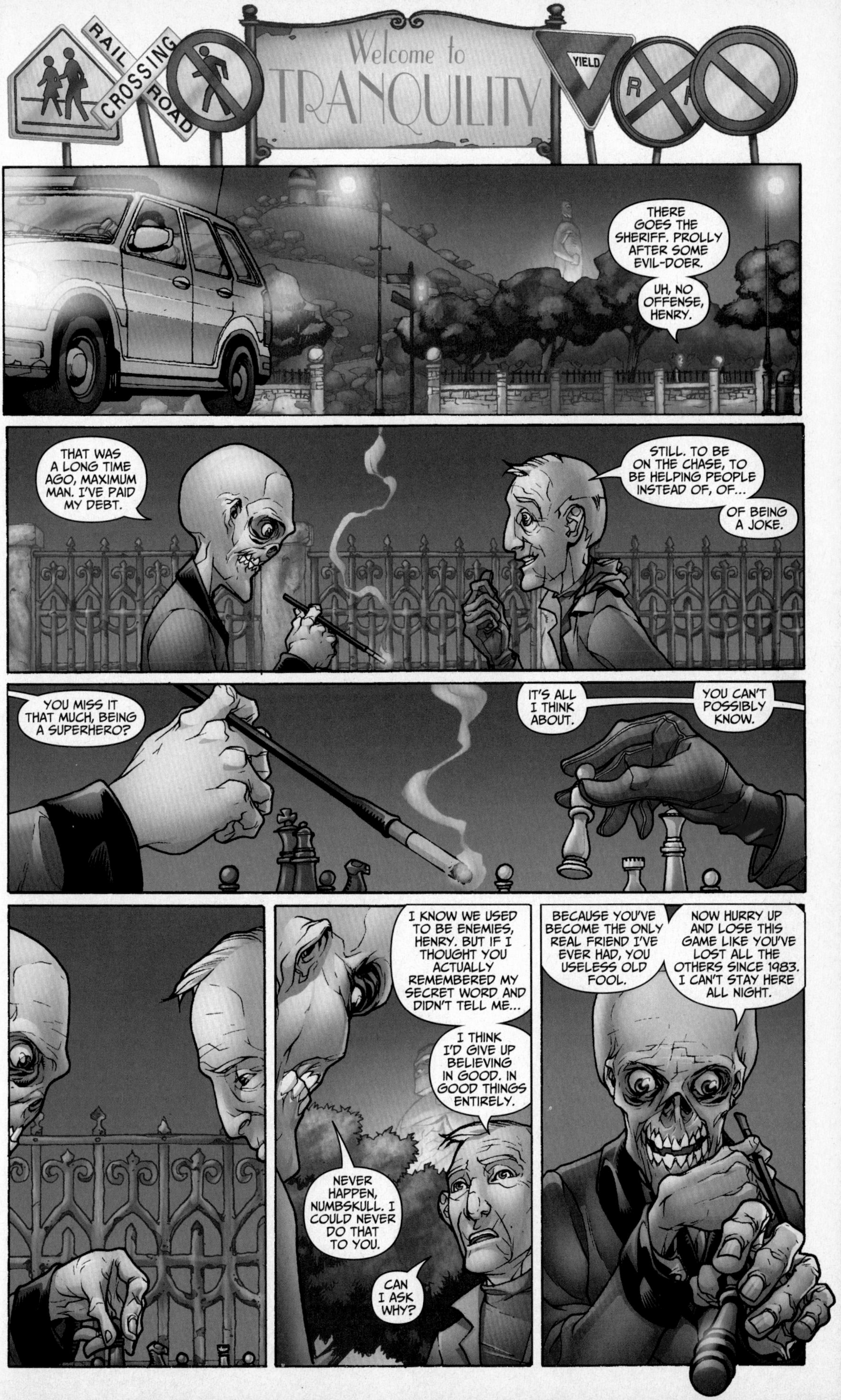
RAIL CROSSING
ROAD
Welcome to TRANQUILITY
YIELD
R R
THERE GOES THE SHERIFF. PROLLY AFTER SOME EVIL-DOER.
UH, NO OFFENSE, HENRY.
THAT WAS A LONG TIME AGO, MAXIMUM MAN. I'VE PAID MY DEBT.
STILL. TO BE ON THE CHASE, TO BE HELPING PEOPLE INSTEAD OF, OF...
OF BEING A JOKE.
YOU MISS IT THAT MUCH, BEING A SUPERHERO?
IT'S ALL I THINK ABOUT.
YOU CAN'T POSSIBLY KNOW.
I KNOW WE USED TO BE ENEMIES, HENRY. BUT IF I THOUGHT YOU ACTUALLY REMEMBERED MY SECRET WORD AND DIDN'T TELL ME...
I THINK I'D GIVE UP BELIEVING IN GOOD. IN GOOD THINGS ENTIRELY.
NEVER HAPPEN, NUMBSKULL. I COULD NEVER DO THAT TO YOU.
CAN I ASK WHY?
BECAUSE YOU'VE BECOME THE ONLY REAL FRIEND I'VE EVER HAD, YOU USELESS OLD FOOL.
NOW HURRY UP AND LOSE THIS GAME LIKE YOU'VE LOST ALL THE OTHERS SINCE 1983. I CAN'T STAY HERE ALL NIGHT.

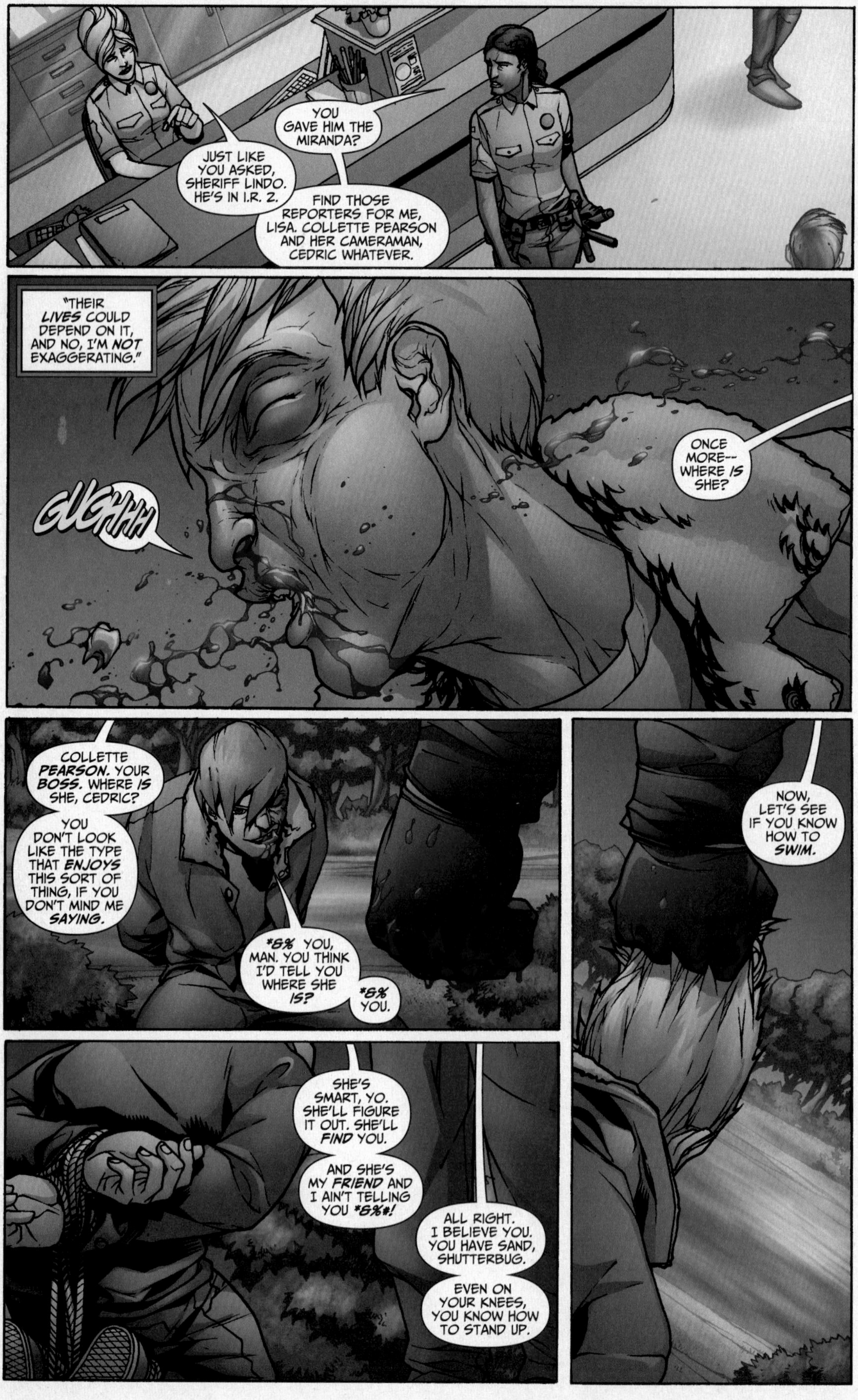
YOU GAVE HIM THE MIRANDA?
JUST LIKE YOU ASKED, SHERIFF LINDO. HE'S IN I.R. 2.
FIND THOSE REPORTERS FOR ME, LISA. COLLETTE PEARSON AND HER CAMERAMAN, CEDRIC WHATEVER.
"THEIR LIVES COULD DEPEND ON IT, AND NO, I'M NOT EXAGGERATING."
ONCE MORE-- WHERE IS SHE?
GUGHHH
COLLETTE PEARSON. YOUR BOSS. WHERE IS SHE, CEDRIC?
YOU DON'T LOOK LIKE THE TYPE THAT ENJOYS THIS SORT OF THING, IF YOU DON'T MIND ME SAYING.
*&% YOU, MAN. YOU THINK I'D TELL YOU WHERE SHE IS?
*&% YOU.
NOW, LET'S SEE IF YOU KNOW HOW TO SWIM.
SHE'S SMART, YO. SHE'LL FIGURE IT OUT. SHE'LL FIND YOU.
AND SHE'S MY FRIEND AND I AIN'T TELLING YOU *&%*!
ALL RIGHT. I BELIEVE YOU. YOU HAVE SAND, SHUTTERBUG.
EVEN ON YOUR KNEES, YOU KNOW HOW TO STAND UP.

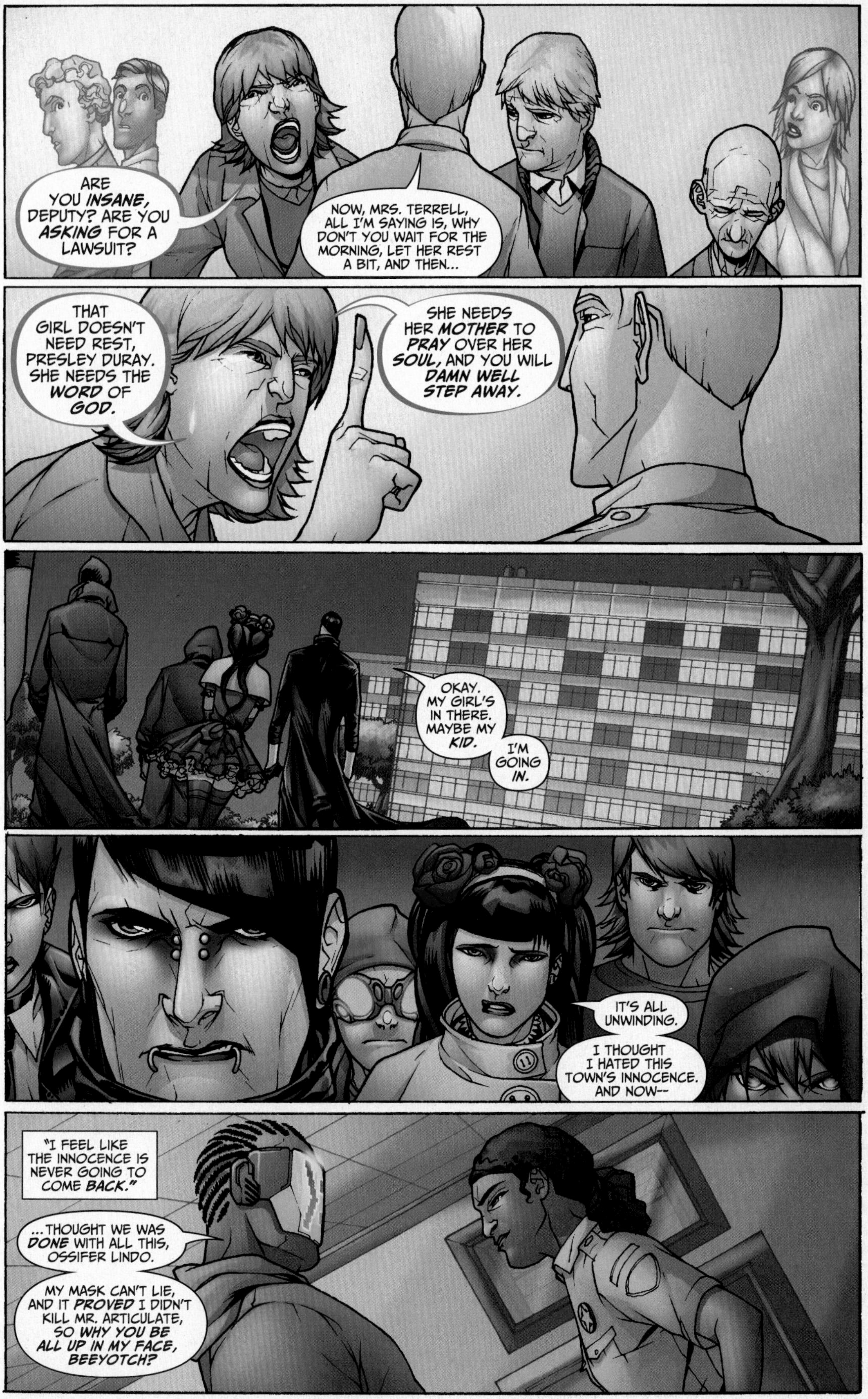

ARE YOU *INSANE*, DEPUTY? ARE YOU *ASKING* FOR A LAWSUIT?
NOW, MRS. TERRELL, ALL I'M SAYING IS, WHY DON'T YOU WAIT FOR THE MORNING, LET HER REST A BIT, AND THEN...
THAT GIRL DOESN'T NEED REST, PRESLEY DURAY. SHE NEEDS THE *WORD* OF *GOD*.
SHE NEEDS HER *MOTHER* TO *PRAY* OVER HER *SOUL*, AND YOU WILL *DAMN WELL STEP AWAY*.
OKAY. MY GIRL'S IN THERE. MAYBE MY *KID*.
I'M GOING *IN*.
IT'S ALL UNWINDING.
I THOUGHT I HATED THIS TOWN'S INNOCENCE. AND NOW--
"I FEEL LIKE THE INNOCENCE IS NEVER GOING TO COME *BACK*."
...THOUGHT WE WAS *DONE* WITH ALL THIS, OSSIFER LINDO.
MY MASK CAN'T LIE, AND IT *PROVED* I DIDN'T KILL MR. ARTICULATE, SO *WHY YOU BE ALL UP IN MY FACE, BEEYOTCH?*

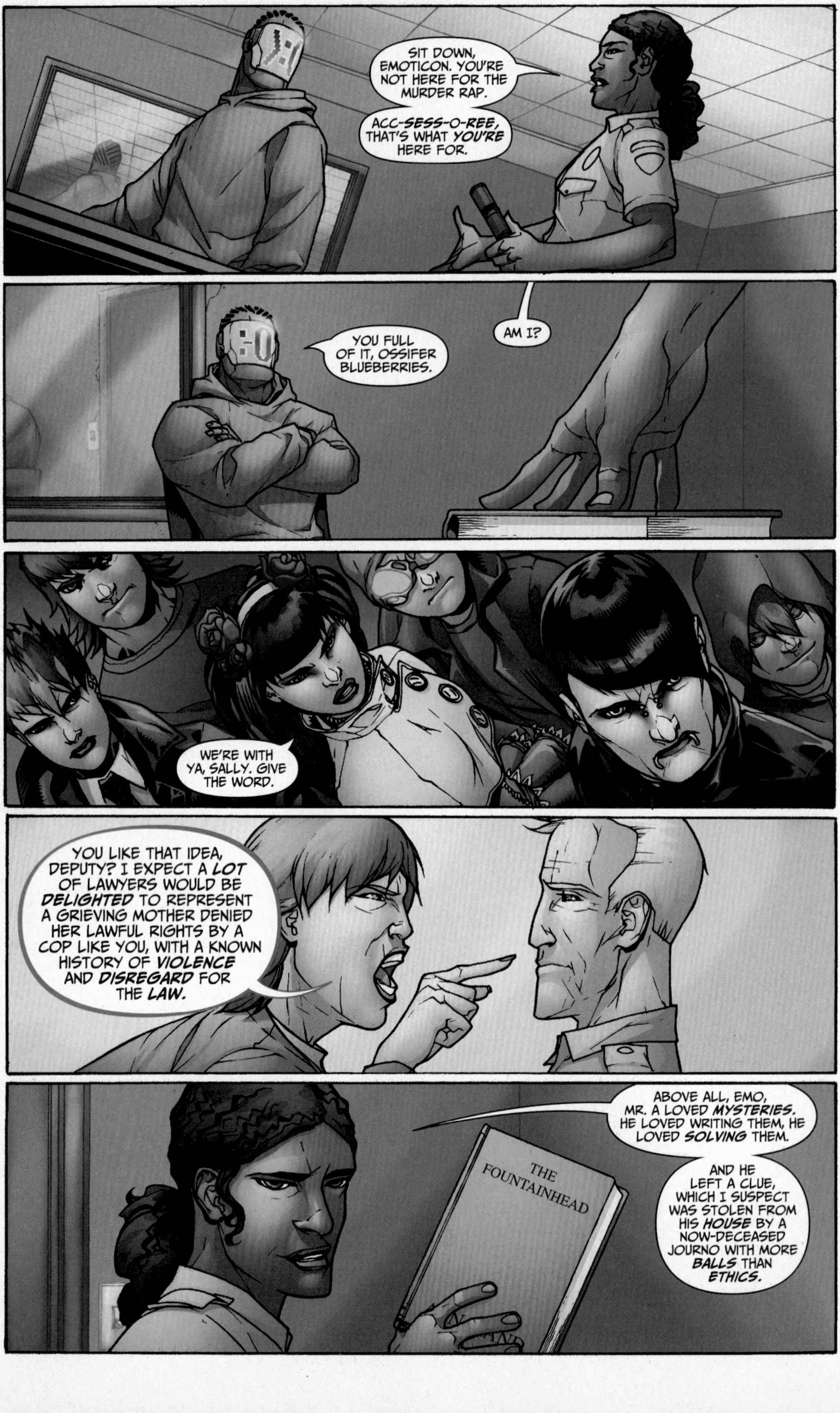
SIT DOWN, EMOTICON. YOU'RE NOT HERE FOR THE MURDER RAP.
ACC-SESS-O-REE, THAT'S WHAT YOU'RE HERE FOR.
YOU FULL OF IT, OSSIFER BLUEBERRIES.
AM I?
WE'RE WITH YA, SALLY. GIVE THE WORD.
YOU LIKE THAT IDEA, DEPUTY? I EXPECT A LOT OF LAWYERS WOULD BE DELIGHTED TO REPRESENT A GRIEVING MOTHER DENIED HER LAWFUL RIGHTS BY A COP LIKE YOU, WITH A KNOWN HISTORY OF VIOLENCE AND DISREGARD FOR THE LAW.
ABOVE ALL, EMO, MR. A LOVED MYSTERIES. HE LOVED WRITING THEM, HE LOVED SOLVING THEM.
THE FOUNTAINHEAD
AND HE LEFT A CLUE, WHICH I SUSPECT WAS STOLEN FROM HIS HOUSE BY A NOW-DECEASED JOURNO WITH MORE BALLS THAN ETHICS.

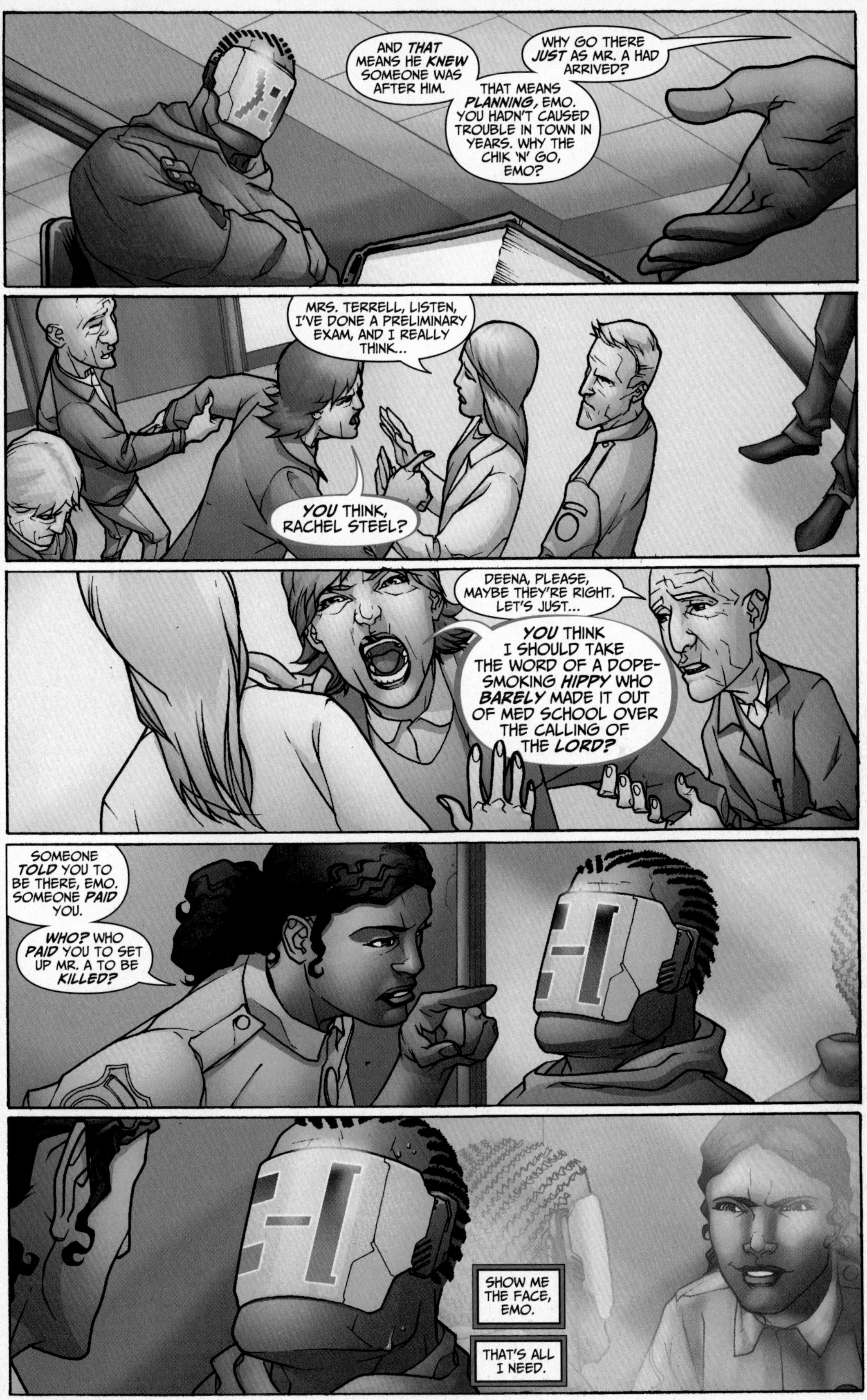
AND THAT MEANS HE KNEW SOMEONE WAS AFTER HIM.
WHY GO THERE JUST AS MR. A HAD ARRIVED?
THAT MEANS PLANNING, EMO. YOU HADN'T CAUSED TROUBLE IN TOWN IN YEARS. WHY THE CHIK 'N' GO, EMO?
MRS. TERRELL, LISTEN, I'VE DONE A PRELIMINARY EXAM, AND I REALLY THINK...
YOU THINK, RACHEL STEEL?
DEENA, PLEASE, MAYBE THEY'RE RIGHT. LET'S JUST...
YOU THINK I SHOULD TAKE THE WORD OF A DOPE-SMOKING HIPPY WHO BARELY MADE IT OUT OF MED SCHOOL OVER THE CALLING OF THE LORD?
SOMEONE TOLD YOU TO BE THERE, EMO. SOMEONE PAID YOU.
WHO? WHO PAID YOU TO SET UP MR. A TO BE KILLED?
SHOW ME THE FACE, EMO.
THAT'S ALL I NEED.

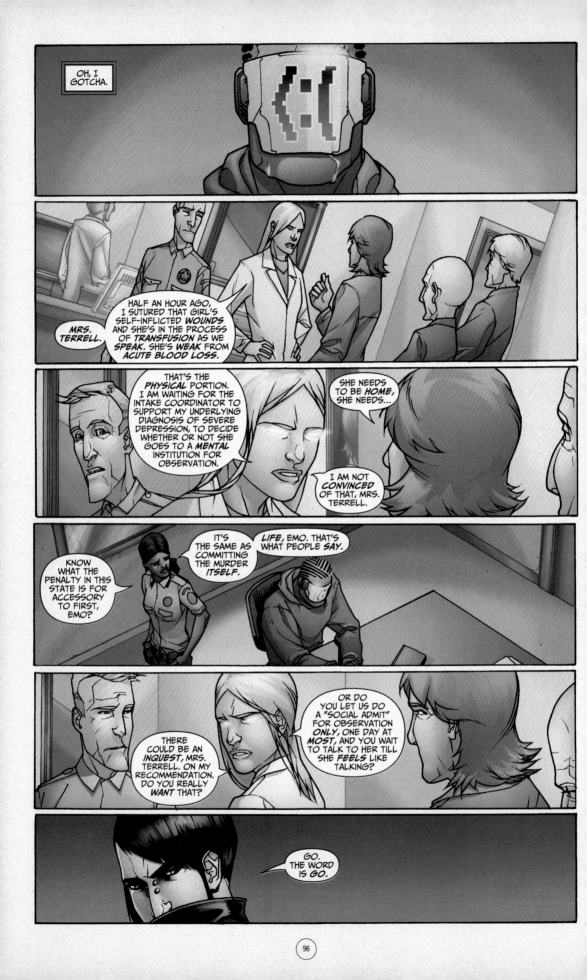

OH, I GOTCHA.

MRS. TERRELL.

HALF AN HOUR AGO, I SUTURED THAT GIRL'S SELF-INFLICTED *WOUNDS* AND SHE'S IN THE PROCESS OF *TRANSFUSION* AS WE SPEAK. SHE'S *WEAK* FROM ACUTE BLOOD LOSS.

THAT'S THE *PHYSICAL* PORTION. I AM WAITING FOR THE INTAKE COORDINATOR TO SUPPORT MY UNDERLYING DIAGNOSIS OF SEVERE DEPRESSION, TO DECIDE WHETHER OR NOT SHE GOES TO A *MENTAL* INSTITUTION FOR OBSERVATION.

SHE NEEDS TO BE *HOME*, SHE NEEDS...

I AM NOT *CONVINCED* OF THAT, MRS. TERRELL.

KNOW WHAT THE PENALTY IN THIS STATE IS FOR ACCESSORY TO FIRST, EMO?

IT'S THE SAME AS COMMITTING THE MURDER *ITSELF*.

LIFE, EMO. THAT'S WHAT PEOPLE *SAY*.

THERE COULD BE AN *INQUEST*, MRS. TERRELL. ON MY RECOMMENDATION. DO YOU REALLY *WANT* THAT?

OR DO YOU LET US DO A "SOCIAL ADMIT" FOR OBSERVATION *ONLY*, ONE DAY AT *MOST*, AND YOU WAIT TO TALK TO HER TILL SHE *FEELS* LIKE TALKING?

GO. THE WORD IS GO.

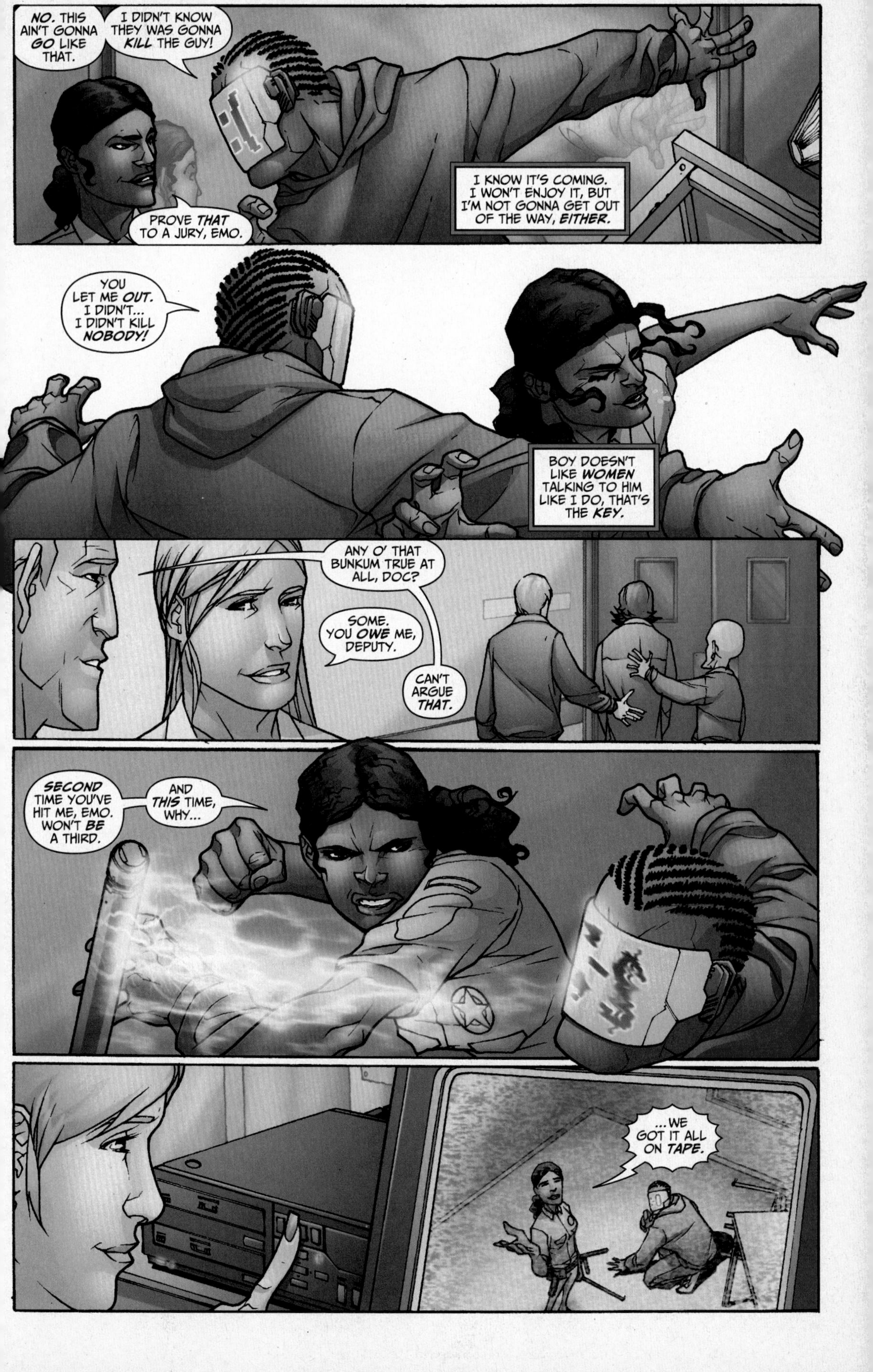
NO. THIS AIN'T GONNA GO LIKE THAT.
I DIDN'T KNOW THEY WAS GONNA KILL THE GUY!
I KNOW IT'S COMING. I WON'T ENJOY IT, BUT I'M NOT GONNA GET OUT OF THE WAY, EITHER.
PROVE THAT TO A JURY, EMO.
YOU LET ME OUT. I DIDN'T... I DIDN'T KILL NOBODY!
BOY DOESN'T LIKE WOMEN TALKING TO HIM LIKE I DO, THAT'S THE KEY.
ANY O' THAT BUNKUM TRUE AT ALL, DOC?
SOME. YOU OWE ME, DEPUTY.
CAN'T ARGUE THAT.
SECOND TIME YOU'VE HIT ME, EMO. WON'T BE A THIRD.
AND THIS TIME, WHY...
...WE GOT IT ALL ON TAPE.

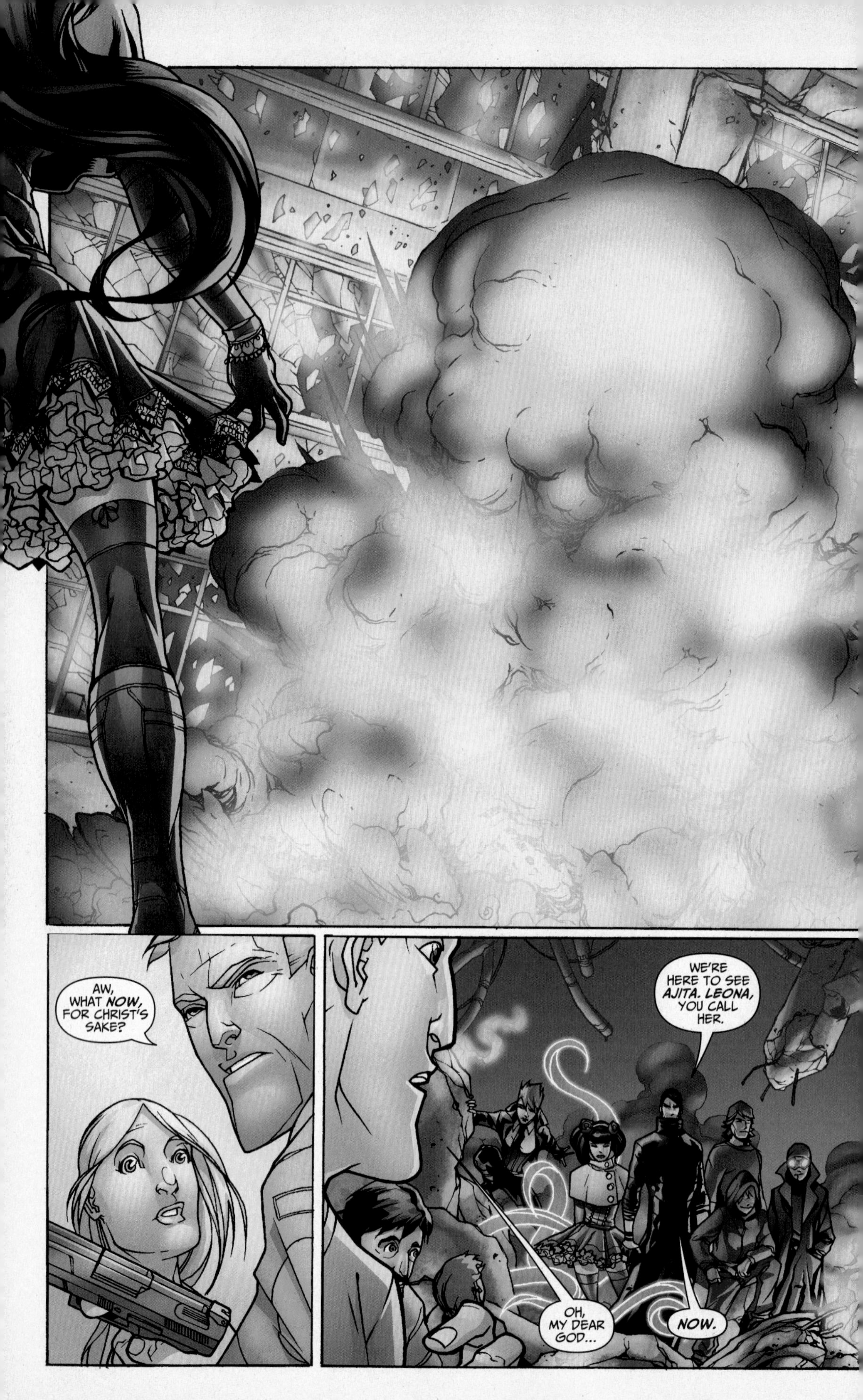
AW, WHAT NOW, FOR CHRIST'S SAKE?
WE'RE HERE TO SEE AJITA. LEONA, YOU CALL HER.
OH, MY DEAR GOD...
NOW.

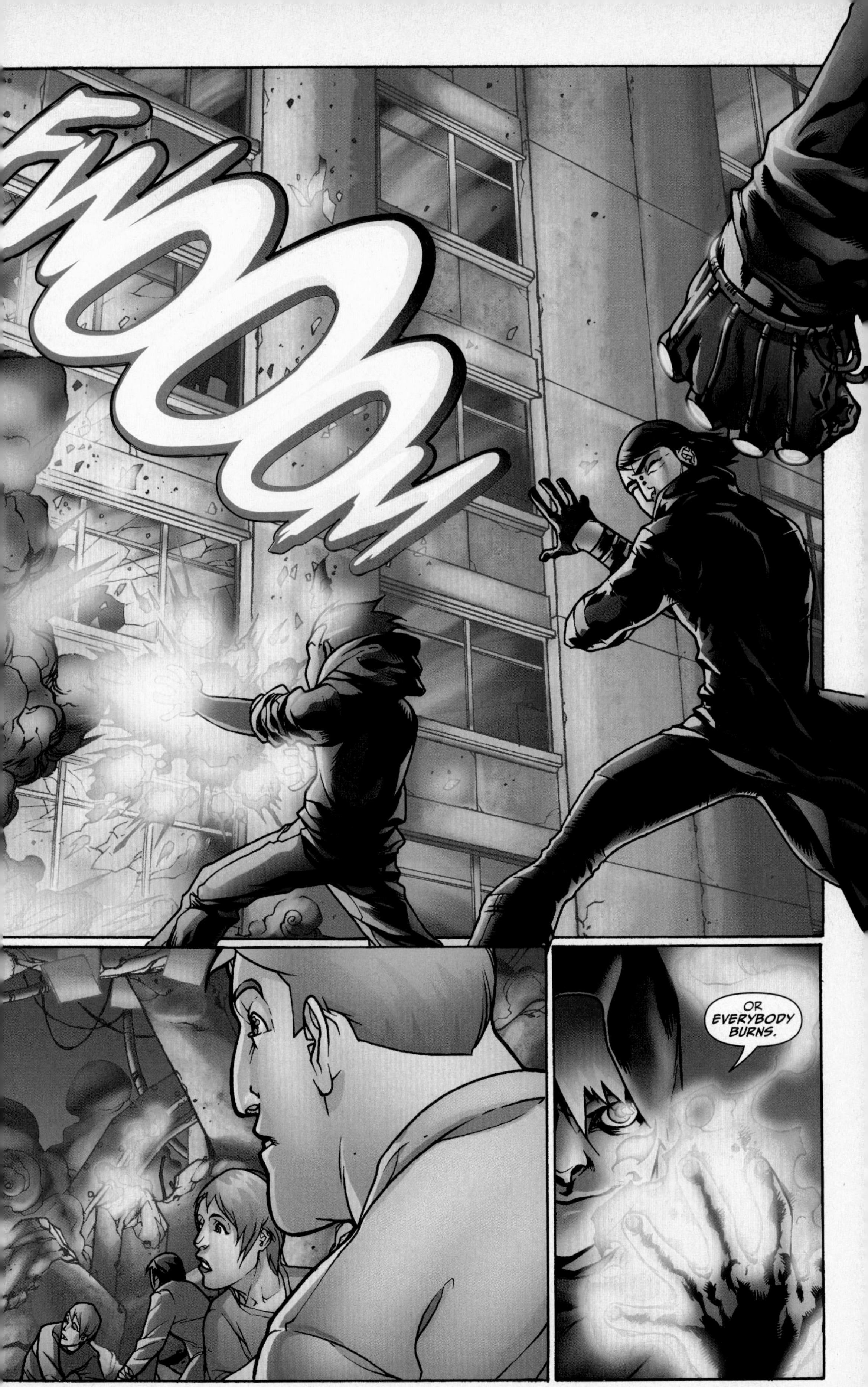
FWOOOM
OR EVERYBODY BURNS.

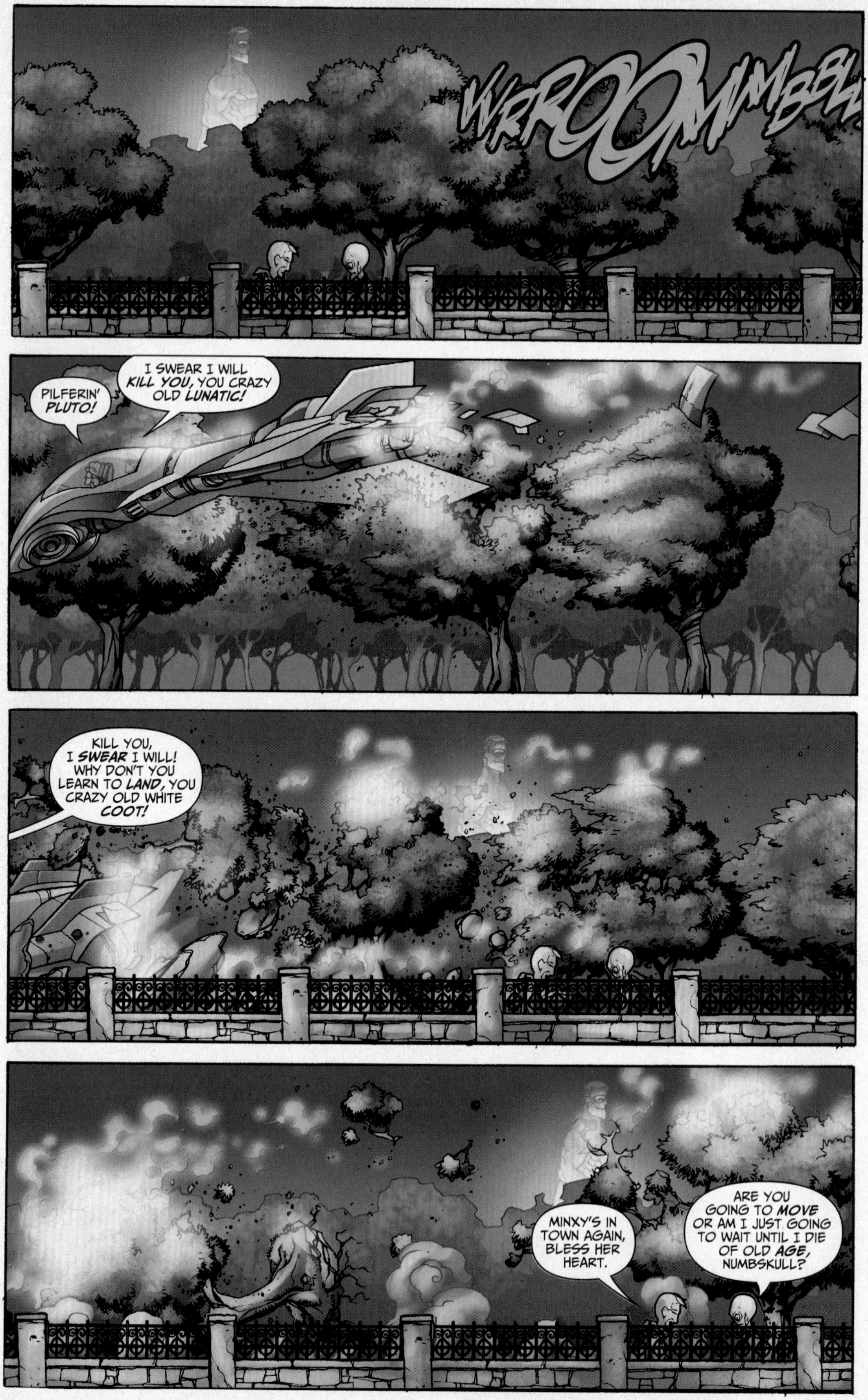
WRROOMMMBBL
PILFERIN' PLUTO!
I SWEAR I WILL KILL YOU, YOU CRAZY OLD LUNATIC!
KILL YOU, I SWEAR I WILL! WHY DON'T YOU LEARN TO LAND, YOU CRAZY OLD WHITE COOT!
MINXY'S IN TOWN AGAIN, BLESS HER HEART.
ARE YOU GOING TO MOVE OR AM I JUST GOING TO WAIT UNTIL I DIE OF OLD AGE, NUMBSKULL?

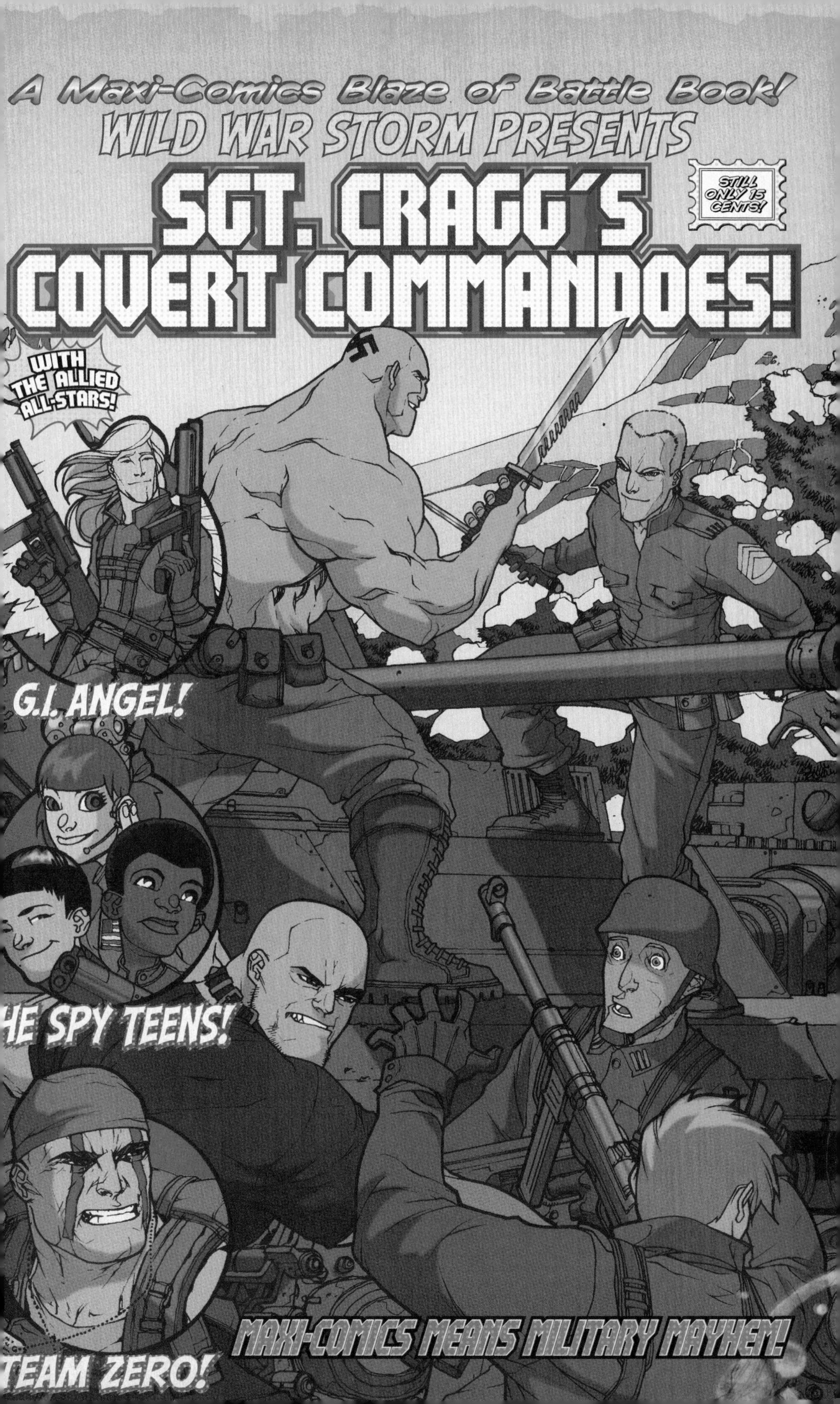
A Maxi-Comics Blaze of Battle Book!
WILD WAR STORM PRESENTS
STILL ONLY 15 CENTS!
SGT. CRAGG'S COVERT COMMANDOES!
WITH THE ALLIED ALL-STARS!
G.I. ANGEL!
HE SPY TEENS!
TEAM ZERO!
MAXI-COMICS MEANS MILITARY MAYHEM!

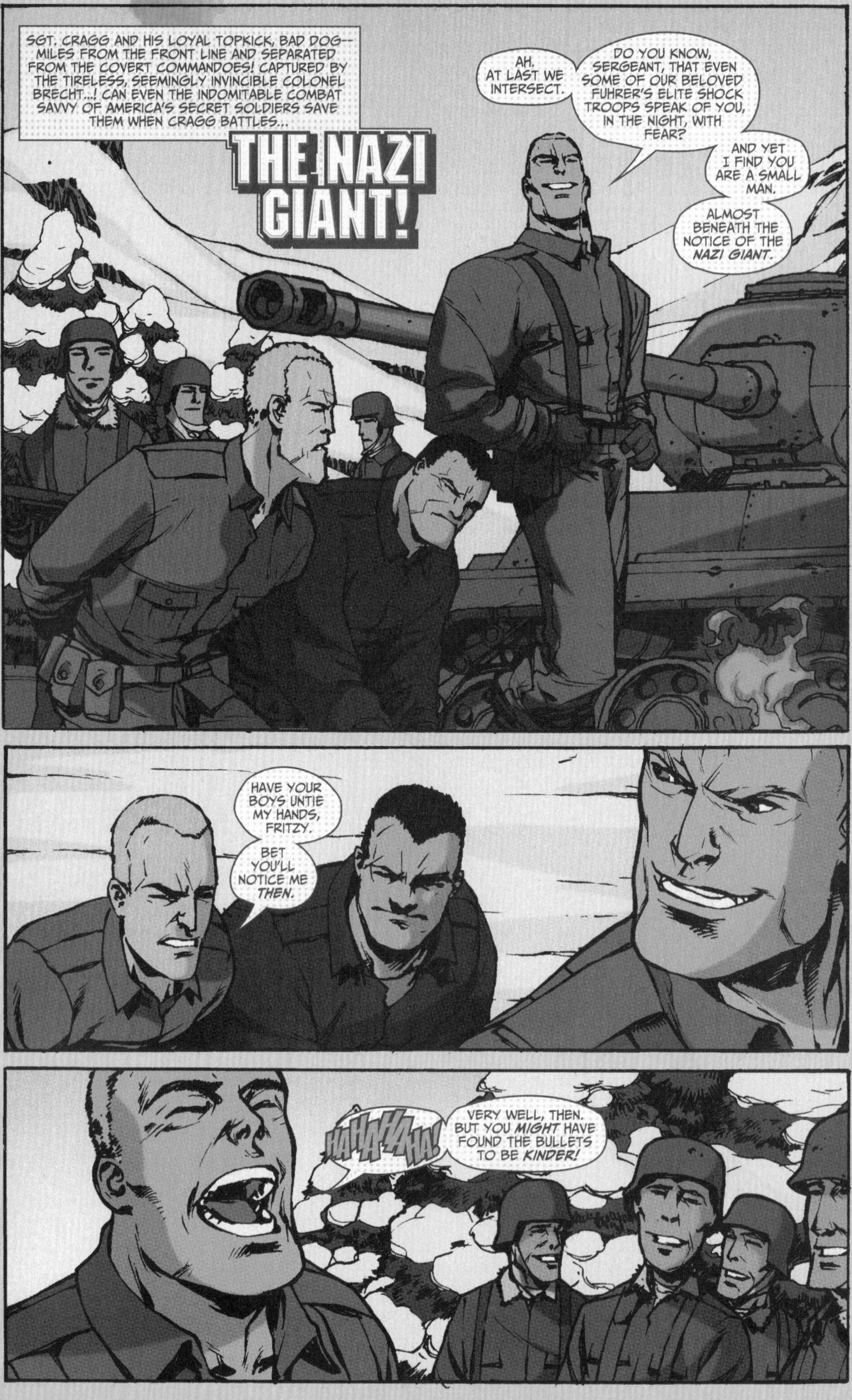
SGT. CRAGG AND HIS LOYAL TOPKICK, BAD DOG--MILES FROM THE FRONT LINE AND SEPARATED FROM THE COVERT COMMANDOES! CAPTURED BY THE TIRELESS, SEEMINGLY INVINCIBLE COLONEL BRECHT...! CAN EVEN THE INDOMITABLE COMBAT SAVVY OF AMERICA'S SECRET SOLDIERS SAVE THEM WHEN CRAGG BATTLES...
THE NAZI GIANT!
AH. AT LAST WE INTERSECT.
DO YOU KNOW, SERGEANT, THAT EVEN SOME OF OUR BELOVED FUHRER'S ELITE SHOCK TROOPS SPEAK OF YOU, IN THE NIGHT, WITH FEAR?
AND YET I FIND YOU ARE A SMALL MAN.
ALMOST BENEATH THE NOTICE OF THE *NAZI GIANT.*
HAVE YOUR BOYS UNTIE MY HANDS, FRITZY.
BET YOU'LL NOTICE ME *THEN.*
HAHAHAHA!
VERY WELL, THEN. BUT YOU *MIGHT* HAVE FOUND THE BULLETS TO BE *KINDER!*

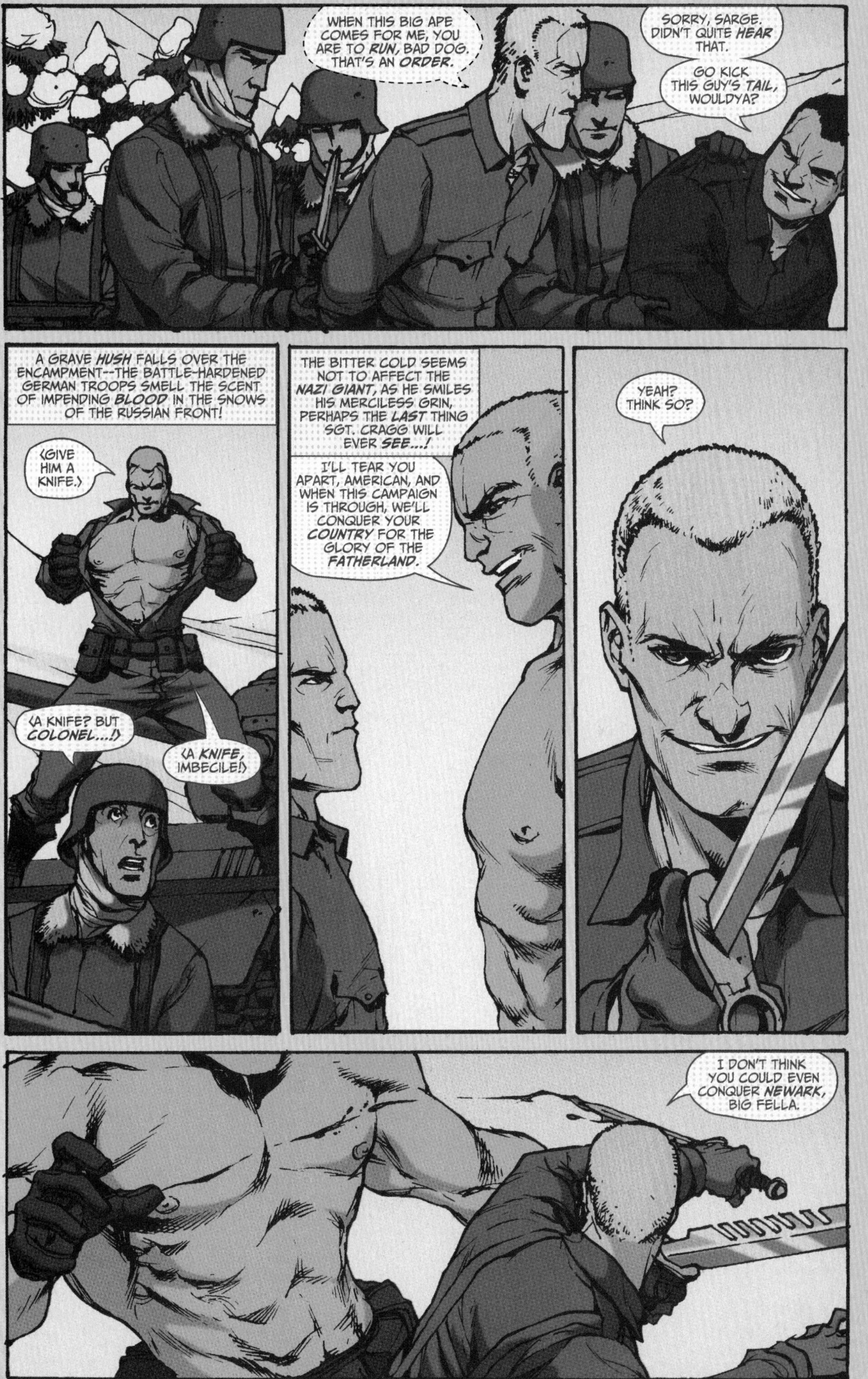
WHEN THIS BIG APE COMES FOR ME, YOU ARE TO RUN, BAD DOG. THAT'S AN ORDER.
SORRY, SARGE. DIDN'T QUITE HEAR THAT.
GO KICK THIS GUY'S TAIL, WOULDYA?
A GRAVE HUSH FALLS OVER THE ENCAMPMENT--THE BATTLE-HARDENED GERMAN TROOPS SMELL THE SCENT OF IMPENDING BLOOD IN THE SNOWS OF THE RUSSIAN FRONT!
‹GIVE HIM A KNIFE.›
‹A KNIFE? BUT COLONEL...!›
‹A KNIFE, IMBECILE!›
THE BITTER COLD SEEMS NOT TO AFFECT THE NAZI GIANT, AS HE SMILES HIS MERCILESS GRIN, PERHAPS THE LAST THING SGT. CRAGG WILL EVER SEE...!
I'LL TEAR YOU APART, AMERICAN, AND WHEN THIS CAMPAIGN IS THROUGH, WE'LL CONQUER YOUR COUNTRY FOR THE GLORY OF THE FATHERLAND.
YEAH? THINK SO?
I DON'T THINK YOU COULD EVEN CONQUER NEWARK, BIG FELLA.

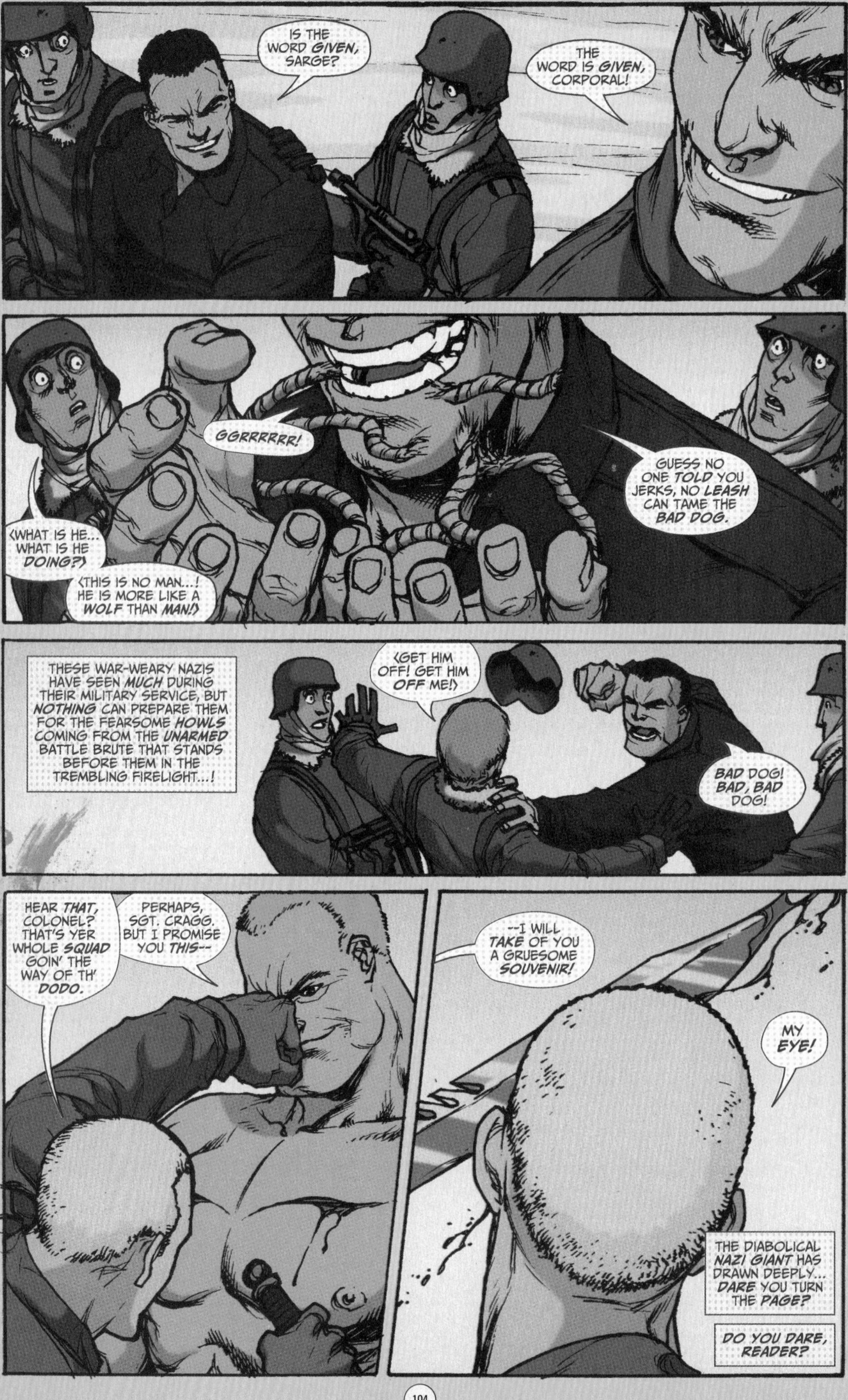
IS THE WORD GIVEN, SARGE?
THE WORD IS GIVEN, CORPORAL!
GGRRRRRR!
GUESS NO ONE TOLD YOU JERKS, NO LEASH CAN TAME THE BAD DOG.
<WHAT IS HE... WHAT IS HE DOING?>
<THIS IS NO MAN...! HE IS MORE LIKE A WOLF THAN MAN!>
THESE WAR-WEARY NAZIS HAVE SEEN MUCH DURING THEIR MILITARY SERVICE, BUT NOTHING CAN PREPARE THEM FOR THE FEARSOME HOWLS COMING FROM THE UNARMED BATTLE BRUTE THAT STANDS BEFORE THEM IN THE TREMBLING FIRELIGHT...!
<GET HIM OFF! GET HIM OFF ME!>
BAD DOG! BAD, BAD DOG!
HEAR THAT, COLONEL? THAT'S YER WHOLE SQUAD GOIN' THE WAY OF TH' DODO.
PERHAPS, SGT. CRAGG. BUT I PROMISE YOU THIS--
--I WILL TAKE OF YOU A GRUESOME SOUVENIR!
MY EYE!
THE DIABOLICAL NAZI GIANT HAS DRAWN DEEPLY... DARE YOU TURN THE PAGE?
DO YOU DARE, READER?

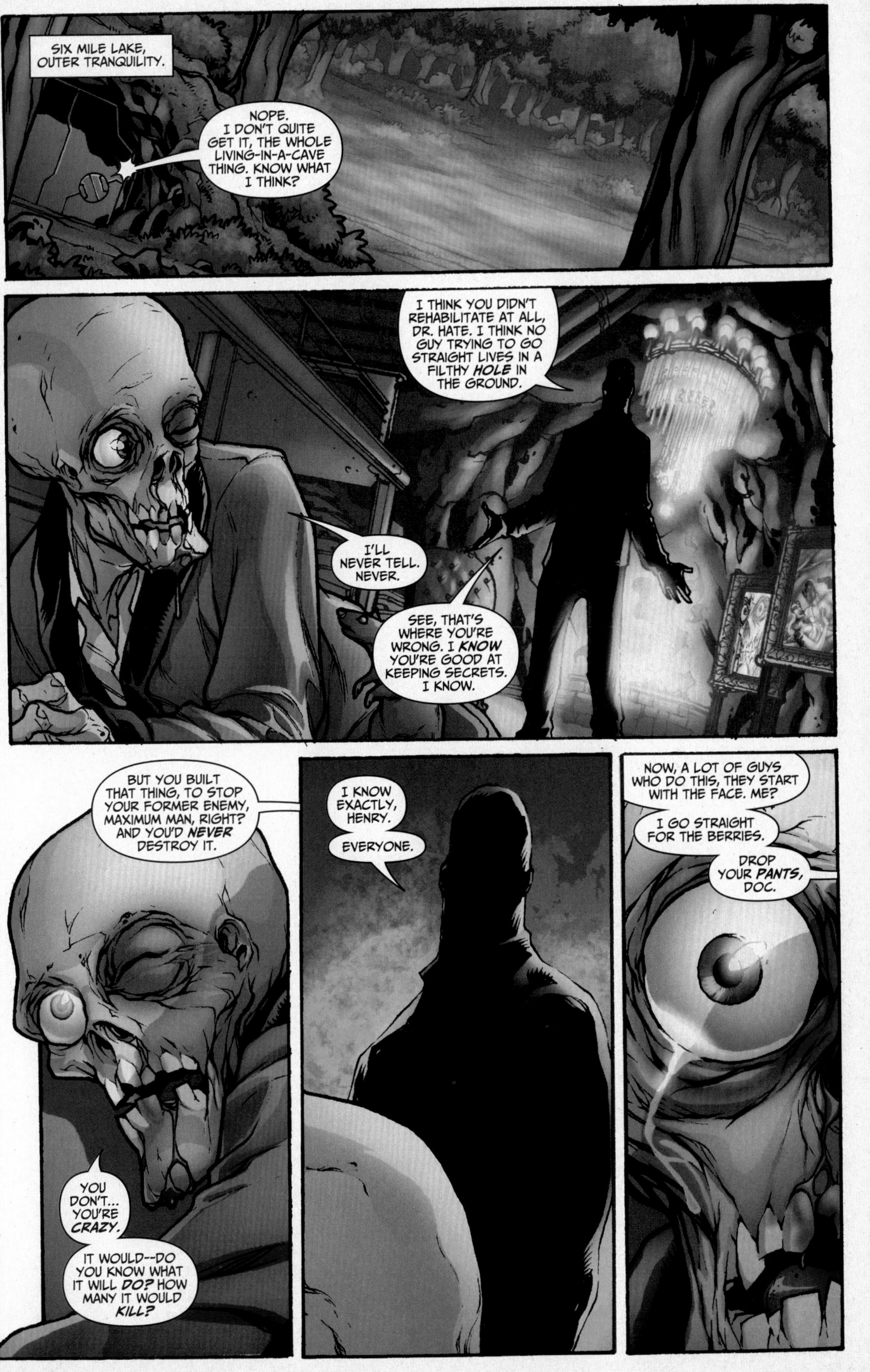

SIX MILE LAKE, OUTER TRANQUILITY.
NOPE. I DON'T QUITE GET IT, THE WHOLE LIVING-IN-A-CAVE THING. KNOW WHAT I THINK?
I THINK YOU DIDN'T REHABILITATE AT ALL, DR. HATE. I THINK NO GUY TRYING TO GO STRAIGHT LIVES IN A FILTHY **HOLE** IN THE GROUND.
I'LL NEVER TELL. NEVER.
SEE, THAT'S WHERE YOU'RE WRONG. I **KNOW** YOU'RE GOOD AT KEEPING SECRETS. I KNOW.
BUT YOU BUILT THAT THING, TO STOP YOUR FORMER ENEMY, MAXIMUM MAN, RIGHT? AND YOU'D **NEVER** DESTROY IT.
YOU DON'T... YOU'RE **CRAZY**.
IT WOULD--DO YOU KNOW WHAT IT WILL **DO?** HOW MANY IT WOULD **KILL?**
I KNOW EXACTLY, HENRY.
EVERYONE.
NOW, A LOT OF GUYS WHO DO THIS, THEY START WITH THE FACE. ME?
I GO STRAIGHT FOR THE BERRIES.
DROP YOUR **PANTS**, DOC.

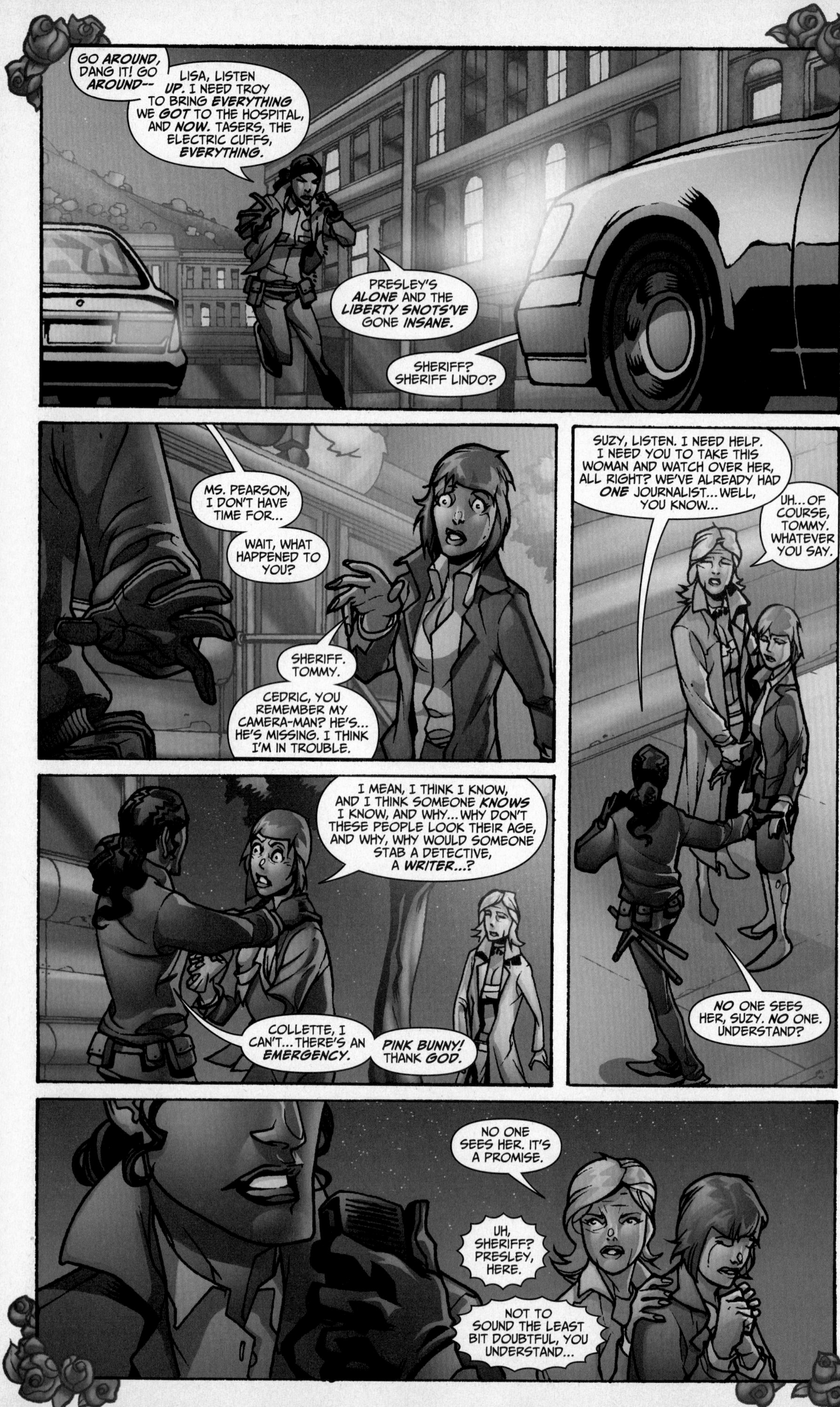
GO AROUND, DANG IT! GO AROUND--
LISA, LISTEN UP. I NEED TROY TO BRING EVERYTHING WE GOT TO THE HOSPITAL, AND NOW. TASERS, THE ELECTRIC CUFFS, EVERYTHING.
PRESLEY'S ALONE AND THE LIBERTY SNOTS'VE GONE INSANE.
SHERIFF? SHERIFF LINDO?
MS. PEARSON, I DON'T HAVE TIME FOR...
WAIT, WHAT HAPPENED TO YOU?
SHERIFF. TOMMY.
CEDRIC, YOU REMEMBER MY CAMERA-MAN? HE'S... HE'S MISSING. I THINK I'M IN TROUBLE.
I MEAN, I THINK I KNOW, AND I THINK SOMEONE KNOWS I KNOW, AND WHY... WHY DON'T THESE PEOPLE LOOK THEIR AGE, AND WHY, WHY WOULD SOMEONE STAB A DETECTIVE, A WRITER...?
COLLETTE, I CAN'T... THERE'S AN EMERGENCY.
PINK BUNNY! THANK GOD.
SUZY, LISTEN. I NEED HELP. I NEED YOU TO TAKE THIS WOMAN AND WATCH OVER HER, ALL RIGHT? WE'VE ALREADY HAD ONE JOURNALIST... WELL, YOU KNOW...
UH... OF COURSE, TOMMY. WHATEVER YOU SAY.
NO ONE SEES HER, SUZY. NO ONE. UNDERSTAND?
NO ONE SEES HER. IT'S A PROMISE.
UH, SHERIFF? PRESLEY, HERE.
NOT TO SOUND THE LEAST BIT DOUBTFUL, YOU UNDERSTAND...

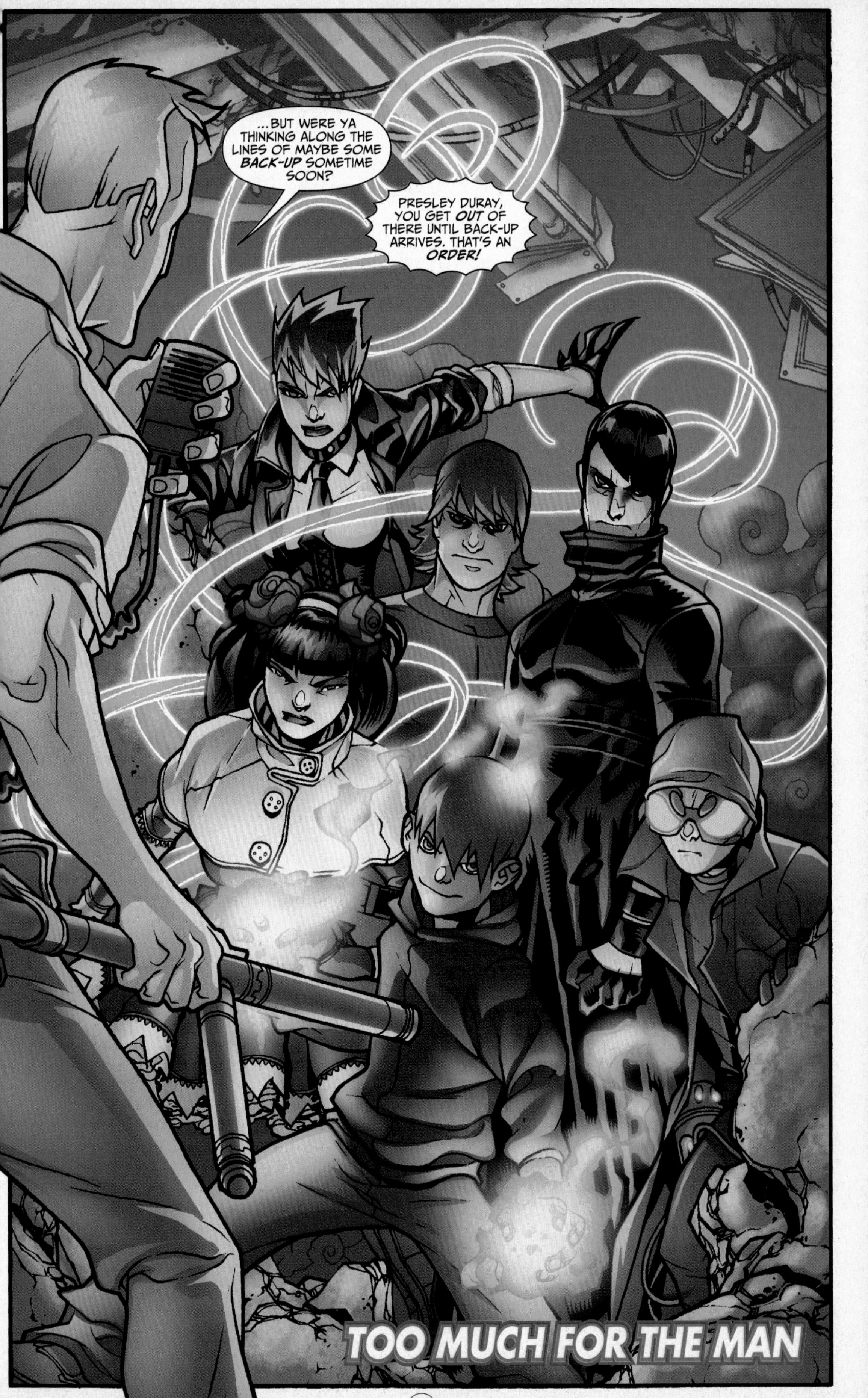
...BUT WERE YA THINKING ALONG THE LINES OF MAYBE SOME BACK-UP SOMETIME SOON?
PRESLEY DURAY, YOU GET OUT OF THERE UNTIL BACK-UP ARRIVES. THAT'S AN ORDER!
TOO MUCH FOR THE MAN

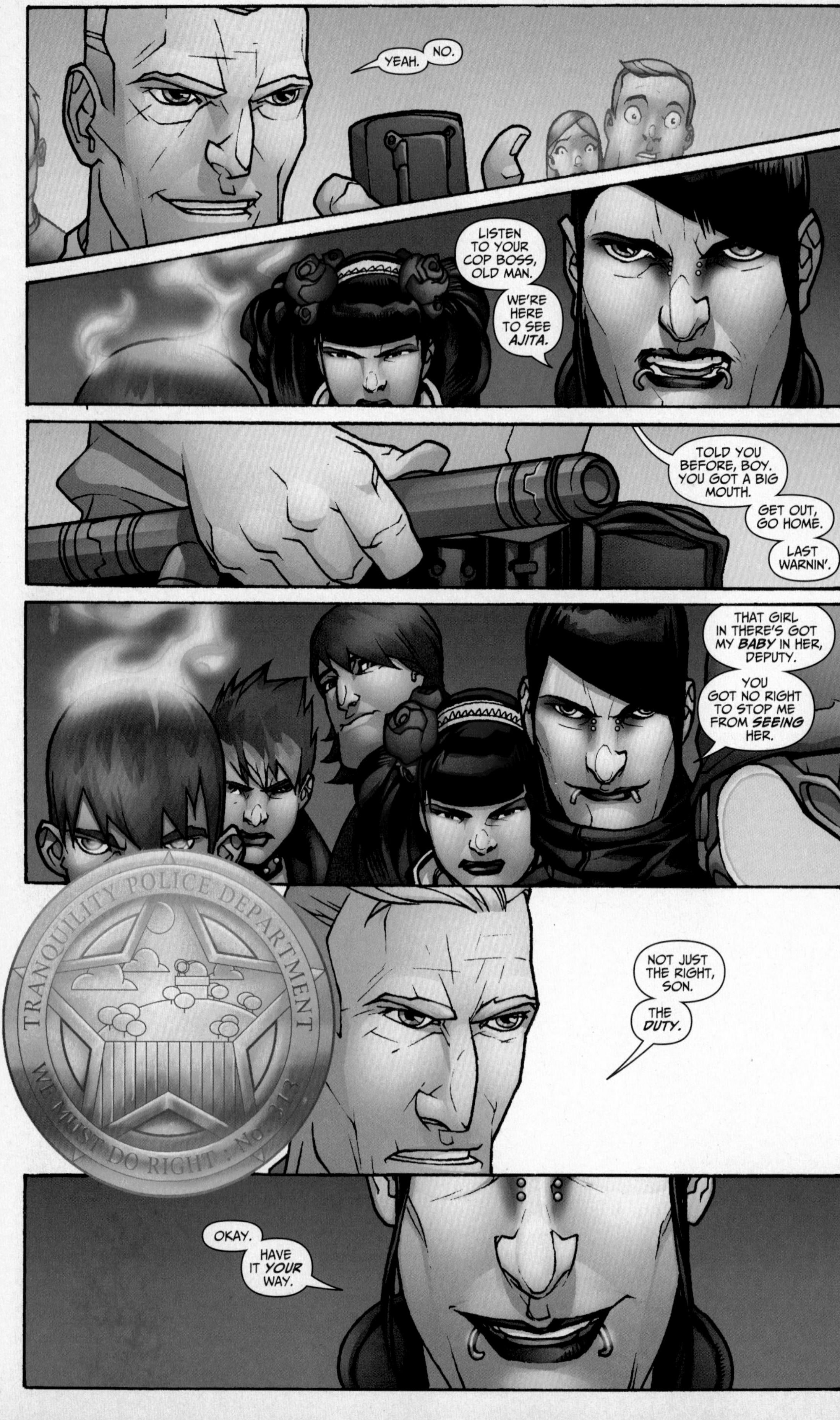
YEAH.
NO.
LISTEN TO YOUR COP BOSS, OLD MAN.
WE'RE HERE TO SEE AJITA.
TOLD YOU BEFORE, BOY. YOU GOT A BIG MOUTH.
GET OUT, GO HOME.
LAST WARNIN'.
THAT GIRL IN THERE'S GOT MY BABY IN HER, DEPUTY.
YOU GOT NO RIGHT TO STOP ME FROM SEEING HER.
TRANQUILITY POLICE DEPARTMENT
WE MUST DO RIGHT : No. 313
NOT JUST THE RIGHT, SON.
THE DUTY.
OKAY.
HAVE IT YOUR WAY.

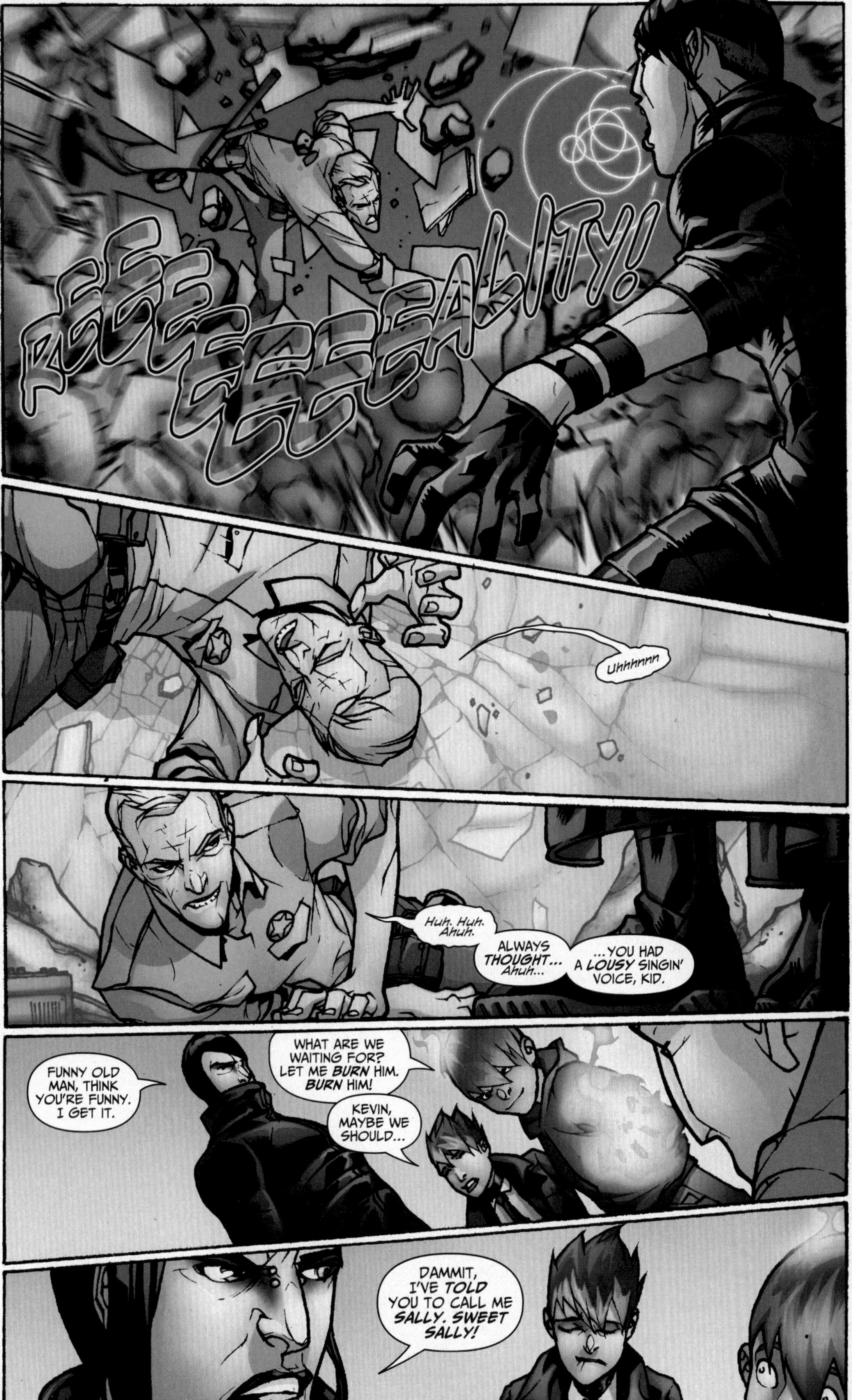
REEEEEEEEEEEEEEEEEEEEEEALITY!
Uhhhhnn
Huh. Huh. Ahuh.
ALWAYS THOUGHT... Ahuh...
...YOU HAD A LOUSY SINGIN' VOICE, KID.
FUNNY OLD MAN, THINK YOU'RE FUNNY. I GET IT.
WHAT ARE WE WAITING FOR? LET ME BURN HIM. BURN HIM!
KEVIN, MAYBE WE SHOULD...
DAMMIT, I'VE TOLD YOU TO CALL ME SALLY. SWEET SALLY!

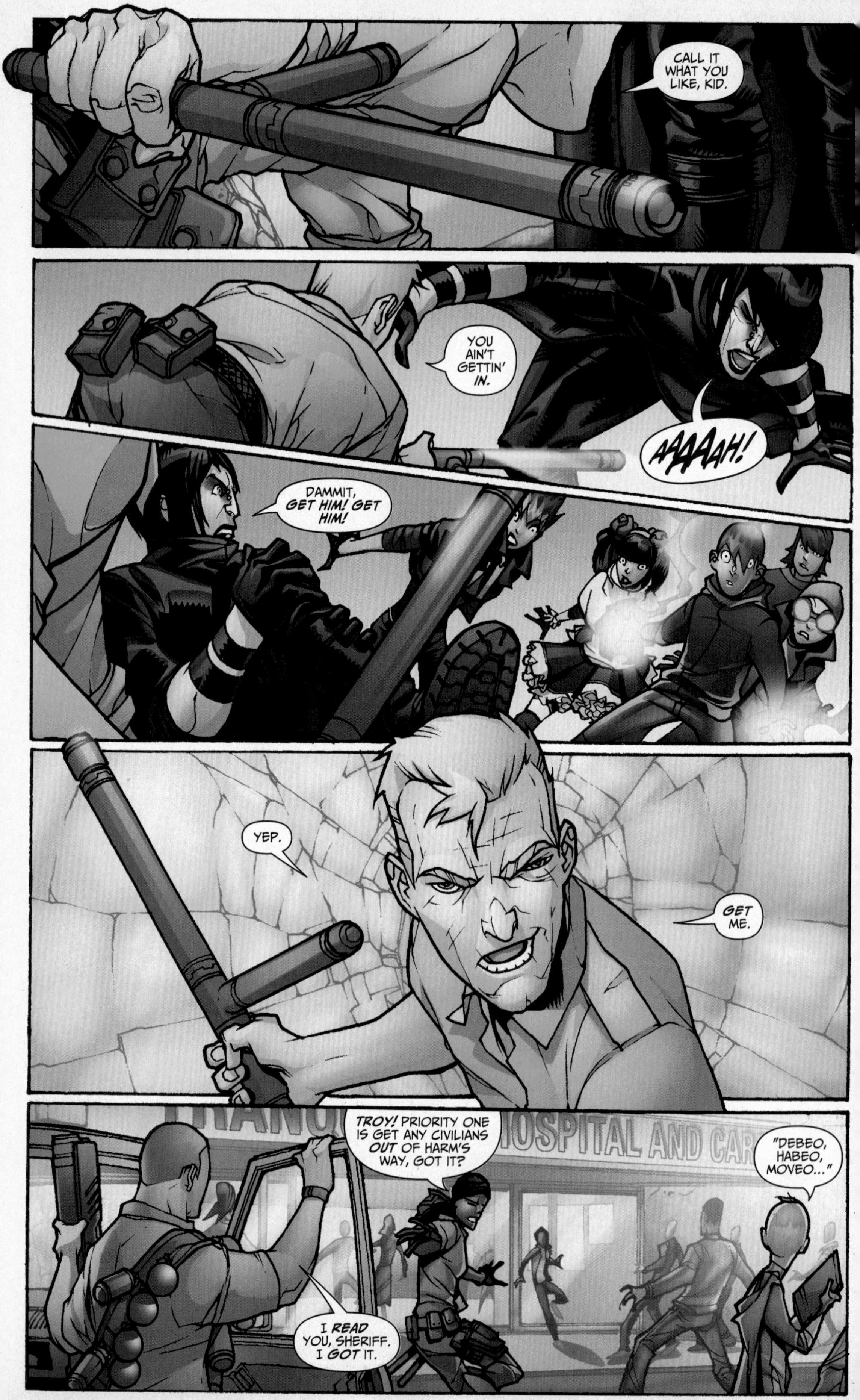
CALL IT WHAT YOU LIKE, KID.
YOU AIN'T GETTIN' IN.
AAAAAH!
DAMMIT, GET HIM! GET HIM!
YEP.
GET ME.
TROY! PRIORITY ONE IS GET ANY CIVILIANS OUT OF HARM'S WAY, GOT IT?
HOSPITAL AND CAR
"DEBEO, HABEO, MOVEO..."
I READ YOU, SHERIFF. I GOT IT.

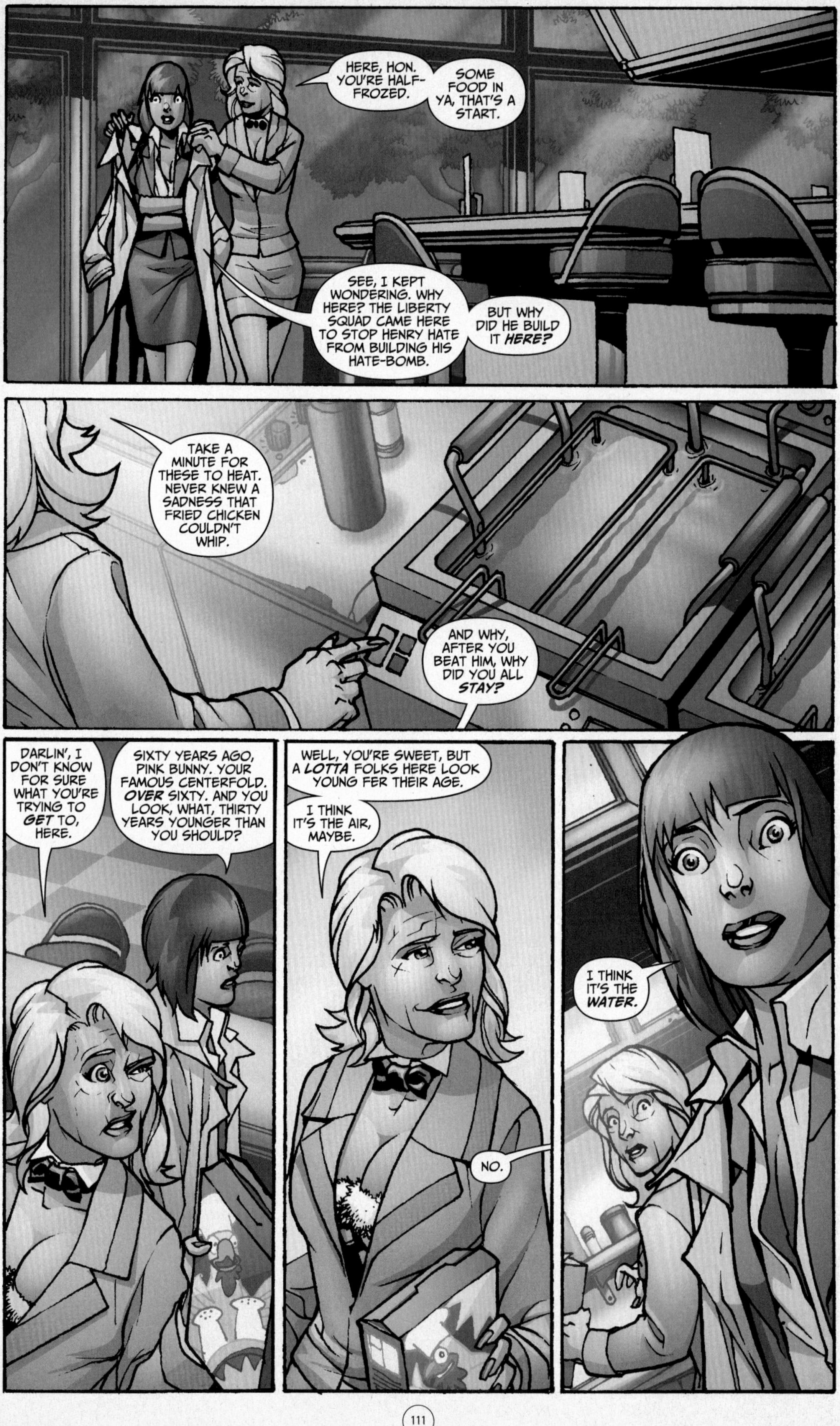
HERE, HON. YOU'RE HALF-FROZED.
SOME FOOD IN YA, THAT'S A START.
SEE, I KEPT WONDERING. WHY HERE? THE LIBERTY SQUAD CAME HERE TO STOP HENRY HATE FROM BUILDING HIS HATE-BOMB.
BUT WHY DID HE BUILD IT HERE?
TAKE A MINUTE FOR THESE TO HEAT. NEVER KNEW A SADNESS THAT FRIED CHICKEN COULDN'T WHIP.
AND WHY, AFTER YOU BEAT HIM, WHY DID YOU ALL STAY?
DARLIN', I DON'T KNOW FOR SURE WHAT YOU'RE TRYING TO GET TO, HERE.
SIXTY YEARS AGO, PINK BUNNY. YOUR FAMOUS CENTERFOLD. OVER SIXTY. AND YOU LOOK, WHAT, THIRTY YEARS YOUNGER THAN YOU SHOULD?
WELL, YOU'RE SWEET, BUT A LOTTA FOLKS HERE LOOK YOUNG FER THEIR AGE.
I THINK IT'S THE AIR, MAYBE.
NO.
I THINK IT'S THE WATER.

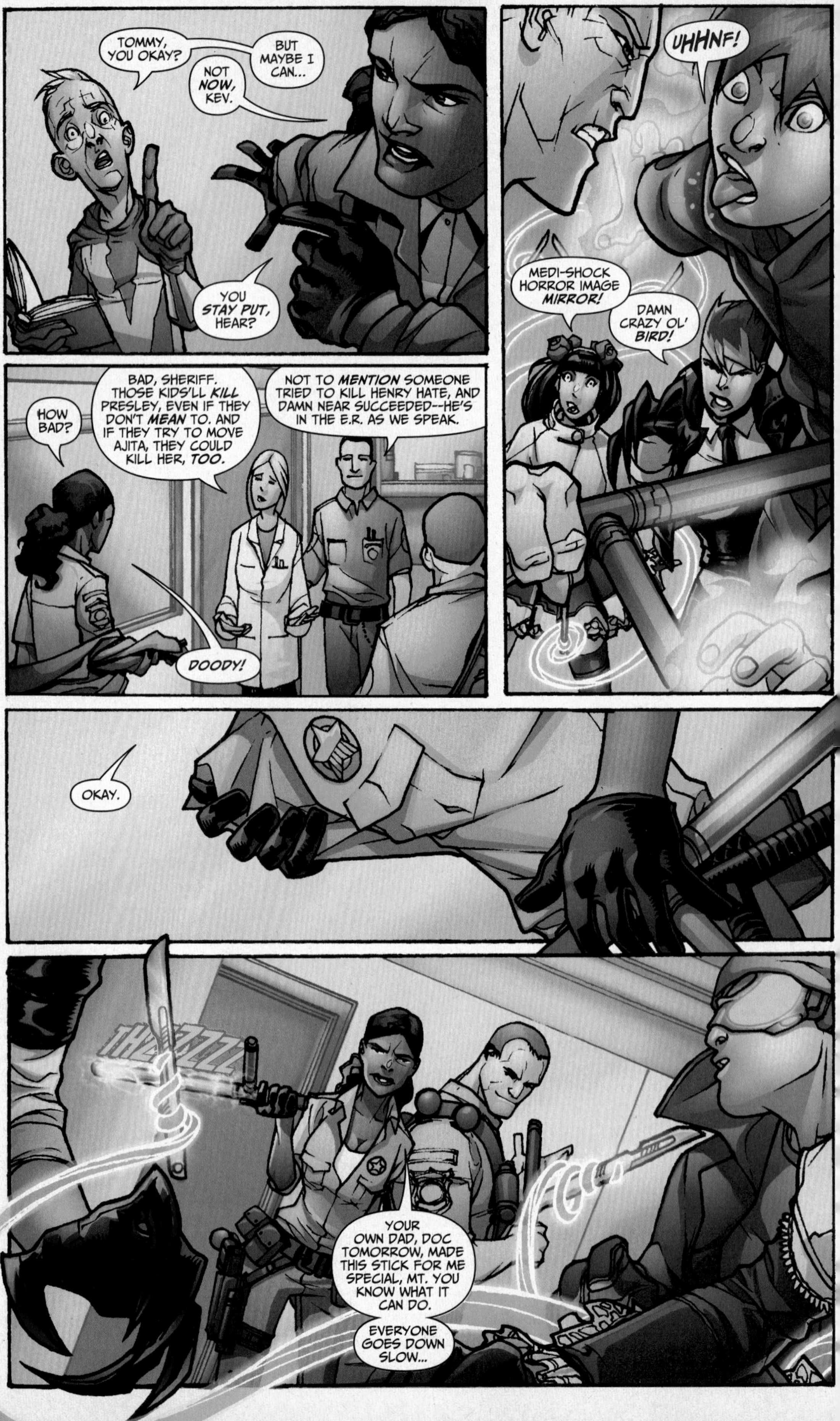
TOMMY, YOU OKAY?
BUT MAYBE I CAN...
NOT *NOW*, KEV.
YOU *STAY PUT*, HEAR?
UHHNF!
MEDI-SHOCK HORROR IMAGE *MIRROR!*
DAMN CRAZY OL' *BIRD!*
HOW BAD?
BAD, SHERIFF. THOSE KIDS'LL *KILL* PRESLEY, EVEN IF THEY DON'T *MEAN* TO. AND IF THEY TRY TO MOVE AJITA, THEY COULD KILL HER, *TOO*.
NOT TO *MENTION* SOMEONE TRIED TO KILL HENRY HATE, AND DAMN NEAR SUCCEEDED--HE'S IN THE E.R. AS WE SPEAK.
DOODY!
OKAY.
THZZZZZ
YOUR OWN DAD, DOC TOMORROW, MADE THIS STICK FOR ME SPECIAL, MT. YOU KNOW WHAT IT CAN DO.
EVERYONE GOES DOWN SLOW...

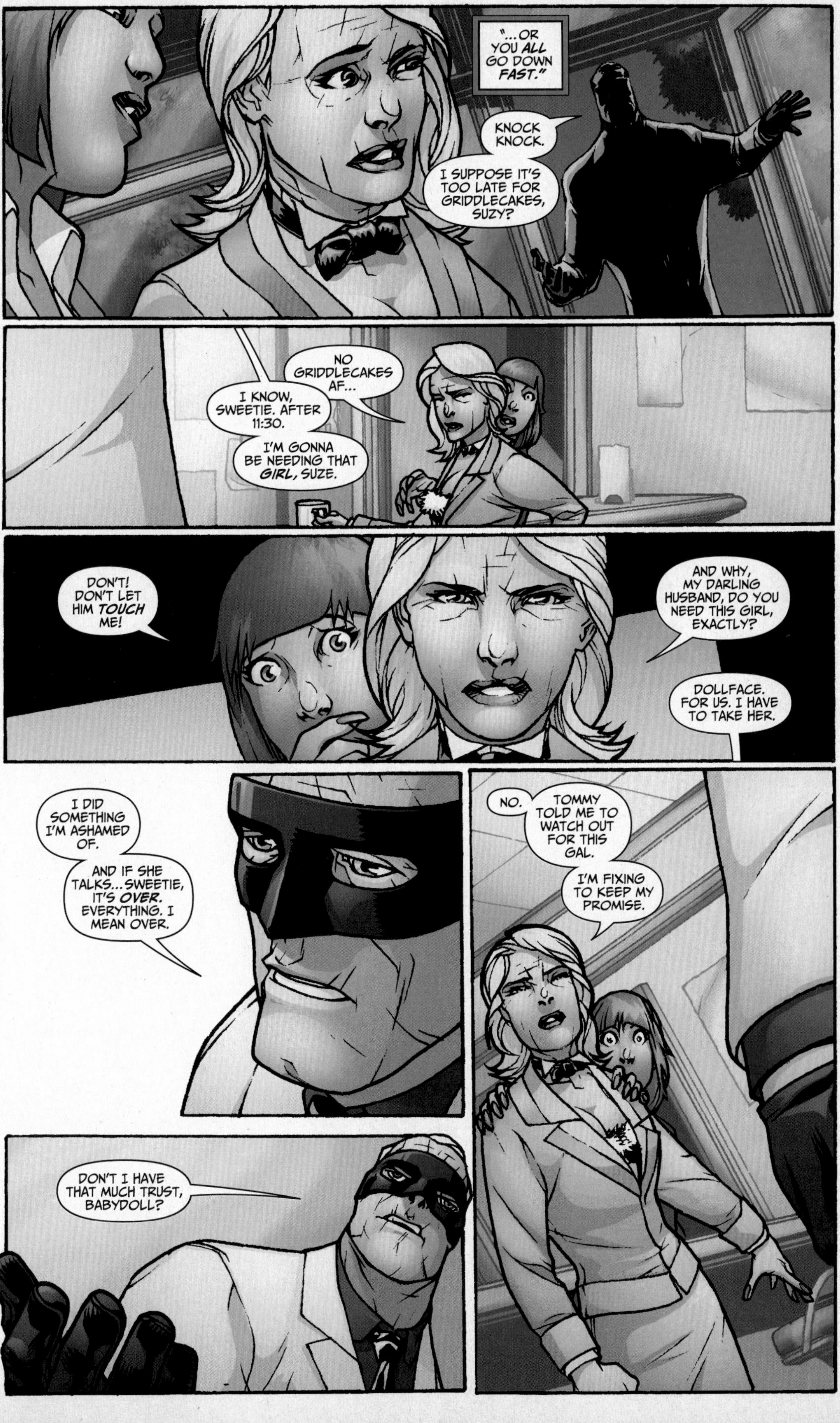
"...OR YOU ALL GO DOWN FAST."
KNOCK KNOCK.
I SUPPOSE IT'S TOO LATE FOR GRIDDLECAKES, SUZY?
NO GRIDDLECAKES AF...
I KNOW, SWEETIE. AFTER 11:30.
I'M GONNA BE NEEDING THAT GIRL, SUZE.
DON'T! DON'T LET HIM TOUCH ME!
AND WHY, MY DARLING HUSBAND, DO YOU NEED THIS GIRL, EXACTLY?
DOLLFACE. FOR US. I HAVE TO TAKE HER.
I DID SOMETHING I'M ASHAMED OF.
AND IF SHE TALKS...SWEETIE, IT'S OVER. EVERYTHING. I MEAN OVER.
NO.
TOMMY TOLD ME TO WATCH OUT FOR THIS GAL.
I'M FIXING TO KEEP MY PROMISE.
DON'T I HAVE THAT MUCH TRUST, BABYDOLL?

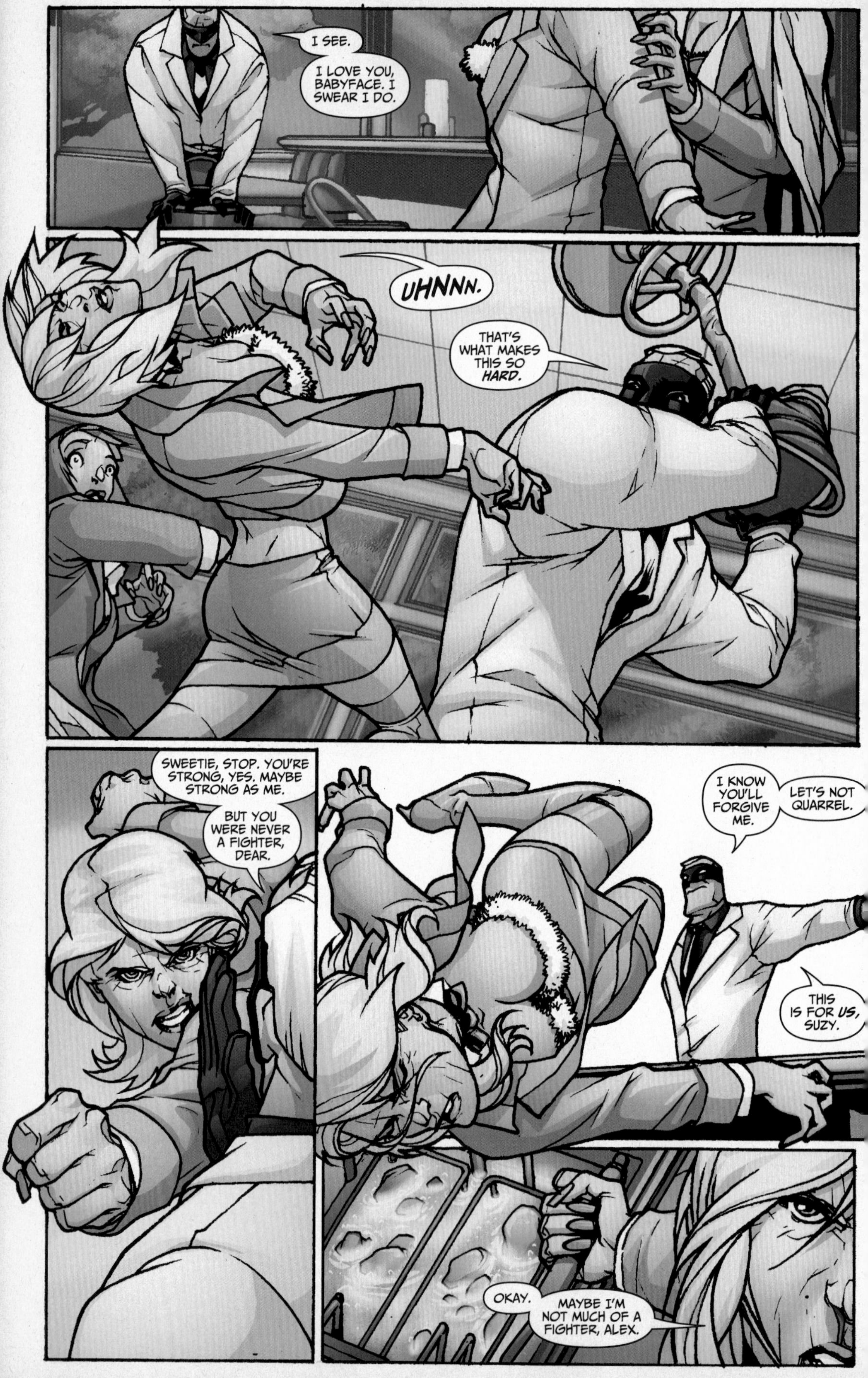

I SEE.
I LOVE YOU, BABYFACE. I SWEAR I DO.
UHNNN.
THAT'S WHAT MAKES THIS SO HARD.
SWEETIE, STOP. YOU'RE STRONG, YES. MAYBE STRONG AS ME.
BUT YOU WERE NEVER A FIGHTER, DEAR.
I KNOW YOU'LL FORGIVE ME.
LET'S NOT QUARREL.
THIS IS FOR US, SUZY.
OKAY.
MAYBE I'M NOT MUCH OF A FIGHTER, ALEX.

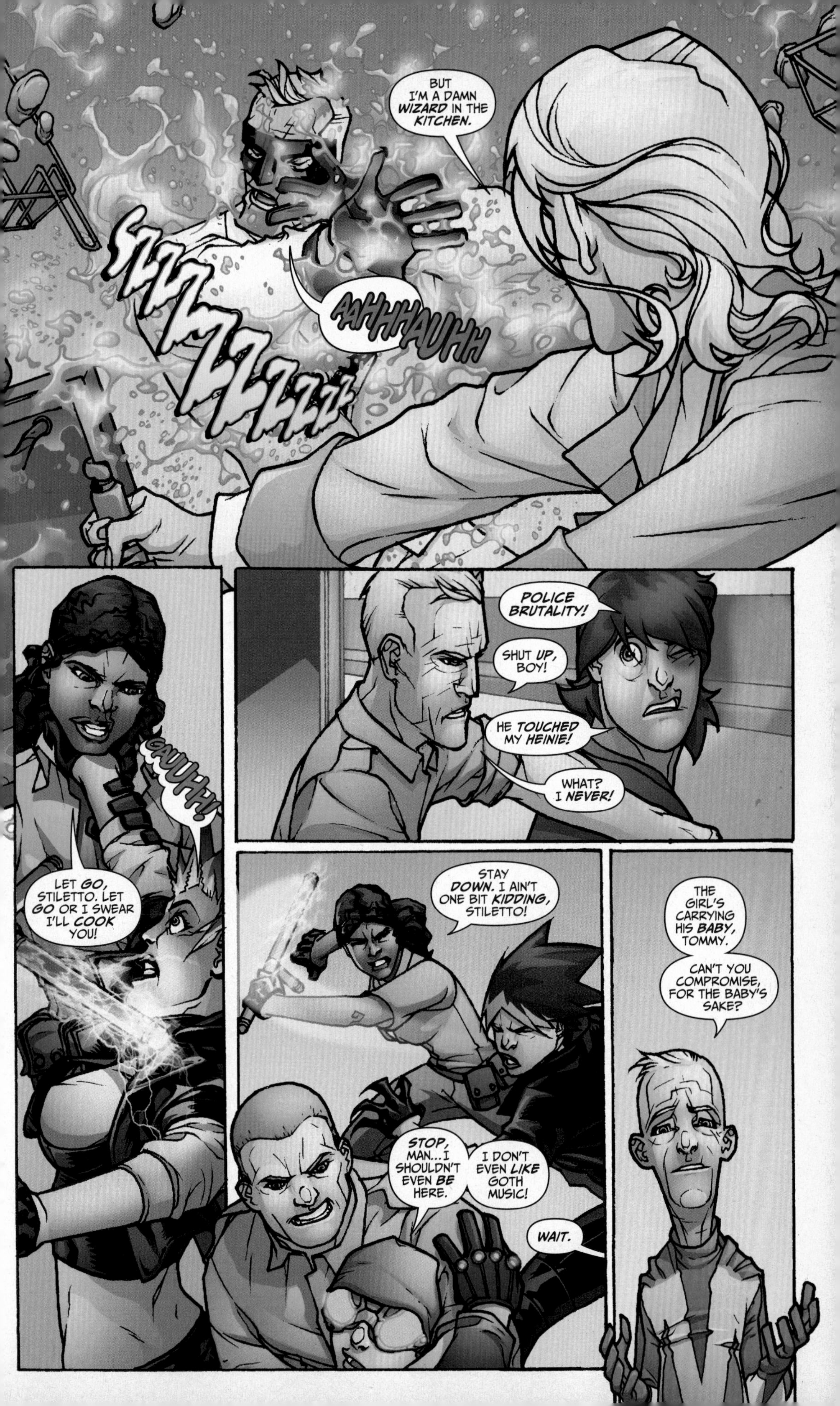
BUT I'M A DAMN *WIZARD* IN THE *KITCHEN*.
SZZZZZZZZZZ
AAHHHAUHH
POLICE BRUTALITY!
SHUT UP, BOY!
HE *TOUCHED* MY *HEINIE*!
WHAT? I *NEVER*!
GAUUHH!
LET *GO*, STILETTO. LET *GO* OR I SWEAR I'LL *COOK* YOU!
STAY *DOWN*. I AIN'T ONE BIT *KIDDING*, STILETTO!
STOP, MAN... I SHOULDN'T EVEN *BE* HERE.
I DON'T EVEN *LIKE* GOTH MUSIC!
THE GIRL'S CARRYING HIS *BABY*, TOMMY.
CAN'T YOU COMPROMISE, FOR THE BABY'S SAKE?
WAIT.

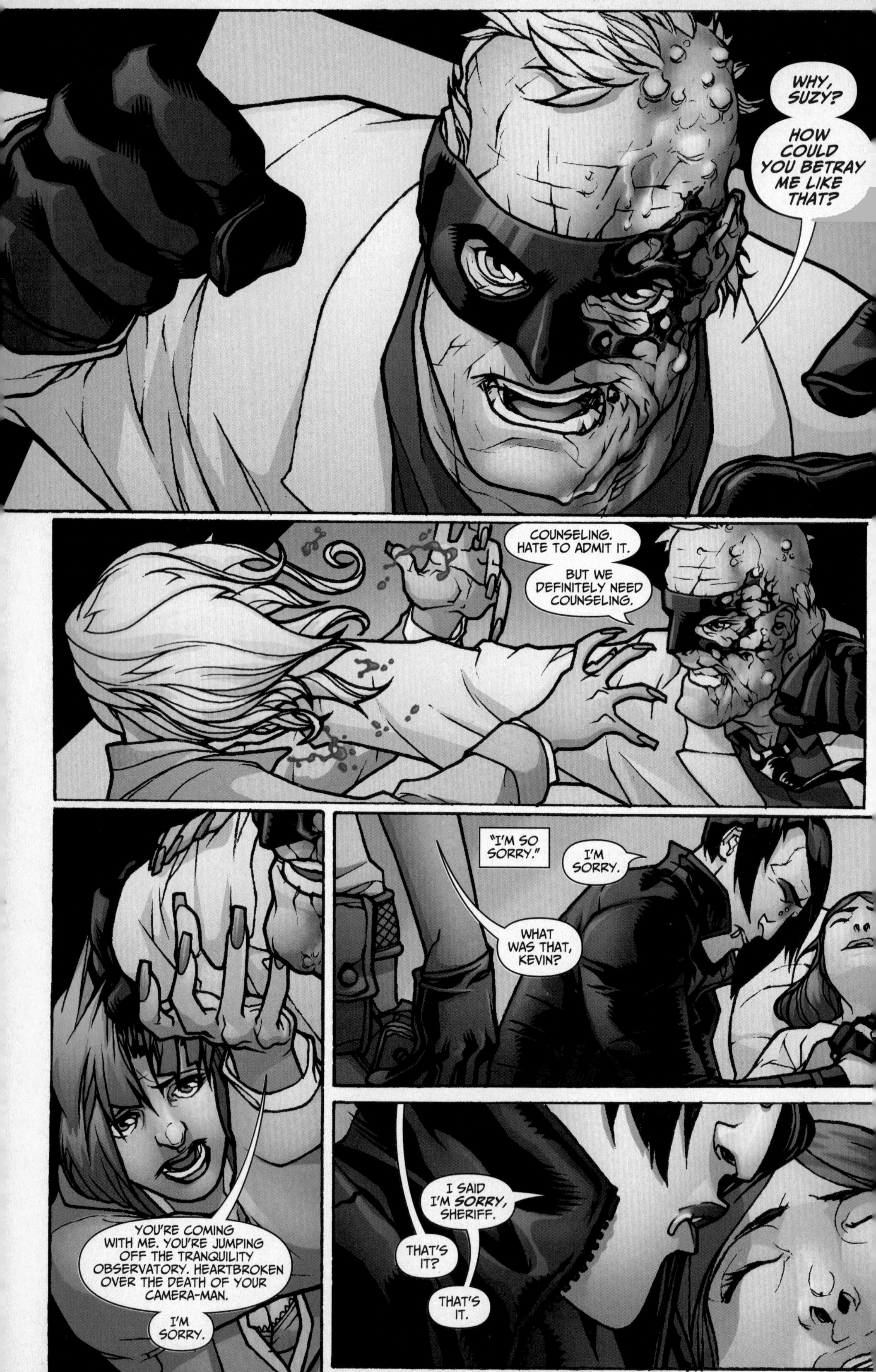
WHY, SUZY?
HOW COULD YOU BETRAY ME LIKE THAT?
COUNSELING. HATE TO ADMIT IT.
BUT WE DEFINITELY NEED COUNSELING.
"I'M SO SORRY."
I'M SORRY.
WHAT WAS THAT, KEVIN?
YOU'RE COMING WITH ME. YOU'RE JUMPING OFF THE TRANQUILITY OBSERVATORY. HEARTBROKEN OVER THE DEATH OF YOUR CAMERA-MAN.
I'M SORRY.
I SAID I'M SORRY, SHERIFF.
THAT'S IT?
THAT'S IT.

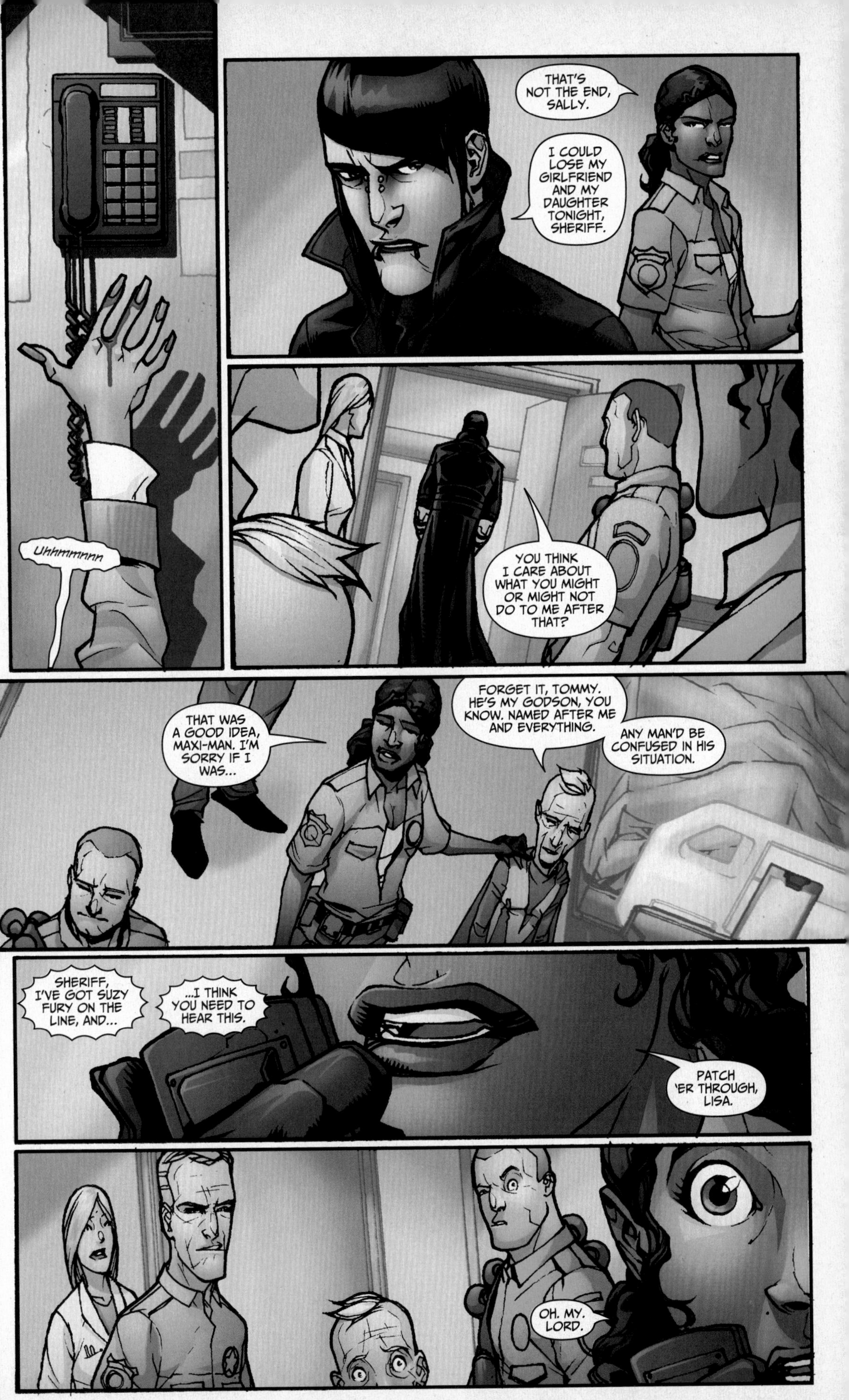
THAT'S NOT THE END, SALLY.
I COULD LOSE MY GIRLFRIEND AND MY DAUGHTER TONIGHT, SHERIFF.
Uhhmmmnn
YOU THINK I CARE ABOUT WHAT YOU MIGHT OR MIGHT NOT DO TO ME AFTER THAT?
THAT WAS A GOOD IDEA, MAXI-MAN. I'M SORRY IF I WAS...
FORGET IT, TOMMY. HE'S MY GODSON, YOU KNOW. NAMED AFTER ME AND EVERYTHING.
ANY MAN'D BE CONFUSED IN HIS SITUATION.
SHERIFF, I'VE GOT SUZY FURY ON THE LINE, AND...
...I THINK YOU NEED TO HEAR THIS.
PATCH 'ER THROUGH, LISA.
OH. MY. LORD.

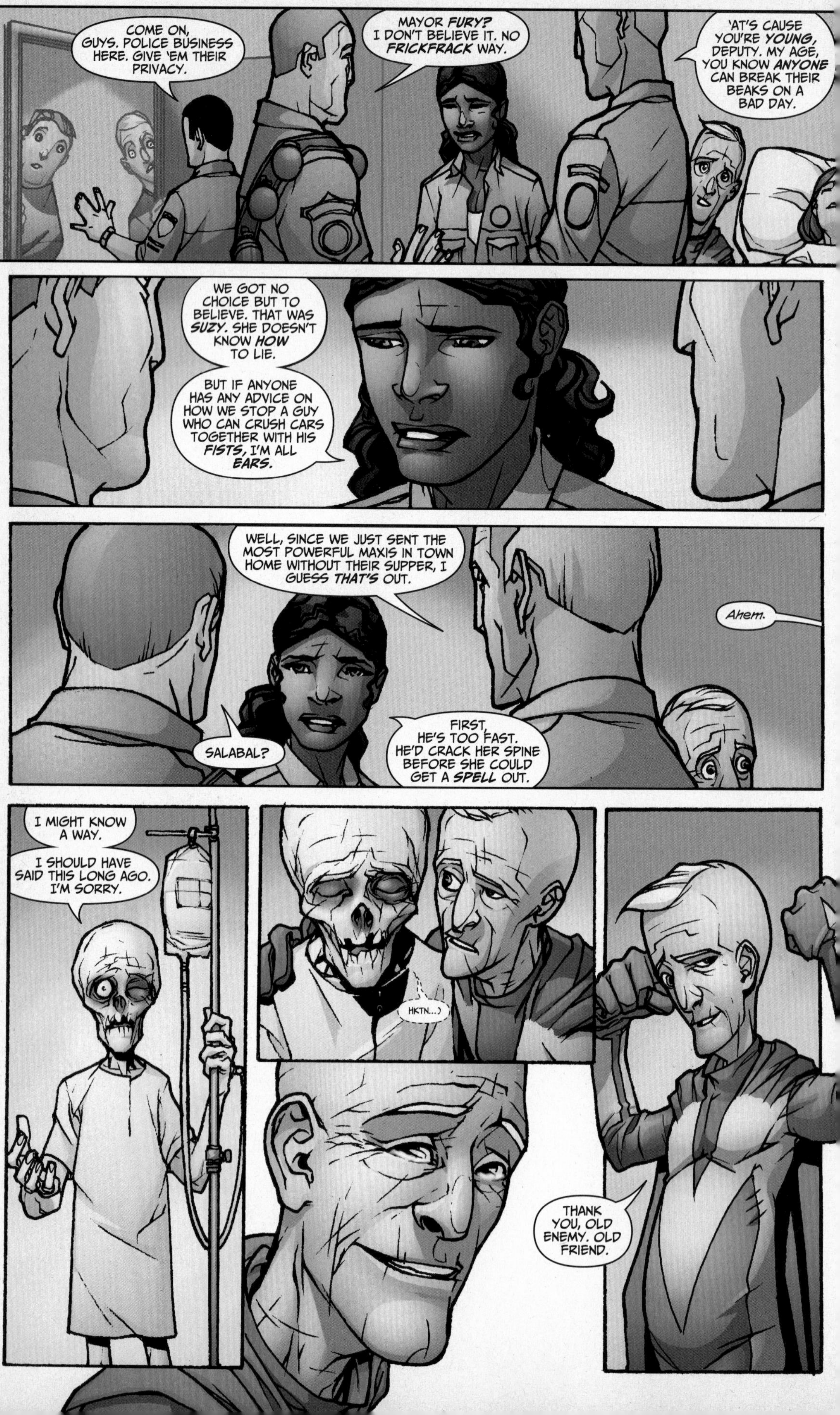
COME ON, GUYS. POLICE BUSINESS HERE. GIVE 'EM THEIR PRIVACY.
MAYOR FURY? I DON'T BELIEVE IT. NO FRICKFRACK WAY.
'AT'S CAUSE YOU'RE YOUNG, DEPUTY. MY AGE, YOU KNOW ANYONE CAN BREAK THEIR BEAKS ON A BAD DAY.
WE GOT NO CHOICE BUT TO BELIEVE. THAT WAS SUZY. SHE DOESN'T KNOW HOW TO LIE.
BUT IF ANYONE HAS ANY ADVICE ON HOW WE STOP A GUY WHO CAN CRUSH CARS TOGETHER WITH HIS FISTS, I'M ALL EARS.
WELL, SINCE WE JUST SENT THE MOST POWERFUL MAXIS IN TOWN HOME WITHOUT THEIR SUPPER, I GUESS THAT'S OUT.
Ahem.
SALABAL?
FIRST, HE'S TOO FAST. HE'D CRACK HER SPINE BEFORE SHE COULD GET A SPELL OUT.
I MIGHT KNOW A WAY.
I SHOULD HAVE SAID THIS LONG AGO. I'M SORRY.
HKTN...)
THANK YOU, OLD ENEMY. OLD FRIEND.

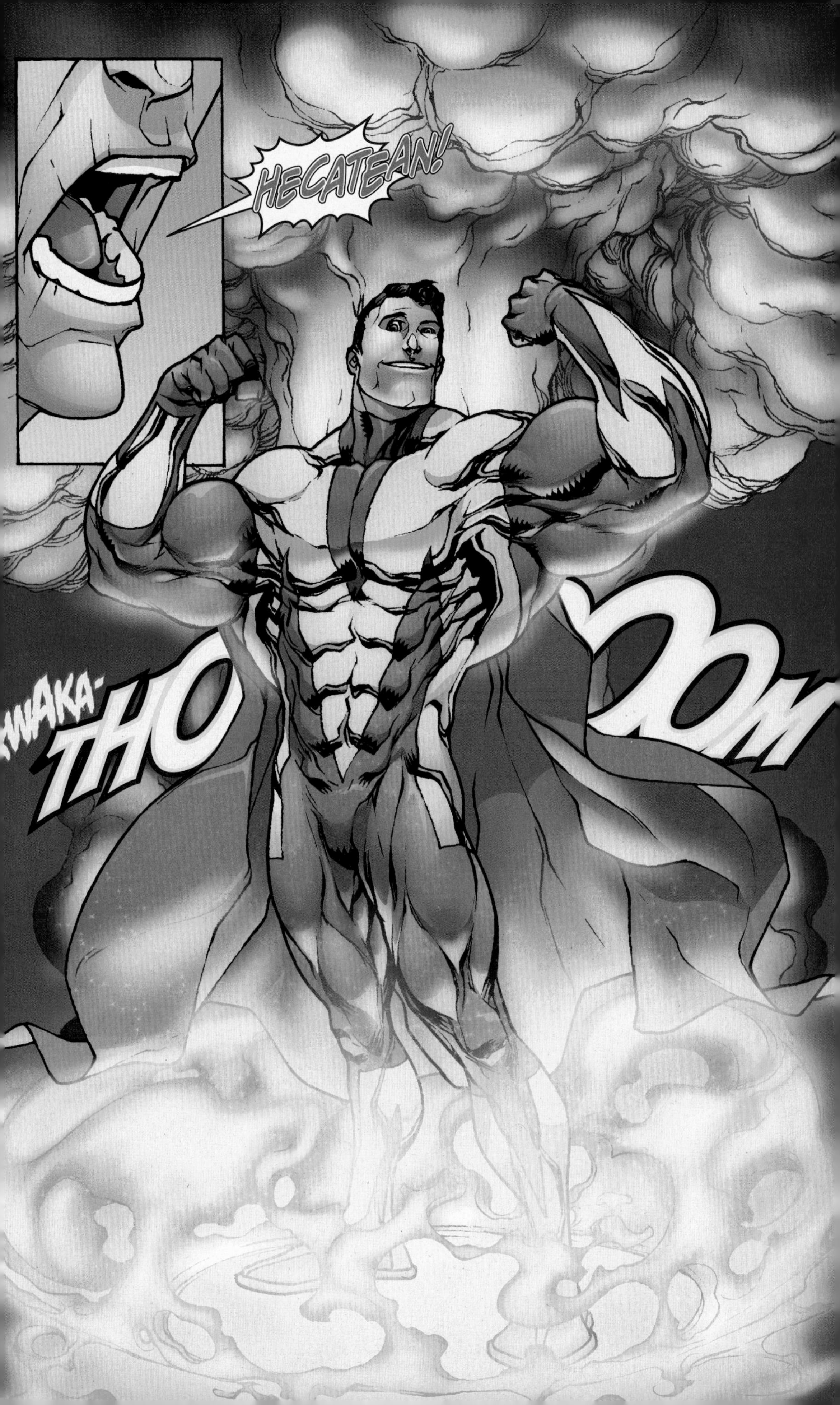
HECATEAN!
WAKA-
THOOOM

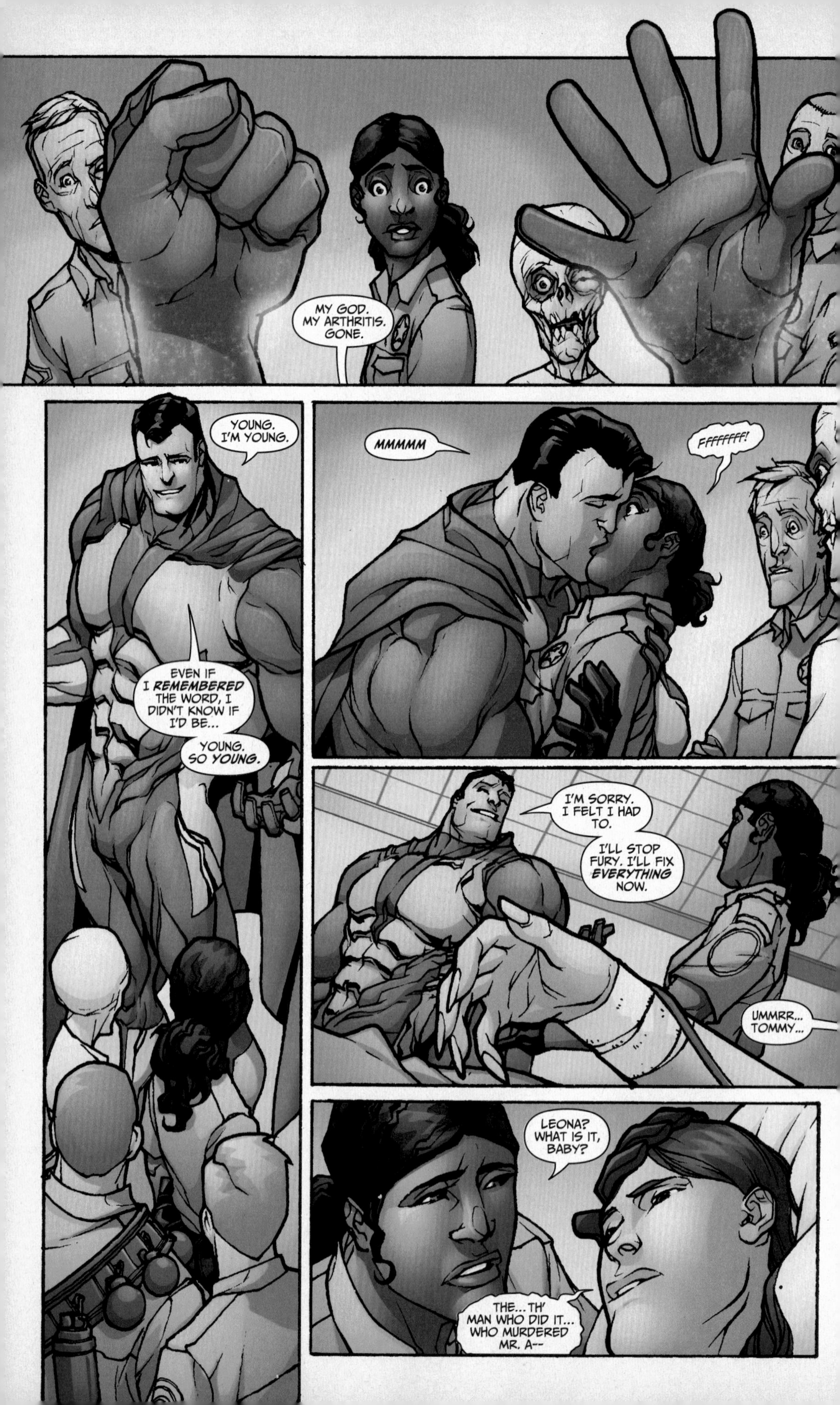
MY GOD.
MY ARTHRITIS.
GONE.
YOUNG.
I'M YOUNG.
EVEN IF I *REMEMBERED* THE WORD, I DIDN'T KNOW IF I'D BE...
YOUNG. SO *YOUNG.*
MMMMM
FFFFFFFF!
I'M SORRY. I FELT I HAD TO.
I'LL STOP FURY. I'LL FIX *EVERYTHING* NOW.
UMMRR... TOMMY...
LEONA? WHAT IS IT, BABY?
THE... TH' MAN WHO DID IT... WHO MURDERED MR. A--

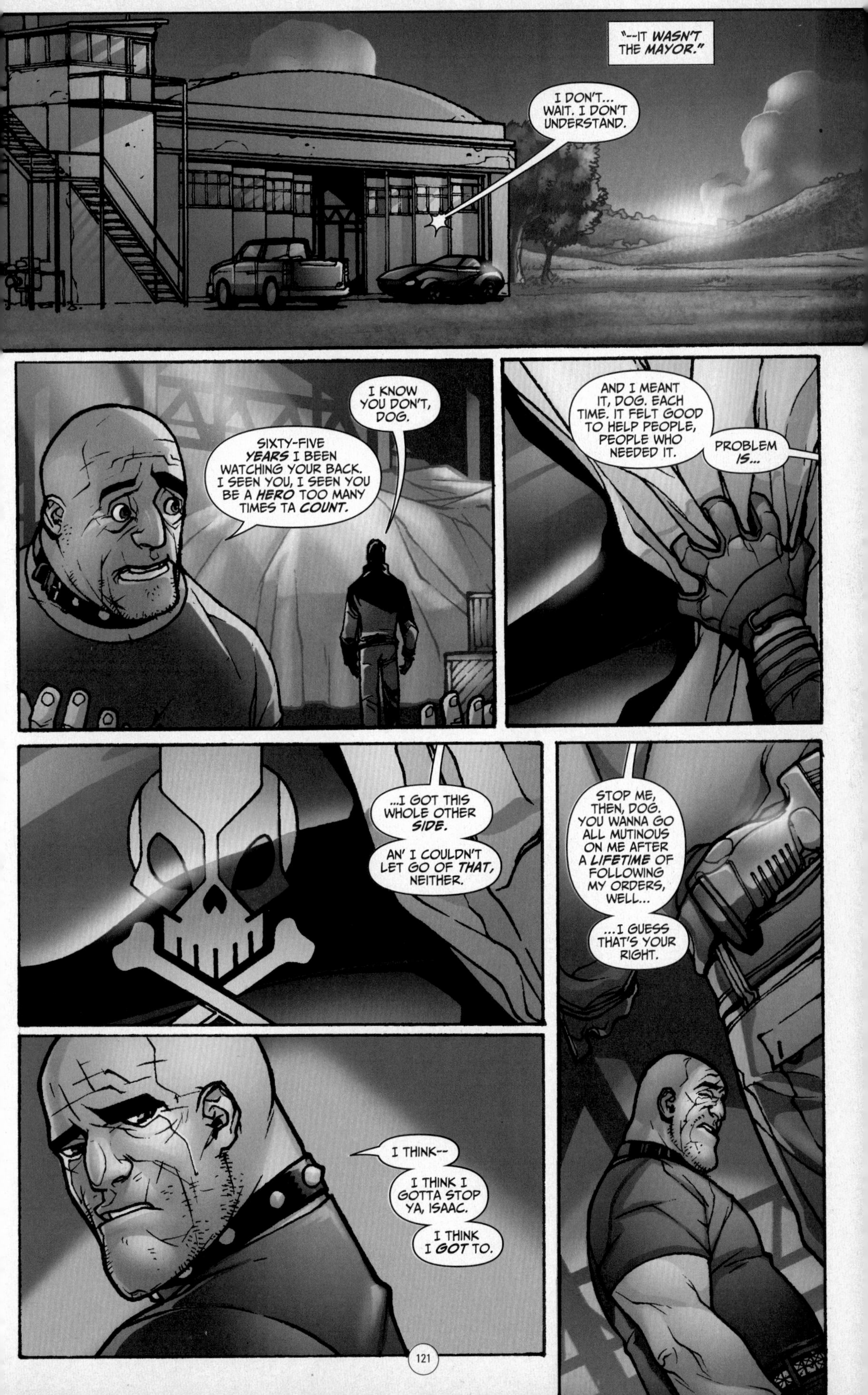
"--IT WASN'T THE MAYOR."
I DON'T... WAIT. I DON'T UNDERSTAND.
SIXTY-FIVE YEARS I BEEN WATCHING YOUR BACK. I SEEN YOU, I SEEN YOU BE A HERO TOO MANY TIMES TA COUNT.
I KNOW YOU DON'T, DOG.
AND I MEANT IT, DOG. EACH TIME. IT FELT GOOD TO HELP PEOPLE, PEOPLE WHO NEEDED IT.
PROBLEM IS...
...I GOT THIS WHOLE OTHER SIDE.
AN' I COULDN'T LET GO OF THAT, NEITHER.
I THINK--
I THINK I GOTTA STOP YA, ISAAC.
I THINK I GOT TO.
STOP ME, THEN, DOG. YOU WANNA GO ALL MUTINOUS ON ME AFTER A LIFETIME OF FOLLOWING MY ORDERS, WELL...
...I GUESS THAT'S YOUR RIGHT.

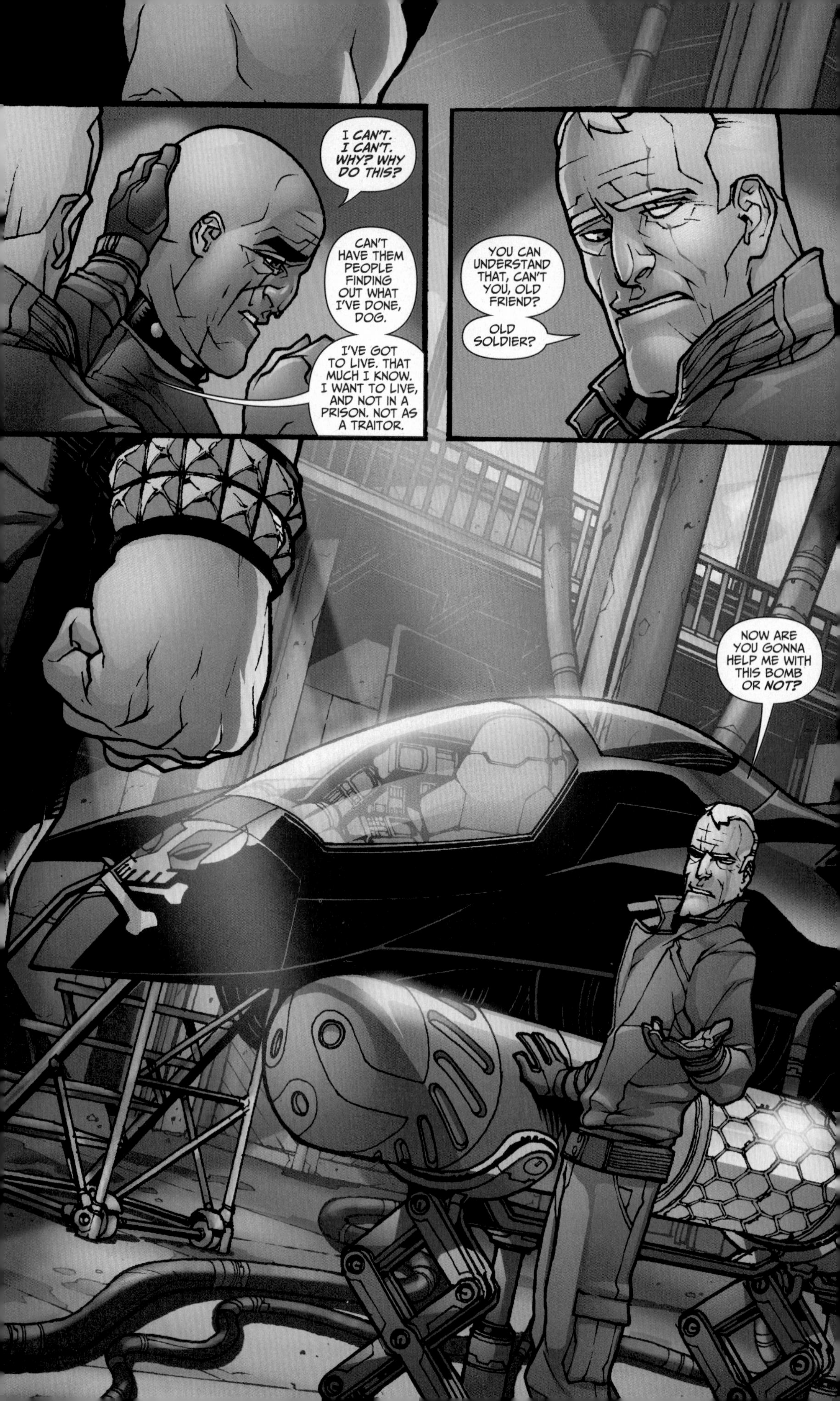
I CAN'T. I CAN'T. WHY? WHY DO THIS?
CAN'T HAVE THEM PEOPLE FINDING OUT WHAT I'VE DONE, DOG.
I'VE GOT TO LIVE. THAT MUCH I KNOW. I WANT TO LIVE, AND NOT IN A PRISON. NOT AS A TRAITOR.
YOU CAN UNDERSTAND THAT, CAN'T YOU, OLD FRIEND?
OLD SOLDIER?
NOW ARE YOU GONNA HELP ME WITH THIS BOMB OR NOT?

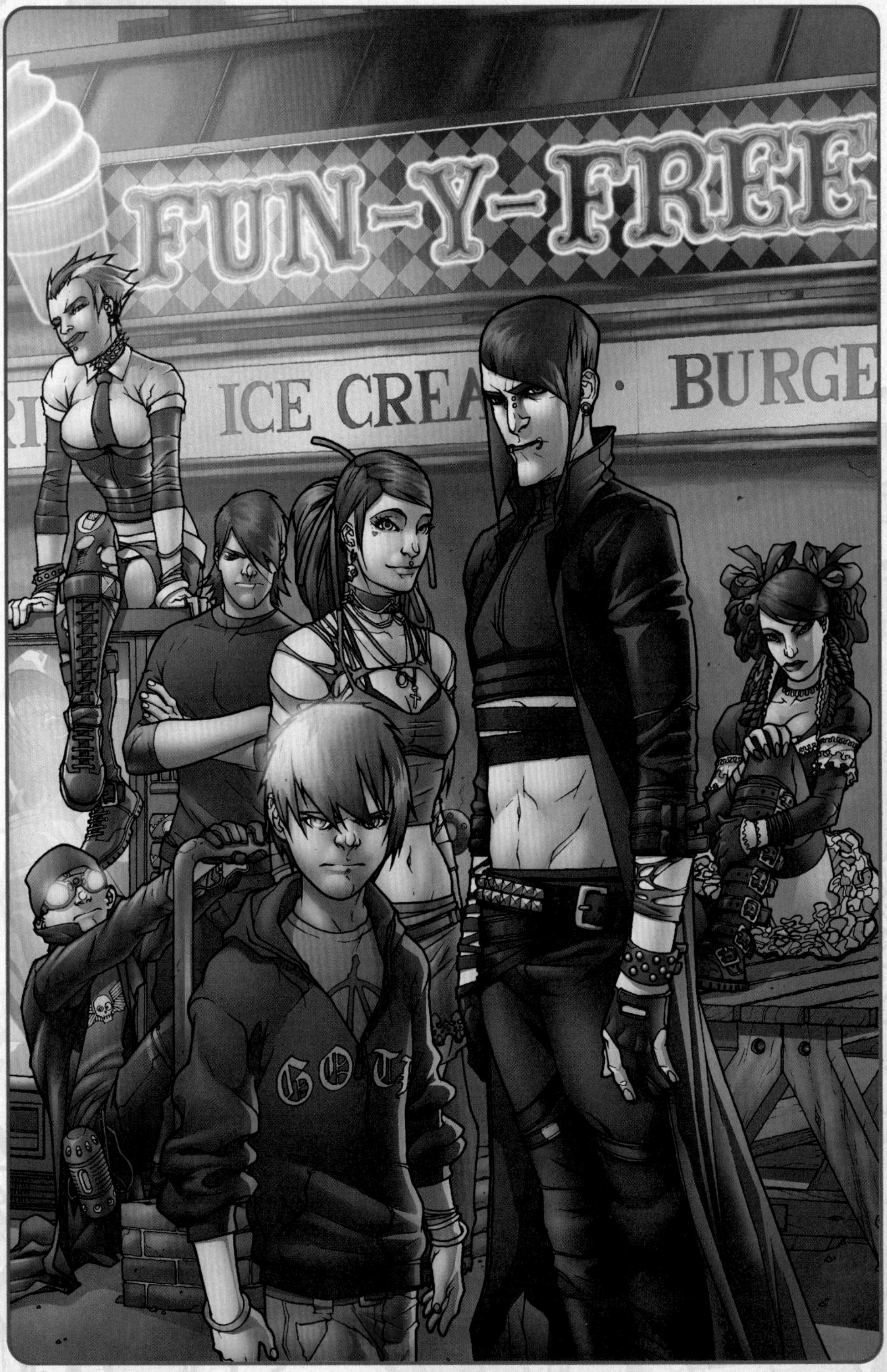
FUN-Y-FREE
ICE CREA
BURGE
GOT

Cover 3

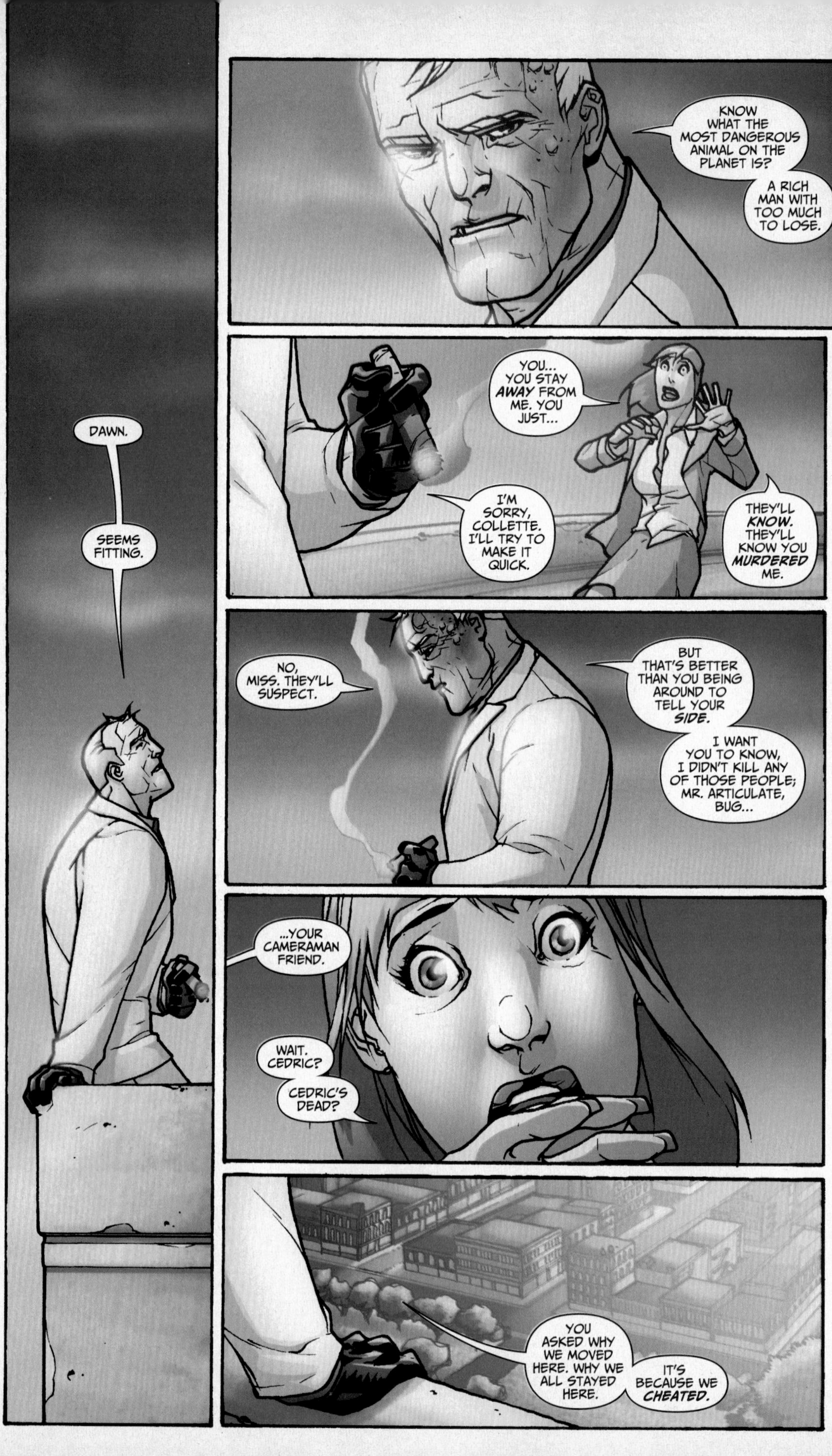

KNOW WHAT THE MOST DANGEROUS ANIMAL ON THE PLANET IS?
A RICH MAN WITH TOO MUCH TO LOSE.
DAWN.
SEEMS FITTING.
YOU... YOU STAY **AWAY** FROM ME. YOU JUST...
I'M SORRY, COLLETTE. I'LL TRY TO MAKE IT QUICK.
THEY'LL **KNOW.** THEY'LL KNOW YOU **MURDERED** ME.
NO, MISS. THEY'LL SUSPECT.
BUT THAT'S BETTER THAN YOU BEING AROUND TO TELL YOUR **SIDE.**
I WANT YOU TO KNOW, I DIDN'T KILL ANY OF THOSE PEOPLE; MR. ARTICULATE, BUG...
...YOUR CAMERAMAN FRIEND.
WAIT. CEDRIC?
CEDRIC'S DEAD?
YOU ASKED WHY WE MOVED HERE. WHY WE ALL STAYED HERE.
IT'S BECAUSE WE **CHEATED.**

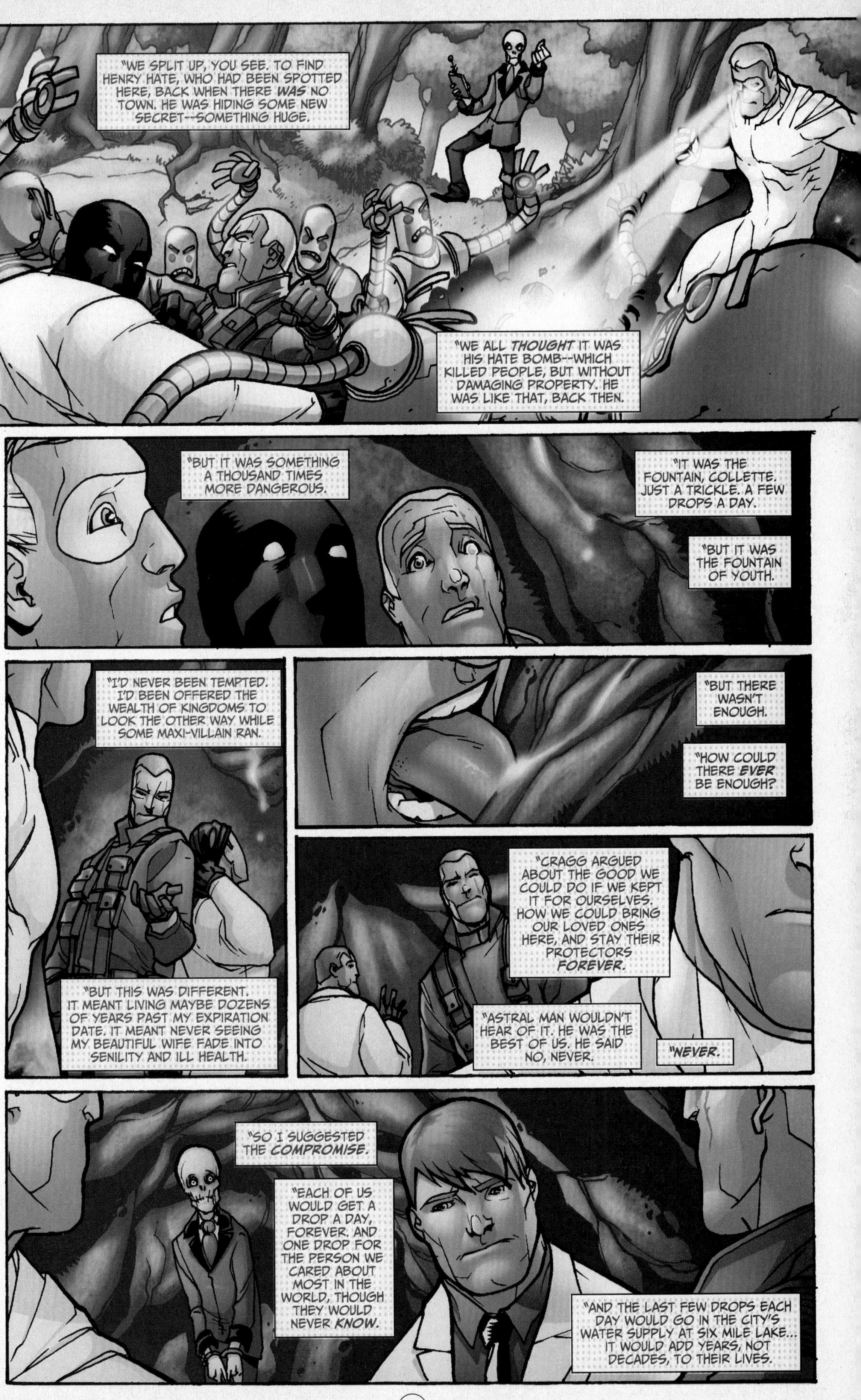
"WE SPLIT UP, YOU SEE. TO FIND HENRY HATE, WHO HAD BEEN SPOTTED HERE, BACK WHEN THERE *WAS* NO TOWN. HE WAS HIDING SOME NEW SECRET--SOMETHING HUGE.
"WE ALL *THOUGHT* IT WAS HIS HATE BOMB--WHICH KILLED PEOPLE, BUT WITHOUT DAMAGING PROPERTY. HE WAS LIKE THAT, BACK THEN.
"BUT IT WAS SOMETHING A THOUSAND TIMES MORE DANGEROUS.
"IT WAS THE FOUNTAIN, COLLETTE. JUST A TRICKLE. A FEW DROPS A DAY.
"BUT IT WAS THE FOUNTAIN OF YOUTH.
"I'D NEVER BEEN TEMPTED. I'D BEEN OFFERED THE WEALTH OF KINGDOMS TO LOOK THE OTHER WAY WHILE SOME MAXI-VILLAIN RAN.
"BUT THIS WAS DIFFERENT. IT MEANT LIVING MAYBE DOZENS OF YEARS PAST MY EXPIRATION DATE. IT MEANT NEVER SEEING MY BEAUTIFUL WIFE FADE INTO SENILITY AND ILL HEALTH.
"BUT THERE WASN'T ENOUGH.
"HOW COULD THERE *EVER* BE ENOUGH?
"CRAGG ARGUED ABOUT THE GOOD WE COULD DO IF WE KEPT IT FOR OURSELVES. HOW WE COULD BRING OUR LOVED ONES HERE, AND STAY THEIR PROTECTORS *FOREVER*.
"ASTRAL MAN WOULDN'T HEAR OF IT. HE WAS THE BEST OF US. HE SAID NO, NEVER.
"*NEVER*.
"SO I SUGGESTED THE *COMPROMISE*.
"EACH OF US WOULD GET A DROP A DAY, FOREVER. AND ONE DROP FOR THE PERSON WE CARED ABOUT MOST IN THE WORLD, THOUGH THEY WOULD NEVER *KNOW*.
"AND THE LAST FEW DROPS EACH DAY WOULD GO IN THE CITY'S WATER SUPPLY AT SIX MILE LAKE... IT WOULD ADD YEARS, NOT DECADES, TO THEIR LIVES.

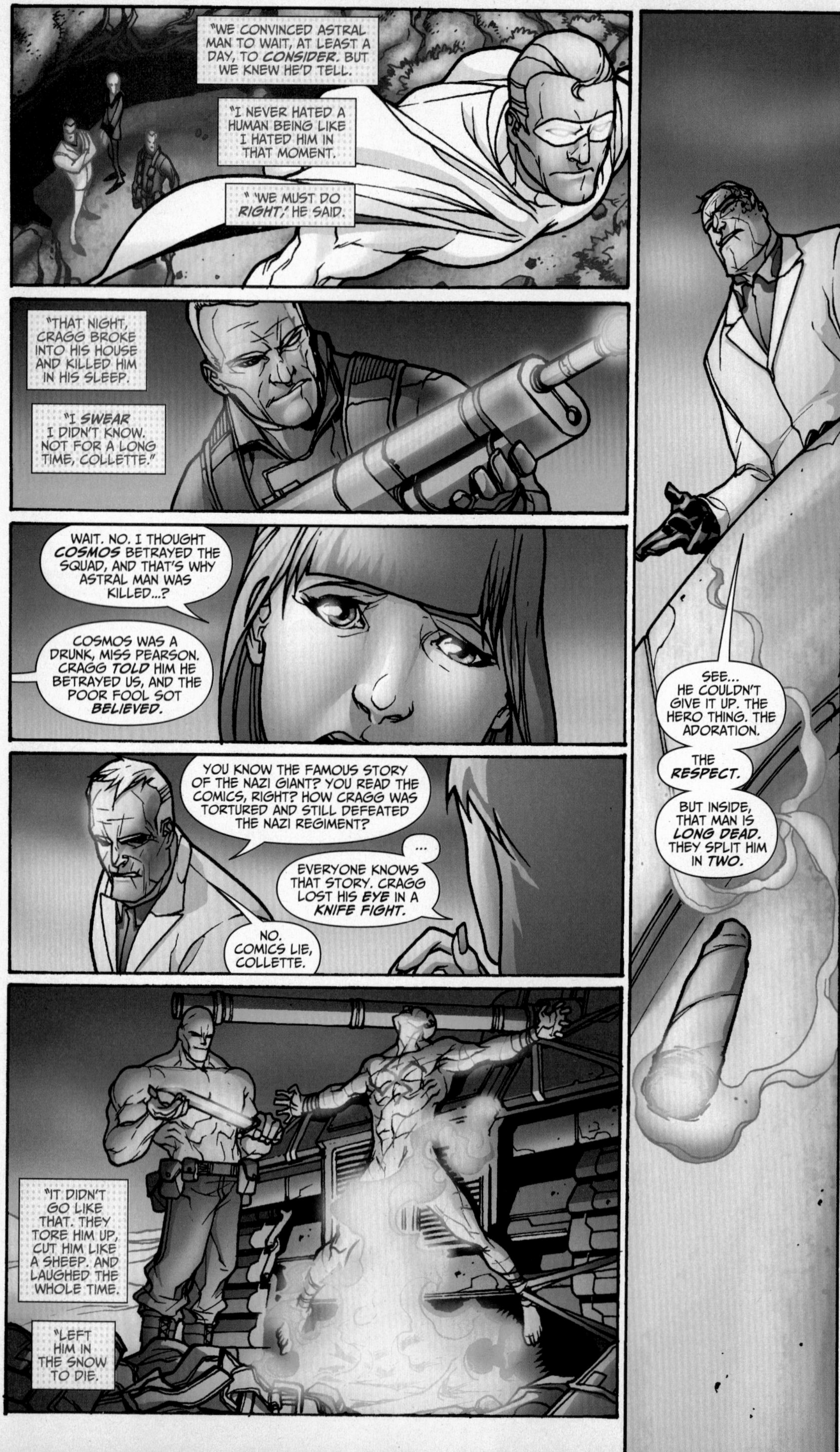
"WE CONVINCED ASTRAL MAN TO WAIT, AT LEAST A DAY, TO CONSIDER. BUT WE KNEW HE'D TELL.
"I NEVER HATED A HUMAN BEING LIKE I HATED HIM IN THAT MOMENT.
" 'WE MUST DO RIGHT,' HE SAID.
"THAT NIGHT, CRAGG BROKE INTO HIS HOUSE AND KILLED HIM IN HIS SLEEP.
"I SWEAR I DIDN'T KNOW. NOT FOR A LONG TIME, COLLETTE."
WAIT. NO. I THOUGHT COSMOS BETRAYED THE SQUAD, AND THAT'S WHY ASTRAL MAN WAS KILLED...?
COSMOS WAS A DRUNK, MISS PEARSON. CRAGG TOLD HIM HE BETRAYED US, AND THE POOR FOOL SOT BELIEVED.
YOU KNOW THE FAMOUS STORY OF THE NAZI GIANT? YOU READ THE COMICS, RIGHT? HOW CRAGG WAS TORTURED AND STILL DEFEATED THE NAZI REGIMENT?
...
EVERYONE KNOWS THAT STORY. CRAGG LOST HIS EYE IN A KNIFE FIGHT.
NO. COMICS LIE, COLLETTE.
"IT DIDN'T GO LIKE THAT. THEY TORE HIM UP, CUT HIM LIKE A SHEEP. AND LAUGHED THE WHOLE TIME.
"LEFT HIM IN THE SNOW TO DIE.
SEE... HE COULDN'T GIVE IT UP. THE HERO THING. THE ADORATION.
THE RESPECT.
BUT INSIDE, THAT MAN IS LONG DEAD. THEY SPLIT HIM IN TWO.

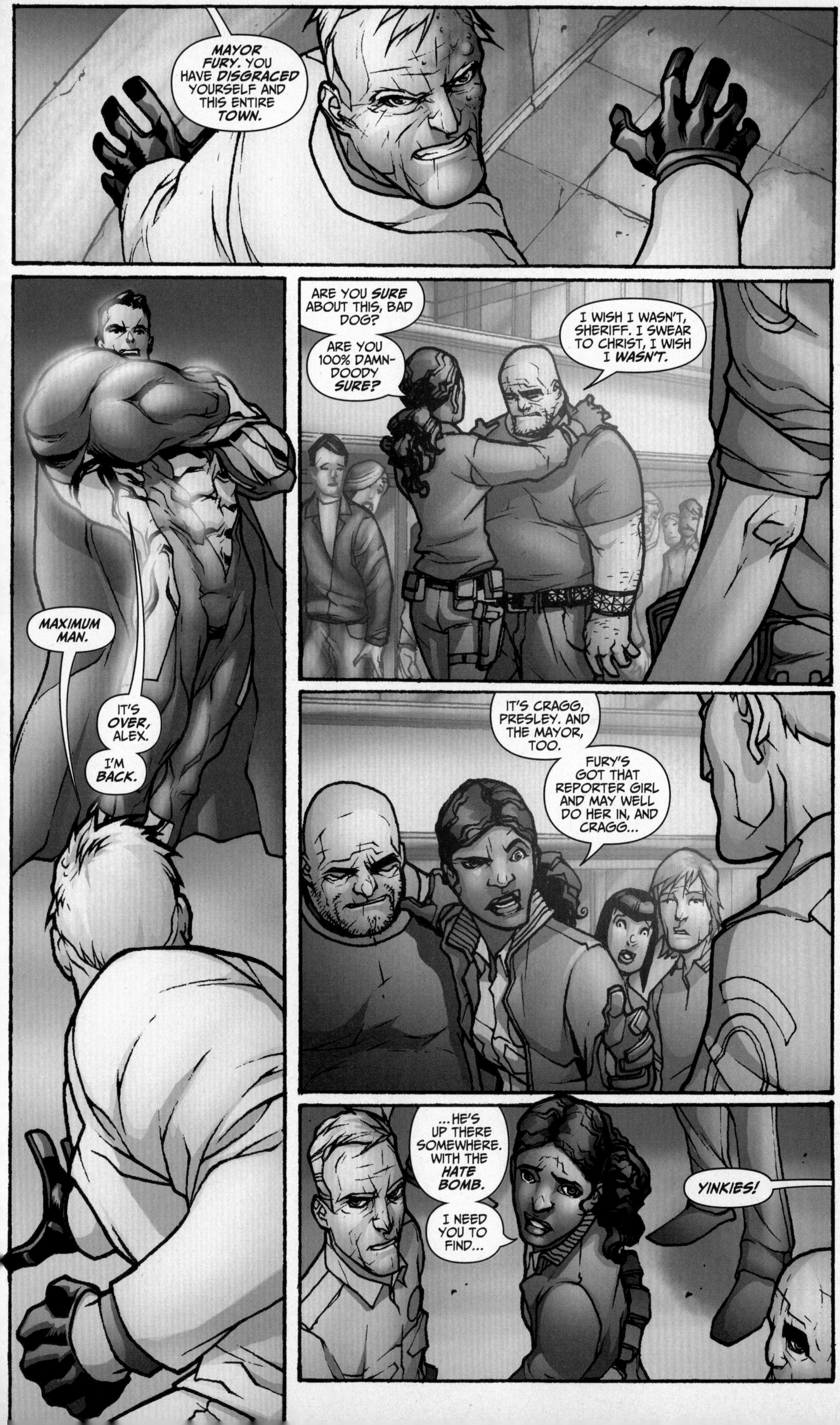
MAYOR FURY. YOU HAVE DISGRACED YOURSELF AND THIS ENTIRE TOWN.
MAXIMUM MAN.
IT'S OVER, ALEX.
I'M BACK.
ARE YOU SURE ABOUT THIS, BAD DOG?
ARE YOU 100% DAMN-DOODY SURE?
I WISH I WASN'T, SHERIFF. I SWEAR TO CHRIST, I WISH I WASN'T.
IT'S CRAGG, PRESLEY. AND THE MAYOR, TOO.
FURY'S GOT THAT REPORTER GIRL AND MAY WELL DO HER IN, AND CRAGG...
...HE'S UP THERE SOMEWHERE. WITH THE HATE BOMB.
I NEED YOU TO FIND...
YINKIES!

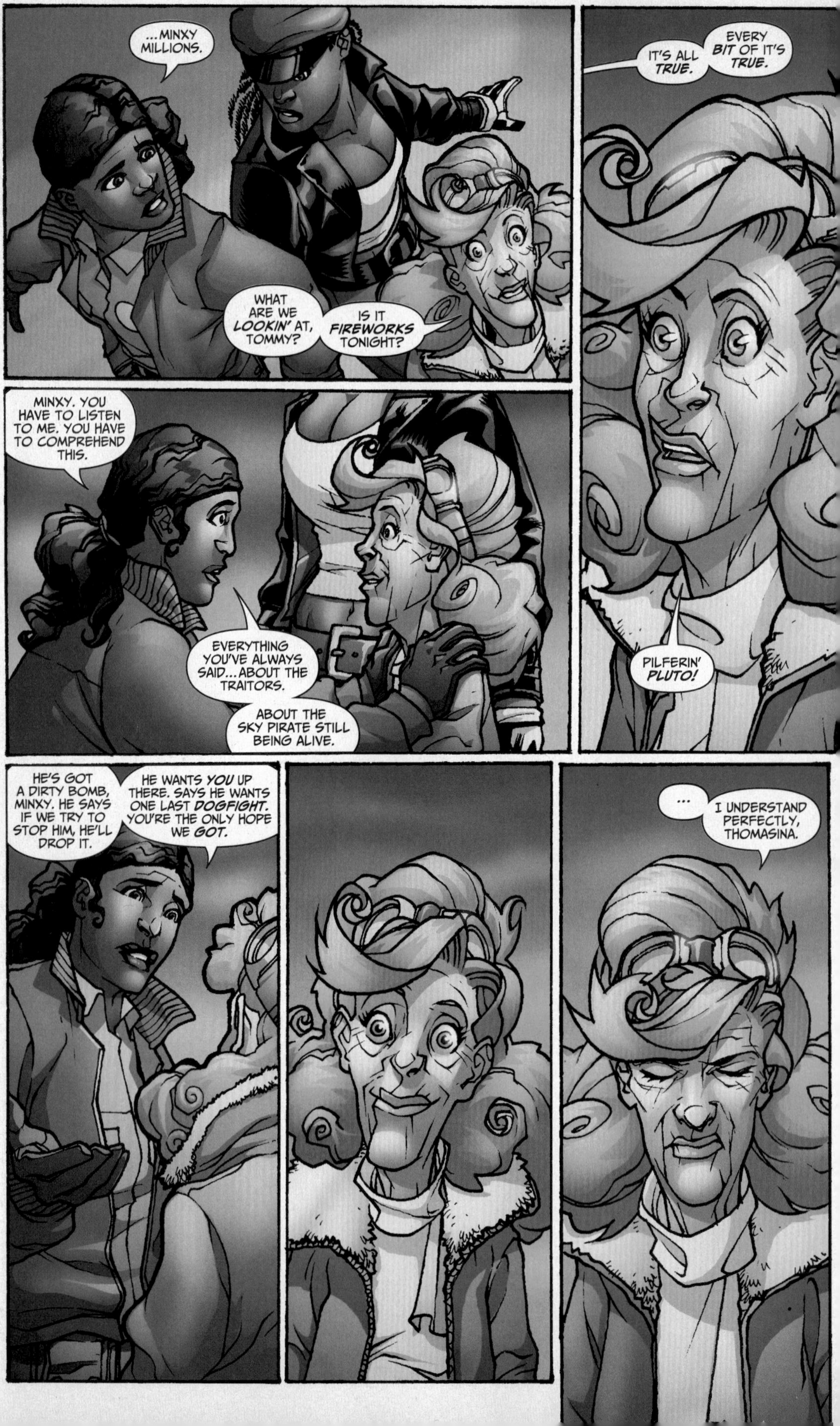
...MINXY MILLIONS.
WHAT ARE WE LOOKIN' AT, TOMMY?
IS IT FIREWORKS TONIGHT?
IT'S ALL TRUE.
EVERY BIT OF IT'S TRUE.
MINXY. YOU HAVE TO LISTEN TO ME. YOU HAVE TO COMPREHEND THIS.
EVERYTHING YOU'VE ALWAYS SAID... ABOUT THE TRAITORS.
ABOUT THE SKY PIRATE STILL BEING ALIVE.
PILFERIN' PLUTO!
HE'S GOT A DIRTY BOMB, MINXY. HE SAYS IF WE TRY TO STOP HIM, HE'LL DROP IT.
HE WANTS YOU UP THERE. SAYS HE WANTS ONE LAST DOGFIGHT. YOU'RE THE ONLY HOPE WE GOT.
...
I UNDERSTAND PERFECTLY, THOMASINA.

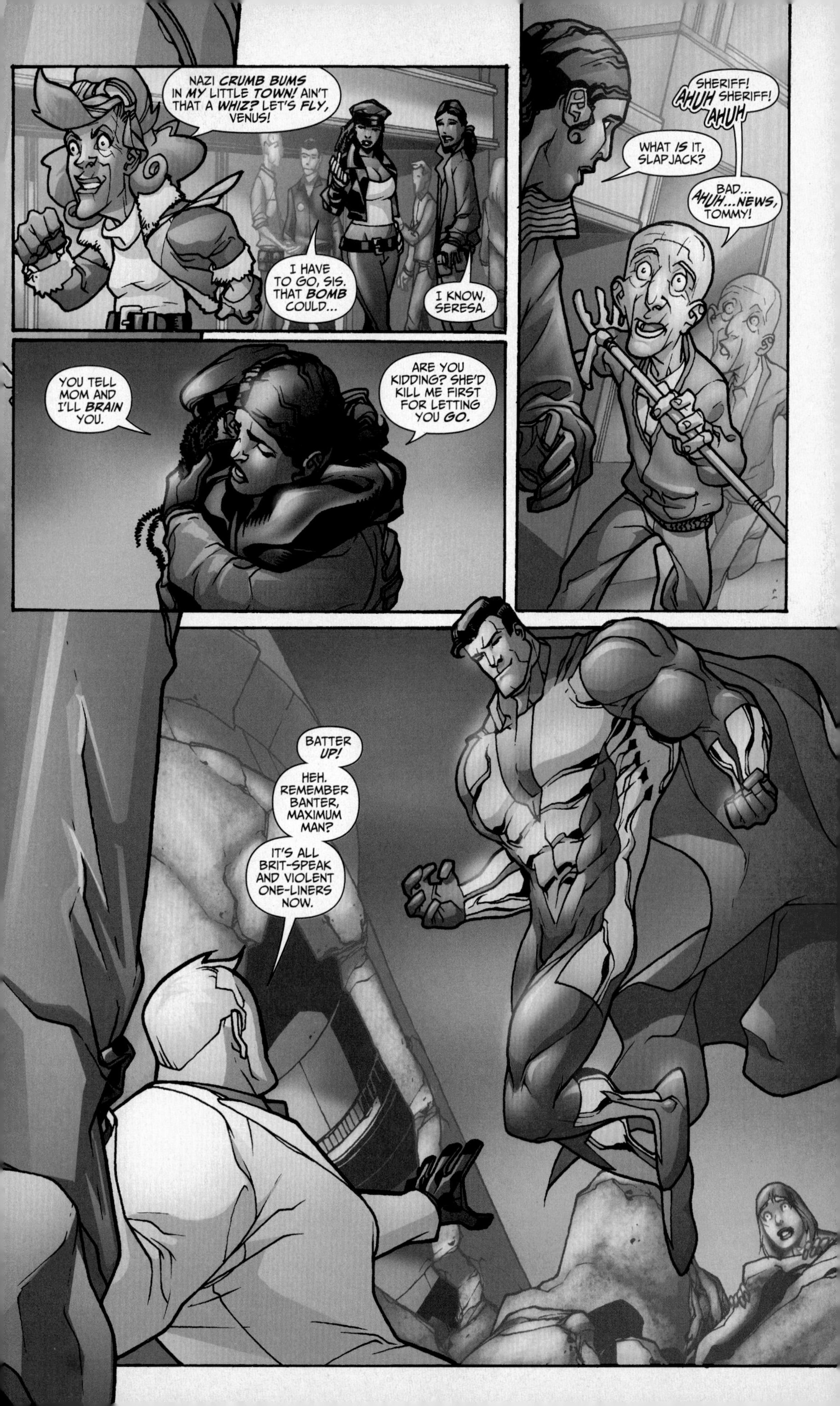
NAZI CRUMB BUMS IN MY LITTLE TOWN! AIN'T THAT A WHIZ? LET'S FLY, VENUS!
I HAVE TO GO, SIS. THAT BOMB COULD...
I KNOW, SERESA.
SHERIFF! AHUH SHERIFF! AHUH
WHAT IS IT, SLAPJACK?
BAD... AHUH...NEWS, TOMMY!
YOU TELL MOM AND I'LL BRAIN YOU.
ARE YOU KIDDING? SHE'D KILL ME FIRST FOR LETTING YOU GO.
BATTER UP!
HEH. REMEMBER BANTER, MAXIMUM MAN?
IT'S ALL BRIT-SPEAK AND VIOLENT ONE-LINERS NOW.

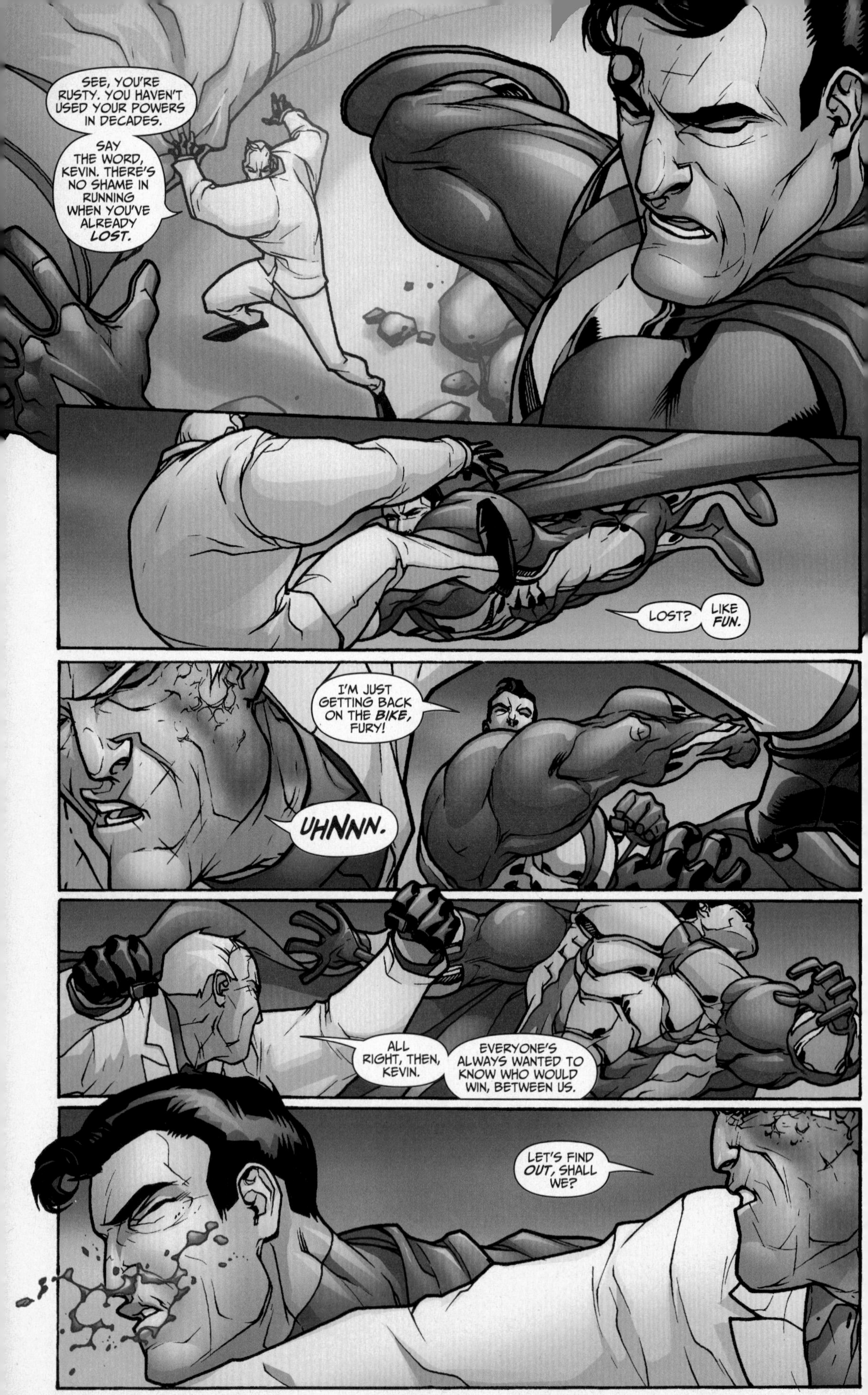
SEE, YOU'RE RUSTY. YOU HAVEN'T USED YOUR POWERS IN DECADES.
SAY THE WORD, KEVIN. THERE'S NO SHAME IN RUNNING WHEN YOU'VE ALREADY LOST.
LOST? LIKE FUN.
I'M JUST GETTING BACK ON THE BIKE, FURY!
UHNNN.
ALL RIGHT, THEN, KEVIN.
EVERYONE'S ALWAYS WANTED TO KNOW WHO WOULD WIN, BETWEEN US.
LET'S FIND OUT, SHALL WE?

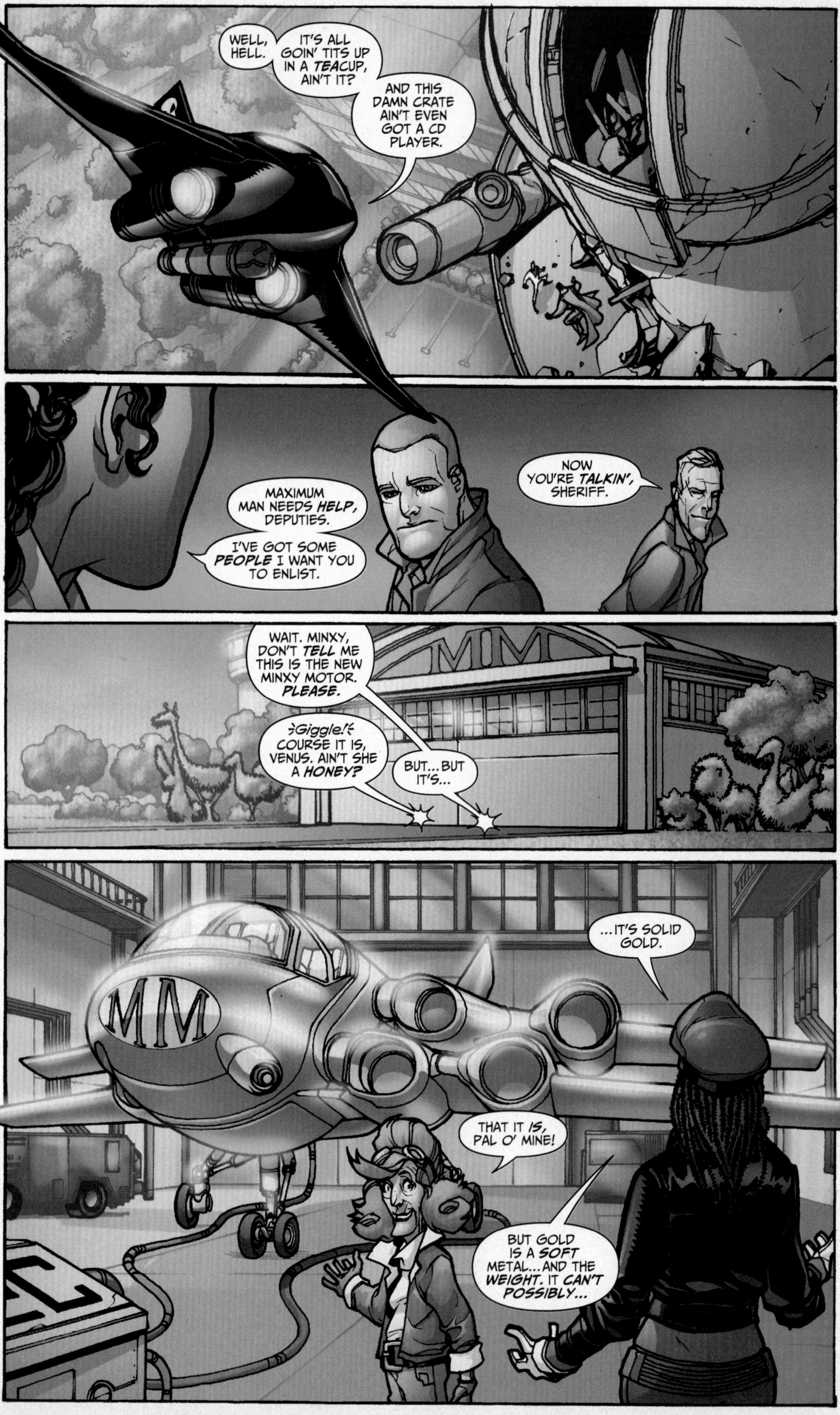
WELL, HELL.
IT'S ALL GOIN' TITS UP IN A TEACUP, AIN'T IT?
AND THIS DAMN CRATE AIN'T EVEN GOT A CD PLAYER.
MAXIMUM MAN NEEDS HELP, DEPUTIES.
I'VE GOT SOME PEOPLE I WANT YOU TO ENLIST.
NOW YOU'RE TALKIN', SHERIFF.
MM
WAIT. MINXY, DON'T TELL ME THIS IS THE NEW MINXY MOTOR. PLEASE.
Giggle! COURSE IT IS, VENUS. AIN'T SHE A HONEY?
BUT...BUT IT'S...
MM
...IT'S SOLID GOLD.
THAT IT IS, PAL O' MINE!
BUT GOLD IS A SOFT METAL...AND THE WEIGHT. IT CAN'T POSSIBLY...

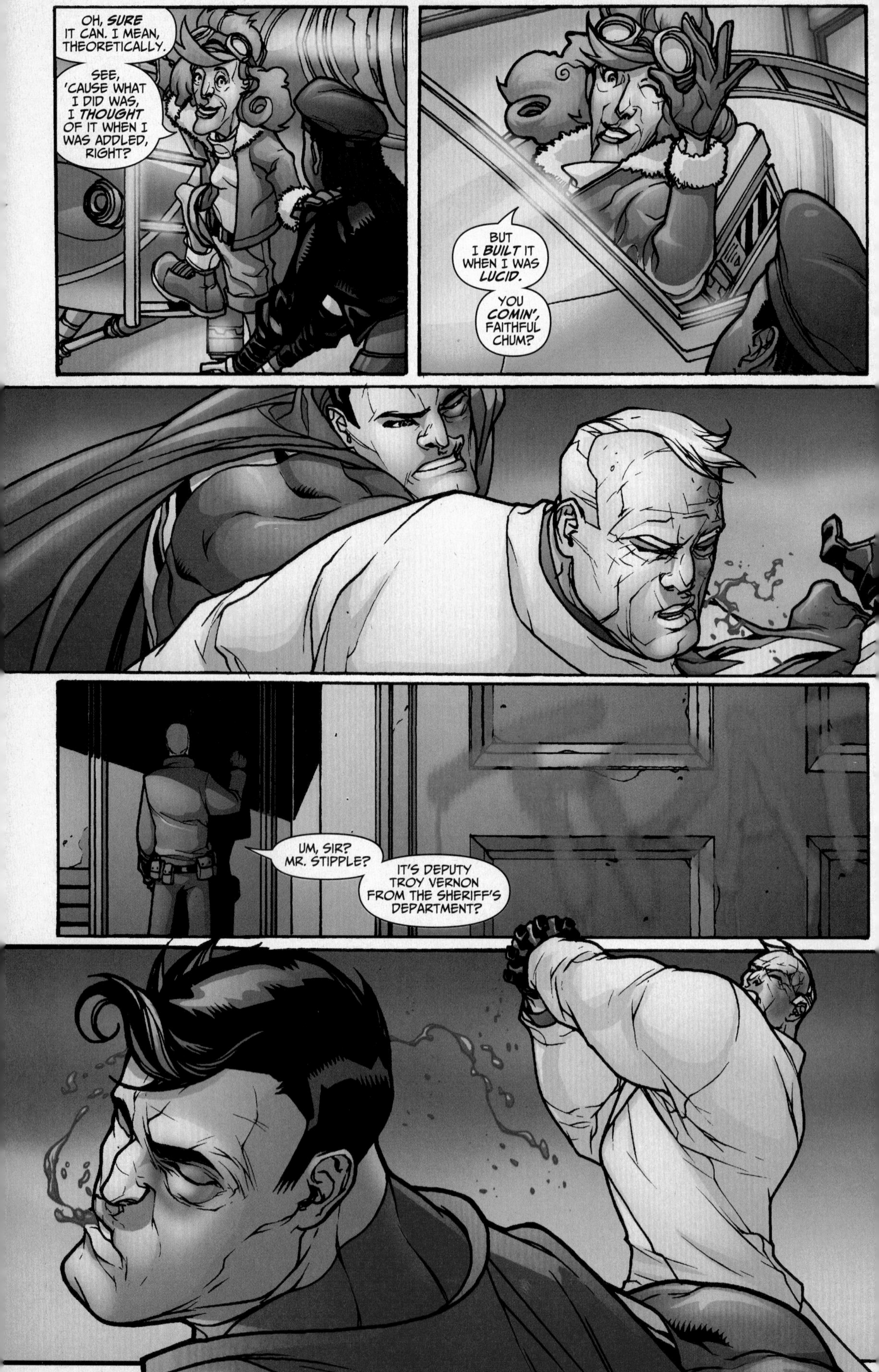
OH, SURE IT CAN. I MEAN, THEORETICALLY.
SEE, 'CAUSE WHAT I DID WAS, I THOUGHT OF IT WHEN I WAS ADDLED, RIGHT?
BUT I BUILT IT WHEN I WAS LUCID.
YOU COMIN', FAITHFUL CHUM?
UM, SIR? MR. STIPPLE?
IT'S DEPUTY TROY VERNON FROM THE SHERIFF'S DEPARTMENT?

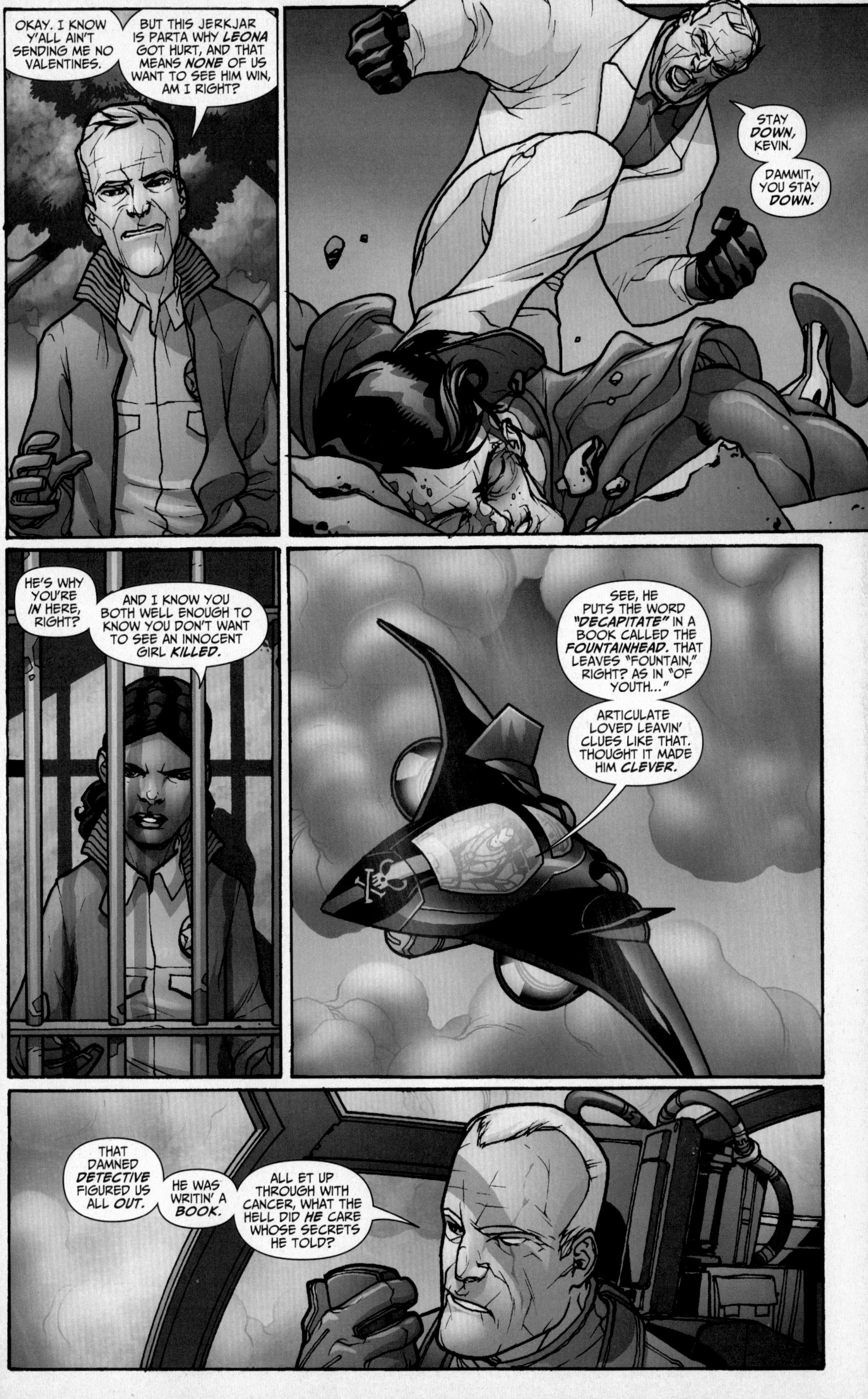

OKAY. I KNOW Y'ALL AIN'T SENDING ME NO VALENTINES.
BUT THIS JERKJAR IS PARTA WHY LEONA GOT HURT, AND THAT MEANS NONE OF US WANT TO SEE HIM WIN, AM I RIGHT?
STAY DOWN, KEVIN.
DAMMIT, YOU STAY DOWN.
HE'S WHY YOU'RE IN HERE, RIGHT?
AND I KNOW YOU BOTH WELL ENOUGH TO KNOW YOU DON'T WANT TO SEE AN INNOCENT GIRL KILLED.
SEE, HE PUTS THE WORD "DECAPITATE" IN A BOOK CALLED THE FOUNTAINHEAD. THAT LEAVES "FOUNTAIN," RIGHT? AS IN "OF YOUTH..."
ARTICULATE LOVED LEAVIN' CLUES LIKE THAT. THOUGHT IT MADE HIM CLEVER.
THAT DAMNED DETECTIVE FIGURED US ALL OUT.
HE WAS WRITIN' A BOOK.
ALL ET UP THROUGH WITH CANCER, WHAT THE HELL DID HE CARE WHOSE SECRETS HE TOLD?

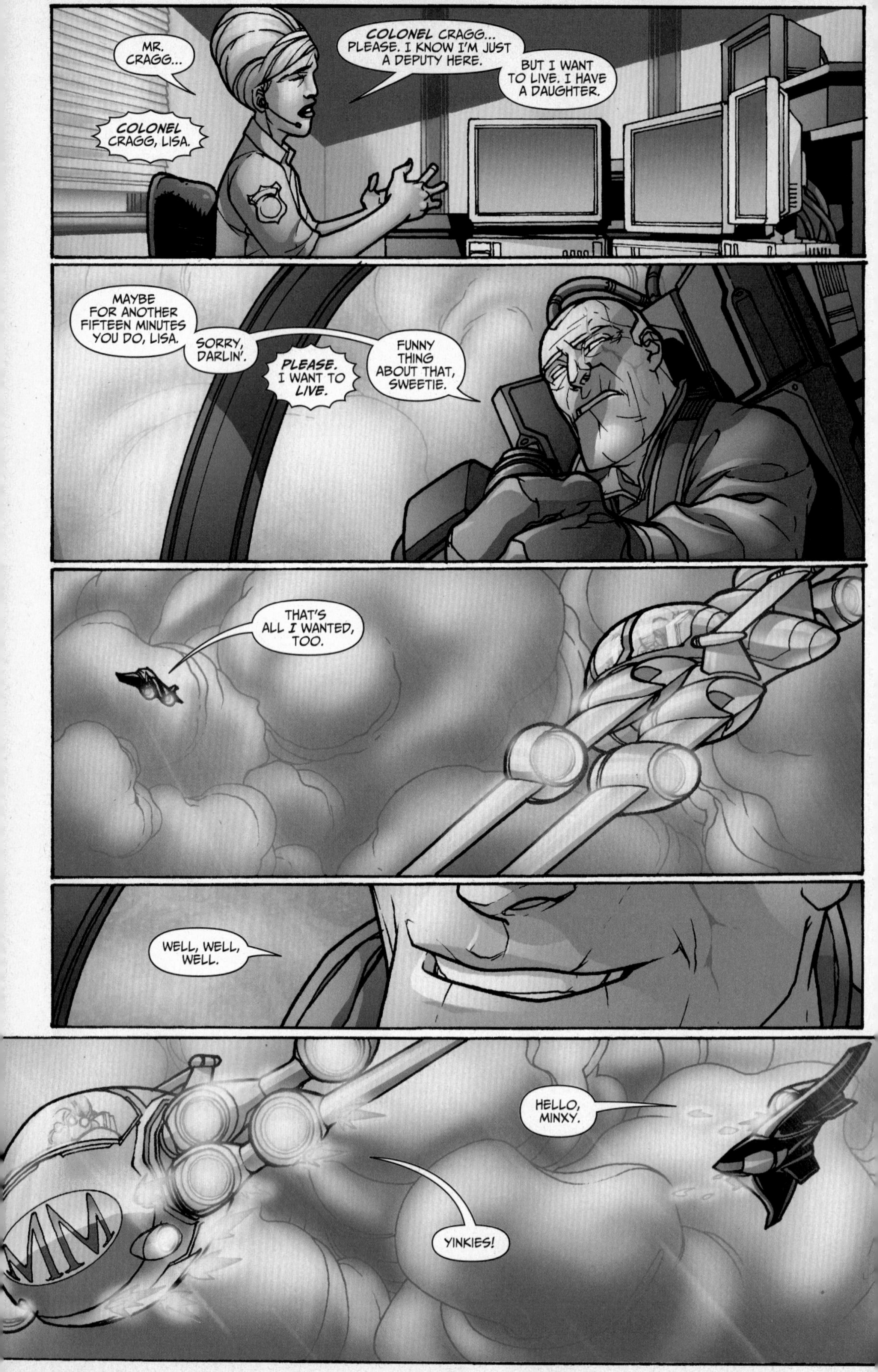
MR. CRAGG...
COLONEL CRAGG, LISA.
COLONEL CRAGG... PLEASE. I KNOW I'M JUST A DEPUTY HERE.
BUT I WANT TO LIVE. I HAVE A DAUGHTER.
MAYBE FOR ANOTHER FIFTEEN MINUTES YOU DO, LISA.
SORRY, DARLIN'.
PLEASE. I WANT TO LIVE.
FUNNY THING ABOUT THAT, SWEETIE.
THAT'S ALL I WANTED, TOO.
WELL, WELL, WELL.
MM
HELLO, MINXY.
YINKIES!

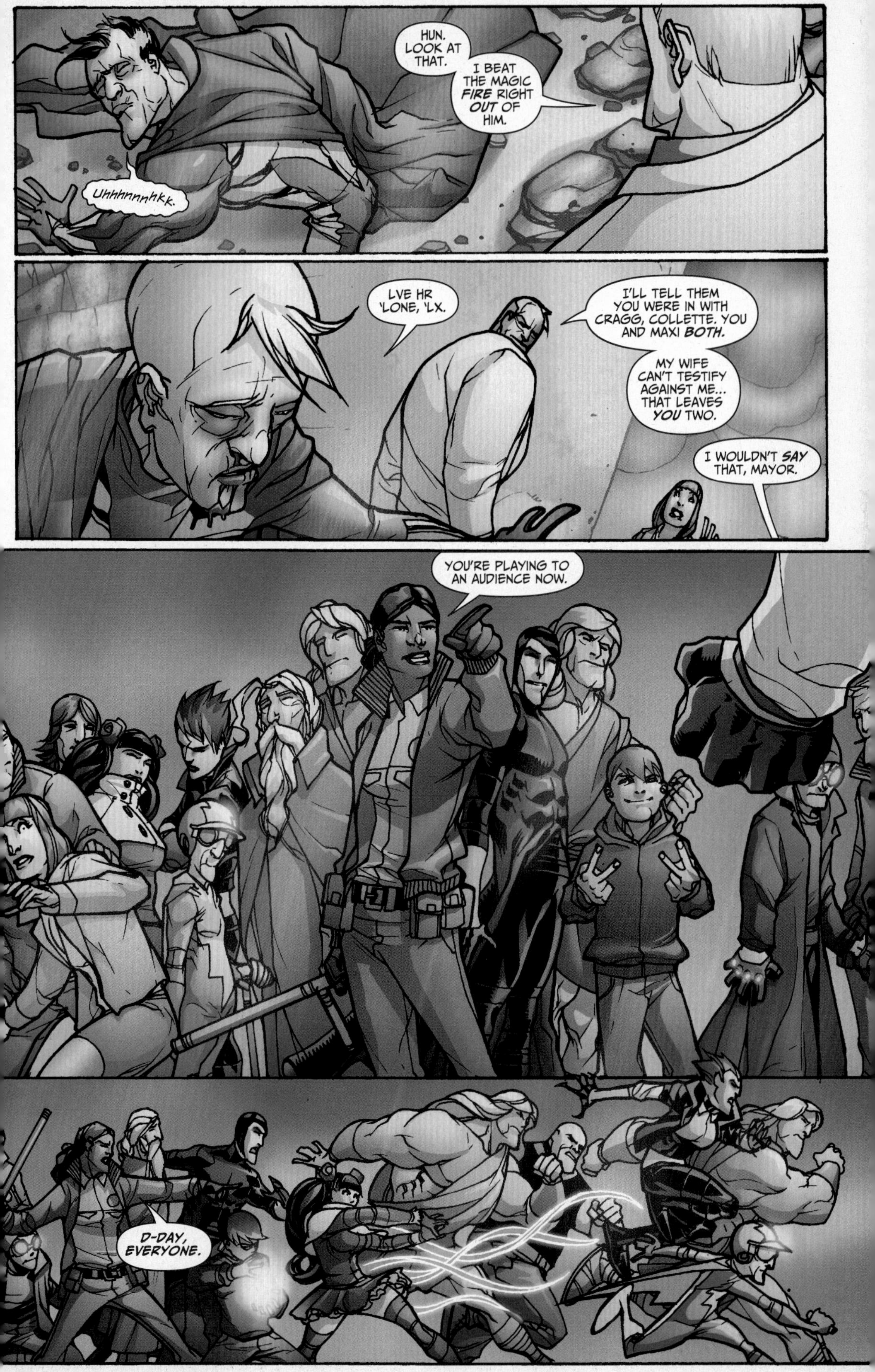
HUN. LOOK AT THAT.
I BEAT THE MAGIC FIRE RIGHT OUT OF HIM.
Uhhhnnnnhkk.
LVE HR 'LONE, 'LX.
I'LL TELL THEM YOU WERE IN WITH CRAGG, COLLETTE. YOU AND MAXI BOTH.
MY WIFE CAN'T TESTIFY AGAINST ME... THAT LEAVES YOU TWO.
I WOULDN'T SAY THAT, MAYOR.
YOU'RE PLAYING TO AN AUDIENCE NOW.
D-DAY, EVERYONE.

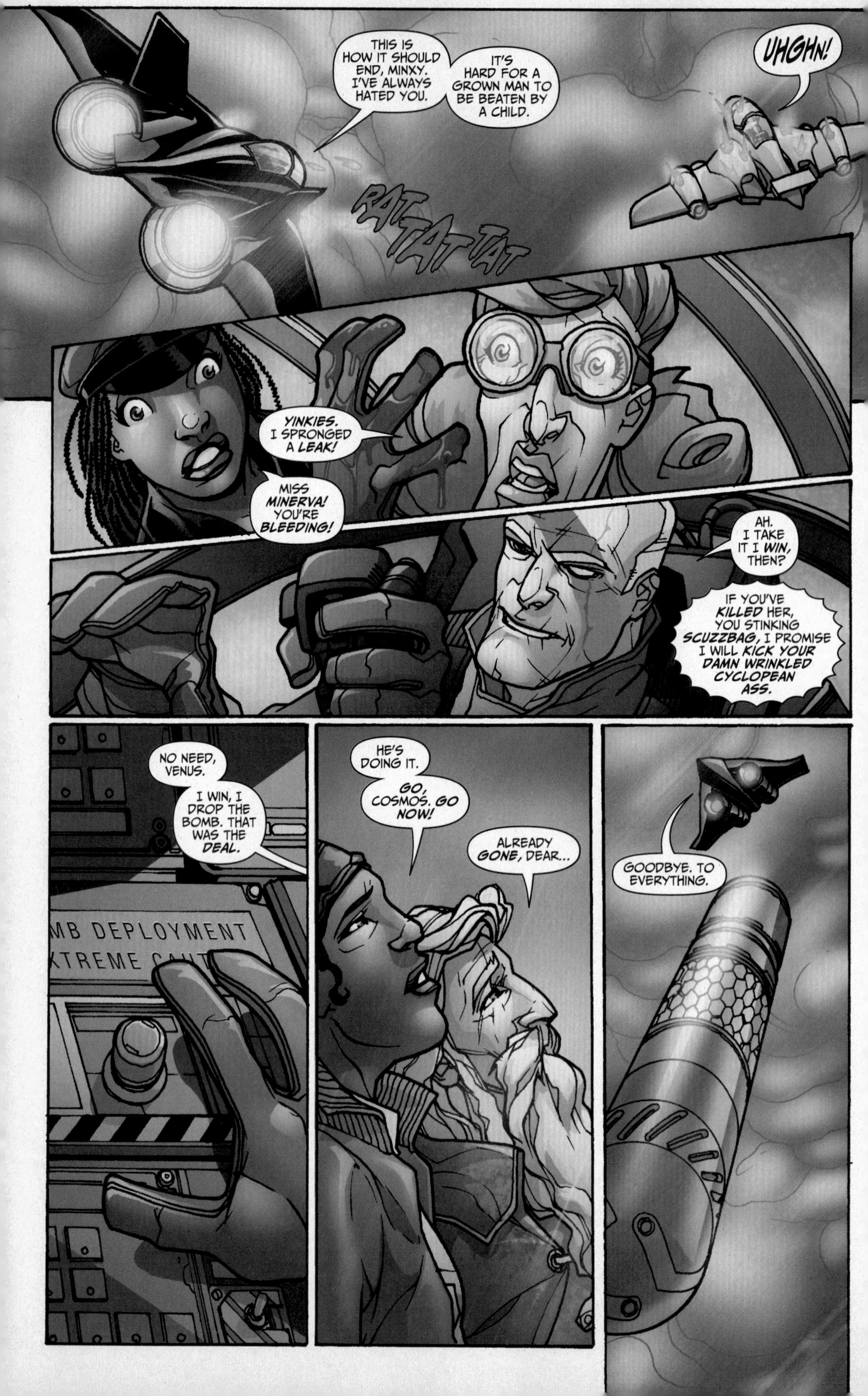
THIS IS HOW IT SHOULD END, MINXY. I'VE ALWAYS HATED YOU.
IT'S HARD FOR A GROWN MAN TO BE BEATEN BY A CHILD.
UHGHN!
RAT TAT TAT TAT
YINKIES. I SPRONGED A LEAK!
MISS MINERVA! YOU'RE BLEEDING!
AH. I TAKE IT I WIN, THEN?
IF YOU'VE KILLED HER, YOU STINKING SCUZZBAG, I PROMISE I WILL KICK YOUR DAMN WRINKLED CYCLOPEAN ASS.
NO NEED, VENUS.
I WIN, I DROP THE BOMB. THAT WAS THE DEAL.
MB DEPLOYMENT
XTREME CAUT
HE'S DOING IT.
GO, COSMOS. GO NOW!
ALREADY GONE, DEAR...
GOODBYE. TO EVERYTHING.

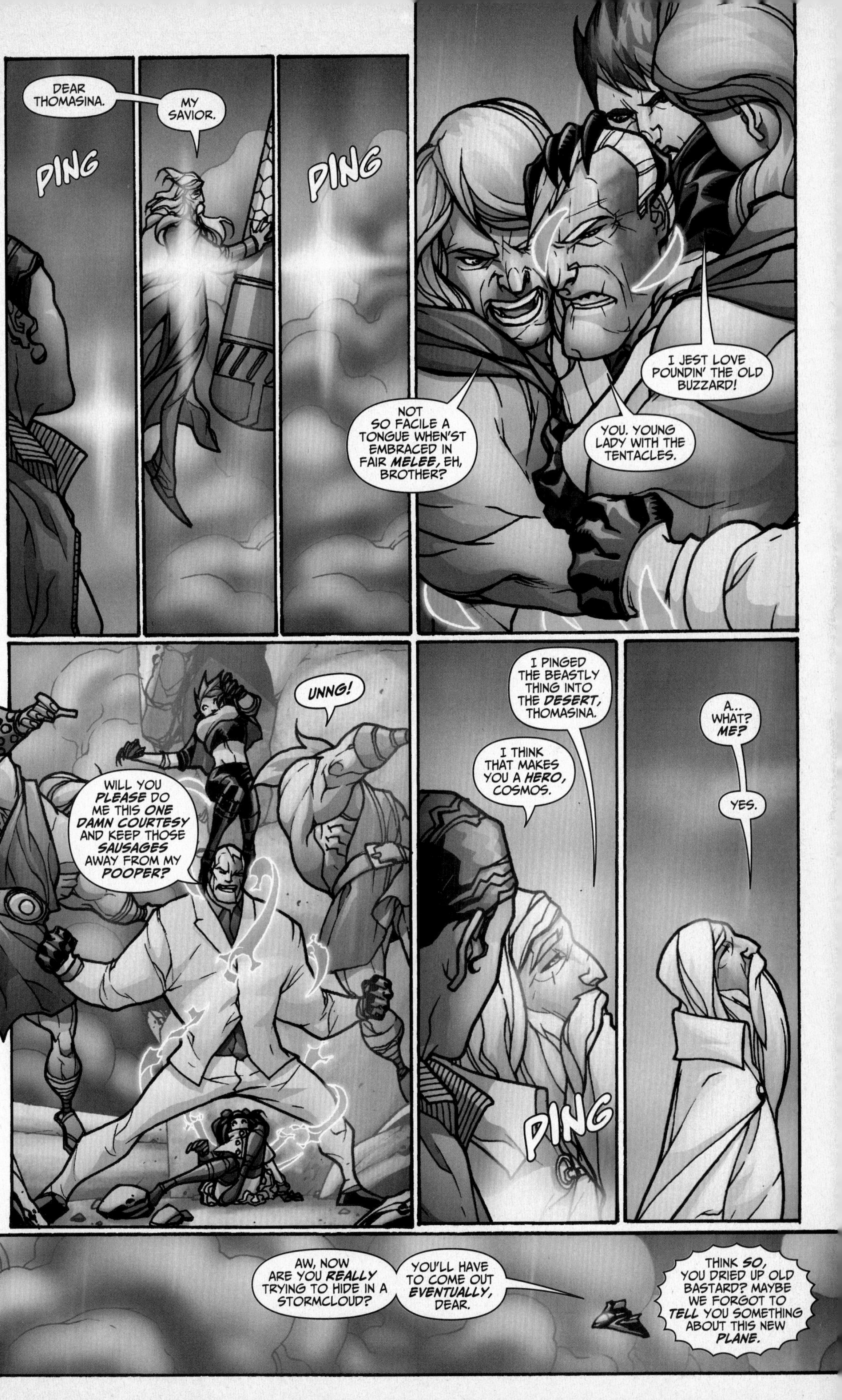

DEAR THOMASINA.
MY SAVIOR.
PING
PING
NOT SO FACILE A TONGUE WHEN'ST EMBRACED IN FAIR MELEE, EH, BROTHER?
YOU. YOUNG LADY WITH THE TENTACLES.
I JEST LOVE POUNDIN' THE OLD BUZZARD!
UNNG!
WILL YOU PLEASE DO ME THIS ONE DAMN COURTESY AND KEEP THOSE SAUSAGES AWAY FROM MY POOPER?
I PINGED THE BEASTLY THING INTO THE DESERT, THOMASINA.
I THINK THAT MAKES YOU A HERO, COSMOS.
PING
A... WHAT? ME?
YES.
AW, NOW ARE YOU REALLY TRYING TO HIDE IN A STORMCLOUD?
YOU'LL HAVE TO COME OUT EVENTUALLY, DEAR.
THINK SO, YOU DRIED UP OLD BASTARD? MAYBE WE FORGOT TO TELL YOU SOMETHING ABOUT THIS NEW PLANE.

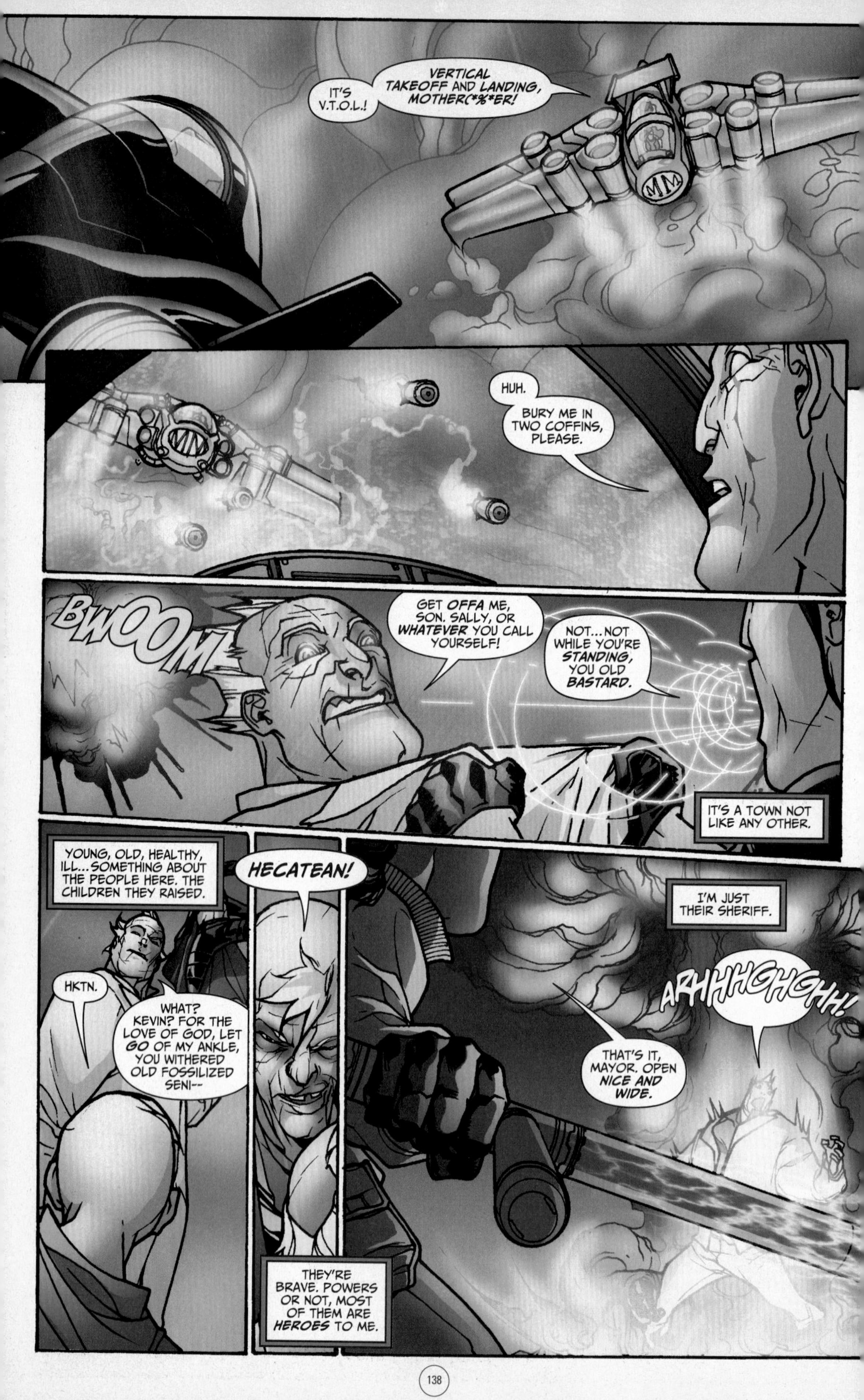
IT'S V.T.O.L.!
VERTICAL TAKEOFF AND LANDING, MOTHER(*%*ER!
HUH.
BURY ME IN TWO COFFINS, PLEASE.
BWOOM
GET OFFA ME, SON. SALLY, OR WHATEVER YOU CALL YOURSELF!
NOT...NOT WHILE YOU'RE STANDING, YOU OLD BASTARD.
IT'S A TOWN NOT LIKE ANY OTHER.
YOUNG, OLD, HEALTHY, ILL...SOMETHING ABOUT THE PEOPLE HERE. THE CHILDREN THEY RAISED.
HKTN.
WHAT? KEVIN? FOR THE LOVE OF GOD, LET GO OF MY ANKLE, YOU WITHERED OLD FOSSILIZED SENI--
HECATEAN!
THEY'RE BRAVE. POWERS OR NOT, MOST OF THEM ARE HEROES TO ME.
I'M JUST THEIR SHERIFF.
ARHHHGHGHH!
THAT'S IT, MAYOR. OPEN NICE AND WIDE.

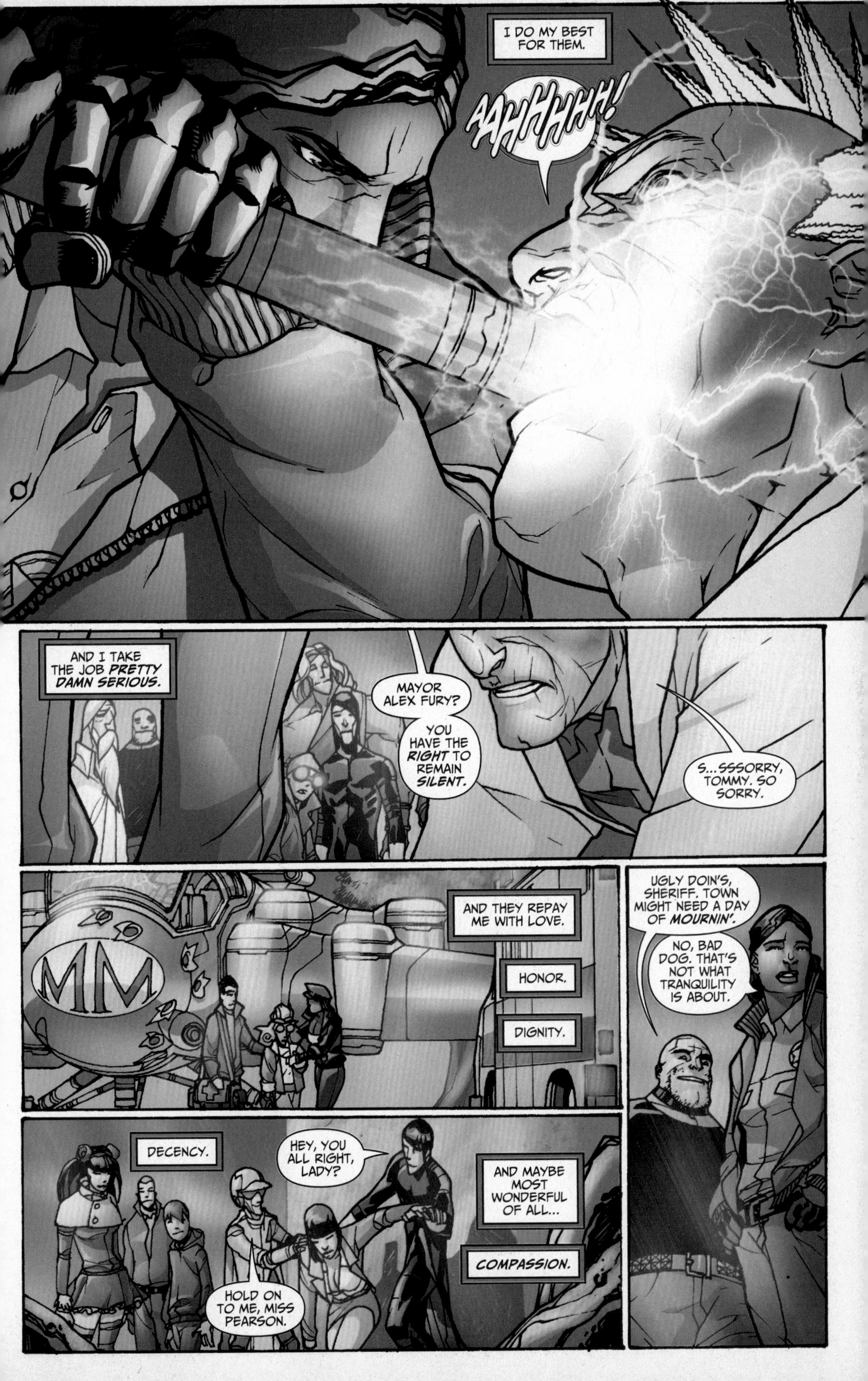

I DO MY BEST FOR THEM.
AAHHHHH!
AND I TAKE THE JOB *PRETTY DAMN SERIOUS.*
MAYOR ALEX FURY?
YOU HAVE THE *RIGHT* TO REMAIN *SILENT.*
S...SSSORRY, TOMMY. SO SORRY.
MM
AND THEY REPAY ME WITH LOVE.
HONOR.
DIGNITY.
UGLY DOIN'S, SHERIFF. TOWN MIGHT NEED A DAY OF *MOURNIN'.*
NO, BAD DOG. THAT'S NOT WHAT TRANQUILITY IS ABOUT.
DECENCY.
HEY, YOU ALL RIGHT, LADY?
AND MAYBE MOST WONDERFUL OF ALL...
COMPASSION.
HOLD ON TO ME, MISS PEARSON.

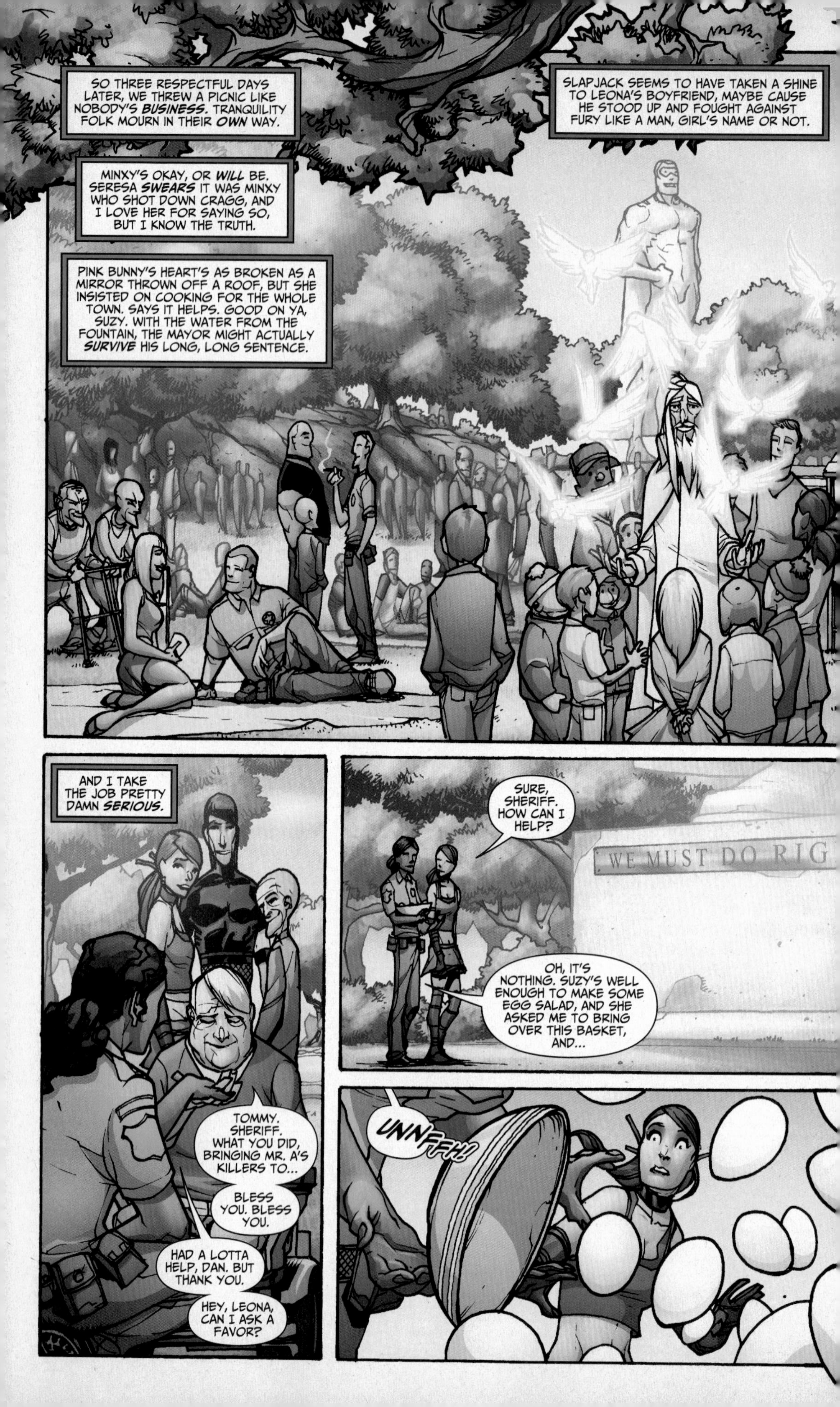
SO THREE RESPECTFUL DAYS LATER, WE THREW A PICNIC LIKE NOBODY'S *BUSINESS.* TRANQUILITY FOLK MOURN IN THEIR *OWN* WAY.
SLAPJACK SEEMS TO HAVE TAKEN A SHINE TO LEONA'S BOYFRIEND, MAYBE CAUSE HE STOOD UP AND FOUGHT AGAINST FURY LIKE A MAN, GIRL'S NAME OR NOT.
MINXY'S OKAY, OR *WILL* BE. SERESA *SWEARS* IT WAS MINXY WHO SHOT DOWN CRAGG, AND I LOVE HER FOR SAYING SO, BUT I KNOW THE TRUTH.
PINK BUNNY'S HEART'S AS BROKEN AS A MIRROR THROWN OFF A ROOF, BUT SHE INSISTED ON COOKING FOR THE WHOLE TOWN. SAYS IT HELPS. GOOD ON YA, SUZY. WITH THE WATER FROM THE FOUNTAIN, THE MAYOR MIGHT ACTUALLY *SURVIVE* HIS LONG, LONG SENTENCE.
AND I TAKE THE JOB PRETTY DAMN *SERIOUS.*
TOMMY. SHERIFF. WHAT YOU DID, BRINGING MR. A'S KILLERS TO...
BLESS YOU. BLESS YOU.
HAD A LOTTA HELP, DAN. BUT THANK YOU.
HEY, LEONA, CAN I ASK A FAVOR?
SURE, SHERIFF. HOW CAN I HELP?
WE MUST DO RIG
OH, IT'S NOTHING. SUZY'S WELL ENOUGH TO MAKE SOME EGG SALAD, AND SHE ASKED ME TO BRING OVER THIS BASKET, AND...
UNNFFH!

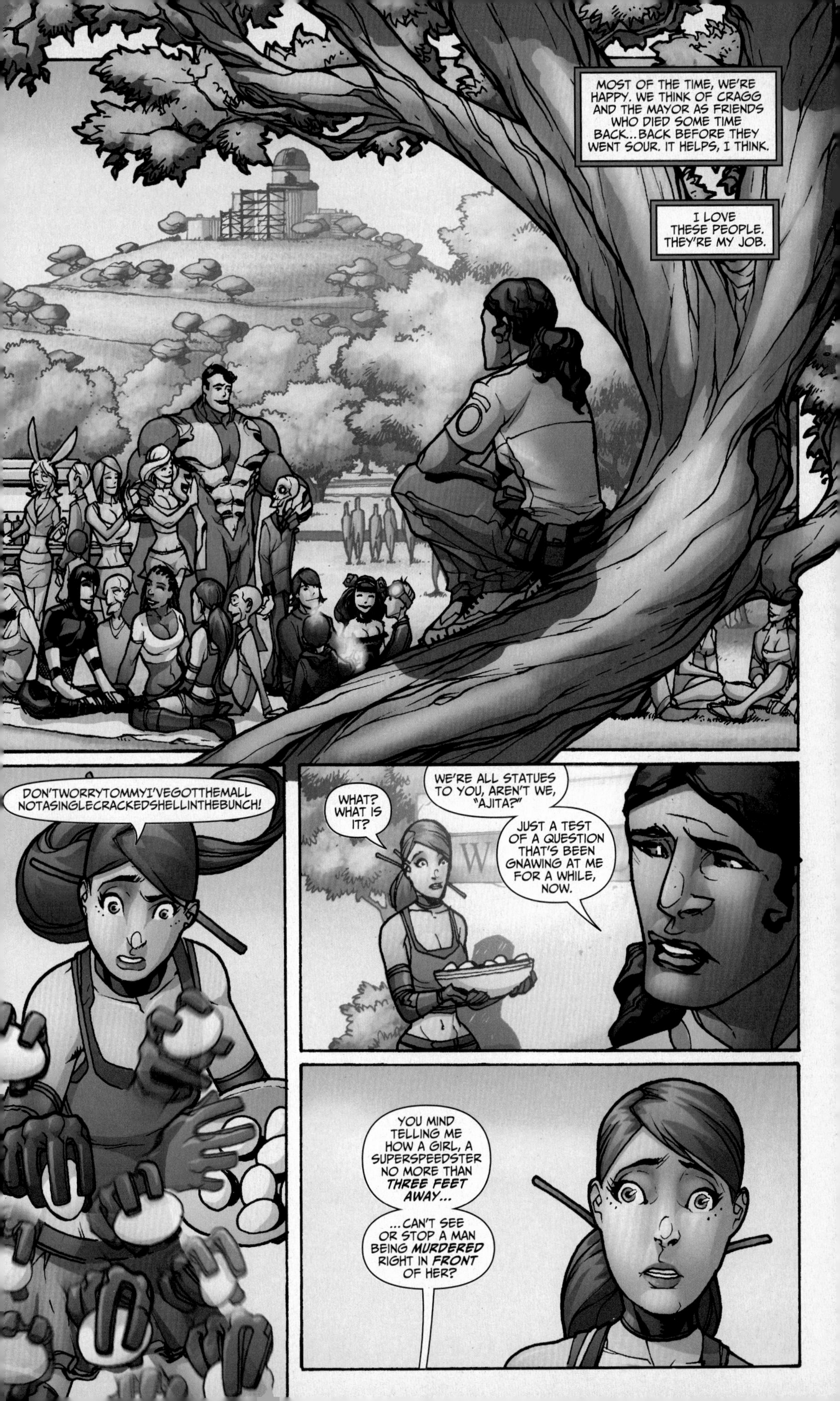

MOST OF THE TIME, WE'RE HAPPY. WE THINK OF CRAGG AND THE MAYOR AS FRIENDS WHO DIED SOME TIME BACK...BACK BEFORE THEY WENT SOUR. IT HELPS, I THINK.
I LOVE THESE PEOPLE. THEY'RE MY JOB.
DON'TWORRYTOMMYI'VEGOTTHEMALL NOTASINGLECRACKEDSHELLINTHEBUNCH!
WHAT? WHAT IS IT?
WE'RE ALL STATUES TO YOU, AREN'T WE, "AJITA?"
JUST A TEST OF A QUESTION THAT'S BEEN GNAWING AT ME FOR A WHILE, NOW.
YOU MIND TELLING ME HOW A GIRL, A SUPERSPEEDSTER NO MORE THAN THREE FEET AWAY...
...CAN'T SEE OR STOP A MAN BEING MURDERED RIGHT IN FRONT OF HER?

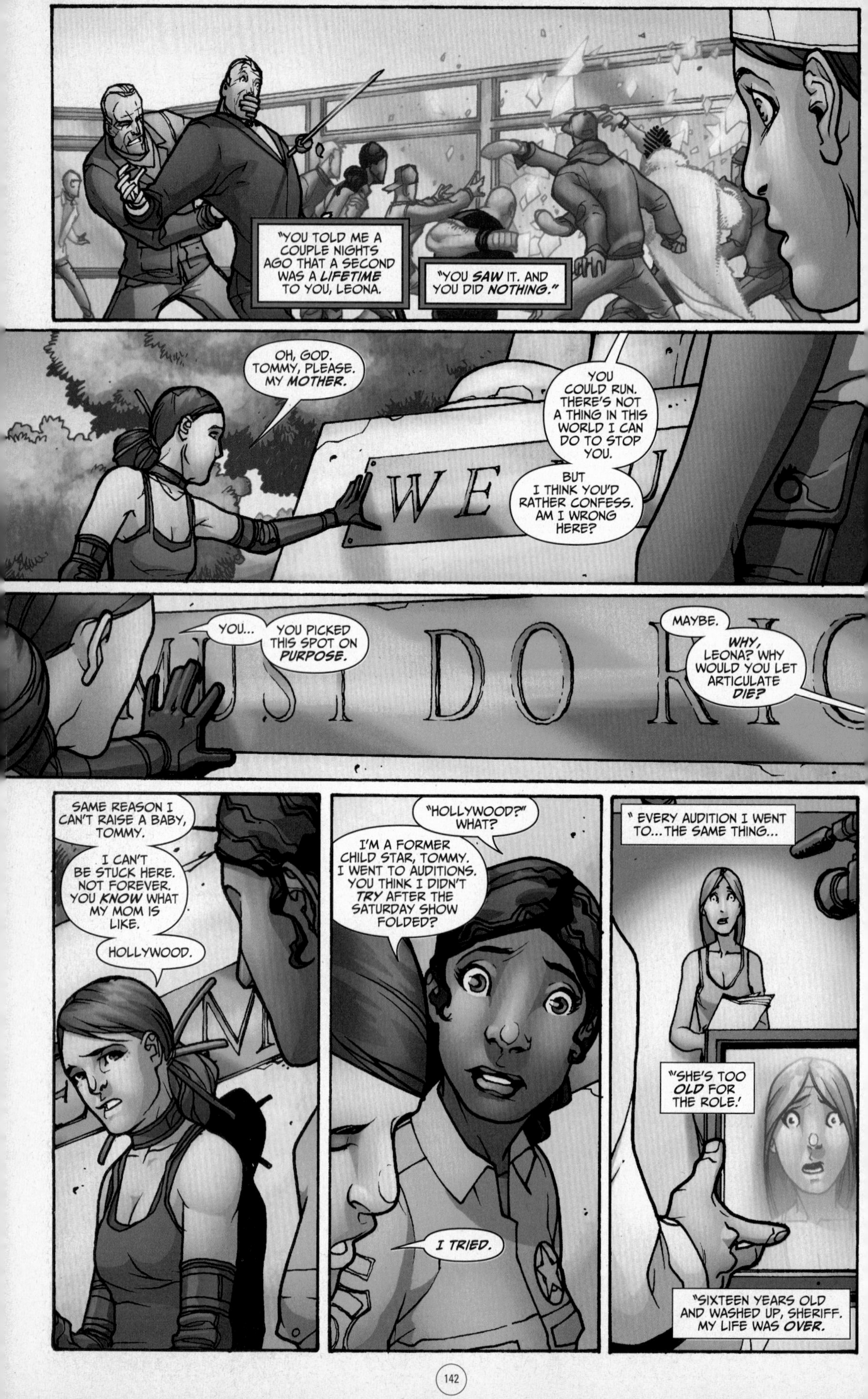
"YOU TOLD ME A COUPLE NIGHTS AGO THAT A SECOND WAS A *LIFETIME* TO YOU, LEONA.
"YOU *SAW* IT. AND YOU DID *NOTHING*."
OH, GOD. TOMMY, PLEASE. MY *MOTHER*.
YOU COULD RUN. THERE'S NOT A THING IN THIS WORLD I CAN DO TO STOP YOU.
BUT I THINK YOU'D RATHER CONFESS. AM I WRONG HERE?
YOU...
YOU PICKED THIS SPOT ON *PURPOSE*.
MAYBE.
WHY, LEONA? WHY WOULD YOU LET ARTICULATE *DIE?*
SAME REASON I CAN'T RAISE A BABY, TOMMY.
I CAN'T BE STUCK HERE. NOT FOREVER. YOU *KNOW* WHAT MY MOM IS LIKE.
HOLLYWOOD.
"HOLLYWOOD?" WHAT?
I'M A FORMER CHILD STAR, TOMMY. I WENT TO AUDITIONS. YOU THINK I DIDN'T *TRY* AFTER THE SATURDAY SHOW FOLDED?
I TRIED.
" EVERY AUDITION I WENT TO... THE SAME THING...
"SHE'S TOO *OLD* FOR THE ROLE.'
"SIXTEEN YEARS OLD AND WASHED UP, SHERIFF. MY LIFE WAS *OVER*.

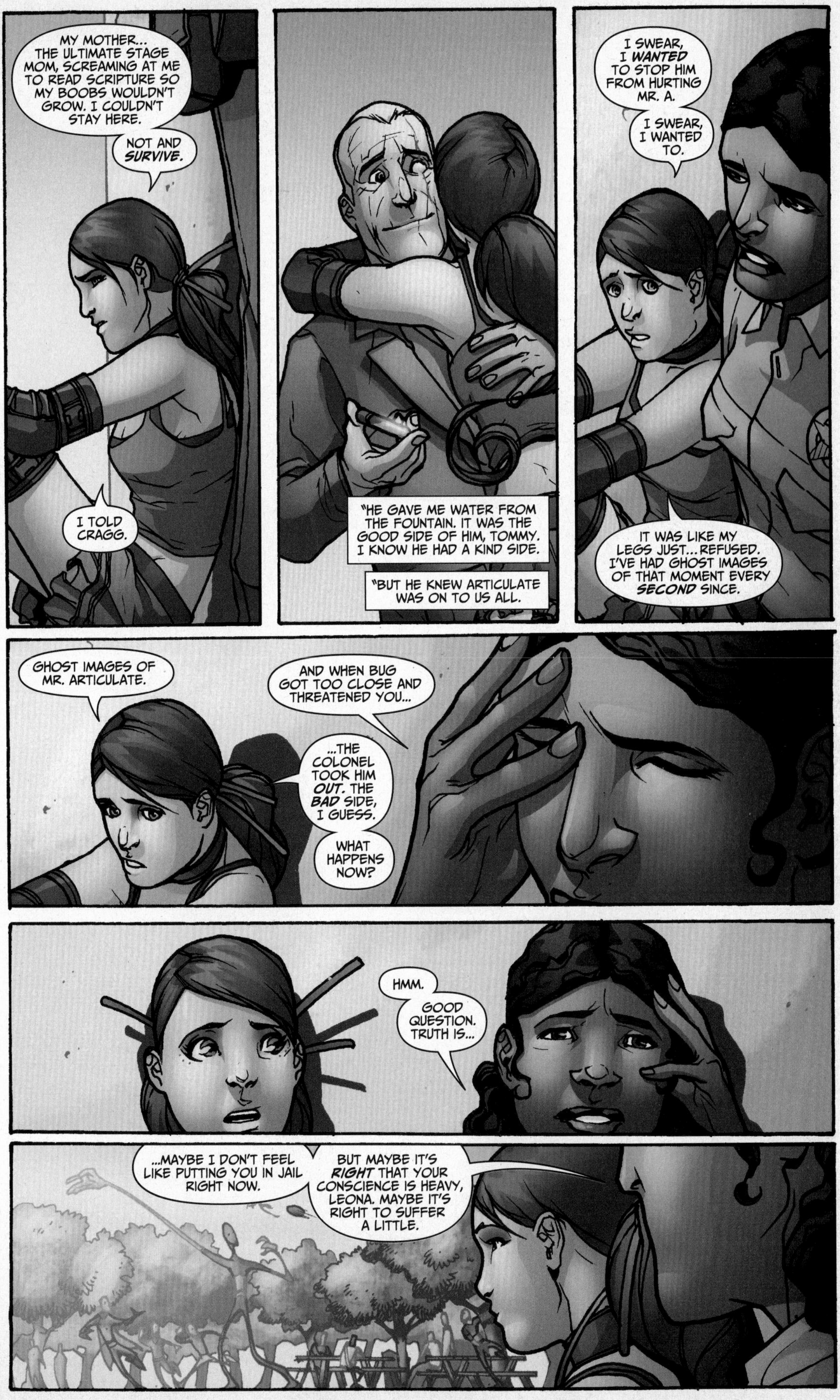
MY MOTHER... THE ULTIMATE STAGE MOM, SCREAMING AT ME TO READ SCRIPTURE SO MY BOOBS WOULDN'T GROW. I COULDN'T STAY HERE.
NOT AND *SURVIVE*.
I TOLD CRAGG.
"HE GAVE ME WATER FROM THE FOUNTAIN. IT WAS THE GOOD SIDE OF HIM, TOMMY. I KNOW HE HAD A KIND SIDE.
"BUT HE KNEW ARTICULATE WAS ON TO US ALL.
I SWEAR, I *WANTED* TO STOP HIM FROM HURTING MR. A.
I SWEAR, I WANTED TO.
IT WAS LIKE MY LEGS JUST...REFUSED. I'VE HAD GHOST IMAGES OF THAT MOMENT EVERY *SECOND* SINCE.
GHOST IMAGES OF MR. ARTICULATE.
AND WHEN BUG GOT TOO CLOSE AND THREATENED YOU...
...THE COLONEL TOOK HIM *OUT*. THE *BAD* SIDE, I GUESS.
WHAT HAPPENS NOW?
HMM.
GOOD QUESTION. TRUTH IS...
...MAYBE I DON'T FEEL LIKE PUTTING YOU IN JAIL RIGHT NOW.
BUT MAYBE IT'S *RIGHT* THAT YOUR CONSCIENCE IS HEAVY, LEONA. MAYBE IT'S RIGHT TO SUFFER A LITTLE.

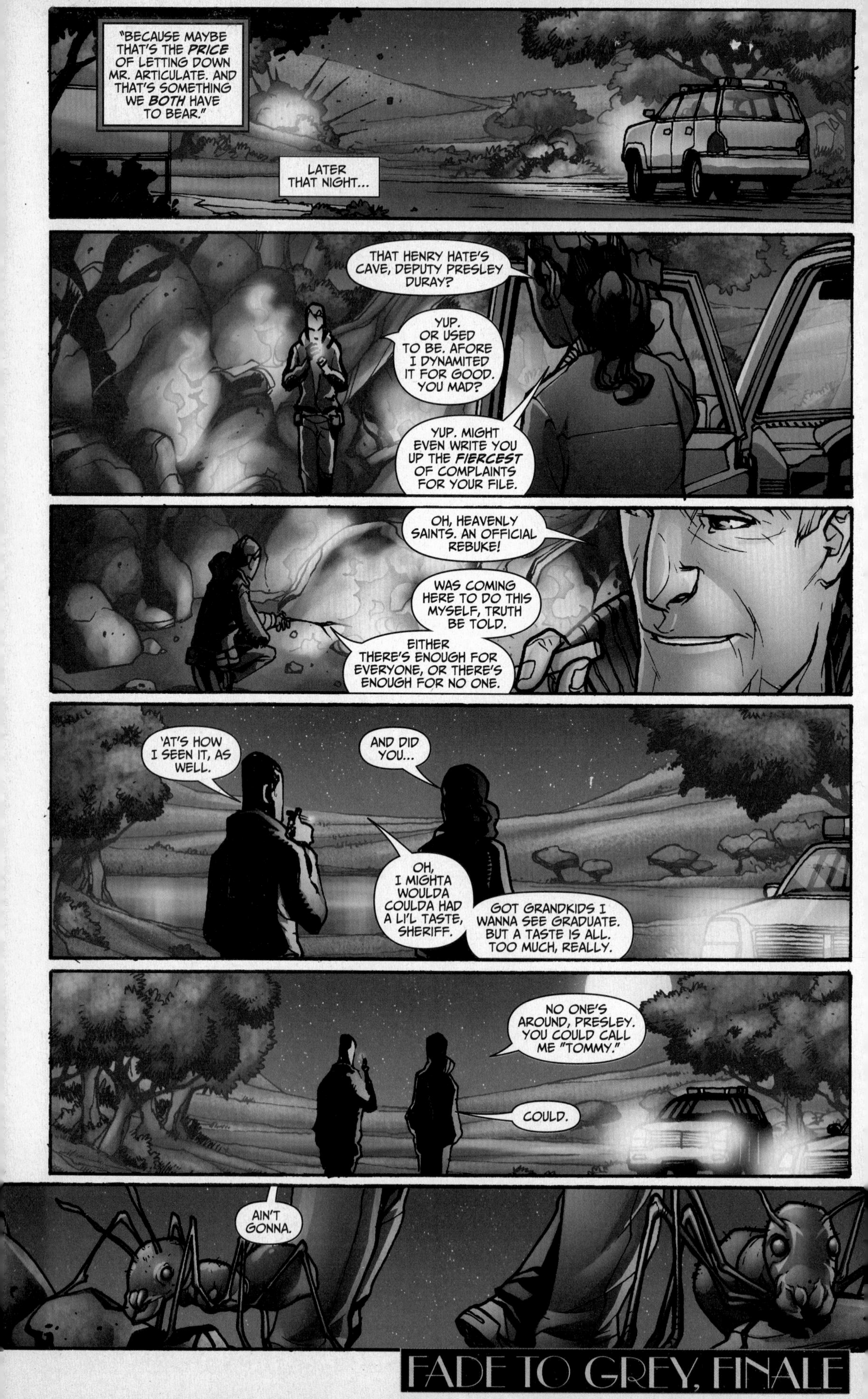
"BECAUSE MAYBE THAT'S THE PRICE OF LETTING DOWN MR. ARTICULATE. AND THAT'S SOMETHING WE BOTH HAVE TO BEAR."
LATER THAT NIGHT...
THAT HENRY HATE'S CAVE, DEPUTY PRESLEY DURAY?
YUP. OR USED TO BE. AFORE I DYNAMITED IT FOR GOOD. YOU MAD?
YUP. MIGHT EVEN WRITE YOU UP THE FIERCEST OF COMPLAINTS FOR YOUR FILE.
OH, HEAVENLY SAINTS. AN OFFICIAL REBUKE!
WAS COMING HERE TO DO THIS MYSELF, TRUTH BE TOLD.
EITHER THERE'S ENOUGH FOR EVERYONE, OR THERE'S ENOUGH FOR NO ONE.
'AT'S HOW I SEEN IT, AS WELL.
AND DID YOU...
OH, I MIGHTA WOULDA COULDA HAD A LI'L TASTE, SHERIFF.
GOT GRANDKIDS I WANNA SEE GRADUATE. BUT A TASTE IS ALL. TOO MUCH, REALLY.
NO ONE'S AROUND, PRESLEY. YOU COULD CALL ME "TOMMY."
COULD.
AIN'T GONNA.
FADE TO GREY, FINALE